Acclaim f

"This book is a classic. Joyce's story has produce praise for a biography – Symon's ... *The Quest fo:* me laugh aloud, and weep, and think. It is sympathetic, in all the right ways, to the monster it portrays."
A. N. Wilson, *Evening Standard*

"*Germany Calling* by Mary Kenny presents a wealth of fascinating new material ... a fascinating, vital account of Joyce's nasty, short and brutish life."
Jewish Chronicle

"Mary Kenny is the perfect biographer for this bizarre figure. [Joyce] was a clever man who could have been a don. Kenny shows, though Joyce's flights of political opinion soared to heights of rancour and bad taste, his core beliefs were not so different to many Irishmen of the period."
The Irish Examiner

"Mary Kenny has written an absorbingly elegant study. To all [Joyce's] shabby dreams, loyalties and cruelties Kenny brings both compassion and a clear mind. A biography whose even-handed beauty of expression combines Irish gravity with Irish spark."
The Guardian

"Popular hate figures are not easy subjects for the biographer. Rebecca West, who sat through Joyce's trial for high treason in 1945, dismissed him as a 'queer little Irish peasant who had gone to some pains to make the worst of himself'. In *Germany Calling* Mary Kenny has painted a more rounded portrait of Lord Haw-Haw, whose propaganda broadcasts for the Third Reich brought him to the scaffold at Wandsworth."
The Times

"Kenny presents for us an appalling man from an appalling time, but such is her narrative skill that we never entirely hate him, seeing in him the possibilities of distinction that were almost obliterated when he went over to the dark side."
The Sunday Times

"A terrific read, and very highly recommended."
Kennys.ie

"Mary Kenny has done her research thoroughly in Ireland, England, Germany and the USA. Her *Germany Calling* is a triumph of enquiry."
Books Ireland

"Kenny makes plausible the idea that a young Irishman with a fine intellect but not much common-sense might fall for the idea, peddled by right-wing English newspapers like the *Morning Post*, that Irish nationalism was a Jewish Communist plot. Kenny has covered the Irish aspect of Joyce well."
The Tablet

"Mary Kenny, with the aid of intelligence files released by the British government and other fresh material, has given flesh to [Joyce's] story. Mary Kenny says she saw in Joyce some of her own flaws … It is, perhaps, this sympathy that has enabled her to produce such a convincing and gripping biography."
Sunday Independent

"No stranger to controversy herself, Mary Kenny does an outstanding job. Highly recommended."
Evening Echo

"Mary Kenny has worked tirelessly to present us with a fascinating portrait of one of Galway's most infamous sons, whose sneering jibes on Berlin radio during World War II, as

Hitler's chief English-language announcer, earned him the nom de guerre Lord Haw-Haw. The real strength of Kenny's book is that it contains a wealth of detail regarding Joyce's Irish roots, which no earlier studies managed to achieve."
Sunday Business Post

"*Germany Calling* is undoubtedly Kenny's best work. Comprehensive and authoritative, it nonetheless manages to be as impelling in its sweeping mastery of material as a thriller. The fact is that *Germany Calling* is a triumph. This sensitive and entertaining biography is the crowning achievement of an unorthodox writer's career."
Irish Independent

"*Germany Calling* is a first-class biography ... [Kenny's] story of Joyce's younger brother Quentin and his forlorn attempt to save [Joyce] is one of the biography's most touching moments. A fantastic and stunning book."
Irish-i

"The British government was on shaky legal ground in hanging American Joyce, but in those days better men were being executed for lesser sins. He was a wretched misfit, who allowed his intelligence to be perverted for the service of monsters."
The Sunday Telegraph

"This life of Lord Haw-Haw is an unexpected triumph ... she achieves the impossible: making Joyce a more likeable figure than hitherto, but also a more impressive one."
The Catholic Herald

"[A] very readable and thoughtful account, with a useful outline of fascism's contemporary appeal as the modernising Third Way ... [Kenny] is surely right to query the legitimacy of his hanging."
The Daily Telegraph

"Reading this book aroused in my mind thoughts about the nature of individual identity, the claims of nationality, and the meaning of treason."
The Irish Catholic

"Mary Kenny has succeeded in maintaining a high level of interest throughout the narrative, giving William Joyce's romantic and marital adventures the prominence that they played in his life. He had a cavalier attitude to his two wives, Hazel and Margaret, but in his own rather odd way he loved them both."
Emigrant.ie

"In *Germany Calling* Mary Kenny certainly recognizes the need to dig deeper and more extensively. She is particularly effective in reconstructing Joyce's early years in Ireland … [and] writes fluently on the personal tribulations that followed his capture by British troops in 1945."
Times Literary Supplement

"Kenny argues, rightly … that Joyce's fate was undeserved: his real offence was to have acquired his nickname, and the legendary repute that went with it. He hadn't been responsible for a single British death, but found himself at the centre of a show trial, which soon afterwards was regarded with some embarrassment. It was essentially a matter of revenge …This is the most thorough study of Joyce's personal life that is likely to be written."
London Review of Books

"This elegant book is a model of its kind and an intriguing story is gracefully told."
Ireland of the Welcomes

GERMANY CALLING

Mary Kenny has been a newspaper journalist and columnist since the 1960s, contributing to, among others, the *Irish Independent*, the *Guardian*, *The Times*, the *Daily Mail*, *The Spectator* and the *Irish Catholic*.

She was born in Dublin, the youngest of four, and, after a period in France, became a reporter on the *London Evening Standard*. A founder-member of an Irish feminist movement in Dublin, she graduated with a degree in French studies at Birkbeck College, London University in the 1990s. In 1997 she published a social history of Ireland, *Goodbye to Catholic Ireland*.

Mary Kenny is married to the writer Richard West and they have two adult sons. She lives between England and Ireland.

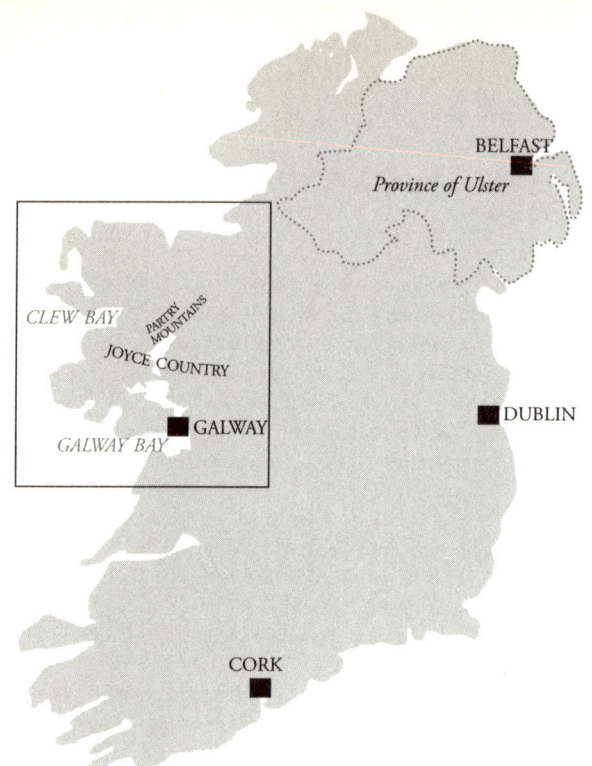

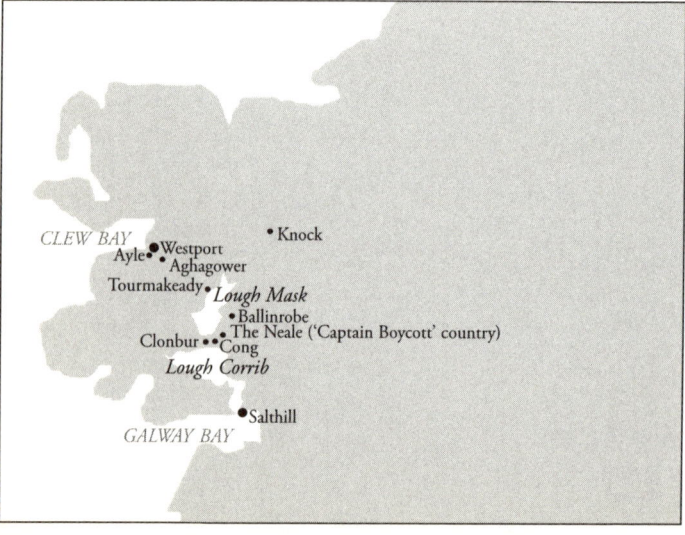

GERMANY CALLING

A BIOGRAPHY OF WILLIAM JOYCE
LORD HAW-HAW

MARY KENNY

NEW
ISLAND

Copyright © 2003 Mary Kenny

GERMANY CALLING
A BIOGRAPHY OF WILLIAM JOYCE, 'LORD HAW-HAW'
First published 2003
by New Island
2 Brookside
Dundrum Road
Dublin 14

This edition published 2004

www.newisland.ie

ISBN 1 904301 59 2

British Library Cataloguing in Publication Data.
A CIP catalogue record for this book is available
from the British Library.

Typeset by New Island
Cover design by Fidelma Slattery @ New Island
Printed by CPD, Ebbw Vale, Wales

10 9 8 7 6 5 4 3 2 1

With special thanks to James Clark

Michael and Doreen Forman of Historia Publishing – the Forman Archive – have a significant and valuable archive pertaining to William Joyce, including 144 prison letters that William wrote to his wife Margaret in the months before his execution. William Joyce's letters to his wife are a brilliant, inventive, comical, sometimes offensive, but always fascinating *tour de force*, worthy of a James Joyce in their puns, linguistic and scholarly jokes drawing on German, Latin and Anglo-Saxon and their reflections on the wartime period. These deserve publication in their entirety of some 150,000 words. I am grateful to Mr and Mrs Forman for allowing me to use short extracts from their remarkable archive, for which they hold the copyright.

Out of Ireland have we come,
Great hatred, little room,
Maimed us at the start.
I carry from my mother's womb
A fanatic heart.

W. B. Yeats, 'Remorse for
Intemperate Speech', 1932

The Immediate Family Tree of William Joyce, 'Lord Haw Haw'

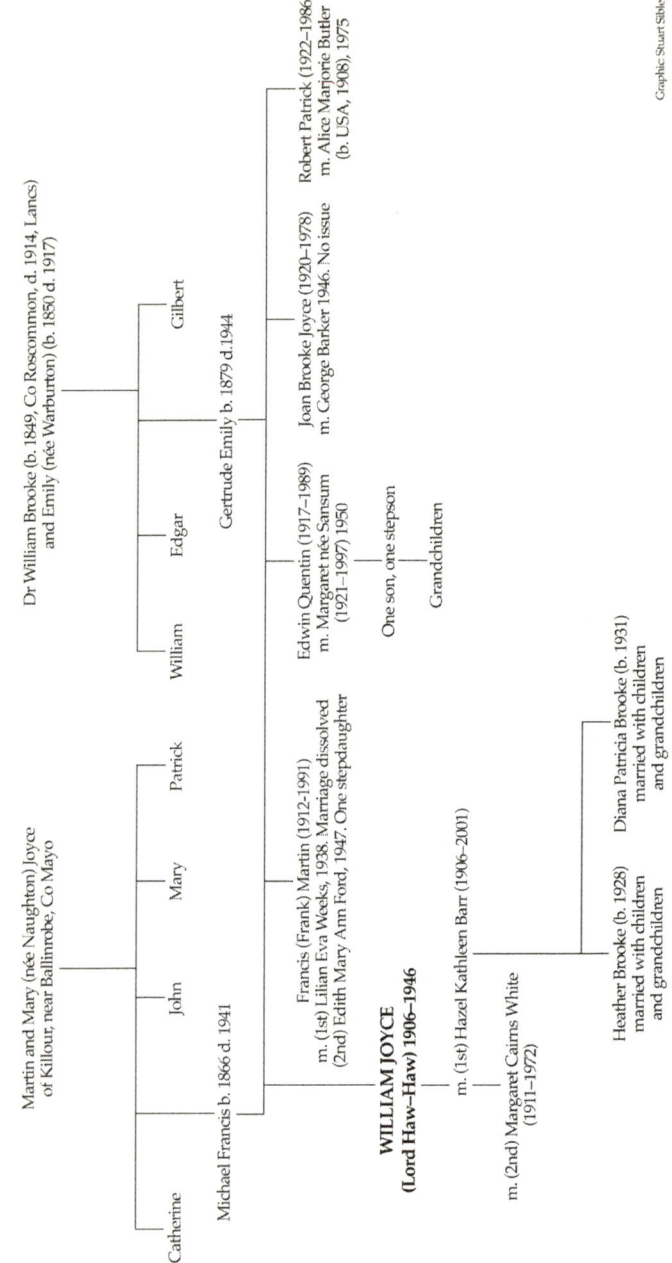

Martin and Mary (née Naughton) Joyce
of Killour, near Ballinrobe, Co Mayo

Catherine   John   Mary   Patrick

Michael Francis b. 1866 d. 1941

Francis (Frank) Martin (1912–1991)
m. (1st) Lilian Eva Weeks, 1938. Marriage dissolved
(2nd) Edith Mary Ann Ford, 1947. One stepdaughter

WILLIAM JOYCE
(Lord Haw–Haw) 1906–1946

m. (1st) Hazel Kathleen Barr (1906–2001)

m. (2nd) Margaret Cairns White
(1911–1972)

Heather Brooke (b. 1928)
married with children
and grandchildren

Diana Patricia Brooke (b. 1931)
married with children
and grandchildren

Dr William Brooke (b. 1849, Co Roscommon, d. 1914, Lancs)
and Emily (née Warburton) (b. 1850 d. 1917)

William   Edgar   Gilbert

Gertrude Emily b. 1879 d. 1944

Edwin Quentin (1917–1989)
m. Margaret née Sansum
(1921–1997) 1950

One son, one stepson

Grandchildren

Joan Brooke Joyce (1920–1978)
m. George Barker 1946. No issue

Robert Patrick (1922–1986)
m. Alice Marjorie Butler
(b. USA, 1908), 1975

Graphic Stuart Sibley

Contents

Acknowledgements

A book is a little like a pregnancy: it is conceived, it grows within the body of the author, it needs to be nourished, fed, developed and cared for. It begins with a seed and ends with an obsession. And to bring it out into the world requires the assistance and support of several experienced editorial midwives. I have many people to thank for their guidance, knowledge, expertise and generosity in helping me bring this project to fruition.

I owe James Clark a particular debt of gratitude. James, who worked as a very young man with William Joyce in Berlin, and who lived through the Third Reich as a witness to history, has been editor, mentor, German expert and collaborator in this project from the start. On three journeys to Germany – Berlin, Apen and Schleswig-Holstein – James has also been a cultivated and delightful companion who protested scarcely at all at my erratic driving on German motorways, crying 'Jesus, Mary and Joseph!' when some catastrophe seemed imminent.

My very special thanks are due to the family of the late Quentin Joyce: his son and daughter-in-law, Michael and Angela Joyce, and his stepson John Quentin Joyce. They not only made available to me a valuable Joyce family archive which has never been accessed before – and was only discovered by the family in 1997 – but also extended most generous hospitality and kindness to me at a difficult time in my own life. Quentin Joyce was William's younger brother, and he fought valiantly to save William from death by execution; as my own darling sister, Ursula, was valiantly facing her own death from cancer just at the time I was reading through Quentin's documents, I could identify painfully with the grief at losing a sibling.

I would very much like to thank Judith Ware, who grew

up as the daughter of Frank Joyce, and has most affectionate memories of all the Joyce family: William's siblings were clever, funny and had their fill of Irish charm, and Judy very kindly made her family pictures available to me – some are reproduced here with her permission.

I researched the life of William Joyce in America, Ireland, England and Germany, and I believe I visited every major location associated with his life. At Wandsworth, my thanks to Mick Lydon, who was principal officer at Her Majesty's Prison and spent a day showing me the outlay of the place Joyce came to call home, including the famous 'execution suite'; and to Stewart McLaughlin, a prison officer who has written a fine history of Wandsworth who helped with details.

In Galway, I was greatly assisted by Ronnie O'Gorman, the proprietor-editor of the *Galway Advertiser* and his assistant Margaret Collins, by Tom Kenny of Kenny's Bookshop – one of the world's great bookshops and art galleries – by Seamus Kelly, who did a fine Radio Telefís Éireann radio programme recalling Lord Haw-Haw, and by Frank Canavan, Headmaster of St Ignatius School. Anne Ryan, the head of William's infant school, now Scoil an Linbh Íosa, went to particular trouble to trawl through the old school-attendance records. Adrian Martyn, a knowledgeable young genealogist, researched the nineteenth-century roots of the Joyce family in north Mayo. I would like to thank Jane Beatty of Loughrea, teacher and local historian, her mother, Kathleen Murphy, and my old school friend Carolyn Hallinan Shiels, who drove me all over Salthill exploring William's boyhood haunts.

Eamonn and Antoinette Waldron, who now live in the former family home of the Joyces, which they have restored to its Victorian perfection, were exceptionally hospitable, and went to some trouble to find the history and deeds of the house.

My thanks to Pat McMahon of the Library of Galway County Libraries, and to Peader O'Dowd of the Galway

Historical Association. To Patricia Naughton, Eithne Griffin and Conor McDonough, who provided recollections of William as a schoolboy. Thanks also to Jimmy Kilbane, who tends Bohermore Cemetery with such dedication.

I also thank interviewees who prefer to remain unnamed, in particular one who provided a key account of William Joyce's necessary departure from Galway.

In Mayo, I would like to acknowledge the assistance of Ger Delaney of the South Mayo Genealogical Research Centre at Ballinrobe, and most especially Jarlath and Anne Duffy of Westport, who provided much background guidance on Mayo life, and who instigated the enchanting Clew Bay Heritage Centre, a museum of Mayo life. Thanks also to Seán Staunton, the editor of the *Mayo News*, and his wife, my cousin Sal, to Sheila Mulloy, of the Mayo Historical Society, who provided such knowledgeable companionship, to John Sheridan at Ballinrobe, to Dermot Keane, the Principal of The Neale National School and local historian, to Tomas O'Toole of Tourmakeady, and most especially to Daniel McGing of Ayle, whose father purchased the public house there from William Joyce's father, Michael. Gerard Moran, of Westport and Brussels, a superb historian of nineteenth-century Mayo, very kindly read my chapter on Mayo and made helpful comments.

In Dublin, Gregory O'Connor at the Irish National Archive was tirelessly diligent in finding papers associated with the Joyce family, some of which have been locked away for years. Dr Deirdre Raftery of University College Dublin provided invaluable background knowledge on education in Ireland in the early twentieth century. Father Fergus O'Donoughue, Father Tom Morrissey and Father Senan Timoney of the Jesuit Order greatly assisted me with research on Joyce's teachers and on the history of Jesuit education in Galway. Proinsias MacAonghusa kindly guided me through his Irish-language interviews with Galway contempories of William Joyce carried out for RTÉ TV in 1976, and remembered details about interviews with Joyce contemporaries then living. I would like to thank our family friends, John Power, for documents he had collected, and Ben Briscoe, who provided a salutary reminder that for Jewish Irishmen Lord Haw-Haw's broadcasts were not quite so amusing. My thanks to David O'Donoghue, the author of *Hitler's Irish Voices*, who is so knowledgeable about the Irish connections with the Third Reich's broadcasts and to Commandant Victor Laing and Captain Pat Brennan of the Irish Military Archive for his help at Cathal Brugha Barracks. I also thank the archivists at RTÉ in Dublin, Barbara Durack, Stephen Darcy and Ian Lee, for their assistance.

In Belfast, I would like to thank Arthur Manton and his colleagues of the Ulster Historical Society who provided a helpful probe on Dr William Brooke.

In New York, I would like to thank Father Leonard J. Tuozzola, who so kindly showed me the archives at All Saints Church in Harlem where the Joyce parents were married, and Father Smith of Brooklyn who found William Joyce's baptismal certificate at Our Lady of Lourdes Church, once Brooklyn's smartest, now burned down. Susan Aprill at the Brooklyn Collection of the Brooklyn Public Library produced illuminating studies of Brooklyn life in the 1900s. Mary Carney of Brooklyn provided help and hospitality.

In England, I would especially like to thank Derek Denton of Oldham, who had assembled some very interesting material on William Joyce's connection with Oldham in Lancashire and kindly put it at my disposal. Derek, his wife Donna and their son John were most hospitable to me. Pat Dimuantes of Lancashire also helped with genealogical research.

I owe a very special debt of thanks to Lawrence Aspden, the Curator of the Special Collection at the University of Sheffield, as well as to Michael Hannon, who was Director of Library Services at Sheffield when I was there. The University of Sheffield has an unparalleled archive associated with the various British Fascist Movements of the 1920s and

1930s – not out of any political bias, but for reasons of historical study. Any papers of mine associated with research into William Joyce's life will be passed on to the University of Sheffield (if these should prove of use).

I would especially like to thank Terry Charman at the Imperial War Museum, who gave me precious time and permission to read through the voluminous BBC transcripts of German propaganda broadcasts available at the Imperial War Museum in Lambeth. I would also like to thank Michael Paterson at the Imperial War Museum, who lent me some very useful books from his private collection, and all the staff in the reading room who were so helpful.

Special thanks to Susan Curtis-Bennett for giving me access to the archive of her father, Derek Curtis-Bennett, who was one of the defence team for William Joyce.

John Warburton of the Friends of Oswald Mosley was extremely kind to me and put a lot of helpful material my way, although the Mosleyites did not approve of William Joyce after he went to Germany. John, now in his eighties, introduced me to several very helpful people, and his own experiences in the 1930s explained to me why many unemployed young men did feel moved to join the Blackshirts. I would like to acknowledge the assistance of Margaret Collins Bowie, who worked with William Joyce and was related to John Angus Macnab, and McNeil Sloane in Australia. Thanks especially to Jeff Wallder for his fund of knowledge in this field, and to Brian Clough of Brighton for access to his archive relating to spies and intelligence during the 1930s and 1940s.

Thanks to Trevor Grundy for his most helpful suggestions; to Dr Brian Harwood of Birkbeck College; and to Alan Kucia at King's College of The Strand in London. Thanks to Peter Morris in Liverpool for his fascinating recollections, and to the late Douglas Trew in Kent, who was at Birkbeck with Joyce.

In Dulwich, South London, the Dulwich historian Brian

Green (to whom I was introduced by Margaret Edwards and Phil Ivory) gave me a most informative introduction to the neighbourhood life of the Joyces. Thanks also to my old Fleet Street colleague Brian McConnell, who helped me with introductions in Dulwich. I greatly benefited from interviews with Russell Vernon, Judith Fitton and Jim Hammer, all of whom had family recollections of the Joyces. At Midhurst, John Dodd and Bob Ratcliffe helped me with background on Alex and Ethel Scrimgeour. At Broadstairs, thanks to Mrs Doris West, who was at school with Joan Joyce, and Mr and Mrs Leslie Waddington-Leat of Herne Bay, who were most hospitable in showing me their home there, 'Joycelyn', which was said to have a secret association with the legend of Lord Haw-Haw.

I would like to thank Richard Jones of the *Daily Mail* newspaper library, who accessed the cuttings file on William Joyce (and Steve Torrington for permission to use this valuable resource). I would also like to thank David Twiston-Davies at the *Daily Telegraph*. I am most grateful to Francis Beckett for his advice and encouragement, and to John Gibson for his material on the trial of William Joyce. I would like to thank David Lewis especially for reading some of the legal material, although any errors which still remain pertaining to the trial are very definitely all mine.

At this point, I should like to say how much I appreciate the forbearance which Jewish friends and connections showed in this project, and many have shown more charity towards the memory of William Joyce than he could ever deserve. The Wiener Library were kindness itself, and I was helped by the *Jewish Chronicle*. I thank Daniel Wolf for his merry company and good-tempered encouragement, and for bringing me together with James Clark. I thank Geoffrey Perry for his assistance and generosity.

In Germany, thanks to the staff at the Deutsches Rundfunkarchiv at Potsdam and to Regina Yates at the Rundfunkhaus, who showed James Clark and me (along with my publisher, Edwin Higel) the restored German Broadcasting House. We express our gratitude to Helmut and Gaby Volkerts at Apen, and to Frau Lisl Kuhlmann also at Apen. In Kupfermühle, Wassersleben, we warmly thank Bodo Daetz, who has restored the Danish heritage of Schleswig-Holstein to its sixteenth-century glory, and who introduced us to Frau Paula Bebenzee who remembered the Joyces in their last days in Germany. Many thanks to John Jungclaussen of *Die Zeit* who made so many introductions possible.

I would like to thank the *Irish Independent, The Irish Times*, the *Irish Examiner*, the *Irish News*, the *Oldie, The Spectator*, the *Connaught Tribune* and the *Mayo News*, all of which published letters from me seeking memories of William Joyce. I would especially like to thank people who wrote to me with their own recollections of Lord Haw-Haw: these are too numerous to acknowledge singly but I was grateful for all of them. I have had some quite amazing letters, all of which will be passed on to the Sheffield Archive as original recollections of a time in history now fading. I would also like to thank the readers of the *Daily Express* who responded with many interesting memories when I wrote about 'Lord Haw-Haw' at the end of 1998. *The Spectator* readers had some especially helpful thoughts about the trial for treason.

I would also like to thank Hilary Rittner for her efficient and cheerful book searches, and Jo Knowsley, who helped me when she was at the *Sunday Telegraph*. Friends in Deal in Kent have been very helpful about books and other material: I thank Joe and Julie Steeples, Colin and Josephine Whittington, Nick McConnell, Audrey and Nick Roethen-baugh, Michael Hill and the late Geoff Axbey. Thanks to Stuart Sibley for interpreting the Joyce family tree in clear diagrammatic form.

Many friends and colleagues helped with suggestions for reading and sources, and I would like to thank Peter Hitchens, Geoffrey Wheatcroft, Miriam Polunin, Daniel

Johnson and Robert Harris. I would like to thank Roy Foster, Declan Kiberd and Patrick Maume for suggestions and directions, dear Lord Deedes for wonderful conversations about the 1930s, and the late Lady Mosley for her courteous correspondence. I owe a most special debt to Murray Sayle, who was the first to urge me to do this book and sent me key sourcebooks. I would like to thank Colette O'Neill of Allied Irish Banks for being so supportive of my circumstances.

Thanks to Dermot Bolger, Ludovic Kennedy, John O'Mahony, Paddy Patterson, Maggie Noach, my computer wizard Francis Hughes and those individuals who spoke to me on the basis of non-attribution.

Emma Dunne, of New Island, and Sean O'Keeffe, have been exemplary editors – imaginative, intelligent, tactful and utterly diligent, and I trusted their judgement implicitly; and my publisher Edwin Higel has been, as ever, wonderfully encouraging and full of enthusiasm. I am most grateful to Fidelma Slattery for a stunning jacket design, and to Joseph Hoban for his brilliant marketing skills.

My brother Carlos Kenny and my late sister Ursula Kenny have been so kind and helpful: my darling sister masked her own suffering for a self-sacrificingly long time to give priority to the William Joyce project. My sons Patrick and Edward West have done a great deal to assist me, with intelligent suggestions and material help with research, particularly with Internet material. My husband Richard West has been unfailingly patient and encouraging, and has put up with a great deal of bad housekeeping over the years for the sake of the rascally Lord Haw-Haw.

✍

With acknowledgements to the following institutions for research facilities: The British National Archive-The Public Record Office at Kew; The Imperial War Museum; The British Library; The Family Record Centre, London; The National Registry Office, Dublin; The Irish National

Archive; The Military Archives of Ireland; The National Library of Ireland; The New York Public Libraries; The Battersea Public Library; The Oldham Public Library; The Galway Public Library; The British Newspaper Library at Colindale

✧

I am exceedingly grateful to all those who have picked up errors of fact (or syntax) in the first edition of this book, and those who added new material: thanks again to James Clark, to Michael Joyce, Tony Duff, Geraldine Wilkinson, Michael Hill, David Twiston-Davies, and Sue Thomson, who assisted with legal material and, again, Murray Sayle. A.N. Wilson very kindly corrected several detailed points of British political history. I should also like to thank again Michael Forman for several corrections, Geoffrey Perry (who arrested 'Haw-Haw' in Flensberg), Charles Lysaght (who researched the last days of Edward Bowlby), and John Yeowell, who knew William Joyce in the 1930s and corrected several points most helpfully. Des Donovan of Bundoran in Co. Donegal told me the surprising story of how Robert Joyce married his mother, which made a previously unknown addition to the family tree. Even more astonishingly, Tully Potter – a fellow journalist from the *Daily Mail* – revealed to me that his mother, as a young teenage girl, had been the mysterious 'Mary' seduced by William Joyce in sensational circumstances which altered the course of Joyce's career: I am most grateful to him for providing this new material, with pictures. My very special gratitude, again, to Terry Charman of the Imperial War Museum, whose eye for detail is forensic, and who gave of his valuable time and expertise in correcting the text for this paperback edition.

There is always something new to be said about a historical character: I welcome comments and further information at my website: www.mary-kenny.com

INTRODUCTION

A Crazy Mixed-up Irishman

*'A queer little Irish peasant who had gone to
some pains to make the worst of himself.'*

Rebecca West's impression of 'Lord Haw-Haw'
in the dock, in *The Meaning of Treason*

Most biographies are, almost by definition, about successful
people. This story is about a man who was a failure, who
made the wrong choices at almost every point in his life, and
ended his days on the gallows – with the negative distinction
of being the last man ever to be hanged for high treason by
the British Crown.

Many of William Joyce's relations are too ashamed of him
even to speak about the connection: his English relatives,
having suffered stigma and verbal abuse – 'Ah, you're related
to the most hated man in Britain?' as has been said to some
of the relatives of Lord Haw-Haw – are ashamed that he was
hanged as a pro-Nazi traitor, and his Irish family associates
are ashamed that he had been so pro-British as a young boy
that he aided and abetted the Black and Tans in Galway in
the 1920s. Among a certain generation of Irish people, the
latter was almost worse than going over to Hitler.

Yet, failure though he was, William Joyce – popularly,

1

almost mythically, known as 'Lord Haw-Haw' – was a significant historical figure: he was acknowledged to be the most memorable of broadcasters from the Third Reich, and in his own perverse way he was something of a media pioneer. His broadcasts, though they could be quite appalling, were also quite often regarded as funny and entertaining. They helped to launch the genre of comedy on the airwaves. Before 'Lord Haw-Haw', broadcasting had been a stuffy and earnest business, and if the BBC announcers did not always wear a dinner jacket when sitting at the microphone, they sounded as though they might have done.

William Joyce demonstrated that radio could be used for political propaganda, yes, but also for invective, plain speaking, rumour, gossip, playlets, sensation, taunts, threats, political satire, local news and even, with dark hilarity at the very end, drunkenness. (He wrote many scripts for other broadcasters using different genres, including Workers' Challenge, a radio station that specialised in robust, proletarian and coarse language which shocked, though also thrilled, the listeners.) William was a kind of radio popular journalist, a spicy and provocative commentator in the style of a Julie Burchill, an H. L. Mencken or a Kevin Myers – the bold and outrageous commentator who says the unsayable.

During wartime, when the press, broadcasters and parliament were loyally – and understandably – behind a coalition British government, Lord Haw-Haw also represented the voice of a silenced Opposition. There were few critical opinions of any weight in the British media at the time of William Joyce's ascendancy, from 1939 to 1942, when deference to politicians and a rather obsequious attitude to the upper classes were the norm. To the working classes who listened to him – Lord Haw-Haw was the first broadcaster to get working-class people listening to the radio – it was sometimes an enjoyable exercise in general irreverence, at least before the Blitz began in earnest.

In Ireland, where 'Lord Haw-Haw' was followed with

delighted dedication, he provided a welcome distraction from the stifling political correctness of neutrality, as well as the satisfaction of seeing the Old Enemy, England, flagrantly scoffed at. Irish neutrality at this time was observed with prim decorum: the war itself was called 'the Emergency', and the Irish State even considered banning toy soldiers for fear they might be used in a partisan way. William Joyce's pugnacious speaking style, boasting of the Reich's successes from the Atlantic to the Siberian steppes, seemed by contrast a brilliantly vivid piece of broadcasting, and some of the most affectionate recollections of Lord Haw-Haw have come to me from those members of the Irish public who remember those exciting radio days.

A biographer must have some sympathy with her subject, and even perhaps some sense of identification with him. I was first attracted to the idea of writing about William Joyce because I have experienced some of that mixed loyalty of being between England and Ireland, and some understanding of being between Catholic and Protestant values. I think of myself as thoroughly Irish, but I am married to an Englishman and have lived most of my adult life in England. I am a Catholic, but I spent a great deal of my childhood with an aunt who had come from an Irish Protestant background; some of the attitudes of the Irish Protestant ascendancy formed part of my early influences.

William's English-Irish mixture was different: his father was an Irish Catholic and his mother a Lancashire Protestant, whose own father always laid claim to be one of the Ulster Brookes. William was three-quarters Irish and one quarter of that was, he claimed, composed of the 'Ulster blood' and the 'Orange chromosomes'. My English husband jokingly suggested, at one point, that I call this biography 'Hitler's Orangeman', a very William-ish provocation. Yet William's personality did show both a volatile Celtic extremism (as a

British secret intelligence report noted in the 1930s) and an Ulster fanaticism. No one loves the British Empire like an Ulster loyalist, but no one can hate the English like an Orangeman who has been disappointed by Mother England.

I chose William Joyce as a subject for a biography because I thought that this English-Irish, Catholic-Protestant identity was something I would understand, historically. But as time went by I began to have the slightly eerie feeling that I had not chosen William Joyce: William Joyce had chosen me. It would be fey to claim that I was being directed from beyond the grave by the ghost of Lord Haw-Haw, but I did come to feel familiar with his spirit.

I had two modes of experiencing William Joyce's presence. In one, I was an elderly teaching nun and Willie (as he was known in Galway) was an exceptionally trying schoolboy. In this reverie, I was forever suppressing the urge to box his ears. Yet, as with most elderly nuns coping with naughty small boys, I couldn't but be amused, sometimes, by his insolence, precocity and provocative antics, and even touched by his total want of common sense. In the second, slightly more disturbing mode, I began to note the similarities between himself and myself, and I could see in some of his flaws my own flaws: the contrariness, the inclination to take everything to extremes, the oddness and eccentricity of character. William was always being rejected and rebuffed, and although he was the author of his own disasters – well, so are we all.

I can understand William Joyce's need for passionate commitment to a cause, and even his inclination to change sides when he grew disillusioned. I can also understand William's exasperation with English mildness and English compromise – William couldn't abide the English obsession with compromise. 'The English are unhappily given to compromise,' William wrote. 'Compromise is the only form of treachery that the Irishman is never prepared to pardon.'[1] William had mixed feelings about being Irish – he was mixed up in his sense of identity anyway – but he admired the fanaticism, or shall we say the absolutism, with which an Irishman is prepared to pursue a cause: and he had that Irish fanaticism himself. But fanaticism, though it can be ugly, is also a search for passion, for total immersion in something bigger than yourself. It is not the safe shallows of compromise and 'the middle way'.

With William's youthful crazy habits, I could also identify. Like him, nothing pleased me more than smoking, drinking, talking, debating and arguing into the night, or indeed sitting up all night bashing a typewriter to meet a deadline. In this, he was in his element: this, and ranting from a platform and, curiously, reading aloud from James Joyce. James Clark once happened upon William Joyce in a studio at the Berlin Rundfunkhaus, and himself reading aloud from *Finnegans Wake*, in the passage about 'Anna Livia Plurabella' (a lyrical text about the rather brackish River Liffey that runs through Dublin). James Clark was startled. *Finnegans Wake* is a famously difficult book, full of nonsense words; but when read by an inspired voice, the whole thing somehow makes music. At that moment, James Clark said, he understood the point of *Finnegans Wake*, and saw, in William Joyce, the Joycean Irishman.

William Joyce had something in common with James Joyce: they were both formed by a Jesuit education, both had something of the 'Jesuit strain … injected the wrong way'; both were connected with Galway; both were indulged eldest sons with a devoted younger brother; both were fascinated by philology, word-play, puns and the intertextuality of Latin phrases interspersed with English; and both were fixated on Jewishness – James being philo-Semitic, William anti-Semitic. Indeed, it is not unusual for people to conflate James Joyce with William Joyce, and more than once their names and identities have been mixed up. This may seem implausible, but I have found it to be so.

When I was trawling through his five and a half years of

broadcasts – he sometimes made two or three broadcasts a day over the course of the Second World War – I saw in William Joyce the part of myself that was the journalistic hack. William *was* an outstanding broadcaster, but he often hacked as well: he just had to churn it out. There were days when he just had to sit down and write a thousand words about, let's say, Germany's disastrous military forays into Russia, and make it sound plausible. Anyone in journalism has at some stage done something similar – produced the requisite number of words because it is the job, it has to be done, and you have no other immediate means of earning a living. For all of his career, drunk or sober, William Joyce met the deadline.

William Joyce was not a particularly nice man, and when he was bad he was horrid. The most disagreeable streak in his personality was his pathological anti-Semitism, which was, as the Irish say, beyond the beyonds. If you said to William, 'It's rainy, today, isn't it?' he would reply, 'Yes, and don't you know the Jews make all the umbrellas, and have a world monopoly in umbrellas, and are using the umbrella market to further their fiendish communist plot by international financiers.' I have come to understand, I think, the source of this fixation, which I explain in the course of the text, but I would not go so far as to say that *tout comprendre, c'est tout pardonner.* I don't think William Joyce should be pardoned for this, particularly in 1945, after the war, when the Nazi concentration camps were being opened up and he showed scant remorse about the consequences of extreme anti-Semitism.

William was a very clever man, academically – he flew through exams and obtained a distinguished First at Birkbeck College, and he possessed a range of eclectic knowledge from medicine to higher mathematics, from Old Norse to the poetry of Horace and the further reaches of physics, chemistry and constitutional law – but he lacked insight, as well as common sense (a not unusual failing in the academically gifted). His friend A. K. Chesterton (a second cousin of the Catholic writer G. K. Chesterton) thought that William might have been clinically insane at certain moments of political arousal: he was 'far indeed from being normal' and had a certain 'neurosis'; one day in the future, Chesterton believed, psychiatric science would figure out his particular personality disorder.[2]

It has to be said anti-Semitism was not uncommon during the 1930s. It was to be found in the work of Virginia Woolf, T. S. Eliot and George Orwell, and in the popular writing of John Buchan, Dornford Yates and Agatha Christie; it can also be found in W. B. Yeats, and one of William Joyce's most ferocious admirers – who almost outdid him in anti-Jewish feeling – was the poet and mentor of poets Ezra Pound. There was a certain element of joking anti-Semitism in the pre-war (but not post-war) lyrics of Noël Coward, and it was evident in the essays of Wyndham Lewis and many other writers and thinkers of the time. For instance, the co-founder of the *New Statesman*, the Fabian Sydney Webb, was at least even-handed in that he thought that both the Irish and the Jews were unfit to breed.[3]

Anti-Semitism was also commonplace among ordinary people, as shown in the Home Intelligence Reports – British government monitors of what people in thirteen regions around the United Kingdom were talking about during the war.[4] As the Holocaust approached a crescendo, in 1943, a frequent attitude among ordinary British people toward Continental Jews was that they were to be pitied for having a 'rough time' – but that 'we don't want them over here'. Throughout the Second World War, grumbling about the Jews, either for allegedly running a black market or for seeming too 'ostentatious' in their lifestyle, was a much-repeated theme.[5] So although William's anti-Semitism was unpardonable, it was an inflated and possibly pathological amplification of a prejudice that many people shared. We must also remember that various racial and group prejudices were commonplace in the recent past: right up until the 1960s, English landladies plying for trade hung a 'No Irish' sign in their front windows, sometimes with the variation, 'No Irish, No Coloured'.[6]

We know that anti-Semitism is odious because we know the deepest pit of evil to which it led; but I came to the view, in the time I spent with the ghost of William Joyce, that it is also unlucky. This is not because there is a world conspiracy of Jews monopolising the media and controlling everything from governments to finance, as William and his colleague John Beckett believed, but because anti-Semitism produces in the individual a negative energy which burns away at all positive gifts and talents.

And William Joyce *did* have good qualities, and interesting ideas, which have been annulled or overlooked by the flare of his violent hatreds. His political ideas were not all loathsome: some of his precepts about education could be endorsed, without alteration, by the most liberal-minded progressives of our day. He wanted to abolish the British public schools and to reduce class size in state schools. 'The purpose of education … is not to make plumbers, doctors or lawyers; it is not to enable every small boy to realise his wish to become an engine driver … The individual purpose is, if we may disclaim unreserved admiration for Epicurus, to make man and woman happy.'[7]

William hated snobbery and the divisions of social class – he had been the butt of English snobbery himself, when rebuffed as a 'common little Irishman' – and he had a genuine feeling for the poor and the unemployed. He had compassion particularly for the dispossessed of Lancashire, where the mills were being annihilated by the forces of what we would now call 'globalisation' – cheaper production in Asia. He campaigned against means testing and declared that 'the fair distribution of wealth is quite incompatible with unlimited profits'.[8] One of the reasons he thought Germany superior to England was that the German working classes of the 1930s had better health, better teeth and the right to have a recuperative spell at a spa. His economic ideas about Ireland's woes were very sensible: he thought that what Ireland needed was lots of money invested in it – which has turned out to be the case.

On a personal level, William had some of the attractive qualities of the absent-minded professor: he had no interest in possessions – he only ever wanted wine, cigarettes, books and a few opera records – and always looked a bit of a mess. He was mechanically incompetent: he couldn't ride a bicycle, dance or play games. He could speak on the radio but could 'barely succeed in receiving a powerful station on the wireless and could never get the tuning really right', according to his friend, John Angus Macnab. While he greatly irritated some people, he commanded the lifelong loyalty of close friends. His friend McNeil Sloane, now an elderly man in Australia, still remembers William with great affection, and Mr Sloane's wife, Rosetta, put flowers on William's grave until her own death.[9]

William Joyce could be very good company when he was on form: he had the Irish conviviality noted by William Shirer, the American anti-Fascist correspondent in Berlin. 'If you can get over your initial revulsion at his being a traitor,' Shirer said, 'you find him an amusing and even an intelligent fellow.'[10] William could certainly be a monster of egotism, but he could also be kind and considerate. One of the warders sent to guard him in his last days called him 'a wonderful man … smiling and courteous, never depressed, never out of temper, always thinking of others, apologising for causing us trouble. We all love him here – there has never been a prisoner like him.'[11] Both A. K. Chesterton and Joyce's best friend, John Macnab, saw in William unusual moods of mildness and even humility. 'When he put aside his jackboots,' said Chesterton, he could emerge 'as a humble person, not without charm and with a delicate sense of irony.'

And he was brave. At a political meeting in Lambeth, south London, as a young boy of seventeen, he had his faced sliced up: this created a livid scar which James Clark recalls looking like 'raw pork'. It marked him badly yet William jokingly called it 'the Lambeth Honour'. When Allied bombs were falling on Berlin, William often went on bashing away at the typewriter, completely unconcerned by the threat to life and limb. When, on one occasion, he did go to an underground bomb shelter, he began singing Irish songs, tipsily, and got into a serious tussle with an influential Nazi. He was subsequently due to be prosecuted for this incident but the documentation was destroyed in a later bombing raid.

William eventually faced his own execution with equanimity. And although he had sometimes been awful to his wife, Margaret (and she had sometimes been awful, in a different way, to him), he did everything to shield her from prosecution. He impressed Commander Burt of Scotland Yard, who brought him back to England for trial, by saying, of Margaret: 'I know you won't try to pin anything on her. She had nothing to do with anything I did.' This was a chivalrous fiction: William and Margaret were a perfectly matched pair of Fascists, and their defection to Germany was a *folie à deux*. But she benefited from a certain reluctance on the part of the authorities to hound a widow, and was never prosecuted on the same charge as William: 'adhering to the King's enemies'. Some surviving Fascists from the 1930s still privately believe that William Joyce did a deal with the British authorities, agreeing to go quietly in return for Margaret being let off the hook.

William Joyce did nearly everything wrong in his life, and certainly had some dreadful views, but he was not without redeeming qualities.

⤜

William had two daughters, and the younger does not wish to have any public connection with him; some of his grandchildren too would prefer it not to be known that their grandfather was the notorious Lord Haw-Haw. But William's elder daughter, Heather, has always been open about her father's memory, which she honours – while dissociating herself completely from his politics. Heather, who was born in 1928, is a retired schoolteacher who, rather as her father did, gives private tuition to youngsters who need extra help for exams. Heather was only seven when her parents were divorced, and after that she didn't see her father again: it was believed, during the 1930s, that a 'clean break' from the non-custodial parent was best for children. Heather remembers William as a good father and a fine teacher – boisterous, talkative, full of life and full of fun. He would tell her stories and sing her songs, including Irish rebel songs (notably 'The Rising of the Moon'). She also remembers that he could fly into a vile temper, which was to some degree responsible for the break-up of his marriage to her mother, Hazel.

Heather is a devout Catholic and has done what she can to atone for her father's vilification of the Jews: she has attended synagogue as an act of reparation, and she persuaded her daughter to spend some time on an Israeli kibbutz. She has also visited Israel with Jewish friends in a spirit of reconciliation. Sarah Ebner of the *Daily Express* has written of Heather: 'She appears to have spent all her life atoning for his [William's] actions.'[12] If that is so, it is all the more affecting that Heather has also continued to show filial devotion to her father's memory. William Joyce did not know how blesssed he was to have a daughter who, right into the twenty-first century, would hold his memory dear.

It was Heather who instigated the reburial of William Joyce, from the shameful yard of Wandsworth Prison, where a convicted felon was ordered to lie, to the quiet green meadow of a Galway cemetery, a space shared with Lady Gregory and the writer Walter Macken. Though advised by family members to 'drop the subject' of Lord Haw-Haw, she has never done so, and she returns to the graveyard every two or three years – travelling by coach from Kent – to tend and clean his grave.

Many people have assisted me in the research of this life of William Joyce and his times, but his daughter Heather Iandolo was the first source, and I owe her much thanks; I also greatly esteem her courageous loyalty to her father's memory, without ever endorsing the unlikeable aspects of her father's cause.

PROLOGUE

A Hanging and Two Burials

*'I am very anxious that you should go to
Galway and see the docks, Long Walk (Spanish
Viertel), O'Brien's Bridge, Nile Lodge, Taylor's
Hill, Lenaboy Castle (Schloss), Menlough on
the Corrib, but, above all, the stretch from
Salthill to Black Rock – the Promenade with
Rockbarton, where we used to live, behind. It
had been my cherished dream to take you to
these places myself. But I can still walk with
you in spirit there.'*

From William Joyce's prison letters to his wife,
Margaret, December 1945[1]

William Joyce, who was born an American and grew up in
the west of Ireland, was hanged for treason by the British
Crown at Wandsworth Prison, London, in the cold dawn of
3 January 1946. His offence was that he had given 'aid and
comfort to the King's enemies' and assisted Germany 'in her
war against our country and our King'. He had done all this
by broadcasting over the radio.[2]

The trial of William Joyce was sensational and notorious
because Joyce was so famous as 'Lord Haw-Haw'. He was

what we would now call a media celebrity. Everyone in London wanted to get a look at him when he was brought to trial in the summer of 1945. He was, wrote Rebecca West in her masterly report of the proceedings at the Old Bailey, 'something new in the history of the world. Never before have people known the voice of one they had never seen, as well as if he had been a husband or a brother or a close friend.' It was as if Anne Robinson or Oprah Winfrey were facing a capital charge in our time.

Joyce's radio voice had become familiar to millions during the course of the Second World War, and been imitated by broadcast and stage comics alike. 'Jairmany calling! Jairmany calling!' the crowd shouted at him, in jeering humour, after his arrest in May 1945, as he was transported on a stretcher into a British military hospital in northern Germany. During the war, comedians would walk on stage and bring the house down with their imitations of his strange but unmistakable, nasal tones, often adding the visual aid of a monocle and a top hat to evoke a toff. All over the United Kingdom and Ireland, people had their own Lord Haw-Haw stories: he had allegedly made references to these people's own locality and was possessed, it was believed, of an almost occult knowledge of circumstances and topography.

A jury of ten men and two women at the Old Bailey decided in September 1945 that William Joyce must hang for treason. They had come to this decision in nineteen minutes. The British Home Secretary, James Chuter Ede, the Prime Minister, Clement Attlee, and King George VI were 'flooded' with appeals for clemency for Joyce from ordinary members of the public. 'Can you not reprieve Joyce?' asked one such appeal. 'He did no harm: he amused a great number of people.' 'Please, King,' wrote someone from North Kensington, 'save William Joyce. There were many people like him that did not believe in the war.' 'Surely enough blood has been shed without this unnecessary and fruitless continuation of cold-blooded murder,' wrote Leslie Harries of Croxley Green in Hertfordshire to the Prime Minister, Clement Attlee.[3] The file of letters and telegrams to the Home Office pleading for mercy for Joyce was three inches thick. At the same time, most of the British public probably accepted the verdict, and many believed that Joyce deserved his punishment.

An Old Bailey jury had found him guilty of treason; an appeal at the Central Criminal Court had failed; recourse to the House of Lords had been unsuccessful; and a final appeal to the Home Secretary was also turned down. The Home Secretary at this time had it in his power to commute the sentence to life imprisonment, but he chose not to. Roy Jenkins, who was himself British Home Secretary between 1965 and 1967, and knew Chuter Ede, observed that:

> Home Secretaries up to at least 1960 thought it was a test of their nerve not to give too many reprieves. Asquith in the 1890s, who greatly disliked the death penalty, let about half of those sentenced hang. Churchill in 1910–11, never an abolitionist but disliking the responsibility, did almost exactly the same. And in 1945 there was the legacy of wartime animosity.[4]

James Chuter Ede, described by Lord Jenkins as 'a decent, but stiff and conventional man', was also new to his job, and relied on the advice of his civil servants to a greater extent than a more experienced or confident politician might do. His chief mandarin, Sir Frank Newsam, who was against repealing the death sentence, advised against sparing William Joyce.[5]

Thus, on 31 December 1945, a civil servant wrote, on behalf of the Home Secretary, to the Governor of Wandsworth Prison:

> I am directed by the Secretary of State to inform you that having had under his consideration the

case of William Joyce, now lying under sentence of
death in Wandsworth Prison, he has failed to
discover any sufficient ground to justify him in
advising His Majesty to interfere with the due
course of the law.[6]

Ten years later, in the mid-1950s, Mr Chuter Ede (later
Baron Chuter-Ede) was to change his mind about the death
penalty, and to favour its abolition; by then abolition was
becoming, itself, a more conventional opinion among the
political classes.[7]

Hartley Shawcross, the handsome and glamorous lawyer
who had prosecuted William Joyce – and had convinced the
jury that, even if Joyce was not technically British, he had
so wrapped himself in the Union Jack that he had morally
claimed the protection of the Crown – was never an
enthusiast for the death penalty. Towards the end of his
career, Lord Shawcross wrote that, although the Joyce case
attracted enormous public and legal interest, and it was his
first appearance as Attorney General, 'it remains in my
mind as one of which I am not specially proud'.[8] He was
never entirely comfortable about the outcome of the Joyce
trial; in this, he was not alone. Other distinguished British
personalities, most notably the historian A. J. P. Taylor,
regarded it as a piece of legal chicanery: indeed, he
concurred with the view that he had heard privately from
some legal experts that it was 'judicial murder'.[9]

Hanging was a secretive business in England in 1946.
While the earlier Victorians had conducted hangings in
public, even making a spectacle out of an execution, the later,
reforming Victorians regarded this as unedifying and
abolished public hangings in 1868. Twenty years later,
newspaper reporters were first discouraged, and finally
barred, from reporting the details of a hanging, largely, it
seems, because some hangings were ill-managed, and even
horribly mangled.

From about 1914 onwards, the whole procedure came

under the Official Secrets Act. After this period, very little information was made available about the process of judicial execution. Press announcements were kept to the bare minimum: every now and then, austere little paragraphs would appear on the inside page of a national newspaper to the effect that an offender, usually a convicted murderer, had been executed. Not until the mid-1950s, when the abolitionist movement was gaining ground, did a hanging become big news: the execution of Ruth Ellis – young, blonde, a mother, and convicted for a crime of passion – turned the death sentence into a sensation.

The *threat* of the death penalty had always brought an element of drama to famous trials. Indeed, it was a legend among Fleet Street crime reporters that the abolition of hanging would diminish the status of crime reporting by removing the drama from it: the notion that a man might swing for his offence had always added an edge to newspaper reporting of a big trial. (One of the classic black comedies of journalism, Ben Hecht's *The Front Page*, places an imminent hanging at the centre of political and media shenanigans with robust hilarity.) And it was certainly a moment of true melodrama when a judge donned the black cap and pronounced the awesome words, as he did to William:

> William Joyce, the sentence of the Court upon you is that you be taken from this place to a lawful prison and thence to a place of execution, and that you be there hanged by the neck until you are dead; and that your body be afterwards buried within the precincts of the prison in which you shall have been confined before your execution. And may the Lord have mercy on your soul.

The press had their splash headlines: 'JOYCE TO HANG'. But once this was announced, the prisoner almost disappeared from view. The decision was made, his life was to be terminated and the world moved on.

Moreover, after the legal decisions were made, the official

veil of secrecy descended. When J. W. Hall, barrister-at-law in the Middle Temple, was composing his legal text-book on *The Trial of William Joyce*, he expressed exasperation at the unyielding secrecy which habitually surrounded the death penalty in the United Kingdom. Writing in 1946, he could discover very little about the conditions in which Joyce went to his death. No co-operation was given from the Home Office, and Mr Hall could get nothing from official sources about the circumstances of Lord Haw-Haw's hanging. Hall was discreetly warned, too, that to publish any detailed report about an execution could lead to prosecution under the Official Secrets Act. When a Major Wallace Blake disclosed in a newspaper article in 1926 the particulars of a hanging, he was charged with a breach of the Official Secrets Act.

Thus it was, complained attorney Hall, that the general public was never properly informed as to the course of a hanging; whether it went well or ill; whether a prisoner died bravely, or whether, as the executioner Albert Pierrepoint has revealed in his autobiography, he may have struggled and sobbed and gone berserk.[10] Under the Official Secrets Act, all such information was censored. J. W. Hall praised, by contrast, the American system, where a certain number of respectable ordinary citizens were admitted to an execution, to bear witness to what was being done in the name of the people. Official witnesses *were* present at British hangings, but all of them were bound to silence under the Official Secrets Act, and none came as an ordinary citizen, but as a representative of church, municipality, state or Crown.

The secrecy surrounding a hanging extended to the informal culture among prison officers. If they had been present at a hanging, they never spoke about their experience. Mick Lydon, the principal officer at Her Majesty's Prison, Wandsworth, from 1969 until 2003, met many 'screws' during his career who were known to have attended one of Wandsworth's 137 hangings (the death penalty had been abolished only in 1965), but only one man would ever admit to it. The apparatus for hanging – an indoor gallows in an execution chamber – was dismantled only in 1993, but Mick Lydon, though a senior prison officer (whose family, coincidentally, came from Oughterard in Galway), was never permitted to see it.

৵

The execution of William Joyce – from what we now know, since more official papers have become available – appears to have gone smoothly. The prison notes of William's last days document a life of serene regularity. It was noted during the preparation for the execution that there was no detrimental change in Haw-Haw's condition, except that his weight had increased in prison. He had weighed 135 pounds when he was admitted to Wandsworth in the late autumn of 1945; when he was hanged, in January 1946, he weighed 151 pounds.[11]

The executioner, Albert Pierrepoint, was most particular about such details. He prided himself on his craftsmanship as a hangman, which, just as Dr Guillotin before him had believed, should be done in a manner which caused the minimum suffering. In their own way, these executioners were enlightened. Pierrepoint, who wrote a laconic autobiography containing much detail about the technical niceties of his trade (with some resentment that he was not paid a fee if a prisoner were granted a reprieve), could despatch a condemned person in seconds. He hanged Ruth Ellis, for example, in eight seconds flat, and was satisfied that she could scarcely have suffered at all. This was achieved through painstaking attention to the details of height, weight and musculature.

Thus, Pierrepoint would measure and weigh an individual with great care – rather as an anaesthetist does before a hospital operation – so that the drop would be exact and the *coup de grâce* instant. When William Joyce was first admitted to prison, for example, it was pencilled in official notes that his height was five foot five and a half inches. Pierrepoint was more precise: Joyce was five foot five and three-quarter inches. His build was described as 'spare but muscular'. The drop, calculated Pierrepoint, would be seven foot six inches. He seldom made mistakes. Albert Pierrepoint's most caustic criticism was directed against unprofessional executioners he had seen abroad, who did not carry out the proper preparations and caused the condemned individual to die a slow and agonised death. He was scandalised that one of the Nazis hanged at Nuremberg had taken twenty-four minutes to die at the end of a rope. Pierrepoint had no feelings for the Nazi in question, but deplored such unprofessionalism in an executioner.

William Joyce's cell, the regular thirteen feet by seven, was located in E Wing at Wandsworth Prison. It exists to this day, as a harmless television staff room – the Victorian grille windows still in place, high above eye level. A collapsible wall opened in the cell to reveal the execution chamber. There was no long walk to the gallows, as frequently depicted in films or ballads.

Joyce's execution, which took place at 9 AM on 3 January (having been deferred from 8 AM) would have been witnessed by the executioner, the executioner's assistant Alexander Riley (also from Manchester, like Pierrepoint), the chaplain and the prison governor. Also present were two prison officers and the High Sheriff of the county. If a prisoner was an ordinary murderer, the Under-Sheriff might represent the High Sheriff, who, in turn, represented the Crown. But for an important hanging, such as death for high treason, the High Sheriff himself would attend; the High Sheriff duly attended the dispatch of Lord Haw-Haw.

William had slept well almost all the time he had been in Wandsworth; only on the night before his execution did he require a light sleeping draught. He saw his wife Margaret for the last time on the eve of his appointment with death. He embraced his brother Quentin, who had done so much for him, and his sister Joan, whom he called 'Little Wolf'. The siblings were in tears; Joyce himself was calm and serene. He was visited by his friends, and old fellow Blackshirts, McNeil Sloane and John Angus Macnab, both of whom would leave England within a couple of years, never to return – Macnab to Spain, Sloane to Australia. It was reported that Joyce was cheerful. He saw the Church of England chaplain, too, for he chose to die an Anglican, like his mother, despite a long and friendly correspondence with a Roman Catholic priest who fought hard for William's soul.

Joyce also had a mystical belief in the theory of 'Gestalt', which was based on holistic approaches to personal growth – but which, with William, also extended to a Zen-like concept of souls drifting off to a higher plane and yet remaining part of those they loved. Strange, perhaps, that he chose a branch of mystical psychology associated with Jewish intellectuals of the 1920s.

On the morning of his execution, William woke early and drank a cup of tea. He changed from his prison clothes into the blue serge suit which he had worn at the time of his arrest in Germany. He washed, but was not shaved. At one minute to nine the prison governor came to William's cell and informed him that his time had come. William walked the fifteen to twenty paces from his condemned cell into the connecting room which was the execution chamber. A hood was placed over his head, along with the noose of the hanging rope; Pierrepoint pulled a lever and a trap door opened underneath Joyce. William dropped, and was dead.

Official records say simply that in facing his execution William Joyce 'made no complaints'. There is an anecdote that he looked at his trembling knees and smiled. The execution was swiftly accomplished: dislocation between the second and third cervical vertebrate occurred and the spinal cord was torn 'completely across', which means that Joyce would have been instantaneously unconscious.[12] Pierrepoint had reason to think that he had done his usual professional job. It has been claimed that the scar on William's face burst open, 'so that on the face of the former orator a second, uglier mouth shortly announced itself, soaking the canvas [underneath] and spreading'.[13] While this is quite probable, no named witnesses are cited.

At Joyce's old school in Galway, St Ignatius, where a Jesuit teacher had prophetically once told young Willie that he would end his life with a rope around his neck, a Mass was said for the repose of his soul; the consecration of the Eucharist was timed for exactly the moment that the noose snapped the cerebral cortex.

The corpse of Lord Haw-Haw was transported to the prison mortuary, and the jury which had convicted William Joyce asked if they could view his mortal remains. They were permitted to do so, again bound by the Official Secrets Act. A coroner officially pronounced that death was due to injury to the brain and spinal cord, consequent upon judicial hanging. And William Joyce, the notorious Lord Haw-Haw, was buried at the dead of night in the prison yard, without any ceremonial, or benefit of clergy or mourners.

This was the rule for the interment of a hanged man: he must be buried within the prison precincts; he must be buried at night; there must be no mourners; and the plot must be unmarked. The ritual was part of the shame and stigma of being a convicted felon. William was buried six feet six inches down, on top of the remains of another hanged man, Robert Blaine, who had been executed for murder just five days before William – and without any public attention whatsoever. Quicklime was not used, but a layer of charcoal separated the corpses and bones of the two men.

✧

And so the notorious Lord Haw-Haw passed into history, though his memory was revived from time to time when some event warranted it. When legal niceties about the constitutional definition of treason were discoursed upon, the William Joyce trial invariably cropped up, as it still does. William Joyce's name was often linked with that of Roger Casement – the British civil servant turned Irish patriot who was also executed for treason, in 1916 – whenever legal experts reviewed the question, still to some extent unresolved, of the meaning of treason.

When Lord Porter, the dissenting judge at the Joyce appeal who voted against the death penalty, died in 1956, his claim to fame was his association with the Haw-Haw trial. When the soldier who had arrested William Joyce, Captain Alexander Adrian Lickorish, died in 1960, he was immortalised as 'Haw-Haw's captor'. When Margaret Joyce remarried, in 1962, to Donald May, an Englishman from Casablanca who had a conviction for minor fraud and a Union Jack fluttering from his private mast, it was newsworthy. When it was announced that Frank Capra would make a movie of the William Joyce story, starring Alec Guinness, the case was again recalled. (The film was never made.) Anniversaries revive the Lord Haw-Haw case every now and then, and radio and television reports about the uses of propaganda invariably feature a clip of his strangely unforgettable voice.

The bones of William Joyce lay in the grounds of Wandsworth Prison for thirty years after his execution. The unmarked burial plot, which had been covered in grass, was, after the abolition of hanging, covered in tarmac. It now forms part of a side road within the prison walls, near a clump of undistinguished sheds sometimes used as dog kennels. The graves of hanged men were unmarked and unrespected as a sign of their shame, and as a continuing punishment for their capital offence. Thus had Roger Casement's remains lain, in an unmarked plot at Pentonville Prison, after he had been hanged in 1916; added to this was the stigma of his homosexual diaries (which the Irish believed were forged as a deliberate attempt to smear him). But history eventually works its alchemy of healing, and in 1965 the remains of

Roger Casement were permitted to be exhumed and returned to Ireland, where he was given a State funeral – a traitor to the Crown, but a hero to the Irish – and reinterred in Glasnevin Cemetery in north Dublin, a place made famous by James Joyce in his great saga *Ulysses*.

The reburial of Roger Casement was also to be a precedent for William Joyce. William's elder daughter, Heather, had for some time been possessed by the idea that, while his bones lay in Wandsworth yard under that unmarked tarmac, her father's spirit was not at rest. The idea of having her father's remains removed to a proper graveyard first came to her while she was crossing Chatham Cemetery in Kent in the mid-1950s, 'around the time of the Suez crisis,' she recalls. 'A voice asked me if I would not have liked my father to be buried in a peaceful cemetery outside prison walls.' It took some years to organise, and the time was not right until after the Roger Casement reburial. Heather subsequently applied to the Home Office for permission to exhume her father's remains and, under the regime of the liberal Roy Jenkins, was granted such permission. She then set about raising money to fund a reburial: she was a teacher of modest means and could not afford to pay all the costs herself. She did pay for most of the funeral costs, but a donor who chose to remain anonymous provided the cash for a headstone.

Heather considered reburying her father in Kent, where she herself lived, but she was advised that in England the grave of William Joyce might attract unwanted attention. It might be daubed by the graffiti of hooligans or attract neo-Fascists, who could turn it into some kind of political shrine. Kent was therefore ruled out, as was the Oldham area, where William's mother is buried and where the British National Party have a foothold. And so it came to Heather that her father's mortal remains should be transported to Ireland, where, she felt, the grave would be undisturbed. William had looked back on his boyhood in Galway, where he had sported and played by the rock pools of the Atlantic Ocean, with great affection.

She made enquiries about a grave in Galway, and her cause was taken up by an enterprising Connacht newspaper, the *Galway Advertiser*, and its proprietor-editor, Patrick O'Gorman, known familiarly as Ronnie. Mr O'Gorman shared the belief, strongly held in Irish culture, that every man and woman is entitled to a decent burial: whatever a man might have done in his lifetime, he deserves respect in death – a belief that, among the Irish, dates back to the ancient Celts.

Ronnie O'Gorman contacted Heather after he saw her interviewed by Gay Byrne in early 1976 on *The Late Late Show*, which at this time was watched by virtually everyone in Ireland. He was impressed by the dignified way in which she had stood by Haw-Haw, not as a Fascist, but as a father. A member of the audience had described Lord Haw-Haw as a 'disgrace', perhaps thinking of the way that his voice had sometimes alarmed Allied sailors at sea. Heather, who is slight in stature and precise in speech, did not contradict this, but accepted what the lady said with humility. But she still wanted to bury her father properly. This is very much Heather's attitude: she accepts hostile judgements against her father as a public character, but she still feels a sense of filial devotion to him as his daughter.

Ronnie O'Gorman felt some sense of association through his own Galway background:

> A friend of my father had been at school with Willie Joyce and had often talked about him, so I had a little bit of background anyway. I was very taken by Heather. She was very fine. And she talked about a visit from an angel, and where most people might scoff, I was quite intrigued. I thought her story was very interesting and I thought her demeanour was very fine. It was a lovely thing to do for your father.

Mr O'Gorman is a fond father himself, and Heather's loyalty touched him. He wrote and offered to help bring Lord Haw-Haw's remains to rest in Galway; he contacted an undertaker in Galway called O'Flaherty – 'if you were any way half-decent or half-gentry at all, the O'Flahertys would look after you' – and they said they would be pleased to do so, for William Joyce. In London, an Irish undertaker, Patrick Ryan, looked after the English part of the transportation arrangements.

And so the process was commenced to rebury Lord Haw-Haw, in the New Cemetery (opened in 1882), at Bohermore Road in Galway, where he would be in the company of Lady Gregory, the co-founder of the Abbey Theatre and mentor to W. B. Yeats; Walter Macken, the popular novelist; the Galway writer Pádraic Ó Conaire, much-esteemed in the west of Ireland; and the family of Nora Barnacle, who became, eventually, Mrs James Joyce. Permission having been granted from the British Home Office, permission was sought, and granted, from the city authorities in Galway. The Lord Mayor of Galway, Brendan Mulholland, to whom the request was made, was 'intrigued' and said that the plan was altogether acceptable.

When the request came to be discussed by Galway Council, there was a dissenting voice when Alderman Fintan Coogan, a member of the Dáil, said that while he respected the dead, as all Irishmen do, he felt compelled to point out that as a young man William Joyce had been known to associate with British soldiers in Galway during the time of the Troubles. This was a delicate point in Ireland. A handful of veteran republicans in the Galway region thought William less than an ornament to Connacht. Yet the feeling in the chamber was strongly favourable towards receiving Lord Haw-Haw. Given that the discussion concerned the dead, and a reburial of a dead man, the council was 'not impressed' by Alderman Coogan's mean-spirited statements: the new mayor, Councillor Mary Byrne, said that a daughter should be allowed rebury her father in a charitable fashion. Councillor Tom Tierney said that there was a lack of Christian charity throughout the world, and that the council should therefore assent to this in a Christian fashion.[14] Ronnie O'Gorman's recollection was that both mayors were rather fascinated by the enterprise.

And so it was that William Joyce was removed from Wandsworth Prison yard on 18 August 1976: the tarmac had to be removed and the body exhumed from plot number 87 at the dead of night – which was still the prison regulation. The remains were transported by Aer Lingus to Galway, where they were laid to rest on a dazzlingly warm August day. William was buried in the Protestant section of Bohermore graveyard, in recognition of his wish to be part of his mother's Anglican faith. Yet Heather chose a Tridentine Latin Mass for the funeral ceremony at the cemetery oratory, preceding the reburial. Her stepmother, Margaret, who died in 1972, had told Heather how much William had loved Latin. When Heather had discussed it with her in the 1960s, Margaret had been enthusiastic about the plan to rebury William's remains in Galway.

The Mass and burial were conducted by a well-known Galway priest, Father Padraic Ó Laoi. Father Ó Laoi was a distinguished author as well as a priest, and he had written a biography of Father Michael Griffin, who, in a tangled way, enters the William Joyce story in the 1920s. Father Ó Laoi was pleased to put the past to rest with this ceremony.[15]

The past is ever present in Ireland, and the Troubles of the 1920s were not forgotten. And yet there was also a feeling among the people of Galway, Ronnie O'Gorman recalled, of what we would now call 'closure': 'Father Ó Laoi said the Mass very beautifully, in Latin, and fulfilled Heather's wishes, I would say, to the last degree.' The British media now reported Lord Haw-Haw's final burial almost affectionately: 'LORD HAW-HAW GOES HOME', 'IRELAND CALLING, IRELAND CALLING!', 'FORGIVE AND FORGET PLEA AS HAW-HAW IS BURIED.'[16]

The coffin was adorned with white lilies as it descended into the Irish earth. 'A few Blackshirts came out of the bushes, standing to attention every now and then when the hearse passed,' Ronnie O'Gorman recalls. 'One wondered at the shadows that passed the cemetery that day.' But in general, it was a genial Irish occasion: a wake. Tea and sandwiches were served afterwards, and Heather went off to north Mayo to visit some cousins, who live near where her grandfather Michael Joyce had been born. She had accomplished what the spirits had asked of her.

And there, towards the entrance of Bohermore, under a spreading yew tree, with the blue hills of County Clare visible across Galway Bay, lie to this day the mortal remains of William Joyce, the man who was 'Lord Haw-Haw'. On his gravestone is written: 'I am the Resurrection and the Life – DONA EIS REQUIEM. William Joyce – 23 April 1906–3 January 1946.' By an odd quirk, the date of William's birth is erroneous by a day: he was born on 24 April.

William Joyce had an ambivalent relationship with Ireland. He hated Irish republicanism, which he regarded as a form of Bolshevism. He also believed, with some justice, that the Irish Rising of 1916 and the Troubles which followed had caused the impoverishment of his family. But his feeling of hatred towards Irish nationalism had modified with time, and Joyce came to accept an independent Ireland.[17]

In his early years he had felt an Anglo-Irish disdain for the Irish tribe and what it represented, but the tribe took him back in the end, and blood and soil exercised their dominion over passports and legalities.

1

Blood and Soil: The Family
Heritage of William Joyce

*'In Ireland, a man carries his family mansion
about him like a snail, and his father's ghost
follows him like a shadow.'*

G. K. Chesterton, *Irish Impressions*

Although he always professed to be against snobbery,
William Joyce took a certain pride in his ancestral heritage.
When, as a precocious lad of sixteen, he applied to join the
British army, he called upon an ancestral line of soldiers and
military men who had dedicated themselves to the defence
of the British Realm. 'As a young man of pure British
descent, some of whose forefathers have held high positions
in the British army,' he wrote, a little pompously, 'I have
always been desirous of devoting what little capability and
energy I may possess to the country which I love so dearly.'[1]
But the country to which he devoted his capability and
energy was not the one he had in mind at the time.

When, on 6 July 1933, he applied for the false British
passport which would eventually hang him, he claimed that
he was born in Galway, in the west of Ireland, which was of
course part of the United Kingdom in 1906. Later, when he
wrote *Twilight Over England*, which was published in

Germany in 1940, he admitted that he was born in the United States, and he presented his ancestral heritage in a more aristocratic light: 'I was born in New York in 1906. My father's people had lived in Ireland since the Norman Conquest. From my mother I inherited English, Irish and Scottish blood.' Although, he told his German readers, he could be called British, he had come to believe that his line was 'more purely Norman than that of most people who trace their descent with finer feelings'.

The Joyces – who have left their name on the map of Ireland, where, to this day, a part of north Galway and south Mayo in Connacht is formally identified as 'Joyce's Country' – did indeed come to Ireland at the time of the Norman Conquest of Ireland, which occurred in 1169. Many scholars, including Sir William Wilde, Oscar Wilde's father, have written about the Norman-Welsh origin of the Joyce clan, who had been 'Joas' or 'Shoyes' in Welsh, and became 'Seoige' (a proper name). The Joyce family settled around Lough Corrib and Lough Mask, a strikingly beautiful part of Mayo, under the protection of the O'Flaherty chieftain. Clans mattered in Ireland, and there is still a sense of the clan tradition. Sir William Wilde, a distinguished medical specialist, had a home in this locality, around Moytura, and loved it for its antiquities: the village of Cong by Lough Corrib was, he observed, a centre of early Christian civilisation.[2]

Sir William Wilde wrote that the Joyces would later specialise in producing some very tall, big, blond men – 'Joyce giants', as they were called – who would be enticed by the court of Frederick the Great to come and serve in Prussia. William Joyce must have been acquainted with this folklore since he also liked to claim some German blood:

> Apart from my absolute belief in National Socialism
> and my conviction of Hitler's superhuman heroism,
> I had always been attracted to Germany. Perhaps the
> attraction was due to the German blood which
> flowed in the veins of some of my ancestors.[3]

It is difficult to find a specific trace of German blood in any of William's direct antecedants, although there was a family tradition that a great-uncle on his maternal side had been associated with the University of Heidelberg.[4] William certainly had a fondness for German culture, and music, from an early age: he claimed that he spoke German from the age of three, picking it up from his Brooklyn German neighbours. Heather recalls her father playing German opera, especially Wagner, to her on the gramophone. Towards the end of his life, William still referred to Germany as 'the Heimat' – the homeland.

Joyce's Country in Galway–Mayo, by the banks of Lough Corrib, is romantic and beautiful: a dreamy, soulful, poetic lakeland with translucent skies over pale water, a landscape evoked most characteristically by the mountainy paintings of the Belfast-born painter Paul Henry. Yet it was a sad and melancholy place. Oscar Wilde often visited his parents' house around Lough Corrib as a young man, but he found it too depressing to linger long, and later complained greatly that his father's tenants were slow to pay their rent.[5]

To be sure, the tenants were tardy with the rent: the poor creatures had no money. Ireland was marked by poverty in the nineteenth century, but hardly anywhere in Ireland was so marked by it as Mayo. Conditions in the county inspired writer, painter and image-maker: George Moore, the author of the first, radical novel about an unmarried mother, *Esther Waters,* hailed from Lough Corrib country. In 1953, south Mayo – and Cong in particular – was the location for John Ford's epic film *The Quiet Man,* starring John Wayne and Maureen O'Hara. Cong has been preserved just as it was in the set of the film.

It was into this region that William's father, Michael Joyce, was born, on 12 December 1866. His exact birthplace was the family home at Killour, in the parish of The Neale; the nearest town is Ballinrobe, ever associated with angling. The Neale has another famous association: it was here that Captain Charles Boycott was the land agent to the Earl of Erne in the early 1880s; he later gave his name to the word 'boycott', used as a noun and verb in eighty-two languages. Captain Boycott was once regarded as the essence of the cruel, mean-spirited and avaricious kind of Englishman who oppressed the Irish poor. Captain Boycott, a collatoral ancestor of the journalist Rosie Boycott, has his own Internet site now. Not only does history pardon all: celebrity pardons anything.

Boycott was not a particularly cruel man, but he was unimaginative and inflexible in seeking to collect rent and enforce evictions at a time of terrible land crises. He symbolises the many misunderstandings between the English and the Irish, and the English insistence on the letter rather than the spirit of the law. He never understood that the people in the west of Ireland did not have the same attitude to legality: in Connacht, they lived by song and story, myth and religion, evasions and deceptions and the circum-locutions of the Celtic mind. This paradigm would arise in the central fact of the William Joyce story: is your identity defined by legality, or by what you think you are, in your own imagination?

But then the people in the county of Mayo had to survive any way they could throughout the miserable years of Queen Victoria's reign. General Gordon of Khartoum once wrote to *The Times* of London comparing – unfavourably – the life of the rural Irish with that of the lowest Indian or Chinese peasant.[6] Around the time that Michael Joyce was born, more than a quarter of the Mayo population lived in one-roomed cabins, which were rated by census commissioners as the lowest category of dwelling. Only one other county – Kerry – vied with Mayo as having such miserable conditions of living.

Mayo had been badly hit by the Great Famine of 1845–50, and the decades that followed were so troubled by evictions, land wars, agrarian outrages and relentless rural poverty that Irish people from elsewhere lamented 'Mayo – God help us!' at its very name. The Famine had devastated the Irish people and left a sorrowful mark on the Irish landscape and character. They lost their native language – Irish went into a rapid decline with the great Famine – as well as much of their population. Ireland, in 1800, had a population on a par with England. By 1900, Ireland's population was less than one-tenth that of England's.[7] William Joyce was an Irish unionist – he opposed the separation of England and Ireland – but came to believe that the break-up of the Union occurred because of the economic neglect of Ireland:

> If one-sixth of the money invested and lost outside the Empire, in South America alone, for example, had been given to Ireland, there might have continued that cooperation between her and England which provided British history with Burke, Goldsmith, Sheridan, Wellington, Boyle, Roberts, French, Beatty and Carson.[8]

The 1870s were not an optimistic era in which to grow up in beautiful but poverty-stricken Mayo. Times got worse as the decade wore on, and by the awful winter of 1878 eviction notices in Mayo had increased five-fold over the average of the previous decade. Another famine was predicted for Mayo in 1879, when the potato crop failed again, and the kelp industry collapsed. A Europe-wide recession – which, elsewhere, would prompt the beginnings of modern anti-Semitism – made matters worse.[9] The reported apparition of the Blessed Virgin Mary at Knock, in north Mayo, in 1879 seems to have brought comfort and consolation to people who were, in effect, living in hovels and clothed in rags. A hundred years later, the faith of the people of Knock would make it a landmark, as Ireland's 'miracle airport', built against all expert prognostications.[10]

The Joyce family were small tenant farmers. Michael Joyce's father, Martin, was illiterate, and signed his son's birth certificate with the mark 'X', but lack of education does not necessarily equate with lack of intelligence. The family were remembered in the locality as very decent folk, and 'an intelligent type of people'. Martin and Mary Joyce (née Naughton) farmed 'twenty-nine acres, two roods and fourteen perches' at Killour in The Neale. The landlord was Richard Cooper, a member of the Anglo-Irish gentry.[11] The property had a total annual valuation of £6 10s, which, though lower than the county average, was not considered negligible. A farm of this size was regarded as solid enough in a county where many Mayo families were living on holdings of less than five acres. And the Joyces' home was a small but solid cottage, not a miserable cabin.

Five children are recorded in the family of Martin and Mary Joyce: Catherine, Michael, John, Mary and Patt – this would have been Patrick, but was spelled 'Patt' in the parish register. Patrick, the youngest, was to inherit the farm: by the beginning of the twentieth century, the Wyndham Land Acts were enabling tenant farmers to buy, at favourable rates, the land they occupied. Patrick's son, Mattie, and his family, still live there.

At that time, in a family of five children, only one could remain on the land: the others would have to fend for themselves – which usually meant emigration to America. There are yearning songs of Irish exile which might indicate that taking the boat to America was a sad event for Irish migrants, but for many young people, America was the land of heart's desire. The British government tried to encourage the Irish to choose Canada, which needed more people. Some did go to Canada, but once they were there, many of them migrated to the United States when they could. The big problem was getting the money for the fare.

'There is at present a desire, amounting almost to a mania, among the juvenile portion of the population of the west of Ireland to emigrate to America,' wrote Vere Foster, a philanthropist of the 1880s, 'but they are without the means of gratifying their desire.'[12] In this mania to emigrate, the young people were supported by their priests – though not by their bishops, who feared the depopulation of Ireland and the moral dangers of life overseas. In 1880, some nine hundred priests on the western seaboard from Donegal to Cork applied to benefactors for financial help to promote emigration. They did this because they were so concerned about the poverty and the lack of opportunity in their parishes. One priest said of the west of Ireland that

> the holdings were so small, the land so sterile, that these people will always be in poverty. I wish to God half the people of this barren territory would emigrate … Penal servitude would be a paradise to many of them compared to their present condition – slaves, drudges and paupers, not half-fed or half-clad.[13]

Michael Joyce, as the eldest son in the family, might have had the choice of staying in Mayo and inheriting the farm, but he seems to have had no interest in agriculture. Daniel McGing of Ayle, near Westport, whose father purchased a public house from Michael Joyce in the early twentieth century, recalled that while Michael was a fine strong man who excelled at anything that involved throwing a ball, 'he wasn't much of a farmer'.[14] Even when he had a pub which had twenty acres of land attached to it, Michael never showed much interest in using the land for agricultural purposes. Michael saw land as real estate, and he liked to improve the property which stood on land. He wanted to go up in the world, and he believed that business, not agriculture, was the way forward.

Michael Joyce grew into a handsome young man, energetic and strong, with one of those chiselled west-of-Ireland faces I have seen in my own relatives in the Connemara region. He took the emigrant boat when he was twenty-one, in 1888, as his younger brother John and his sister Mary would do also. They would have departed from Galway or from Derry in the North: Westport had also been a translatlantic port until the mid-1880s.

Michael was always a man with ambition – which is not, in itself, to be disparaged. His politics were also, perhaps, a little unusual for an Irish Catholic, and a Mayoman, at this period. Unlike many of his compatriots, and most of his peers, Michael was not an Irish nationalist; he was a pro-British unionist in his political leanings. Indeed, he did not at all care for the drift of Irish political activity in the 1880s.

The Land League had been founded in 1879 – perhaps significantly, almost in the same week as the apparition at Knock – with the ostensible aim of reducing rents, but with the longer-term goal of banishing British landlordism in Ireland. Charles Stewart Parnell became the leader of the Irish party at Westminster in 1880, and the spirit of Irish nationalism increased from this time on.

While many of the Irish saw England as a cruel oppressor – a view echoed and sometimes amplified by the Irish in America – Michael, as a businessman, saw the British Empire as a civilising influence which, everywhere it went, sought to establish law and order, just as the Roman Empire had once done. Lawlessness was a continual problem in much of rural Ireland at this time.

Landlords, and those belonging to the 'landlord class', were continual objects of assault and assassination: in Michael Joyce's own townland of The Neale, Lord Montmores, a local small landlord and magistrate, had been horrifically murdered in 1880. His body was found riddled with bullets; when it was suggested that the corpse be taken from the road and placed in a nearby cottage, 'the terrified cottager begged that it should not enter his house, in case he himself might be murdered for affording it shelter.'[15] The refusal to shelter the dead was also considered shocking, as it went against Irish traditions of respect for a corpse. This was the measure of how powerful the forces of lawlessness could be in Ireland.

In 1882, the country was aghast at two separate murder cases. In Dublin, the notorious 'Phoenix Park murders', when Lord Frederick Cavendish and T. H. Burke were suddenly set upon and assassinated. In County Galway, a whole family of Joyces were killed in cold blood in the grisly Maamtrasna murders – a criminal act rather than a political crime, which, for more than a century afterwards, remained the subject of communal silence in the locality.[16]

Such incidents portrayed Ireland as a place that was hopelessly mired in the most depraved crime and disorder; the image was not far from the reality. According to the Irish criminal and judicial statistics for 1880, crime in Ireland outstripped crime in England in all categories except forgery, attempted suicide and 'offences against morality' – which mostly meant homosexual acts.[17]

Michael had a lifelong horror of crime – and poverty – and developed a corresponding respect for the police and for authority. He always esteemed the constabulary; they would later do business with him in Galway. A local Royal Irish Constabulary sergeant would describe Michael Joyce as 'one of the most respectable, law-abiding and loyal men in this locality, and one who has been consistently an advocate of the "pro-Allied" cause since the beginning of the [1914–18] war.'[18] These values were transmitted, with added intensity, to his son William.

✎

An Irishman who admired Britain and the British Empire might, we could imagine, prefer to emigrate to England; but for an ambitious young man, to join the Catholic Irish in Britain was hardly a step up the social ladder. The Catholic Irish in Britain had a very lowly status indeed. They were regarded as the poorest of the poor, savages who slept with their pigs. It was Friedrich Engels who coined the latter stereotype, which endured right into the middle years of the twentieth century. The anti-Semitism which William Joyce would profess, although fierce and nasty, seemed scarcely much worse than the manner in which the Irish had been portrayed in English iconography and popular literature.

It was possible, but difficult, for a Catholic Irishman to move up in the world in England, away from the poor Paddies, and the simian creatures labelled 'Irishmen' who illustrated the pages of *Punch* and *The Times*. The Irish who went to England were saddled with this stereotype; the Irish who went into the melting pot of America had more opportunity of upward mobility. In America, all immigrants were in the same position of having to work their way up to respectability. More importantly, perhaps, in the case of Michael Joyce, the Irish who went to America had the chance to make money.

The America that Michael Joyce came to, in 1888, was tough but exciting. The poor and the huddled masses indeed swarmed forth, just as the Statue of Liberty invited them to do. New York City, where Michael landed, was a rabbit warren of tenements, of slum dwellers crammed into rookeries at extortionate rents, of two-cent restaurants and seven-cent lodging houses.[19]

Poverty and overpopulation characterised the living conditions of many immigrants, but life was beginning to improve for the Irish in America by the mid-1880s. By 1884, some 40 per cent of New Yorkers were of Irish extraction; nearly a fifth of these lived in Brooklyn.[20] Twenty-five per cent of whites in Brooklyn had Irish mothers, which also indicated a degree of intermarriage with other ethnic groups. The Irish were rising because they had relatively higher literacy rates than other immigrants, but also because they had mastered the political machines of East Coast America and learned how to trounce their immigrant competitors – the Italians, the Russian Jews and the Chinese.

In previous decades, there had been WASP (white Anglo-Saxon Protestant) prejudice against the Irish – similar to that which obtained in England – with 'no Irish need apply' signs in the advertising columns of the newspapers. By the 1880s, this had largely disappeared. The great chronicler of immigrant life Jacob Riis describes the Irishman in New York at this period as 'the true cosmopolitan immigrant. All-pervading, he shares his lodging with perfect impartiality with the Italian, the Greek and the Dutchman … and objects equally to them all.' In this mêlée of new American life, the Irishmen dominated the saloon bars and used these to further their political schemes; the Germans became obsessively domesticated; the Jews saved money; and the poor Italians and Chinese became street scavengers.[21]

Opportunities in the building trade were booming all over the United States, and Michael began, as many other Irishmen did, as a builder. He worked for the Naughton Construction Company in Brooklyn, with which there was some famliy connection; for the Griffin Iron Works; and for the Pennsylvania Railroad, as a freight-checker.[22] He travelled around between New York and New Jersey in the course of following the building trade. At this time he also began to use his middle name of 'Francis' and signed himself 'Michael F. Joyce', in the American style. (Francis was a baptismal name; he was registered at birth as plain 'Michael'.) Michael acquired an American accent, which he always thereafter retained, although it was a light accent, with west-of-Ireland inflexions. Later, he would be called 'Poppa' by his children and grandchildren, in the American style.[23]

Moreover, within four years of arriving in America, Michael Joyce took the preliminary steps towards becoming an American citizen. All our acts have consequences, and this decision of Michael's was to feature dramatically in the trial of his son William more than fifty years later. On 22 July 1892, Michael Joyce signed a formal declaration that it was

> his bona fide intention to become a citizen of the United States, and to renounce for ever all allegiance and fidelity to any and every Foreign

> Prince, Potentate, State and Sovereignty whatever, and particularly to the Queen of the United Kingdom of Great Britain and Ireland, whose subject he has heretofore been.[24]

Two years later, on 25 October 1894, he was duly sworn in as a citizen of the United States in Hudson County, New Jersey.

In a way, it seems contradictory that Michael Joyce, the great admirer of the British Empire, should renounce queen and country as emphatically as this avowal required. There was no *requirement* on those who immigrated to the United States to become American citizens, and many immigrants did not do so, or did not begin the process until they had been in America for perhaps ten or twelve years.[25] Until 1906, there were no uniform standards of naturalisation across the Union, and until 1914 there was no necessity for those living in America to hold a passport when travelling abroad.

But Michael almost certainly decided to take up American citizenship because it was good for business, and it served his striving ambition. Although immigrants could do a whole range of jobs without being citizens of the United States, they could not enter any government, state or city business unless they had acquired citizenship. The Irish-American grip on City Hall business had solidified by the end of the nineteenth century, but when contracts were put out to tender, those with citizenship were given preference. Michael Joyce was unlikely to have been particularly good friends with the Tammany Hall Irish who were increasingly securing government and state contracts, as the core of this Irish-American community were anti-British Irish nationalists; on the other hand, by becoming an American citizen, he could qualify for business tenders.

Some years later, Michael Joyce would advise a friend by letter that it was always more advantageous to be an American citizen when working and living in America.[26] So his political allegiances were not entirely fixed, and were sometimes dictated by circumstances: he was an Irish loyalist, but when it came to advancing in business, he was also an American citizen.

❧

For the next ten years, Michael Joyce remained a bachelor. In Ireland, post-Famine, it was the practice for men to marry late. Once out of Ireland, however, opportunities to marry were more plentiful. Trawling through the records of other young Irishmen named Michael Joyce who appear in the American census of 1900, it seems that most of them married young, and by their thirties were usually fathers of four or five children. America has always been a high-marriage (and pro-natalist) society, but Michael Joyce held back from such commitment; he was perhaps too focused on working hard and making money to give time to courtship and family. And perhaps Michael was waiting for a bride who would be fitting for his upward social ambitions.

During this time, Michael was prospering sufficiently in the United States to return to the west of Ireland several times on holiday. He visited both Mayo and Galway on these trips. And it so happened that an Irish-born doctor, William Brooke, a resident of Lancashire, along with his daughter Gertrude Emily were also in the habit of visiting the west of Ireland during the summer months.

Dr William Brooke had been born in County Roscommon in 1849, of an Ulster Protestant family. He graduated from the Royal College of Physicians in Edinburgh in 1872 and from the University of Ireland in 1874.[27] Dr Brooke was not just a general practictioner: he held several important government appointments in the Manchester area. He was Medical Officer for Health at Crompton, near Manchester; Medical Officer to the Poor Law Authority; and Public Vaccinator. He was a man of standing in the community, and though he died in 1914, there are still respectful memories of his ministrations in

41

Lancashire.[28] William Brooke's wife, Emily (née Warburton), came from more modest stock in Lancashire; her father had been a mechanic.

It was a tradition in the family that Dr William Brooke was a kinsman of the Fermanagh Brookes, landed gentry who produced many soldiers and buccaneers, as well as Lord Brookeborough, iron-willed Prime Minister of Northern Ireland in the mid-twentieth century (and scourge of Catholics). William often referred to his 'Fermanagh blood' but no genealogical link has been found between Dr William Brooke and the Fermanagh Brookes. It is more likely that William Brooke was related to the Brookes of Dromavana, who flourished in the Irish midlands and around Cavan – which is also, properly speaking, Ulster.

'William' was not a family name with the Fermanagh Brookes, but it was a frequently used name with the Dromavana Brookes – who produced the eighteenth-century scholar Charlotte Brooke and the Westminster Member of Parliament Peter Brooke, subsequently Lord Brooke (Northern Ireland Secretary from 1989 to 1992). The 'Fermanagh blood' represented to William a stubborn Ulster strain of Protestant Loyalism. He should probably have referred to 'the Cavan-Longford blood'.[29]

Certainly, Dr William Brooke's association with Ireland was always strong: his mother Ann, also born in Ireland in 1812 lived with the family, as did an infant cousin, Madeleine Brooke, for a time. Dr William Brooke would return to Ireland on an annual fishing holiday, as his son Gilbert recalled. It was on one of these vacations when Dr Brooke, accompanied by his daughter Gertrude, first met Michael Joyce, at the Skeffington Arms Hotel, in Eyre Square, Galway.[30] And presently, Gertrude Brooke and Michael Joyce arranged matters so that their respective Irish holidays would coincide: a courtship had begun.

But from the beginning, there was an underlying discord on the question of religion. The Brookes were not keen on marriage to a Roman Catholic. At this time, for a Protestant, to marry a Catholic was to lose social status. The Catholic Church also stigmatised 'mixed marriage', and would introduce, in 1908, a decree, *Ne Temere*, insisting that any children of a marital union be brought up as Roman Catholics, which subsequently had the effect of inhibiting marriages in general.

Nonetheless, Gertrude Emily Brooke and Michael Joyce were smitten with one another, and became engaged. Gertrude Emily, known as 'Queenie', was twenty-five in 1904, and for an English girl, she was at an age where marriage was expected. While the Irish postponed marriage, English girls married early: past her mid-twenties, a lady might be considered to be 'on the shelf'. Queenie was small and delicate in stature, and did not need to work – the mark of a young woman of means in those days. There was also some talk of a dowry, which would not have been unusual at this time: her parents certainly left a handsome sum of money eventually, and Gertrude and Michael would benefit from this in the period of the First World War.

In Queenie, Michael Joyce had certainly made 'a good match'. Deferring his marriage until he was thirty-nine had paid off: he had found a bride of suitable social stature to correlate with his ambitions – a doctor's daughter (and a lawyer's sister, since Queenie's brother Edgar was a solicitor). This was not his only motive in getting married, however: Michael Joyce loved Queenie and was always devoted to his wife.[31] As for Queenie, she was an intelligent woman, and intelligent women need men who are striving and challenging. The religious differences between the two would last all their lives, and this situation did not have a good impact on their children, but the marriage itself was not unhappy – contrary to claims by Gertrude's youngest brother, Gilbert. On all questions but religion, Gertrude and Michael remained solidly united.

The wedding was duly arranged for May 1905, and

Gertrude sailed to New York, with her middle brother Edgar, who was four years older than her, for the event. Dr Brooke insisted that Edgar, a qualified lawyer, should accompany his sister, to ensure that all proprieties were observed. Mrs Brooke seems to have entertained worries with regard to her prospective son-in-law. Gertrude arrived in New York just three days before the wedding, sailing on the Cunard line *SS Campania.* She had two hundred and fifty dollars in cash, which was an agreeable amount of pocket money at a time when five cents would purchase a modest dinner.[32]

Michael might have been self-conscious or even a little vain about his age: he claimed to have been born in 1868, whereas the records show that he was born two years earlier. A cousin of his, Mary Naughton, was a witness at the wedding and might have noticed that her thirty-nine-year-old cousin was claiming to be thirty-seven. On the other hand, the Irish born in the mid-nineteenth century could be vague about matters like birth-dates; official records were not introduced until the 1860s. Charles O'Malley, the Irish Party MP, opens his autobiography with the declaration that he was born 'some eight or nine years after the Famine of 1846 or '47'. Even educated people in the mid-nineteenth century sometimes did not know their exact birth dates.

The wedding was to take place at the Church of All Saints in Madison Avenue at 129th Street in New York on 2 May 1905. It is a beautiful church – now, alas, closed – with an exceptional organ designed by the architect of St Patrick's Cathedral, James Renwick. Situated in Harlem – near where Michael lived, at 114 East 123rd Street – it was popular with the Irish, and sometimes known as 'the Irish Cathedral'. Michael and Queenie's entry in the register there is surrounded by the names of O'Rourkes, Fitzpatricks and Callaghans. When it emerged that Michael and Gertrude could not be married at the central altar of this church, but only in the presbytery (a deliberate strategy to deter 'mixed marriages'), Gertrude's brother Edgar tried to persuade Gertrude to call it off. But no: Father C. F. Crawley proceeded with the wedding ceremony of Michael Francis Joyce and Gertrude Emily Brooke, and eleven months later, the infant 'Lord Haw-Haw' was born.

William Joyce's arrival in the world, on 24 April 1906, came six days after the great San Francisco earthquake, and the newspapers at the time of his birth were aghast by the scenes of horror, violence and distress occasioned by the event. On the day that William was born, at 1377 Herkeimer Street, Brooklyn, New York, which was by now the couple's home, the local newspaper, the *Brooklyn Daily Eagle*, was much exercised by subsequent earth tremors. Brooklyn, like other parts of the United States, had immediately set up a relief fund to help the victims of the earthquake, and the Catholic churches in the locality were active in soliciting assistance for the 'Frisco Disaster'.

Herkeimer Street was a pleasant New York surburb in 1906, with white clapboard houses and a neighbourly feel. It has deteriorated somewhat since, and seems a little flyblown now. The house where William Joyce was born is what we would call a maisonette, being a domestic residence of two floors, on the corner of Herkeimer and Eastern Parkway. The number 1377 no longer exists as a street number: being on a corner, it has been amalgamated into the building on the next street, and the lower floor is a shuttered-up shop.

According to family tradition, William was born worryingly underweight – it is said that he weighed only two pounds at birth.[33] He was always of slight stature, so this is quite probable. His low birth-weight may have given some concern to his mother and father: he was probably much fussed over. He was registered with the State of New York as William Joyce, on 3 May 1906. But it was a fortnight before he was christened, at the Church of Our Lady of Lourdes at De Sales Place in Brooklyn. It would have been unusual to wait for two weeks for a baby's christening, particularly in Catholic tradition, where an infant was baptised as quickly as possible, for fear that it would die and be consigned to Limbo, that spiritual no-man's-land of the unbaptised.

It is said that there were disagreements between the parents about the christening: that his mother didn't want to let baby William out of the house, since he was poorly – although the weather was seasonally mild. The Church of Our Lady of Lourdes was distinguished as the tallest Catholic church in Brooklyn. It also had a reputation for special cures, and was adorned with discarded wheelchairs and crutches, as in the shrine of Lourdes in France, and was perhaps chosen by William's parents among several local Catholic churches for that reason. If so, it conferred on William robust health at least from puberty, and a narrow escape, twice, perhaps three times, from death before the age of twenty-five.

Later, William claimed that there was a family quarrel over his name: his mother wanted him called 'William Brooke Joyce', in recognition of his Protestant Ulster forebears, but his father's family smuggled the baby away to the church and had him named merely William Joyce. The Christian name 'William' certainly came from the Brooke side – both Queenie's father and her eldest brother were 'William'. Queenie finally got 'Brooke' into one of her children's baptismal names when her fourth child was born, and christened, Gertrude Joan Brooke Joyce. As a widow, after William's death, Margaret Joyce began to sign her documents 'Margaret Brooke-Joyce', as if to revive the Brooke connection in William's honour. William was so proud of the Brooke blood that he insisted that both his children had 'Brooke' for a middle name.

William was a hugely cherished child; indeed, he was probably thoroughly spoiled from conception. Queenie didn't like America, and even when she was pregnant with William, she turned to the child in her womb as a source of comfort. 'I inherited the unambiguous dislike of my mother for the

Americans,' William wrote in a German newspaper in 1944. 'She told me: "I shall never in my life forget how lonely I have felt in America. Even before you were born you were my only comfort in this atmosphere of strangeness, lack of interest and hostility."'[34] So, when he was born, it seems that William became the whole focus for her daily life. The couple did have friends and relations in America – Michael's brother John was now in Brooklyn, and there were Joyce cousins – and visitations were exchanged with Irish and English friends. But even the cousins noticed how especially proud Michael and Queenie were of little William, who, from infancy, showed signs of intelligence and precocity.[35] William's claim that he learned German at three from Brooklyn neighbours may be something of an exaggeration, but people did remark upon his remarkable mental aptitude from a very early age indeed.

There are enormous advantages to being an only child, or the first child in a family, and a first child who is an only child for a relatively long time in his life will have a strong sense of himself and his place in the universe. William remained, all through his life, the lodestar of the family, though heaven knows he must have broken their hearts. At the end of his life, when William Joyce spoke about 'the children' in his family, he meant his younger brothers and sister (not, significantly, his own children). As he was an only child until he was six, the other siblings always seemed like little children to his more senior and precious self.

Why did Michael Joyce and his wife decide to leave the United States in 1909? Partly, perhaps, it was that Queenie was unhappy there, in the maisonette in Brooklyn, surrounded by German and Danish-speaking neighbours. Moreover, it seems that Michael encountered some problems at work, or quarrelled with a colleague, which caused him, suddenly, to depart.[36] At Naughton Construction, his partner was a Mr Freedman, with whom he may have fallen out. There is some evidence that Michael Joyce was, or became, anti-Semitic while he was in America; this could be a factor in William's later pathology.

There was a large rise in the Jewish immigrant population in the New York area from the 1890s, and from the early years of the twentieth century this was particularly marked in Brooklyn. The coverage of Jewish affairs increased in the Brooklyn newspapers around 1909, and the neighbourhood of Brownsville, of which Herkheimer Street was just on the fringes, was fast becoming a Jewish stronghold, and indeed 'a dynamic working-class Jewish community'. In the areas around, 'English and Irish residents responded violently to the increasing Jewish population and many Protestant landowners in these areas refused to sell to Jewish developers'.[37] But the Jewish communities grew just the same: the builders who were winning contracts for development, by 1910, and the businessmen dominating the trade associations included Isaac Levinson, Morris Weinberg, David Isaacowitz, Abraham Kaplan, Moses and Samuel Bernstein, and Max Feldman; the bankers were Armand Cohen, William B. Roth and Julius Josephson.[38] Moreover, not only was Brownsville more and more Jewish as the century progressed; it also became radical and left wing. Margaret Sanger opened up her first birth-control clinic in Brownsville because of the socialist character of the area.

Such themes – increased, or even perceived, Jewish domination of business life, coupled with Jewish left-wing radicalism – were a key element of twentieth-century Fascism, and it is not at all improbable that hostility to the expanding numbers and alleged power of the Jews in America was a strong element of William Joyce's childhood. In any case, by now, Michael Joyce had made enough money to set himself up in business in Ireland, at a time when business prospects were greatly improving in the old country. And there is evidence that by 1910 Michael was already buying real estate for rent in Ireland.[39]

Indeed, the Ireland of 1909 seemed a different country altogether than the miserable isle of the 1870s and 1880s. The Irish economy had begun to improve, quite remarkably, from around 1904, and there was a great deal more optimism around. Ireland was being compared, favourably, to Denmark, a similar small country whose economy was based on agriculture. London had decided to 'kill Home Rule by kindness', and many reforming measures were taken to improve the state of the country. There was a surge in interest in 'improvements' in husbandry, and in housewifery too, as the tenant farmers were permitted to buy the land they had farmed, and this all fuelled the economy. Shops were flourishing as never before. In 1909, Lloyd George introduced the basic pension for men and women over seventy; this was perhaps the most useful social advance that ordinary people had ever known, and gave many old people dignity and status – and removed the fear of the workhouse. In 1908, a Mayoman, Martin J. Sheridan, won two gold medals for discus-throwing at the London Olympic Games, which cheered the whole country up hugely.

My own mother was born in 1902, in Galway, and she recalled the period just before the First World War as being extraordinarily promising. In the arts, there was a flowering Celtic renaissance, and in every sphere of Irish life things seemed to be getting better. Many memoirs and auto-biographies of this period make the same observation and underline the sense of optimism and excitement that pervaded Irish life at this time. It made sense for a man like Michael F. Joyce to return to his native place in such an era, and so he did, making the journey in October 1909, to be followed by Gertrude and baby William in November.

The Joyces lodged for a while at Ballinrobe, and then settled around Killour and The Neale, not exactly in the place where Michael was born, but a little further north, near to the pretty town of Westport. It was here, at Ayle, about five miles from Westport, that Michael Joyce purchased a pub in 1910. The premises still stand – a handsome road-house with a large bar and an entertainment room on the main road between Lough Mask and Westport. It now bears the name of 'Digger Jay's' and is much in demand for musical and social occasions. The pub was a shrewd choice by Michael: it has always done good business.

It was there that the Joyces came to remake their lives in Ireland – in the beautiful Mayo countryside where, it seemed, the wretchedness of the Victorian age might now make way for a sparkling new Irish future in which Michael and Queenie Joyce hoped that England and Ireland might go forward together in prosperity.

2

A Jesuit Boyhood; A Time of Troubles

'The Irishman is never so Irish as when he is English.'
G. K. Chesterton, *Irish Impressions*

Michael Joyce ran his pub business at Ayle, near Westport, energetically. He improved the house itself: the roof had been made of thatch, but he replaced it with modern slate. Michael and Queenie were regarded as 'great hosts' when they entertained, and Queenie impressed family and friends with her hospitality. Michael's younger brother Patrick Joyce, who took over the family farm at The Neale, regarded Queenie as a very kind person, and 'a good friend'.[1] He thought his brother Michael had done well in his marriage, the religious factor notwithstanding.

At the age of three, an adored only child, little Willie Joyce was propped up on the bar, and was much admired as an articulate child and a little dote, according to local lore. Under the eaves of his bedroom, he was placed in a fine big wooden rocking cradle, where he was lulled to sleep by his mother, and consoled by her soothings when he took fright at the spiders which haunted the child's room. For many a long year, he remembered those spiders with a child's horror.[2]

Little Willie Joyce didn't like Mayo: he said so later in his prison letters to his wife Margaret. After his death, he said, she might go back and live in Ireland, perhaps in Galway, or possibly somewhere around Dublin, which he described as being 'touched by the Renaissance'. But *not* in Mayo. Perhaps it was the spiders in the corner of his bedroom, at the foot of Croagh Patrick, the holy mountain of St Patrick. Perhaps it was the isolation, for the pub his father owned was – and is – a detached house on a road that could be lonesome. Perhaps it was the mixed marriage of his parents, which he must have become aware of in Mayo, as his mother walked to the local Protestant church in Ayle on a Sunday, while his father took Willie, by pony and cart, to the Catholic church at Aghagower. Michael Joyce was not fanatical about religion, but he was an observant Catholic, and the feasts of the church – particularly Easter – held meaning for him.[3]

Queenie must have had some inner conflicts about this: she was conscientious about fulfilling her promise to bring up her son – and her subsequent children – as a Roman Catholic.[4] Nevertheless, William must have unconsciously picked up, from an early age, the idea that loyalties can be in conflict. Queenie may have been personally liked in Mayo, but Protestants as a group were sometimes regarded with hostility, and vice versa: a local Protestant landowner at this time refused to employ Catholics and brought his own staff from England and Scotland.[5]

Queenie must have felt that her values were a little under siege, for she had a strong attachment to her father's Ulster Protestant traditions: her favourite holiday resorts were Portstewart, in what she would have called County Londonderry, and Portrush in Co. Antrim on the northern tip of the Ulster province.[6] And just as William had been her main comfort in America, now, in Mayo, she must have held fast to him as the main focus of her life in a fairly remote part of the west of Ireland. It was unusual at this time that William should be an only child for such a relatively long period: birth control, except by abstinence or coitus interruptus, was not routinely practised, and Catholics and Anglicans at this time had more or less the same adherence to the biblical injunction to 'go forth and multiply'.

But if William had been a sickly baby, as family sources report, and an especially adored one, Michael and Queenie may have taken measures of conjugal abstinence to reduce the chances of having another child too soon. In any case, the status of being an only child had an impact on William's personality: he always had the confidence and self-belief of the unique child. He also benefited from the Freudian affirmation that 'no man can fail, who is a hero in his mother's eyes'.

The education of William might have been one of the reasons why the Joyces moved from Ayle only two years after settling in there. Beautiful though it was, Ayle was remote for a child's schooling. In 1911, William was five, and well ready for school, since he was already reading fluently. Even at four, he amused the local shopkeepers by reading all the labels behind the counter in Westport shops. It was also said, in the neighbourhood, that Queenie didn't feel contented in the area, even though she was liked. The Joyces were welcoming hosts, and Queenie was a good cook – which was much admired at a time of culinary simplicity among ordinary people. She put up a wonderful dinner for the McGings when John McGing came to take over the pub from Michael Joyce in 1911. Daniel McGing, who grew up in the pub, subsequently recalled that 'Mrs Joyce didn't fit in, but all the same she was hospitable.'

Daniel McGing was also told by his parents that Queenie's brother Edgar sometimes came to visit from England. At one level, his visits provided company for Queenie, but at another, they were a worry, for Edgar was 'known to be an alcoholic' and was to die of drink-related causes in 1918, aged forty-three.[7] He had been omitted from his mother's will in 1917, possibly because of his alcoholism.[8]

Michael Joyce was to return to Ayle again, when he was involved in the transport business in Galway. He ran one of the first special coach tours between Galway and Croagh Patrick, and the coach party would stop at the pub at Ayle that was subsequently owned by the McGing's.

Yet there was a cloud over the Joyces' departure from Ayle. One night a man drinking in the bar became seriously intoxicated, and Michael Joyce, as the landlord, ejected him, as was his entitlement. The drunk in question was turned out into the road, and was found dead, on the threshold of the pub, the following morning. There was 'talk' about this unfortunate episode. 'The people turned against Joyce then,' says a veteran resident of the area, Tomas O'Toole, who has run a pub in nearby Tourmakeady all his life. 'The man had been drunk – very, very drunk, yes. But he shouldn't have been put out to die. Someone should have seen he was brought home safely.' The death of the man may not have been Michael Joyce's fault, but it went against him just the same: Michael's politics may not have helped. The Irish had a special word of contempt for individuals who preferred British rule to Irish independence movements: *shoneen*.

For a short period Michael and his family moved to his property at Tourmakeady, a few miles away on the western side of Lough Mask. Like Ayle, it is a very pretty place, but it could also be achingly lonesome. Tourmakeady is a Gaeltacht (Irish-speaking area): here the Irish language hung on despite the success of English all around it. Unerringly, the pro-unionist Joyces had picked a part of Mayo which was, even at that time, nourishing the Irish-Ireland and Sinn Féin movement. Tourmakeady was much favoured by Irish cultural nationalists, and was visited, on bicycle tours, by Patrick Pearse, the guiding spirit of the 1916 Rising, and Thomas Ashe, the Irish republican who would die on hunger strike in 1917.[9]

At Tourmakeady, the Joyces lived in a fine white house on a hill, later to become the doctor's house for the locality. By the autumn of 1911, Queenie was pregnant with her second child, who would be born in Westport on 29 June 1912. The baby was christened Francis Martin and was known as Frank. William seems to have welcomed the arrival of his baby brother: looking back on his childhood from his prison cell, he felt a nostalgic affection for Frank because he was a welcome playmate. Maybe he was glad to be no longer an only child.

Later that year the family commenced its planned move to Galway; the move was completed in the spring of 1913. In March, Willie Joyce was enrolled at the Convent of Mercy school in Francis Street – still a thriving primary school in central Galway to this day (renamed as 'Scoil an Linbh Íosa' – 'the School of the Infant Jesus').[10]

Willie, as his name appears on the school rolls, entered the Mercy Sisters' care in March 1913; his father's profession is given on the rolls as 'architect'. This was somewhat in contrast to Willie's immediate classmates, whose fathers plied more modest trades, being labourers, coach-builders, butchers, clerks, employees in the hotel business, drivers and suchlike. It was also, perhaps, indicative of Michael Joyce's ambitions that he inflated his status as a builder into the grander bracket of 'architect'. William maintained the fiction in Germany, when asked to give his father's profession on official papers, even though, by 1940, Michael F. Joyce's situation was much reduced.

It was noted in the school annals that this appearance at Francis Street was Willie's first experience of school: he had not attended a school in remote Tourmakeady. (Children were not obliged to attend school until the age of seven at this time.) The Joyces were now living – temporarily, it seemed – in Eyre Square, in the centre of Galway, but Michael Joyce was preparing to buy an elegant house in Rutledge Terrace at Rockbarton in Salthill, one of the most attractive spots on Galway Bay, a mile from the centre of Galway. Michael's real-estate investments were paying off, and he was realising his ambitions of social and financial success, which seemed set fair to continue indefinitely in the optimistic time just before the First World War.

Although William was a bright little boy, he was not, at first, a regular school attender. Indeed, he completed only forty-seven days' attendance in his first school year (a complete attendance would have been a hundred and sixty-nine days, and most schoolchildren managed more than a hundred and fifty). Reasons for poor school attendance varied, from chaotic family life to child labour. But the Joyces were keen on education, and a more likely reason for William's absence from school was that he was frequently ill. He may have been unsettled and his mother may have been over-protective. Indeed, his attendance was so irregular that Willie was struck off the school roll later in 1913; this occurred when a child's school attendance dropped below par. He was readmitted again, and then again struck off for absences. He settled down the following year, and his attendance doubled.

The Mercy convent school then would have been a practical, primary school, with a strong basis of rote-learning in reading, writing and arithmetic, and of course a strong overlay of religious values which would have permeated the ethos of the school. There is a beguiling photograph of the young Willie Joyce enrolled in the 'Sodality of Angels': he is dressed as a particularly angelic little altar boy.

The school would have worked from a basic British curriculum – which had been revised in 1900 – but a more Irish flavour was beginning to colour education in Ireland at this time. Most of the clergy would have been moderate Home Rulers rather than extreme republicans, since republicanism itself was anathematised by the Church as a fiendish descendant of the godless French Revolution. But whether the Catholic Church liked it or not, Irish nationalism was increasing in support and enthusiasm, and from about 1907 or 1908, the national movement was becoming an ever stronger feature in Irish education. The Irish language was made compulsory for entry into the National University of Ireland in 1910; in schools, it was still optional, but school inspectors were 'at liberty to use Irish in conducting the school examinations', and they did so. Young William Joyce may have imbibed something of this spirit of Irish nationalism, in a criss-cross kind of way: he was, as a young man, vehemently pro-British, but he was a British nationalist, and he always approved of the idea of nationalism. When William said he was a National Socialist, he meant he was both a nationalist and a socialist.

The basic curriculum of William's primary school would have been 'Manual Instruction, Drawing, Object Lessons and Elementary Science, Singing, School Discipline and Physical Drill', which were compulsory where teachers held the relevant certificates. The primers of English prose and poetry were romantic and high-minded: Tennyson, Wordsworth, Edmund Burke.[11] At a personal level, it is likely that William was indulgently treated by the nuns who taught him. He later said that the Sisters of Mercy had adored him. This is highly plausible: the convent had a majority of little girls and a minority of little boys. Nuns had a reputation for being sweeter to little boys, and more inclined to make pets of them; this was possibly the expression of a thwarted maternal instinct in a culture where the mother–son relationship was especially valued.

'The child is father of the man,' wrote Wordsworth: in the morning-time of our childhood appear the beginnings of our mature selves. From his infant school-days, William Joyce had a fascination with news and current affairs. 'He would amaze the other children by bringing all the news into the school each day,' says Eithne Griffin of Galway, whose mother Anne O'Sullivan attended primary school at the same time as William.[12] He would always have the latest developments from the outside world, and he even sometimes brought newspapers, or newspaper clippings.

Later in her life, when Anne O'Sullivan heard 'Lord Haw-Haw' over the airwaves, she recalled the small boy of seven and eight who had been so quick to inform the children of the latest amazing happenings in the outside world, at a time when many children in the school would not have had a daily newspaper in their home, and would have been easily impressed by his superior knowledge.

Willie Joyce was a born journalistic commentator – fascinated by the unfolding of contemporary events, with an urge to add his opinion to their interpretation. There must have been something around him, in the home, which sparked off this interest: 'I was brought up by my parents,' William wrote, 'in a creed of fanatical patriotism which the English people found very hard to understand. From my earliest days, I was taught to love England and her Empire. Patriotism was the highest virtue that I knew.' The reaction to the political events around him must have been heard by his precocious little ears from the age of reason.

William could scarcely have grown up at a more political time. From 1912 to 1914, Ireland was in a continual ferment, fevered with political excitement. In 1912, Prime Minister Asquith introduced the Third Home Rule Bill in the House of Commons. This was to give Ireland a measure of independence, but was violently opposed in Northern Ireland: half a million Ulster loyalists signed a 'Covenant' against Home Rule, some in their own blood. We can imagine Queenie and Michael discussing this – in front of seven-year-old Willie – probably in passionate support of the Ulster unionists.

In 1913, the Ulster Unionist Council, led by Edward Carson, prepared to set up a 'provisional government' as a form of resistance to Home Rule. The Ulster Volunteer Force was formed in Belfast with the same object, and in Britain, the League for the Support of Ulster was established. In

Dublin, a 'Citizen Army' was formed under the leadership of James Connolly, a Scottish-born communist: the Citizen Army was regarded by the British security authorities as a proto-Bolshevik movement. Again, we may suppose that the Joyces, who took a daily newspaper, commented on this news, and looked on Connolly with alarm.

The fever pitch of political excitement in Ireland at the time was not incongruent with the optimism of the period. Indeed, it was all part of the same sense of confidence and heightened expectations. The Galway newspaper the *Connaught Tribune* – which little William was studying and clipping from so assiduously – was full of confident articles about opportunities for expansion in the Galway area. Most especially, it noted the tremendous growth in transportation of all kinds. A tramline was being laid between Galway and its seaside outpost – a mile away – at Salthill; the proud boast of this line was that it was the most western tram service in Europe. There were hopes that the Galway docks might be revived; they had declined in activity with the growth of Liverpool, Southampton and Queenstown (now Cobh). These aspirations for Galway's translatlantic potential appear in James Joyce's *Ulysses,* in which Mr Deasy, the schoolmaster – and Orangeman – laments the way in which Liverpool has sabotaged the Galway harbour scheme by affirming the primacy of England.

Personally, and financially, things were going well for Michael and Gertrude Joyce and their little family of two boys. On 29 October 1913, Michael completed his purchase of 1 Rutledge Terrace, in Rockbarton by Salthill – a delightful mid-Victorian family home in a short cul-de-sac terrace – for the sum of six hundred and fifty pounds.[13]

The terrace of eight houses was originally built in 1850 as holiday homes by a Mr Rutledge, who had constructed the soldiers' garrison at nearby Renmore, and built the terrace from the rubble that was left over. The Joyces' home now belongs to Eamonn and Antoinette Waldron, who moved to this address in 1995 and restored it to perfection; in the summertime, young children can still run safely down to the seashore and paddle about among the shallow rocks and sands.

Moving to 1 Rutledge Terrace would have placed the Joyce family among the well-to-do classes in Galway. By the time William entered secondary school, at the Jesuit foundation of St Ignatius, Sea Road, Galway, in 1915 – which took boys from the age of nine – William was already growing into a boy with an air of childish arrogance. His self-assurance had developed into self-certainty and his brains and precocity encouraged an air of superior disdain. He strutted about and thought highly of himself; he already had strong opinions which he wasn't shy of voicing. The political talk at home may have prompted him to look down on the 'mere Irish', in the way that British tradition had done for so long. Yet he must have had a sweet side too, as a young child. On one occasion, he went during the summer holidays with his brother Frank to visit his Lancashire family in the Oldham area of Manchester. 'William used to play with my sister and myself at our house for hours at the time,' wrote Mrs Harriet Buckley in 1976. 'He was a grand boy and had lovely parents.' Another neighbour, Mrs Butterworth, said that 'William was a very nice boy': he would willingly sing and play the piano upon request and was unfailingly polite to all the neighbours.[14]

❧

Observing the impact of a Jesuit education on James Joyce, Kevin Sullivan wrote:

> The Irish Jesuits left on Joyce a psychological, moral, religious, intellectual and even social impress … In his mature years, settled with his

family in Trieste and looking back on his days at
Clongowes, he still felt 'admiration and gratitude
for the care of my tutors'.[15]

Much the same could be said of William. William – like
James – turned his back on the Catholic aspect of his Jesuit
education, but he retained other elements of it.

I went to school in Ireland where the Jesuits, with
whom I had differences, gave me the benefit of
their splendid educational system. However
recalcitrant I may have proved in some matters, I
have good reason to be grateful to them for what
they did for me.[16]

William never identified himself as a Catholic in his adult
life, but he always described himself as a Jesuit boy.

William Joyce's Jesuit school, St Ignatius College in
Galway, was established in 1860 (initially at Eyre Square) 'to
do something for the gentry in helping to educate their
children'. It didn't have quite the status of Clongowes –
sometimes called 'Ireland's Eton' – but it was thought of as
the best school in Galway, where it is known simply as 'the
Jez'. It removed from central Galway to Sea Road in 1863,
and is still there, next door to the Church of St Ignatius
Loyola, the sixteenth-century Spanish soldier who turned his
attentions to God and became the founder of the Jesuit
order.[17]

William had indeed cause to thank the Jesuits: they gave
him a rounded education, with an extra-curricular emphasis
on chess (which he always liked), drama and debating, in
which he honed his speaking skills. The teachers were almost
all Jesuit priests, whose outlook on life was zealously Catholic
yet politically tolerant. Many of the priests were men of
distinction: the Prefect of Studies, Father John Barragry, was
a graduate in philosophy of Valkenberg University in the
Netherlands. Father Patrick Nolan, the history and
geography master, was also a history graduate of Valkenberg,

and of St Mary's College, Stoneyhurst; he had taught at Belvedere College Dublin, and at Clongowes Wood, and had been a friend of Father Willie Doyle, the Jesuit priest who died on the Somme, where he had administered the last rites to dying soldiers.[18] Father Pat Nolan seems to have made an impact on William Joyce: William remembered him with gratitude from his condemned cell.

Father Andrew Macardle, the rector of St Ignatius, was an energetic and capable manager who greatly expanded the school, and enhanced the number of scholarships to university won by Jez boys. Father Henry Foley, who was to become rector in 1919, was a noted public preacher on social issues, on which he was ecumenical and progressive. Joyce's schooling was neither racist nor Fascist: it was, by the standards of the time, enlightened and liberal. Conor McDonough of Castlebar, whose father Tom attended the Jez with William Joyce, described the Jez education as encouraging good manners and a tolerant interest in other faiths and people. None of William Joyce's peers at the Jez that I could trace showed any evidence of Fascism or anti-Semitism in their subsequent careers.

William found learning easy, and shone in English, French, German and Latin. The Jesuits always had a tradition of encouraging clever pupils, and on one occasion he wrote such an impressive essay about a day out on Lough Corrib that it was ordered to be read aloud to all the senior boys as a model of English writing. The other pupils were greatly impressed by this – indeed it was 'the talk of the school', according to one of his classmates. 'He was a clever sort of lad,' wrote William Naughton, a classmate who always liked Joyce and admired his intelligence. 'He was fond of using big and strange words.' When the Corrib essay was read aloud, 'that was the first time any of us had heard the word "scow" to describe a boat,' Naughton recalled. (The boys were then in 2nd Prep, and would have been about twelve years old.) William's manner of speech was much remarked upon too. When he was only ten years of age, he had said to William Naughton's parents – when the boy was absent with a cold – 'Do tell Billy to take care of himself, Mrs Naughton. After all, one's health is one's most precious possession.'[19] This was repeated with much amusement at the quaintness of the child's turn of phrase, and the earnest little-old-man air with which he enunciated it.

William had a great interest in Napoleon as a young boy, showing his early penchant for heroes and hero-worship. He also boasted that he had joined the Baden-Powell Boy Scouts, who were regarded as 'very British': in fact, there were no Boy Scout groups in Galway at that time. Nonetheless, William managed to get hold of 'the Scouts khaki shirt, the tie through a ring and scout badge (like the fleur-de-lys)', the last of which he wore in the lapel of his coat. He liked to demonstrate the different Scout signs and signals with his fingers. Anything military, or paramilitary, always pleased him, although he does not seem to have had the kind of fastidiousness associated with soldiers' spit-and-polish. His appearance, William Naughton recalled, was 'unwashed and untidy, the dirty lining of his school cap sticking out at the back of his head.' He 'never played games, but was strong physically.' He was also fascinated by unusual mental experiments, and got involved with mesmerism and hypnotism, repeatedly trying to hypnotise classmates and cronies.[20]

William always made it plain – indeed boasted – that he was pro-British, which is a paradox in view of his fate as a traitor to the Crown. Tom McDonough, who lived in another house in Salthill also owned by Michael Joyce, remembered that William 'took after his mother's side and was very pro-British'. He would always defend the honour of the Empire. 'I remember one time, we used to play together in Rockbarton and that time we were discussing the merits of the American navy and the British navy, and I was sticking up for the American navy [laughter], and Willie Joyce threw out and kicked me on the shin.'[21] Tom McDonough was also a 'returned Yank'; despite the fights, he was fond of young Joyce, his playmate.

Margaret Joyce, William's second wife, claimed that the Jez school was tough on 'Will' as a boy: that the Latin Master in particular was a tyrant and once tied the young William to a radiator. But then William must have been quite a trying youngster too. He was increasingly pugnacious as he grew into his teens, combative, argumentative and impatient. He was also courageous and willing to stand up for his controversial opinions. At the age of fourteen, he declared that he would no longer accept the Catholic Church as his religion, although he had been baptised into it; he would, instead, embrace his mother's faith, the Church of England. Margaret claims he gave cheek to the Bishop of Galway and argued theology with him, which he was well capable of doing.[22]

William's critique of the Catholic Church was, in a way, a kind of gallant defence of his mother. He declared that he could not accept the Catholic maxim of *extra ecclesiasm nulla salus* – that outside the church there could be no salvation.

> On hearing this formulation, W. said to the preceptor: 'My mother is a Protestant and a sincere Christian. Do you mean that she is sure to be damned unless she joins the Catholic Church?' The preceptor said he did mean just that ... From that moment he was merely to pick holes in Catholic doctrine.[23]

William's friend John Angus Macnab, who was a most orthodox Catholic convert, took the view that William had been right and his preceptor had been in error.[24]

William continued to be a handful: on one occasion in chapel, he swung the censer so vigorously that the incense was scattered all down the aisle. He also acquired a broken nose when fighting a boy who had called him an Orangeman – alluding to his pro-British proclivities. That 'Orangeman' insult left a lifelong impression on William: the broken nose accounted for the nasal tone in his voice which was so perceptible in his broadcasting. Indeed, he always had trouble with his adenoids because of it.

There were more serious charges than the spirited naughtiness of the rebellious schoolboy: it has been claimed, though never confirmed, that William drew a gun on a boy he was fighting with, a gun he had procured from a Royal Irish Constabulary (RIC) barracks of which his father was the landlord. 'One day, William Joyce spotted a boy with the [republican] tricolour on, he told him to take it off, the boy refused, there was a scuffle and Joyce produced a gun,' wrote Michael d'Arcy in a Jesuit magazine in 1982.[25] William was reported to the headmaster for this episode and, according to Michael d'Arcy, asked to leave the school. However, there would be an even more urgent reason why William would leave St Ignatius very precipitately indeed.

'In one sense, he was a boy beyond his years, but emotionally, he never seemed to grow up,' recalled E. L. Kineen in 1941. 'He was a morose and lonely little fellow at all times … For all his brightness, there was something missing in Willie. I cannot precisely define it, but he was not the normal type of healthy schoolboy.'[26] Kineen remembered how Joyce the schoolboy would give impromptu speeches in the playground, warning his playmates about the growing dangers of Communism.

William had a boyish fascination with soldiers and military events, which may well have been nourished by his history teacher, Father Patrick Nolan, who excelled at teaching military history and would reconstruct ancient battlefields with pernickety attention to detail. Indeed, William's interest in soldiers would not have mattered at all if his life had been more or less normal. Richard Thomas Moynan's charming picture *Military Manoeuvres*, completed in 1891 and hanging in the National Gallery in Dublin, shows small, barefoot Irish boys in an Irish town imitating the marching of the redcoats. Before the Troubles which commenced in 1919, there was nothing particularly amiss about a young boy liking the British military.

Eithne Griffin of Galway was told by her own mother (born at the beginning of the twentieth century) that young boys in the Galway area often followed the military around: it was a laddish pastime. Indeed, committed Irish republicans themselves admitted as much: the British army 'always put on such a good show', according to one classical Irish republican memoir,[27] and it could be gratifying to watch their military manoeuvres. But the years of Willie Joyce's adolescence were not normal. The First World War had started, and Home Rule had been suspended for the duration of the war.

The constitutional nationalists supported the Crown, and at least a hundred and fifty thousand Irishmen went off to fight in France. John Redmond, leader of the Irish parliamentary party in the House of Commons – and a Clongowes man – pledged Ireland's support with the words: 'With our brethren in the north, we will ourselves defend the coasts of our country.' But militant nationalists, led by Patrick Pearse, Bulmer Hobson and Éamon de Valera, decided in 1915 that they would mount a rising for the old historical reason that 'England's difficulty is Ireland's opportunity'. This occurred, as the world knows, at Easter 1916, and the sixteen men involved in its organisation – including Roger Casement, who was tried for treason in conditions which would prefigure William Joyce's own trial to come – were executed.

Political attitudes in Galway in 1916 would have been very divided. My mother remembered how unenthusiastic people were initially about the Easter Rising. She vividly recalled that shopkeepers were unable to get provisions because of the 'rebellion', and this caused widespread vexation. Most people were not supportive of the rebels, and certainly the Bishops and leaders of the Catholic Church were initially highly critical of them. As time went by, however, there was a gradual but perceptible shift in attitudes. The Catholic Church was exercised by the unwise decision by the British government to impose conscription on Ireland in 1917, and there was a nationwide Novena to Our Lady of Lourdes to halt the measure. (Our Lady of Lourdes duly obliged – assisted by the whole spectrum of political protest in Ireland: conscription was abandoned.) As matters developed in 1918, 1919 and 1920, what had been previously a boyish turbulence in Willie began to bring him into the more dangerous waters of espionage, and even touched on the subject of murder.

In 1918, after the end of the First World War, Sinn Féin swept the country – or rather, significantly, the twenty-six counties which would become Éire – in a general election. Countess Markievicz, a full-blooded republican (and denounced by a Catholic bishop as a Bolshevik), became the first woman elected to the British parliament. Yet the Ulster problem remained doggedly intractable – as it is to this day – and most of the northern province remained unionist. In 1919, Sinn Féin convened the First Dáil, but it was not recognised by Westminster. Michael Collins then decided that the only way to wrest independence from the British was to fight them for it. So in 1919, the 'armed struggle' by Irish republicans was effectively launched by a republican gunman, Dan Breen. When the British took retaliatory action, the War of Independence had begun.

∗

In 1920 William Joyce was coming up to fourteen years of age: he now had another brother, Quentin – christened Edwin Quentin – who was born 28 August 1917, and for whom William would always be the big hero, and on 18 May, 1920, his mother gave birth to a daughter, Gertrude Joan Brooke. William's brother Frank, born in 1912, was now also enrolled with the Jez.

Michael F. Joyce was the respected patriarch of the family, with property in Galway and Mayo, some of which he leased to the RIC. By 1920, Michael had also become one of the first shareholders in the Galway Omnibus Company, which had such great hopes for bringing new transport structures to the west of Ireland. He also took a job as the manager of the Omnibus Company in 1920. Although Michael was optimistic enough to start this new career in transport, he must have felt increasingly anxious about the turn of events in Ireland. His horror and fear of lawlessness, which had been such a menacing part of his background in the 1870s and 1880s, must once again have been aroused.

The Royal Irish Constabulary, which was, in effect, a client of his (they rented property from him), was, like other British institutions, quite obviously losing ground: they were unable to police the country, as, progressively, the courts were unable to implement law and order. It was because of this failure of the conventional forces that the London government sent to Ireland reinforcing troops theoretically under the command of the RIC – the notorious Black and Tans.

When the Troubles began, in 1920, 'it was then that things started to get hot', Tom McDonough recalled. It was one thing for Willie Joyce to follow soldiers around when he had been a young boy; it was quite another for him to attach himself to the hated Black and Tans, who were ill-disciplined killers, and not infrequently drunk. For Galway people of the generation who experienced these Troubles, it seemed that the Nazis could not have been worse than the Black and Tans. A Galway historian remembers his Sinn Féin aunt excoriating Willie Joyce as 'a scut' for his teenage association with the Black and Tans, but softening towards him quite affectionately when he broadcast for Hitler.[28]

Many witnesses in Galway remembered seeing Joyce sitting on the Crossley tender vehicles used by the Tans. Because he was small, it has even been claimed that he was adopted as their mascot. Tom McDonough, William's schoolmate, recalled that Willie now gathered a little gang of boys around him to support the Crown forces. 'Willie Joyce organised a group of the RIC men's children,' McDonough recalled. 'I remember once in Dominic Street in Galway, I was looking in a window, and he came up to me, and he had all these youngsters with him, you know. He came up to me and he said "If anything happens any of my men [laughter], your house will go up!" He did, yes.'[29] At this, his parents should perhaps have exercised more control over the headstrong and provocative young William. Things were becoming dangerous. But perhaps his parents had no control over him: teenage boys are often beyond parental control. Possibly they were absorbed by the care of their three other children, who included a toddler and a baby.

Perhaps they felt even more stubbornly pro-British themselves: the Irish version of history understandably concentrates on the horrors of the Black and Tans, and their associates, the Auxiliaries (known as 'the Auxies'), but the IRA were no slouches, either, when it came to the business of killing. The *Illustrated London News* of this period is full of the most lurid reports about mayhem in Ireland, with illustrated pictures of hapless young English officers murdered in 'circumstances of peculiar brutality'. The Anglo-Irish watched in dismay as their houses were burned out, their people sometimes murdered in lonely farm-houses – although many of them were also appalled at the conduct of the Crown forces.[30]

And so it was that William – fuelled by his family's 'fanatical' (according to himself) patriotism – attached himself to this force, at the age of fourteen, in 1920. He hung around Lenaboy Castle, where the Crown forces were stationed, and was seen, many a time, sitting with them on their lorries. It was believed, at the time, that Joyce went around Galway with the Tans, pointing out houses and individuals who had republican connections.[31] Whether this is true, or an exaggeration, it was in character for him to be provocative and outrageous, and, once he had embraced a cause, to take it to extremes.

Memoirs written by ex-Black and Tans seem to discredit William's value to the Crown forces, however. Indeed, according to Douglas Duff, who was an RIC sailor fighting with the Royal Marines against the IRA during the Troubles, William was regarded as a complete pest. On one occasion, a party of 'Auxie' cadets, along with some RIC men, were about to be carried across the Shannon estuary – between Galway and Clare – in a small craft known as a fishing smack. As they were casting off, a young civilian suddenly leaped aboard. 'I recognised him at once,' Duff wrote in his memoir.

> He was one of our greatest embarrassments in Galway City. His trouble was fanatical patriotism to England and a burning wish to fight against the Irish 'rebels', as he always called them. He often tried to smuggle himself into our lorries … we laughed at him, but we used to chase him fairly fiercely for, if he had been killed or wounded, his ending would have caused the man in charge of the patrol a lot of trouble.

On this particular occasion, Duff recalled, they simply booted young William Joyce off the vessel – Duff himself gave William 'a terrific kick in the stern' – and let him swim ashore.[32] Twenty years later, the former Black and Tan realised that the notorious Lord Haw-Haw had been the miscreant he had booted into the Shannon estuary.

Even these antics, of trying to attach himself to the Tans, might have passed off as teenage nonsense if William Joyce's name had not been associated, at least by rumour, and possibly through mistaken identity, with the murder of Father Michael Griffin. This incident has remained a significant episode in the history of Galway city; Griffin Road, a principal road in Galway, is named after the murdered priest.

There was a schoolteacher in Barna – a seaside resort, bleached-white like a Greek island, on the road west out of Galway – named Patrick Joyce who was also known to be pro-British, though he was no kin to Michael Joyce. Patrick Joyce's house was raided by persons unknown and he was kidnapped by the IRA. Subsequently, the Crown forces in 'lorry loads' swooped on the Barna district in a house-search for the disappeared Pat Joyce. 'They terrorised the people,' according to Padraic Ó Laoi's biography of Father Griffin. They shot farm animals, and dealt savagely with those they interrogated. 'They posted up notices in the west of the city and in Barna, threatening dire reprisals unless [Patrick] Joyce was returned unharmed. On learning of the kidnap, Father Griffin called to Mrs Joyce to comfort and console her.' Michael Griffin was a nationalist with a great interest in Irish language and culture, though he was not in any way actively involved with republicanism.

Patrick Joyce was not found: not until 1998 when his remains were finally uncovered, in the bogs around Barna. But the fact that his kidnap had so exercised the Crown forces seems to indicate that he was somehow associated with the British authorities. On 14 November 1920, Father Griffin also disappeared, after a game of cards with some fellow priests. Someone came to his door and summoned him as if for a sick call. He responded, and was never seen again alive. A week later his body was found in a boggy grave at a Barna crossroads.[33] Father Griffin was almost certainly murdered by the Black and Tans as a reprisal for the killing of Patrick Joyce.

There is absolutely no evidence that young William Joyce was involved in any collaboration with the Tans over this killing, but in a small community, rumour can be as powerful as fact, and for many years afterwards rumours circulated that

Willie, along with another teenage boy, had tipped off the Black and Tans about the whereabouts of Father Griffin. In a lecture given at the Loughrea Historical Society in 1998, the lecturer, local historian and teacher Jane Beatty, again claimed that William Joyce had been instrumental in Father Griffin's disappearance, while acting as a spy for the Black and Tans.[34] But there has never been any concrete evidence to support this, and others who knew what was going on in Galway at the time have said that William had no connection with the Griffin case. Proinsias Mac Aonghusa, the broadcaster and Irish-language scholar from Galway, investigated the rumour in 1976, when there were still many people alive who remembered the events: he was told by Old IRA men he spoke to that William Joyce was not guilty by association of the Father Griffin murder.[35]

Nevertheless, from this time on William was in big trouble. By the age of fifteen, he had witnessed a policeman with his brains blown out, and later in life, when he had a drink or two taken, he would return to this image, which had imprinted itself on his teenage brain. 'He saw battle, murder and sudden death at a very early age,' as MI5 noted in their intelligence report on William Joyce.[36] He was considered a pest by the British forces, and a danger to nationalist sympathisers by Irish activists: by December 1921, the IRA took the decision to liquidate him with a sniper bullet.

A young Galway IRA lieutenant, aged twenty-eight, was ordered to assassinate William Joyce on his way home from school in the first week of December. The lieutenant took up position on the route between the Jez, at Sea Road, and Salthill, just a couple of miles west. The December days were short, and darkness would start to fall by mid-afternoon, when the schoolboy would be coming home.

However, Michael Joyce had by this time taken the precaution of moving his family away from Salthill and into another property he owned, at Victoria Place, just behind Eyre Square in central Galway.[37] The young IRA lieutenant waited in vain for his target. Years later, in the 1980s, the former IRA sniper told his son – who was by then a prominent Galway politician and a member of the Irish government – about the aborted assassination of the man who was to become 'Lord Haw-Haw'. In fact, the old man said, it was not without a certain relief that he had put away his Lee Enfield, sparing William's life. But, a message, to the effect that the IRA would not fail a second time, was transmitted.[38]

William was immediately hurried out of Galway. He took the train for Dublin, and was on the mailboat from Kingstown, County Dublin forthwith. He fled to England, alone, at the age of fifteen. He probably considered himself a political refugee – and not for the last time, either.

3

From Erin to Empire;
From Anti-Fenian to Anti-Semite

*'Anyone who has attended a Communist
meeting can testify that the most bitter and
vindictive elements are Jewish aliens and
Southern Irish.'*

Morning Post, 4 July 1925

We can imagine the defiant frame of mind of the fifteen-year-old William Joyce as he sailed across the Irish Sea on Friday 9 December 1921.[1] He was almost certainly accompanied, on the chugging old mailboat, by a number of other British loyalists who had also decided that there would be no place for them in an independent Ireland. British loyalists – mainly Irish Protestants – would soon be fleeing 'in trainloads', according to a loyalist newspaper of the time, some in a hurry to escape the burning-out of the old gentry houses, many in fear of being shot as 'spies', the catch-all description for anyone unlucky enough to incur the displeasure of the Irish Republican Army. Some fled, as depicted in William Trevor's *The Story of Lucy Gault,* because of a single incident which destroyed neighbourhood trust.

The sovereignty of the British Crown was formally withdrawn from the Irish Free State in January 1922 at a symbolic ceremony at Dublin Castle. Michael Collins handed the Lord Lieutenant a copy of the Treaty, signed in December, which agreed to the foundation of the Irish state. (Lord Fitzalan, the Lord Lieutenant, remarked to General Collins that he had kept him waiting seven minutes: Collins quipped that after seven hundred years, this was scarcely significant.) In February, seven southern Irish regiments which had served the Crown from the Battle of Waterloo to the Boer War were disbanded: to the regret of some Irishmen who had served these regiments, 'a splendid military record was closed'. Many loyalists felt that, once the British forces had left Ireland, they would have little protection from those Irish republicans who had sworn to 'get every fucking Orangeman out of the country'.[2] The conflicts we have learned to call 'ethnic cleansing', of hunting minorities out of newly formed nations, were at this time being enacted all over Europe. Post-1919, some twenty-five million Continental Europeans found themselves uprooted from states in which they were regarded as unpopular or alien minorities.

All his life William wanted to be some kind of a soldier: from boyhood he had admired Napoleon, the little gunner who had risen to become emperor through military glory;[3] another of his heroes was Cromwell. Before he departed from Galway, Joyce had signed up to join the Worcester Regiment; on 8 December 1921, he was accepted and declared fit by the medical officer.[4] The commanding officer might have entertained suspicions when this undersized young boy claimed to be eighteen years of age, but he may also have realised that William was a pro-British loyalist in trouble with the IRA, and signed him through.

William must have felt sustained, on that mailboat, by the idea that his soldierly ambitions were about to be realised, for he was due to join his regiment at Norton

Barracks, near Evesham on the River Avon (and not far from Shakespeare's birthplace, Stratford-upon-Avon). He probably dreamed that he would embrace, at last, the true British patriotism and ardent feelings of Empire that he had been brought up to revere. He almost certainly spent Christmas itself with his Brooke relations in Oldham in Lancashire, where he was on friendly terms with many of the neighbours, familiar from childhood holidays, and where folk thought of him as such a nice young boy.

In his application to the Worcesters, William had given his birthplace, truthfully, as New York, and his parents' nationality as 'British', even though this was not technically correct. Michael and Queenie thought of themselves as thoroughly British, and claimed, on documents, to be so, although they had already been cautioned by the authorities in England for not registering as 'aliens' when on British soil.[5] So there was always this fiction in William Joyce's background: his father was an American but concealed that fact whenever he could. This did not matter so much in Ireland, where 'returned Yanks' were commonplace and where people did not have the same English regard for the letter of the law; but it mattered in England.

William gave his date of birth, wrongly, as December 1903, and his age, thus, as eighteen. He gave his religion as Church of Ireland, which was not the denomination into which he had been baptised, though it was, now, broadly his faith of choice. It was noted that his complexion was fresh, his eyes grey, his hair fair, and his weight 8 stone 2 pounds. He had a slight scar under his left eye, though he did not have the great gash on his right cheek which was to mark him so memorably. His teeth were in good condition.

On joining the Fourth Battalion of the Worcesters, William found himself once again regarded as an oddity. He had been 'odd' in Galway because he had been seen as 'an Orangeman' among the Galway boys; now he was considered just as odd among the men of the Worcesters because he seemed so comically, patriotically, British. He was described by comrades as 'a queer fish'.[6] The British patriotism which he had been so unwise as to flaunt in Ireland was out of place, in rather a different way, in the England of the early 1920s.

After the end of the Great War of 1914–18, people were tired of the patriotic message, and resentful of the politicians who had preached it so ardently while men were being slaughtered on the battlefields in its name. In 1922, the historian A. J. P. Taylor wrote; 'People wanted a quiet life. They did not want any more to be a world power with this glamour and excitement.'[7] Willie Joyce's naïve and provincial ultra-patriotism was a source of caustic hilarity to the other recruits, and they ragged him mercilessly: they would get him to jump out of bed at night and stand to attention by whistling 'God Save the King'. Eventually, according to William's friend Angus Macnab, 'his sense of humour came to the rescue, and he got more sleep.'[8]

Yet in his eagerness to be in uniform, he donned damp fatigues and developed a bad case of rheumatic fever as a result. Before the introduction of antibiotics, this could be dangerous: Macnab claims that it nearly killed him. It also apparently halted his growth. 'He never grew after the age of sixteen and his constitution was never the same again,' wrote Macnab, who was to become William's closest and most trusted friend. At the military hospital where Joyce was treated, his real age was discovered, apparently by an Irish doctor who recognised him from the time he had lived in Galway. It was noted on his regimental record that his birth certificate was dated 24 March 1906 – although this too was slightly erroneous, since he was in fact born on April 24 that year – but in consequence, he was 'Discharged. Having made a misstatement as to age on enlistment.'

William left the army on 20 March 1922. Many a young man had fibbed about his age on joining up in 1914, and it was accepted casually enough in wartime, but not, it seems, in times of peace. Perhaps the army would have readmitted

William if he hadn't already earned such an odd reputation for himself. William must have been disappointed, but his dream of being a soldier endured; he would continue to cherish military ambitions until the last years of his life, when in bizarre circumstances in Germany, his military ambition would be fulfilled.

But for now, he returned to Lancashire, where he lodged with his Brooke relations, first at 20 Albert Street in the curiously named Mumps, which is by way of being a suburb of Oldham, and subsequently at 86 Brompton Street in Oldham itself.

᷾

Michael and Queenie were no doubt relieved to get William out of Galway in December 1921; Queenie was in any case pregnant with her last child, who would be born prematurely in February 1922.[9] At this point, Michael Joyce may well have wanted to remain in Ireland, even though some of his property had been attacked, and he felt the need to move closer to Galway, and away from the more outlying Rockbarton in Salthill. Michael was now fifty-five: he had begun his working life once in America, and again in Ireland. Besides, some people were optimistic that the 1921 Treaty would bring peace to Ireland and restore Anglo-Irish relations to the cordial state they had been in before the First World War.

Michael himself seemed to be enthusiastic about his new venture with the General Omnibus Company. He had high hopes that the General Omnibus Company would greatly enhance Salthill, opening it up to tourism and trade. Salthill had been a charming but simple little village, surrounded by fields, until the early years of the twentieth century.[10] What it needed was a reliable transport service; Michael Joyce believed that modern transportation was a vital aspect of economic development. He had not only become manager of the omnibus company; he was also among the first fifty investors to buy shares in it. (His forecasts for Salthill turned out to be right: property there is now as expensive as in the most fashionable parts of Dublin.)

Michael believed in the modern concept of the coach trip, too: he brought one of the Galway Omnibus coaches up to Mayo on special outings, and on pilgrimages to Croagh Patrick. Whenever possible on these trips, he would stop at his old pub at Ayle, where passengers would have a drink and a comfort stop.[11] And however pro-British Michael Joyce was in his politics, like most businessmen he was prepared to make adjustments to reality: he seemed ready to accept the new Irish State. In 1921, he described himself as 'British' on the Omnibus Company's ledger papers; in 1922, he gives his nationality as 'Irish Free State'; in 1923, he calls himself simply 'Irish'. He also showed a certain flexibility in his attitude to his own social status. In the first ledgers, he gives his occupation, rather grandly, as 'gentleman'. (Most of his cohorts describe themselves more prosaically as grocer, merchant, dentist, clerk or draper, for instance.) By 1926, Michael had stopped calling himself a gentleman, and described himself simply as a 'bus manager'.[12]

While Michael, Queenie and the younger children stayed on in Galway, William was finding that England was not the Arcadia which Irish loyalists often portrayed it to be. The great British Empire on which he had set so much store was not quite as he had imagined. Not only had his fellow squaddies seemed so disrespectful of patriotism, but the condition of England itself was anxious and uncertain. The Empire on which the sun was said never to set was, at its heart, racked with poverty, unemployment, political mediocrity and dishonest patronage.

The old cities of the industrial north of England, such as Manchester and Liverpool, were showing all the signs of imperial and economic decline, and working-class life was grim. Unemployment, at a time when the dole was niggardly and stigmatised, was a national bugbear. The *Illustrated London News* of the early 1920s depicted miserable pictures of working men trudging the streets in search of work, returning crestfallen to haggard womenfolk. 'All day they walk in search of work, and return home ... weak and dispirited, after a vain quest.'[13] By 1922, there were already nearly two million unemployed, mainly among the working classes, while the papers and magazines carried photos of the 'Bright Young Things' of Mayfair, with their 'unladylike' bobbed hair styles and sexily short hemlines basking in a life of plenty.

Many a working-class Fascist was formed in Lancashire towns like Oldham, which had once been the hub of the British Empire's world cotton trade and was now a down-at-heel locality where clogs and shawls were standard apparel. (Oldham has of course been the scene of racial conflicts between Asian and white British youths in recent years.) The mills of Lancashire were closing down in the 1920s, by virtue of the transfer of investment to India, which was frequently ascribed to heartless decisions made by the money men of the City of London. 'By 1923,' wrote John Charnley, a Blackshirt who wrote a beguiling autobiography of his Lancashire childhood, 'the Indian Dhooty, a type of thin muslin which had been the "bread and butter" of much of Lancashire's trade, had already been transferred to India's sweatshops.' Charnley saw this as the asset-stripping of England in the quest for the cheap labour of 'globalisation'.[14]

This picture of English decline must have cut deep into William Joyce's teenage psyche: it was a theme he would return to all his life. Even in uncredited German radio commentaries in English during the Second World War, a William Joyce script was identifiable by its frequent allusions to Lancashire's parlous situation, and the 'international financiers' who, he claimed, were the cause of this decline. In fact, it was the familiar cycle, which we have seen often in our time, of trade moving on, technologies changing and the developing world becoming more competitive. Joyce would – piquantly, like Winston Churchill – remain an implacable opponent of Indian nationalism and Indian independence.

Among the politically aware, there was much discontent with the political system and with established politicians. The latter were considered to be either untrustworthy characters, like David Lloyd George, or mediocrities of the 'Second XI', those left after the most brilliant potential leaders had been slain in the Great War. And there was much bitter grumbling about 'war profiteers' – the 'hard-faced men who look as though they had done very well out of the war', in the celebrated phrase first coined by Stanley Baldwin, invoked by the economist John Maynard Keynes.

Many of the ordinary people who had fought in the First World War did badly, economically, out of it; many of those who did not fight profited. Businessmen came much more to the fore, while the old landed gentry, like the old northern proletariat, declined. Lloyd George, the Prime Minister who had 'won the war', quite shamelessly sold political honours – estimates of the amount he raised by selling knighthoods and peerages range from £1 million to £6 million. William, who was addicted to reading newspapers and news magazines, would have come across many articles in the popular press about the 'sleaze' of British politics in the 1920s, and the contempt that was displayed for Parliament. For example, the magazine *John Bull* noted that the New Year's Honours List for 1922 apparently contained no honours for men who had served in the Royal Navy, but 'Mr Midas Moneybags has been raised to the peerage for "conspicuous public services".'[15] Quite soon a new theory would grip William Joyce's mind at its most formative, and would obsess his values until the very end of his life: that the troubles and disorder of the world of his youth were to be blamed on Communists and Jews, who were, in his eyes, one and the same.

William, having left school precipitately at fifteen – possibly as a result of having been asked to leave – and having been sacked from the army, was now faced with the dilemma of what to do with his life, at a time when jobs were not easy to come by. It was not particularly unusual for a young person to leave school at such an early age – the school-leaving age had only just been raised to fourteen, in 1918 – although leaving school hastily, just before Christmas, must have been a little irregular. In more normal circumstances, the Jesuits might have expected a boy of William's intelligence and ability to stay on at school and take his Matriculation at sixteen or seventeen. He would have left school with just the Junior Inter Certificate, which was an examination carried out in three parts at around the age of fourteen, fifteen and sixteen; he would not have completed the final section. The Junior Inter was regarded as a reasonably good level of education at this time, but William's mother dearly wanted him to become a doctor, like her father, and a Matriculation exam was required for medical studies.[16]

William, in his odd sort of way, had a certain flair for anatomy and physiology. He once broke his collarbone while skating in Scotland, and set it himself. He believed he had a cure for cancer: he advanced the theory that as cancer 'was an anarchic disorder of the normal cell-growing function, it should be curable by rebalancing the cell-producing glands'.[17] He experimented with plants, treating them with calcium solutions, and apparently succeeded in producing abnormal cell growths in plants analogous with a carcinoma in human anatomy. So he was perhaps not opposed to the suggestion that he should study medicine.

And so it was decided, either by William himself or by his relations – or by both – that the Battersea polytechnic, then at Battersea Park Road in south London, would be the best place for him to continue his studies. It had been founded in 1891 as a technical school, but had expanded into a college with a broad curriculum, with an especially good reputation for engineering, mathematics and the sciences. It was not expensive, and hostels and digs were found locally for the students. After his discharge from the army in the spring of 1922, William applied to Battersea Poly to study mathematics and chemistry, commencing in the autumn term.

His first of many homes in London was in digs at 10 Longbeach Road, in the Lavender Hill area of Battersea,[18] a pretty street constructed between 1893 and 1895 as a housing development for 'artisans and labourers', according to records in the Battersea Public Library. Battersea was at this time a lively working-class neighbourhood: the people were generally described in local-history records as 'rough-and-ready types with hearts of gold'; though it wasn't without refinements, and there was a particularly active local chess club, which might well have attracted William. He also made friends in his Battersea digs with people who would be loyal to him years later when he was imprisoned as a traitor.[19]

Battersea was also strongly politicised: Charlotte Despard, who threw her lot in with the Irish revolutionaries and became Maud Gonne's best friend, had been active in the Battersea Trades Union council in 1918–19. The borough had had the first black mayor ever in England, elected in 1912. In 1922, the local Member of Parliament was the well-known Indian communist and anti-imperialist, Shapurji Saklatvala, whom William immediately took against. Saklatvala must have enraged William Joyce when he wrote: 'The British Empire is made up of the aristocratic and cunning "dirty dogs" of Great Britain, who will assail any country at any time … to keep in bondage all the bullied nations.'[20] Saklatvala was, indirectly, to mark William Joyce for life: it was at a meeting organised for the Indian Communist's Tory opponent that William received his trademark facial scar.

❧

But, as in his regiment, William was not to prosper or to 'fit in' at Battersea Poly. His time there was also a disastrous chapter. He made a poor impression on his teachers: he did not apply himself to his work, and his political leanings did not find favour. 'He seemed to hold rather extreme views on politics and upheld the use of force as a method of spreading opinions,' the principal of Battersea Poly, George O'Riordan, wrote sniffily.[21] Again, William struck the English as odd: he was put down, early, as a 'politico' – a person with political obsessions – which, in the 1920s, was not considered respectable in British academic life. In the 1920s, it was still considered rather 'bad form' to argue about either politics or religion in genteel society; William delighted in arguing about both.

By contrast, the Battersea students concerned themselves – outside of the curriculum – with dances, football and hockey. They published whimsical little articles such as 'A Dissertation on Umbrellas' and 'A Dissertation on Suet Puddings' in their student mags. Debates did not attract a great deal of support, and were conducted, in any case, with suburban good manners: a principal debating forum was the Domestic Science Debating Society.[22] All this was a long way from the guerrilla warfare which William had lived through in Ireland.

By 1923, he was a college drop-out. He would never have made a doctor like his grandfather, anyway: he had the brains for medical science but did not have the temperament for dealing with sick people. And for some reason – perhaps because his head was too full of politics and he was too troubled, alone and immature – he couldn't, or wouldn't, concentrate. Perhaps he simply missed his parents, or having family members around him. It was not until his parents came to England, and he joined them to live in the family home at Dulwich, a pleasant and well-favoured suburb of south London, that he at last settled down and applied himself successfully to study – at Birkbeck College, part of London University.

By 1923, the Joyce family had decided to leave Galway

and go to England. Having endured the worst of the Troubles in Ireland, they decided to move just as the Civil War came to an end – the hardline republicans were for the moment defeated and the Irish Free State established. Perhaps Queenie sensed that her troublesome eldest son needed a stabilising force in his life. It was a juncture when the other children could reasonably easily transfer to English schools. Frank, aged eleven, had attended the Jez in Galway for two years, but was of an age when he could enter an English secondary school.[23] Quentin was just coming up to six, and had not yet gone to school; Joan would be three that summer; the baby, Robert, was just a year old. Michael Joyce sought to disengage himself from Ireland gradually, however, as there were serious financial considerations at stake. Moving to England was not, as it turned out, a wise move financially, and Michael was now really too old to start his working life for a third time.

He was in negotiation with the new Irish Free State (in conjunction with the departed British authorities) over compensation for his property which had been destroyed during the Troubles. His house at Capaduff East, Tourmakeady, County Mayo had been burned down by the IRA during the night of Wednesday 12 May or early in the morning of Thursday 13 May 1920. He was claiming the sum of £1,500, plus costs, in compensation 'for malicious damage' incurred.[24] These negotiations dragged on for several years, and there was much correspondence between the Irish branch of the Colonial Office in London and the Ministry of Finance in Dublin. It was initially agreed that Michael should receive £1,210 plus £34.13s in costs, but the full sum was never paid.

After two years, in October 1922, a hundred pounds was advanced to Michael Joyce by the British government, against the eventual compensation payment; in July 1923, a further hundred was advanced to him; and in August 1923 another hundred was paid. But when the final judgement was made by Saorstát Éireann on 17 January 1924, the compensation to be paid was reduced to £480, plus costs. As Michael Joyce had already received £300 in advance, the balance was £180, plus costs of £36.15s, plus interest, and minus income tax, which came to £220.2s.

This gradual doling out of sums of money suggests that Michael was in need of the cash to transfer his wife and four children from Ireland to England, and of course to support his eldest son William in London. The mean sum awarded would rankle with the Joyces for ever after. In 1940, when Queenie had cause to write to the Home Office, she pointed out bitterly that 'we lost all our money in Ireland' and that this was largely because of their patriotic adherence to the Crown.

This was broadly true. Michael Joyce's property had been burned down because it was rented by the Royal Irish Constabulary. And it is very likely that he was under-compensated because of his allegiances too, since the amount decided upon was made within the Irish jurisdiction. Saorstát Éireann did not intend to give generous handouts to the pro-British who were leaving the country. If Michael had stayed in Galway, he might have eventually done better. He was, within the town, a citizen of some standing, and if he had been 'pro-British', so were others who eventually accepted the new state. But once he left Ireland, he never again recaptured that status as a man of property and a 'gentleman'. When he died in 1941, Michael Joyce was a door-to-door vacuum salesman, aged seventy-four, and his eldest son William had broken his heart.

In the summer of 1923, Michael and Queenie, with their children, made the move to England. Michael retained his investments – fifty pounds in one-pound shares, which made him among the more substantial investors – in the Galway Omnibus Company until 1936, although he began selling some of the shares in 1934. He also retained his property at Rutledge Terrace until September 1930, when he sold it for

£550.[25] Perhaps Michael still had thoughts of returning to Ireland at some point, for he did not officially change his address, in the Galway Omnibus ledger book, from Ireland to England until 1927. He also retained an affection for the province of Connacht; he transmitted this affection to his son Quentin. Quentin always spoke of Ireland as 'the old country', in deference to his father's memory; when he eventually purchased a home of his own he called it 'Connemara'.

The Joyce family went, initially, to Oldham and stayed with Queenie's relations, even lodging, briefly, with some of her Oldham neighbours. A neighbour, Mrs Butterworth of Bath Street in Oldham, recalled helping to get a house ready for Mr and Mrs Joyce. They 'stayed with my mother-in-law until they got 1 Brompton Street ready … They had just come over from Ireland and they had nowhere to go. They were a very nice family.'[26] In 1923, the Joyces would move to 7 Allison Grove in East Dulwich – an admirable address. And William, who had now got himself into Birkbeck College in London to study English and history, would move back with his parents and siblings until he was ready to marry, at the age of twenty-one. This seems to have given his life some measure of stability.

William Joyce showed no evidence of anti-Semitism when he was in Galway – indeed, according to the census, there was only one Jew in Galway when William was growing up.[27] None of William's schoolmates who have been traced ever mentioned anti-Semitism as a factor in the school, or in the culture of Galway at this time; some of them were most puzzled by William's later *idée fixe* on this subject. Criticism of the Jews was not unknown in Catholic culture, particularly within the context of France in the early years of the twentieth century, when some conservative Catholics blamed left-wing Jews for the secularisation in French education and society that was taking place. In Limerick, there had been anti-Jewish boycotts around 1904, when it was claimed that Jewish moneylenders were becoming too powerful. But none of this touched Galway.

As has been noted, there may have been an element of hostility towards the Jews in the Joyce family from their American experience: ethnic rivalries were a lively part of New York society, and in Brooklyn, the expansion of Jewish immigrant life was a factor in the growth of anti-Semitism. Michael Joyce did on occasion refer to Jews as 'Yids'.[28] But the virus of pathological anti-Semitism entered William Joyce's bloodstream with particular ferocity, I believe, when he came to England as a lone teenager, his life threatened, without a proper home, with a brilliant brain but scant common sense; and at a time when there was a strong strain of anti-Semitism in the air. William's odd character had been noted by many who knew him: his Fascist colleague A. K. Chesterton thought he was slightly psychologically disturbed, and it is possible that he had some sort of personality disorder.

The Russian Revolution of 1917, followed by a civil war lasting until 1921, had shaken, and terrified, bourgeois society: this revolution not only led to the murder of the tsar and his famly in horrifying circumstances; it announced the abolition of private property, and the establishment of official atheism and the dictatorship of the proletariat; the last of these three was perceived in Europe as being synonymous with the rule of the mob.

Another theme was emerging alongside this fear and horror of Bolshevism. This was the notion that the Red revolution, which looked as though it could sweep the world, was essentially a Jewish revolution. Many books of propaganda hammered at the theme that most of the leading Russian Communists were Jews. In March 1919, *The Times* of London stated plainly: 'Most Bolsheviks are Jews.'[29] Stories circulated to the effect that the Jews had murdered the tsar and his family. In 1920, a British edition of a forged – yet widely believed – book called *The Protocols of the Elders of Zion* appeared. This claimed to be the political and economic programme of an organised Jewish plot to take over the world. Although its authors were pre-revolutionary Russian anti-Semites, there were otherwise perfectly intelligent persons, such as Henry Ford, the motor-car pioneer, who believed this dangerous nonsense implicitly.[30]

It was true that some radical revolutionaries, like Leon Trotsky, born 'Bronstein', and Rosa Luxemburg were Jewish; it was also true that, for a time, communism had a particular appeal for young Jews who had been subjected to anti-Semitic pogroms and restrictions under the tsars. In England, Poland and America, many communist activists and intellectuals were Jewish. But the suggestion that there was a Jewish conspiracy or plot was ludicrous. Yet *The Protocols* ran into many editions all over the world.

These themes were discussed repeatedly in the media which William Joyce would have read in the early 1920s: *The Times* and the *Morning Post* were full of such allusions.[31] And the *Morning Post* (which was amalgamated with the *Daily Telegraph* in 1937) made repeated claims that 'Jewish Bolsheviks' were behind the Troubles in Ireland.[32] William would probably have identified with the editorial position of the *Morning Post* because it made a special cause of supporting the 'suffering Irish loyalists' and launched appeals for funds to help pro-British Irish people who had had to flee from the IRA.

Sinn Féin, claimed the *Morning Post*, was backed by 'Ireland's Red Army'; these were communists, often aided and abetted by 'aliens' (a codeword for Jews). The Irish nationalists and Jewish Bolsheviks were, they went on, together plotting to overthrow the British Empire: 'Anyone who has attended a communist meeting can testify that the most bitter and vindictive elements are Jewish aliens and Southern Irish.'

In January 1922, just when William was at his loneliest and most vulnerable – a rejected rookie soldier with few connections and a compelling newspaper habit – the *Post* was reporting that the Communist Party of Ireland, in its newspaper the *Workers' Republic,* was all set to establish a Red regime in Éire. One of their reports ran:

> In Dublin, anxiety about Bolshevism is quite indescribable. On the railway I travelled in the same compartment with several Bolshevist agents. Three of them were talking the vilest German and by the look of them I should say that they were Russian Jews. They got out at the stations and had evidently understandings with the railway porters, whom they were urging on to strike. Such is the state of Ireland, abandoned by British rule.[33]

These influences were also supposedly worming their way into England: the country was 'flooded with aliens – Bolsheviks from Ireland to New York and Frankfurt.' And the Jewish international financier was behind it all: 'Jewry ... supported and sympathised with the rebellion in Ireland.' The *Post* quoted with satisfaction Brigadier-General Prescott-Decie, who said: 'If you traced the Bolshevik from Ireland to New York to Moscow, he would take you back to Frankfort, to the Jewish international financier.' The brigadier-general was addressing an organisation called 'The Britons' that was to become a key 'ultra-loyalist, ultra-patriotic' group, attracting influential anti-Semites and xeno-phobes during the 1920s and 1930s.

The idea that the Jews were behind the Irish revolution was at the centre of an influential book called *The Alien Menace*, written by A. H. Lane and published in 1928. Lane picked up many of the allegations that had appeared in papers like the *Morning Post* (and to a lesser extent, the magazine *John Bull*) and gathered them together. 'The Irish rebellion and the manner in which the British government finally surrendered to murder is an illuminating though tragic example of the power acquired by an Alien-directed movement,' Lane wrote.

'The Irish were and are incapable of organising such a movement without foreign aid and guidance. The Irish revolution was aided and abetted by the Socialists and Communists of Britain who ... were pursuing the historic role laid down for them by Karl Marx.' Marx, said Lane, had ordered that the British Empire could be destroyed from Ireland – through Ireland 'the primal condition for the proletarian revolution in England would be fulfilled.' The 'Prussian Jew, Karl Marx', had planned the destruction of the British Empire through the fomenting of bloody revolution in Ireland.

To William, this must have seemed the logical explanation of everything that had occurred: the reason why Ireland was lost to the Empire, and India was in danger; the reason why his life had been threatened and his parents had lost their property. His world-view was set at that moment, and in this respect it never changed. His anti-semitism took hold of him when he was a student in London in 1922–23, when such prejudices were at their most excitable, and it was set in stone. Later, the Bolshevik–Irish theme faded in the British media, as it became clear that the Irish Free State was of its natural inclination deeply conservative, and the Communist Party of Ireland was no match for the power of the Catholic Ireland.

William became associated with an early Fascist group, the British Fascisti (founded by the feminist Rotha Linton-Orman, who was inspired by Mussolini) in 1923, but though he attended meetings, he seems not to have been a full member of the party.[34] Rotha Linton-Orman was a colourful character who came from a distinguished military family and looked like Radclyffe Hall, the well-known lesbian author of the 1920s; Linton-Orman deplored the fact that Britain, after the Great War, was falling into such decline. The British Fascisti attracted soldiers and ex-soldiers, but it might have been a little too 'Home Counties' genteel for William, for it also attracted many titled ladies and gentlemen.

William might have been an extremist, but he was also a radical. He seems to have been interested in the Conservative Party for much of the 1920s, partly perhaps because they had a more realistic chance of being in government than a minority party: one of his ambitions was to become a Member of Parliament.[35] He believed that the Tories needed 'reform', and that he was the man to do it. In 1922, he had worked as a Conservative Party volunteer for Lord Howe, a kinsman of Lord Curzon (who, coincidentally, was Sir Oswald Mosley's father-in-law).[36] And it was in the cause of defending the Conservative Party that William received the livid scar that ran across his face from ear to mouth.

There was to be a British general election in October 1924: the first minority Labour administration, under Ramsay MacDonald, had been in power for ten months, and was seeking re-election. William felt strongly that Battersea's Communist MP should suffer a resounding defeat, and offered his services to a local Conservative speaker, Jack Lazarus, in stewarding a Tory meeting on the evening of Wednesday 22 October. The general election was accompanied by an increasing degree of rowdyism and hooliganism, which had not been a feature of British public politics previously, and was greatly deplored. According to the Conservative press, much of this disruption was aimed at Conservative candidates and was caused by socialists and 'Reds'.

Trouble was expected at Battersea, and William Joyce was not back-ward in coming forward in such circumstances. Apparently he told his mother that morning that he had a presentiment that he 'would finish the evening either in hospital or in the police-station charge room'. Queenie said that if it had to be one or the other, she would prefer him to be in hospital than to be on the wrong side of the law, and asked him not to go out equipped with any kind of weapon himself. William agreed.[37] But it seems that during the course of the meeting he was set upon by a gang of youths: one of them took out a cut-throat razor and slashed William's face. The *Evening Standard* reported the incident as the front-page splash the following day (relegating to the inside pages Marie Stopes' controversial appeal for birth control to the House of Lords). This, said the *Standard*, was an appalling example of 'rowdyism', and evidence that the Conservatives now had to battle for free speech against 'three hundred hooligans'.

'The man Joyce, one of our supporters, fell down, his face covered in blood,' the Tory, Jack Lazarus, told the paper.

> I am told that a spanner was also used in the fight, but I did not see that. No arrests were made bec-ause by the time the police came in the rowdies had quietened down again and so distributed them-selves that it was impossible to tell who had inflicted the razor wound.

Mr Lazarus had requested that the police be stationed outside the Lambeth Baths buildings, where he was speaking. There were also detectives and stewards inside. Mr Victor Fisher was speaking from the platform when the attack occurred. 'They noisily took exception to what he was saying,' according to the *Evening Standard* reporter.

> Suddenly there was a rush down one of the gangways, a scuffle with the stewards, and in the middle of it, the flash of a razor. Mr Lazarus vowed to have the Public Order Act enforced after these scenes of disorder, as a result of which Mr William Joyce of Allison Grove, Dulwich, had had to be confined to hospital.[38]

With this attack on his face with a razor, young William Joyce made his first appearance in the public prints, at seventeen years of age, his young broth-of-a-boy face staring out from the front page of one of the newspapers. The papers reported that he was recovering the next day, but again, Angus Macnab had a slightly different version of events.[39] The injury that William had received was very serious, wrote Macnab, and required twenty-six stitches to his face. Macnab claimed that William was 'on the danger list' for a fortnight: 'WJ asked for a discharge from hospital but the doctor refused it. On the morning of 11 November, he obtained some clothes, absconded from the hospital and took his place [at the Remembrance Day service at the Cenotaph].' He laid a wreath at the Cenotaph, apparently, and shortly afterwards collapsed. He was taken to the home of a young woman – Hazel Barr, who was later to become his wife and the mother of his two daughters.

The scar on William's face was raw and disfiguring. It was what people first noticed about him – that, and his 'dwarf-like' size. When Rebecca West saw William Joyce in the dock, on trial for his life at the Old Bailey in 1945, she observed the scar as the most noticeable characteristic of his physiognomy: 'There was nothing individual about him except a deep scar running across his right cheek from his ear to the corner of his mouth … It gave a mincing immobility to his mouth, which was extremely small.'

Unfairly, it was frequently assumed that he had received this scar as the result of a street brawl, or that he somehow deserved it. A clergyman who knew William Joyce at Birkbeck, the Reverend W. P. Webb, claimed in 1945 that 'I distinctly remember him getting his scar when he tried to break up a Communist meeting in the Mile End Road.'[40] This was simply not true: William was the victim of an unprovoked attack. The *Daily Mail* featured a close-up photograph of William after the event, the whole side of his face and neck copiously bound in bandages. 'Victim of Hooliganism', ran the caption. 'The supporters of the Socialists are hitting below the belt in their efforts to prevent the truth reaching the electors from Conservative platforms.

Not content with organised rowdyism, razor attacks have been made on their opponents.'[41]

In fact, William accepted the physical disfigurement manfully. He did not seek to hide it and occasionally referred to it in speeches and texts. He had a nickname for everything, and he nicknamed the scar 'the Lambeth Honour'. But it was not the physical disfigurement that mattered to him so much as the metaphorical significance of the scar: ever afterwards, William claimed that his attacker – his would-be murderer, as he believed, since the razor was apparently initially aimed at his throat – was a Jewish communist. This fitted perfectly with his world-view and all his conspiracy theories. It is likely that the 'rowdies' were young left-wingers; it is possible, even probable, that some may have been Jewish. And yet William's ally and defender, the Tory organiser Jack Lazarus, was also Jewish, which clearly showed that not all Jews were 'Reds' – or out to get him.

But William chose to believe, always, that a 'Jewish communist' had tried to kill him when he had sought to defend free speech at Battersea, just as an IRA gunman had tried to kill him for – as he would put it – simply affirming his loyalty to the Crown. For a lad of seventeen summers, William had already experienced his share of violence and danger.

4

A Married Man

'Men cannot live without dogmatical beliefs.'

Alexis de Tocqueville, *Democracy in America*

Living with his parents once more helped young William Joyce to focus his mind on his studies, but the association between politics and some sort of violence was now firmly set in his head. During the Irish Troubles he had seen an assassinated policeman dying in a pool of his own blood, his brains seeping out on to the pavement, and this image, imprinted on his inner eye at the age of fourteen or fifteen, sometimes came back to him in later life.[1] When he was very drunk in Berlin, he would mention it to Margaret.

Shortly before the razor attack he had, it seems, known a young man in the British Fascisti – a youth called Pearson – who was found dead in a pond in south London, apparently as a result of political violence.[2] This may have been more of a mishap, since deaths from politically motivated attacks were extremely rare in England, but William interpreted Pearson's death as another attack by the 'Reds' on 'British loyalists'.

William enrolled at Birkbeck College, a faculty of the University of London especially catering for mature students, in 1923. He was one of the youngest of the students, many of whom were individuals in their later twenties and early thirties who had missed out on further education because of the First World War. Birkbeck, now as then, admits students on entrance examination alone, and allowed working people to study part-time. Fees were modest, and sometimes students were assisted by bursaries or local-authority subvention.

Douglas Trew, who was born in January 1905, was enrolled at Birkbeck in the mid-1920s, studying for a law degree while working as a bank clerk. Birkbeck was then situated in Bream's Buildings, between Fetter Lane and Chancery Lane near Fleet Street in London. 'They were all working people – the students,' he recalled. 'Many of them people working in the City or in various firms, either for science degrees or something of that sort. Or schoolteachers working to get a degree to supplement their teachers' training.' Indeed, the Birkbeck records show that the majority of students at that time were schoolteachers. 'It was a very busy place,' Mr Trew remembered. 'At that time, after the 1914–18 war, it opened its doors in the daytime [as well as in the evening] and it was filled with ex-soldiers coming back from the war. When I got there, it was a very, very lively place, with plenty of clubs and societies.'[3]

William was reading English, with history as a secondary subject. In contrast to Battersea Poly, at Birkbeck 'there was a great interest in politics, because all the ex-servicemen took a keen interest in politics,' Trew recalled. This was not William's street agitprop, but respectable British political discourse: the students were Conservative, Liberal or Labour – the latter now a rising tendency after the first Labour government of 1923. Communists and Fascists, or other extremists, did not figure. The fear of Bolsheviks articulated by the *Morning Post* had not yet penetrated student circles, although it would do after the General Strike of 1926.

William worked hard at Birkbeck. 'He was as fanatical in

his studies as he is in other directions,' reported the MI5 spymaster Charles Maxwell Knight, 'and several times during his scholastic career he reduced himself to the verge of a nervous breakdown.' He had a remarkable brain for academic work: he possessed a brilliant memory – he could always quote any poem he had read with attention, and could even commit to memory a piece of prose. He mastered a variety of languages, including Latin and some Greek, and higher mathematics were no trouble to him. He also had the mathematician's affinity for music, and could reproduce, on a piano, almost any piece of music he had heard.[4] William's intelligence was such that he was often regarded as a bit of a genius by his immediate circle of friends.

He got involved in other aspects of student life, too. Although he had no interest in sport in general, he later claimed that he had joined the boxing and fencing clubs. Still nursing a desire for soldiering, he also joined the London University Officer Training Corps. And he continued to play chess, a hobby that would endure until his last day on earth, in the condemned cell at Wandsworth Prison. William was a skilled chess player, but he had one strange quirk: he could only play a defensive game and could only play with the black pieces. It amazed his friend Angus Macnab that William displayed no aggression whatsoever when it came to the chessboard: 'In this respect he showed a curiously defeatist mentality. To beat him, all one had to do was to avoid making any howlers and go on pressing the attack: he would merely defend, never make a counter-attack.'[5]

Birkbeck had a mock parliament which the students ran as a political forum; William attended it from time to time. He spoke as a Conservative but, according to Douglas Trew, quickly bored the audience with his anti-Semitic tirades: 'He hadn't got to speak for more than a few sentences before everybody was telling him to sit down. His theme was always the same – anti-Jewish.'

Despite his academic ability, William's 'oddness' persisted

and he didn't cut much of a figure with his fellow students: the gash on his face, his very short stature, his shabby suits and what Mr Trew calls his 'obvious' Irishness hardly added up to an alluring personality in the eyes of his peers. Outside of college life, he was even formally reprimanded by the British Fascisti for his immoderate language. 'You allowed yourself to give vent to an expression of opinion concerning the members of the Council which was unwarranted, uncalled for and utterly unpardonable,' he was told in a letter from British Fascisti headquarters in December 1924. Had he been been a member of the party, he was informed, he would have been asked to leave because of his 'ill-considered and ill-judged remarks, coupled with subsequent loud-voiced interruptions'.[6]

Against this pattern of troublesome behaviour was the contrasting evidence of academic brilliance: he emerged from Birkbeck with a First Class degree – one of only two in the faculty of English to do so in the academic year 1926–27. The man who came second, William Lees, remained a good pal of his.[7] It was said that William Joyce had produced the best paper on Shakespeare the university had seen in the twentieth century.[8] He also wrote papers on Milton, answering the question 'What do you take to be the process which led Milton from *Paradise Lost* to *Samson Agonistes*?' and discussing 'the satiric theory and practice of Dryden'.[9] He was fond of Dryden: during the most difficult moments of his trial, he kept his self-control by mentally reciting Dryden to himself.

William would also be rewarded, in another department of his life, by the love of a woman, Hazel Barr. Hazel was one of three daughters of a family from Canterbury – her father was a dentist who had served in a Scots regiment in the First World War – all of whom were destined to be long-lived. She would have been called – in the parlance of the time – a young girl of good family, who had been educated at Lady

Margaret school in Fulham. The family were High Church in London (although they had been Low Church in the country), and thoroughly Conservative. Hazel remained interested in politics all her life. In the 1920s, she and her older sisters were most exercised about the Russian Revolution: they were 'very excited about Russians, and Russian spies, and expected Russians to arrive in London with snow on their boots at any moment'.[10]

Hazel and her family were 'very patriotic' and keen on supporting the British Empire. It was certainly possible that she was present at the Cenotaph in November 1924 when William apparently fainted, still in the throes of recovery from the twenty-six surgical stitches applied to his face. It would have been convenient, too, for her to remove him to her parents' flat just down the river at Chelsea, where she could tend to his wound. And as Hazel was studying pharmacy herself, she would have had the paramedical skills to be of some assistance. As well as the bond between nurse and patient, William and Hazel also had something else in common: Hazel was attending Birkbeck College as a part-time student.

And so, it seems, Hazel Barr and William Joyce fell in love. Their daughter Heather says that Hazel was initially fascinated by William: 'his knowledge, wit, charm'. It is often the case that women don't mind 'oddness' in a man if he makes them laugh. William was, as Heather commented, 'really struck on' Hazel, who was taller than him, intelligent, and something of a cool English rose. Hazel was working at Mr Balfour's chemist's shop at Shepherd's Bush; William took to visiting her there. Some of their courtship also took place at political meetings in Hyde Park.

Both sets of parents, however, were against the match. William and Hazel were only twenty. William's second wife, Margaret, claimed that the Joyce family never really liked Hazel; perhaps she was a little too reserved for the talkative Joyces. But perhaps second wives are not always the kindest judges of first wives – Margaret was also inclined to exaggerate the age difference between William and Hazel – which was only one month – to Hazel's disadvantage. But the real objection was that they were too young and William was in no position to support a wife and family – a conventional expectation of a man at the time. He was still a student, though by the mid-1920s he was earning a little money through part-time tutoring.

Neither set of parents was present when the wedding of William Joyce and Hazel Kathleen Barr took place at Chelsea Register Office on 30 April 1927, just six days after William's twenty-first birthday – the earliest date on which they could marry without the consent of parents. (Hazel had turned twenty-one just a month previously.) After the simple, early-morning ceremony, which was afterwards blessed by a High Anglican priest, Father Eaves, they each went home to their respective parents as though nothing had occurred. William and Hazel had chosen a civil wedding ceremony because, their daughter suggests, this was what 'bright young things' of the 1920s did.[11] And yet perhaps it indicates that for Hazel – who was of a religious turn of mind, and requested the Church of England blessing afterwards – there wasn't a total commitment to this marriage. The way was open for Hazel to remarry without canonical objection, since she had never been sacramentally married to William Joyce; indeed she eventually did remarry in church.

When the marriage of William and Hazel was eventually revealed to their parents, it was as a fait accompli, and the respective families eventually accepted it (although the first reaction of Hazel's mother was to swoon). The Barrs even provided William and Hazel with living quarters: the young couple began their married life together at 44 Jubilee Gardens in Chelsea, in a flat owned by Hazel's family. William moved London addresses many times, but he always liked best that area of Chelsea and Westminster encompassed by the postal codes of SW3, SW7 and SW1.

William never showed any interest in social status (or in material possessions, for that matter), yet in marrying Hazel Barr, in the eyes of the world, he was marrying upwards. He was the odd little Irishman with the funny face; she was the well-spoken young English lady from the Home Counties, with an address in fashionable Chelsea.

At the time of the marriage, William was only just completing his studies at Birkbeck, and about to embark on postgraduate work for an MA. The head of the English Language and Literature department, H. H. Lobban, had a high opinion of young Joyce. Typically, however, William complained that a Jewish lecturer at Birkbeck took against him; he even claimed that she used his research work without acknowledgement (admittedly a not unknown practice).[12] Since William made little secret of his anti-Semitism, he could hardly expect a Jewish member of staff to warm to him, but in any case, the allegation may not have been true, and it has not been possible to ascertain whether any relevant member of the Birkbeck staff was Jewish.

But Birkbeck was good to William Joyce: he may have struck other students as weird, but he flourished as an intellectual, sharpened his already bright wits and expanded his reading. He conceived a special admiration for the nineteenth-century conservative intellectual Thomas Carlyle. Carlyle remained a lifelong influence on William; Joyce regarded the Scottish writer as an early Fascist. He wrote:

> Thomas Carlyle ranks first amongst British heralds of the British revolution … in all the vast extent of Carlyle's writings there is nothing that could be regarded as other than the product of a National-Socialist mind. He himself had the spirit of National Socialism long before it existed.'[13]

Whether Carlyle would have claimed to be an intellectual

ancestor for Fascism is unknowable, but the ingredients of William's National Socialist philosophy are there. Carlyle was clever, sarcastic and authoritarian; he loathed snobbery and what he described as 'materialism', was a Germanophile, patriotic and something of a racist; he believed in a spiritual order apart from orthodox religion and had a strong social conscience in regard to poverty.

Carlyle also developed the idea of 'the hero' as an object of 'hero-worship', a word he coined: he believed that men need heroes, who can be gods, poets, priests, kings or warriors. This was one of William's core beliefs. Temperamentally, he himself always needed heroes: Napoleon, Cromwell, Oswald Mosley and Adolf Hitler all became, in turn, William's special hero and the object of his hero-worship.

William also developed an interest in philology and linguistics during his time at Birkbeck. In the year that he graduated from Birkbeck, William had two articles published in respected magazines associated with London University: in the spring of 1927 he appeared in the *Lodestone*, the journal of Birkbeck College.[14] Even more impressively, he had an article accepted by the *Review of English Studies*, an academic quarterly journal of English literature and language. The article, which appeared in 1928, was on the philological subject of 'The Mid Back Slack Unround Vowel [a] in the English of Today'; the essay was essentially a commentary on north of England pronounciation.[15]

He drew on his Oldham background for this discourse: 'As a northerner I am keenly sensitive to the difference between the Low Front Slack [ae] of Received Standard and the corresponding sound, as in "hat" in the north.' The article shows a keen ear for linguistic nuance on the part of its author; it is written knowledgeably, but without the pedantry or jargon that marks some academic work. Perhaps significantly, Joyce compares English sounds with the 'purer' German ones, identifying the 'a' in the German verb 'machen' as 'a true "a" sound'. (He identifies the word 'laugh' as an example of the serious differentiation of speech between the north and south of England.) William's interest in philology was obviously significant in terms of his life's calling as a radio performer and platform speaker.

Around 1927 or 1928, as a young married man and then a father, William Joyce might have taken the route of respectability of becoming an academic. He also tried to become a diplomat. He made his application to the Foreign Office in April 1928, writing from 44 Jubilee Place in Chelsea, where he and Hazel still lived. On paper, William should have been a suitable candidate: he had an excellent degree and a wide range of accomplishments. He spoke good French, excellent German, good Latin, some Greek and some Italian, and was a scholar in old Germanic languages such as Anglo-Saxon, Icelandic, Gothic and Old Norse. William's character referees were Reverend Cuthbert C. Keet, BA, BD PhD, the vicar of St James's in Hampstead Road, a High Anglican priest who was very likely a connection of the Barr family, and Sir Frederick Hall, KBE, DSO, a Tory member of parliament. Sir Frederick had been Conservative candidate for Dulwich and was quick to write to Willliam's mother after he had read about the Lambeth razor attack: he offered her his 'very sincere sympathy that he should have been the victim of such cowardly Bolshevik methods.'[16] William also got a good reference from the head of English and principal of Birkbeck College, Dr George Senter.

William disclosed in his Foreign Office application that he had been born in New York, but hoped that this would merit a dispensation. He pleaded that 'the circumstance [of his birth], over which I had no control, was due to business reasons which prevented my mother from crossing the Atlantic, as she had hoped to do, before my birth.' He added, anxiously:

> Sir Frederick Hall will assure you of my patriotism
> and devotion to the King; and if necessary, several
> Members of Parliament of high standing will gladly

> corroborate his information ... I can produce,
> should you require it, sufficient evidence of my
> integrity and constant patriotism to justify the
> authorities in making any exceptions necessary.[17]

He was, in fact, granted a dispensation from the Foreign Secretary on account of his American birth.

What damned William's chances of even sitting the examination to enter the Foreign Office was a dreadful reference from the principal of Battersea Poly. William Joyce had not distinguished himself at Battersea, wrote George O'Riordan: he held 'extreme views and upheld the use of violence in political action ... Our very vivid recollection of Mr Joyce is that he was entirely unfitted for a responsible position, and particularly for the Foreign Office or Diplomatic Service.'[18] However brilliant William was academically, this completely scuppered his chances. Moreover, the anxious, exaggerated, over-patriotic language which he used in his letters of supplication did not find favour.

Against William's protestations of his Britishness, his avowals of 'patriotism and devotion to the King' and his apology that he had not served in the Great War (he was only eight when it began), some Foreign Office mandarin scribbled on his application: 'A little oily, don't you think?' William Joyce was very definitely 'Not One of Us'. Had he been an upper-class English communist, rather than a *déclassé* Fascist, and Irish to boot, it is probable that his chances of advancing in the Foreign Office might have been much better.

William always claimed, especially to his second wife, Margaret, that he had been rebuffed by the Foreign Office because he was a working tutor, with no private income: there was an expectation that people in the diplomatic services would have private means. This was not so, but he preferred to believe this rather than admitting that he was rejected because of his character defects, as well as the prejudices of the system. As Rebecca West noted, years later, William Joyce simply was not the kind of person who, in

England, would ever have been entrusted with any position of authority, however outstanding his academic achievements might have been.

⁓

William and Hazel's first child, Heather, was born on 30 July 1928, a little over a year after their wedding. Hazel had a difficult pregnancy and a very painful childbirth: William wept during his wife's long labour, with the distress of a young father who realises, for the first time, perhaps, how distressing it can be to enter the world.[19] But Heather was his pride and joy, and although he was only to be with her until she was seven, this was enough time for him to bond with her, and to reveal to her his best side – the high-spirited, clever, fun-loving father who told stories, sang songs and could be greatly beguiling. When he was coaching a former army officer in political speaking in 1932, he wrote: 'I adore my eldest little girl.'[20] Heather remembers occasions of merriment and good cheer in their home, with, eventually, the grand-parents being fondly involved with the children.

In the early years of the marriage, William was teaching and tutoring at the Victoria College. He quickly proved to be good at this job; he was also doing some academic research with a view to continuing a full academic career. But he couldn't leave politics alone.

In the late 1920s, he made a serious effort to develop his links with the Conservative Party and even began to cherish the hope that he might one day be chosen as parliamentary candidate for the very desirable seat of Chelsea. Indeed his loyal friend Macnab claimed that, 'but for domestic troubles, it is exceedingly likely that he would have been nominated as candidate for Chelsea in the early 'thirties'.[21]

From 1928 until 1930, William became active in the Conservative Party of Chelsea; he was also the chairman of the Chelsea Junior Imperial League, an organisation that attracted potential young Tories. He seems to have moderated, at least initially, his blatant expressions of anti-Semitism.[22] Some time later, William explained that one must be more careful in expressing anti-Semitic feelings with the upper classes than with ordinary folk – because the British upper classes were, he said, so intermarried with Jewish grandees that half of them were half-Jewish themselves.[23]

For a short time between 1928 and 1930, it even looked as though William might become the kind of Englishman he secretly wished to be, at least in one part of his psyche: a respectable right-wing Tory with some academic distinction, married to a High Church wife with a property in Chelsea, and a family man. He made friends with Members of Parliament and spoke about his connections within Westminster; he believed he had some influence there.

He had impressed the Chelsea Tories with his 'unique gift of oratory' and willingness to work hard for a cause. They also liked his energy and enterprise, and, being a teacher, he was good with the young people of the 'Imps' (the Junior Imperial League); he increased the number of young people attending the league.

Gradually, however, William began to overstep the mark, as was his wont. He increased the discipline among the Imps, and then commenced military drilling in the meetings. His speeches became gradually more authoritarian, and he introduced these mild Tories to an 'aggressive nationalism' that is not at all the English style. 'He demanded absolute silence for some time at the beginning of each meeting, even if he were not speaking,' recalled Hester Marsden-Smedley in 1973.[24] 'One day there was some giggling at the back. Joyce shouted indignantly and ordered the offenders out.' When he was not obeyed, he sent for the police, an episode which turned quite farcical. At an inquiry afterwards, William accused a young Tory in Chelsea of 'softness and decadent Jewish influence'. He had overstepped the mark again. He even on one occasion reduced Hester Marsden-Smedley to tears – which, she said, no man had ever done before.

Mrs Marsden-Smedley, who was a grand matriarch of Kensington and Chelsea Conservatives (after the two boroughs merged), knew that William would have to go and awaited her opportunity to push him; such an opportunity duly came. She had met Hazel, and liked her. 'Pretty, shy, a devoted mother, she took little part in her husband's activities through his wish,' Mrs Marsden-Smedley recalled. One day Hazel came to Hester Marsden-Smedley in tears and told her that William 'owned to having seduced one of his pupils, was in love with her and wanted a divorce to marry her.' The pupil in question, who seemed to be involved with the Chelsea Junior Imperial League, was 'young, pretty and of a well-known, distinguished family'. In the late 1920s, divorce was still held in some circles to be a slight stigma, but Joyce declared (truthfully) that he was only doing what those who called themselves his betters did.

'The opportunity was too good to miss,' Mrs Marsden-Smedley recalled. 'We pounced, moral pressure was brought to bear on him and he was allowed to resign, which he did with customary flamboyance.' William's public version of events was that he had sought to 'reform' the Conservative Party but that it proved to be unreformable. Privately, he knew he had seriously misbehaved. He confessed, in a letter to his pupil C. C. Lewis – whom he coached in political rhetoric – that he was aware that he somehow lacked a 'moral sense'. He wrote that he had 'lost his lemon' with the Chelsea Tories.[25] He continued to believe that if he hadn't done so, he might have become the MP for Chelsea.

The full story of William Joyce's affair with this young woman has now emerged. The girl in question – Mary Ogilvy – was indeed young and pretty: she was only sixteen years of age when Joyce first met her, in 1927. He was already married. Mary's father, who was by this time dead, was Walter Tulliedeph Ogilvy, the younger son of a baronet: the family was fully represented in *Debrett's Peerage*, which meant a great deal in Chelsea in the 1920s. Mary was intelligent, musical and artistic, as well as being pretty. She had come to London with her mother from Co. Durham, probably with the intention of being a debutante, but there may not have been sufficient funds to carry out this plan. It is possible that during Mary's time in London, where she was supposed to be studying art, her mother Nora (herself the daughter of a canon in the Church of England) was sometimes absent, and Mary may have been rather unsupervised.

In any case, Mary became involved with the Chelsea Tories – the family tradition was High Church, High Tory – and some time before her seventeenth birthday, in 1927, William Joyce seduced her. Indeed, he deflowered her, in a dramatic scene that she never forgot. She knew nothing whatsoever about sex, had never seen a naked man before – let alone a naked man in a state of erection. The seduction was traumatic and shocking: and it imprinted itself on her psyche indelibly. She fell under William's spell completely. She was dominated by him over the following months – possibly more than a year – until Hazel Joyce went to Mrs Marsden-Smedley and the affair came to light. It was then hushed up, as smartly as possible, with the despatch of William from the Chelsea Tories, and the bundling off of Mary abroad, first to Austria and subsequently to Paris (where she studied music and the history of art).

Mary subsequently married Bryan Potter, whose family was associated with the Prudential insurance business. She had six children, and after the war, they went to South Africa – Mary certainly remained on the right of the political spectrum. Her life there a strange mixture of the frivolous and the intense. She was party-loving, a fabulous hostess, enjoyed society and gossip, and had many affairs during the course of her life. Yet she was also something of a failed artist: she tried to write radio plays, she loved music, and she was a sculptress in a small way.

When William became notorious as Lord Haw-Haw, Mary feared that her name might emerge in the newspapers in connection with his, but it never did. As an old lady – she died in 1996, in Johannesburg – she told her son Tully the whole story. William had remained a fixture in her memory, something unforgettable, but also something dark. He certainly had behaved as a bounder, in deflowering a sixteen-year-old girl while his wife was pregnant, and yet he retained a genuine affection for her. When William's life began to fall apart in a crumbling Berlin, he recalled with a kind of nostalgic passion the memory of Mary Ogilvy.

William's parents had been right in thinking him too young and too immature for a life of quiet married domesticity. At home, William liked to have people in, and to stay up half the night talking, drinking and arguing. There was no end to the hospitality and carousing. Aside from the suspicion that he had had an affair with a student, this compulsive greg-ariousness wore Hazel down. The couple had moved house from Jubilee Place to 41 Cedars Road in Battersea, and then in 1931 back to the Chelsea area, to 27 Bramerton Street. Wherever they were, there were strangers coming and going: it was not a lifestyle that young wives with small children generally find congenial.

There must have been financial strains too. William was supporting his family by tutoring, but he never cared about money, and seldom had much of it. His parents, Michael and Queenie, must have been finding life in Dulwich something of a struggle, with three children still in full-time education: Frank, William's next-eldest brother, was eighteen in 1930 and training to be a radio engineer, while Quentin, aged thirteen, was enrolled at Mercer's School in Holborn. The parents considered Alleyn's School in Dulwich – the best school in the area, apart from Dulwich College – for Quentin, but they could not afford the fees. Joan was just eight and Robert five. The Joyce house in Dulwich would have cost something in the region of £1,000; in 1930, they finally sold their home in Galway for £550. There was no cash to spare. Michael and Queenie started a small grocery shop in south London – Michael was ever the businessman – but although it would survive for a few years, in the end it failed in the general economic climate.

And then in July 1931, Hazel gave birth to a second daughter, Diana; perhaps this was a reconciliation baby after the Chelsea affair. She was born 'looking as Irish as anything, with her mop of dark hair'.[26] But Diana seems to have less happy memories of her early life with her father than Heather, and has little desire to be associated with him publicly. By the time she was three or so, her parents' marriage was frayed and irascible. There were bad-tempered outbursts from William; he would go for long walks to work out his spleen. Moreover, he exhibited no attachment to his second child: he mentions Heather in letters and other reflections, but never makes any reference to his younger daughter. There is a family theory that Diana simply looked too raven-haired and Irish for her father's affection, whereas Heather looked English, even Aryan.

William had developed an interest in the relatively new field of educational psychology, and had applied to King's College in the Strand on 26 May 1932, from which he must have hoped to emerge with a PhD. He was by now working thirty-two hours a week as a tutor of languages and history at the Victoria Tutorial College at 89 Eccleston Square, Victoria, in London SW1. William was a gifted teacher: his friend 'the Master' Macnab said that William was able to impart knowledge in special subjects even in areas where his technical knowledge was not remarkable: for instance, he was able to impart his grasp of Latin texts to his students, even though he was not an outstanding Latinist. One of William's less admiring pupils called this particular approach 'bluff': 'He had a good deal of bluff to support the cleverness,' the student recalled.[27] His experience in teaching was leading him to take a special interest in the psychology of teaching.

He registered under Professor Francis Powell Aveling, a distinguished Canadian and former priest with an impressive array of publications to his credit. Aveling pioneered work on educational psychology but was also drawn to various mystical theories on consciousness, mental energy and the immortality of the soul. William was to attend lectures at King's College, near the Aldwych in the Strand in London, on Thursdays from five thirty to eight thirty in the evenings. His tuition fee at King's was to be three pounds per term.[28]

William and Hazel were now living at 41 Farquhar Road in Upper Norwood, overlooking Crystal Palace; the house was within walking distance of William's parents in Dulwich. Heather remembers visiting her Joyce grandparents on a Sunday, and how she became a special pet of her grandfather, Michael Joyce, whom she knew as 'Poppa'. If Heather was naughty, Poppa would always defend her, saying that she was a high-spirited child. William seemed very keen on his postgraduate studies at King's College: Professor Aveling was his new hero. Without Hitler's dramatic rise to power in Germany, William might have lived a normal span of life as Dr Joyce, philologist and psychologist, with eccentric views and a scarred face but an established reputation as a teacher and even, perhaps, as a pioneer of educational psychology. Instead, history led him in quite a different direction.

The 1920s had been an era of economic shocks and chronic unemployment but it had also been a decade of excitement for the post–Great War generation. 'In no similar period have such tremendous changes swept across the world,' wrote Winston Churchill of the reign of George V, which reached its apogee in the 1920s.

> In none have its systems, manners and outlook been more decisively altered; in none have the knowledge, science, wealth and power of mankind

undergone such vast and rapid expansion. Indeed,
the speed at which the evolution of society has
taken place baffles all comparison.[29]

The aeroplane proclaimed a new era of international
travel: Stanley Baldwin, the Conservative Prime Minister for
most of the 1920s, believed that the aircraft had done away
with Britain's frontiers, and possibly its defences. In literature
and the arts there was a new candour, which some regarded
as disturbing and pornographic. In Germany, historians such
as Oswald Spengler saw in these trends the decadent phases
of a dying civilisation. To those who were already inclined
towards anti-Semitism, it was disconcerting that Jewish
influences seemed to be so culturally and political dominant
in post-war thinking. 'During the 'twenties ... men were
moving into a world whose main intellectual energy has
come from members of the German–Jewish community,'
according to *The Oxford History of the Modern World.*[30] Marx,
Freud and Einstein were the giants of the post-war world.

The General Strike of 1926 seemed, at first, to pose a
threat of revolution – William affirmed his Conservative
patriotism by enlisting as a Special Constable at the time – but
in fact proved quite the contrary: the Left was trounced, the
radical miners were defeated and Britain retained its stable,
even stodgy, political character. Fear of communism was still
an issue, yet, overall, towards the end of the 1920s it looked as
though the world was gradually returning to normality.

Then, in October 1929, the event which would
effectively shape the 1930s took place. While Europe
struggled with unemployment and post-war malaise,
America had been glamorously prosperous during the 1920s,
at least for its most successful citizens. While the British
Empire seemed to be fraying, the prestige of American
influence and money expanded everywhere. New York
replaced London as the banking centre of the world, and
from the mid-1920s values on the New York Stock Exchange

rose and rose. Share prices continued their inexorable rise throughout the spring and summer of 1929. But in the last week in October, shares began to slide, and despite efforts by senior financiers to shore up the stock exchange, blind panic set in and the Great Crash began. Billions were wiped off share values, families were ruined, businesses were destroyed, and industry and markets were shaken to their foundations.[31]

As well as triggering the Depression in the United States, the Wall Street Crash, with its soup kitchens and the haunting song 'Brother, can you spare a dime?', had reverberations all over the world, most significantly in Germany, which had been the beneficiary of American investment. This investment was now withdrawn, and Germany, which was only tentatively recovering from its ghastly inflationary troubles of the 1920s, was once again plunged into a new cycle of unemployment, loss of savings, decline of the middle class and destruction of the respectable working class. Berlin would become a city of teenage gangs where crime soared, as did suicide, prostitution and drug abuse.

The Crash convinced millions of people around the world that capitalism was doomed. Individuals had been reduced to begging because great fortunes and great investments had depended upon the brokers of Wall Street and the greed of the speculators. This was, many concluded, no way to run an economy. Membership of communist parties increased hugely throughout the western world; the Soviet Union was one of the few countries to escape the consequences of the Crash.

In England, some of the best and brightest young people would now become Communists. Oxford and Cambridge became seedbeds for Marxism. And where communism flourished, Fascism arose in response, and indeed vice versa. The two ideologies were not in fact very different. Radical Catholics became Fascists because the atheism of the Communist Party precluded their adherence to communism.

Essentially, both communism and Fascism were primarily concerned with delivering an alternative to the free-market system which seemed to have served the world so ill.

The 1930s would be the age of extremism, and that excited William Joyce. With one extreme gesture, he cast aside his promising academic career and threw himself wholeheartedly into the newly formed British Union of Fascists.

5

With the Blackshirts: The 'Mighty Atom'

> *'The Irishman must talk; somehow he must*
> *shatter the mystery that separates him from his*
> *neighbour and from eternity.'*
>
> Charles Arthur Boycott, *Boycott: The Life Behind the Word*

William always knew that he was capable of becoming a notable public speaker. He had given playground speeches to his school fellows in Galway. At the age of thirteen, he had spoken against communism in the school playground.[1] As a young man, fresh to England, he had watched soapbox orators at Hyde Park Corner in London, and knew he could do it as well as any of them. Then, one day, a soapbox speaker at Hyde Park Corner was haranguing his audience about Ireland, and the long British oppression of the Irish; William promptly mounted a soapbox of his own and gave his alternative, loyalist version of the history of Britain's relationship with Ireland.[2] On another occasion, his parents, taking a walk in Hyde Park on a Sunday, were surprised to hear a voice that struck them as familiar. It was William, their son, treating the passing public to his political viewpoint.[3]

The British Union of Fascists was launched by Oswald Mosley in October 1932. Although he was at a loose end politically, William did not join the party right away. He waited for another ten months, during which time he continued to focus mainly on his postgraduate work at King's College in London. Perhaps William was also trying to save his marriage, which was frayed and tempestuous. And before he joined the new Fascist party, he acquired for himself a British passport.

William applied for his passport from his address at 41 Farquhar Road, in south London, declaring that he had been born at Rutledge Terrace in Galway, which was, of course, part of the United Kingdom in 1906. Birth certificates were not required as proof of British birth: an Englishman's word was his bond, and references from two respectable persons were sufficient. He duly received his passport on 5 July 1933: he was number 125943. It would be noted at his trial for treason that even though William was American by birth, he had *sought* the protection of His Majesty, and therefore owed the Crown his allegiance. In 1933, William Joyce would have had no quarrel with that notion, for he proclaimed from every available rooftop his super-allegiance to His Majesty.

He joined the Mosley movement on 17 August 1933 as a party member.[4] But initially, he clearly did not intend his membership of the party to interfere with his academic goals: in the autumn term, he enrolled for another year at King's College. He even increased his study-times at King's to three evenings a week in 1933–34: his term fees rose from three to five pounds. Then, suddenly, in November that year, he informed his tutor that he would not be finishing his PhD because he felt called to devote himself more fully to politics. His tutor, and other friends, tried to dissuade him from throwing away his academic future in this way, but having made up his mind, William was adamant.[5]

William's interest in the psychological work of Professor Aveling seemed somewhat faded next to his newfound hero-worship of Oswald Mosley, the founder of the British Union of Fascists. A. K. Chesterton said of William Joyce that it was in his nature to be 'an idolator': in Mosley, in 1933, he had found an object of veneration. Soon after he joined Mosley's Fascists, William said of his leader, reverently: 'There is no greater man that God has ever created.'[6]

Mosley was certainly a charismatic character. He was regarded by some as an opportunist, and his judgement often led him astray, but in his early years he had shown courage, vision and leadership. He had come from a background of squires of the shires – the hard-riding country gentry who disdained metropolitan values – and had been a daring air ace during the First World War. He had been a Conservative MP, and crossed the floor of the House of Commons in 1920 in protest against the conduct of the Black and Tans in Ireland. Mosley and William Joyce might have disagreed on this subject, although Mosley's reasoning was both humane and practical. But it was a characteristic gesture by Mosley: he was socially fearless. He had the confidence of the upper-class buccaneer. He was, said an associate, an 'Englishman of the Carolean tennis court, of the duelling ground rather than the Pall Mall Club'.[7]

Mosley was not another bespectacled, predictable, desk-bound politician: he was a man of action, and his strong card was 'youth'. 'Youth!' would be the great Fascist call to arms: Benito Mussolini's marching song was *Giovinezza!* (*'Giovinezza! Giovinezza! Primavera di bellezza!*' – '*Youth! Youth! Beauty's springtime!*')

In challenging the 'old gang' in England, Mosley had a point: English politics at the time was full of time-serving nonentities and, worse, unimaginative people who had not understood that the world had changed since 1929 and the onset of the Depression, and that fresh economic thinking was required. The economist John Maynard Keynes saw that new ideas were needed in the sphere of economics, and so did Oswald Mosley.

After becoming a Labour MP – eighty Labour constituencies had invited him to be their Member – Mosley broke away from Labour to launch a 'New Party', in search of a 'third way'. Then, on a visit to Italy in 1932, he underwent a 'conversion experience' when he saw Mussolini's corporate state. There was nothing unusual about this: from the middle of the 1920s, Fascist Italy had been regarded as a remarkable success and had drawn admiration from Winston Churchill, George Bernard Shaw, Sir John Reith, Professor Walter Starkie and many other luminaries.[8] In its early stages, aspects of Mussolini's Italy were impressive, with, for instance, energetic slum clearances and health programmes to eradicate TB. Neither was it either racist or anti-Semitic in the beginning: the Chief Rabbi of Rome was among the first people to join the Italian Fascist Party. In some ways too, Fascism was 'modern': it embraced the motor car, the airplane, scientific experiments and new architectural design.

Mussolini's success spawned many imitators: there had been, from 1923, the British Fascisti – subsequently called the British Fascists – founded, as has already been mentioned, by the feminist Rotha Linton-Orman. This group had become ineffective and fragmented, and when Mosley launched his own British Union of Fascists, he would now take over, or politically kill off, what remained of the luckless Rotha's following (she would die of drink in 1935, having ruined her family's fortune on the cause of British Fascism).[9] There were other British Fascist organisations, including Arnold Leese's Imperial Fascist League, founded in 1929. These groups would remain bitter rivals of Mosley's, and many of them were even more extreme than his organisation. But the British Union of Fascists was to become, during the 1930s, by far the most successful of the Fascist groups in Britain. It would also attract many more people than the Communist Party of Great Britain, although the Communists were more influential and indeed, paradoxically, more upper class in their composition.

✑

When William quit King's College in November 1933, he plunged immediately into his new life as a speaker for the British Union of Fascists. He was still doing some teaching at the Victoria Tutorial College, but it was on a flexible enough basis to allow for his political engagements. Almost immediately after leaving his university life, William was performing as a political orator. Oswald Mosley, for all his vigour and potency, did not always enjoy good health, and on 20 November 1933, when due to address a meeting at Streatham in south London, he fell ill with phlebitis; Joyce deputised very ably. Six days later, William addressed an audience of over five thousand at Liverpool Stadium; from this time on, he travelled up and down Britain speaking on behalf of Fascism.

As a speaker, his talent was immediately apparent – when he was in the right milieu. Many who saw him speak, in those early days of the British Union of Fascists, described him as an electrifying orator. Even Hester Marsden-Smedley, who had effectively had William expelled from the Chelsea Conservatives, admitted that she had never seen anyone so brilliant on a public platform.

John Beckett, formerly a Labour MP, was virtually converted to Mosley's Fascism by hearing an address by Joyce. In 1934, John, 'in a mood of disillusionment, went to a BUF meeting at Paddington Baths,' according to his son Francis Beckett.

> Mosley was ill, and the meeting was taken by a young man called William Joyce, of whom John had never before heard. He described the effect: 'Within ten minutes of this twenty-eight-year-old youngster taking the platform I knew that here was one of the dozen finest orators in the country.'[10]

John Beckett compared Joyce to Winston Churchill, in terms of political rhetoric. Beckett, an impulsive, passionate man who had been shattered by his experience in the Great War, joined the BUF straight away. For Beckett, William Joyce became, for a while, *his* hero.

Peter Morris, a doctor's son from Lincolnshire who was born in 1916, and who followed his sister Sylvia into the Blackshirt movement in the 1930s, heard William Joyce speak 'between ten and twenty times' in the 1930s. 'He was a character,' Morris recalls.

> He was known as 'the Mighty Atom'. He was an excellent speaker. He gave the impression of strength. He was short, and thick. He was as broad as he was long. His chest was terrific, his waist was small, his legs were terrific, his arm muscles were terrific. He had worked his body. And he was such a charismatic character. Both on the platform and in little groups of people, he always dominated every group.[11]

Margaret Collins, one of two Catholic sisters who came to work at the BUF headquarters, first encountered William Joyce when she was 'eighteen or nineteen,' she recalls. She noticed how much at ease William was when facing a large and noisy crowd. He loved public speaking and felt at home on a public platform. He must have yearned for this outlet during his time spent beavering away at academic studies.

Oswald Mosley must have recognised in William Joyce a compelling quality – although he never liked Joyce personally – because by early 1934, he had hired William as his propaganda director, at a yearly salary of £300 – a very decent income at the time. (Members of Parliament earned £400 annually; an office clerk would earn £77 a year). This meant he could give up his tutorial job at the Victoria College. It would also mean a lot of travelling for him up and down the country – which, in the circumstances, Hazel may have welcomed.

Within months of joining the BUF, William was being widely described by the mainstream newspapers as one of the stars of the Fascist movement in Britain; he was even nicknamed 'the Professor' because of his know-all armoury of information.[12] He could also be witty with hecklers. In a north of England town, a particularly fierce working-class woman shouted at him, 'You're a right bastard!' He quickly retorted, 'Thank you, mother', to much laughter.

A year after joining the BUF, William was regarded as a future leader of the British Fascist movement, which seemed, in its early days, to be destined for great things. In the first six months of 1934, Lord Rothermere of the powerful *Daily Mail* group had given enthusiastic backing to the Blackshirts – as the BUF followers were sometimes called because of the distinctive black shirts which they wore. Rothermere did this partly to annoy the socialists, partly in an attempt to create a bulwark against communism, and partly because he believed in Mosley's gifts. Membership of the BUF quickly reached about fifty thousand: it seemed to have a dynamic appeal to the younger generation.

This early period of British Fascism is sometimes known by historians of the period as 'the respectable phase'. Fascism challenged unbridled capitalism, proposed a unified corporate state and promoted patriotism. There was also an element of idealism, and of egalitarianism, in the Fascist creed: in February 1933, the weekly publication *The Blackshirt* proclaimed that the policy of the BUF was:

> All shall serve the State and none the Faction. All shall work and thus enrich their Country and themselves. Opportunity shall be open to all, but privilege to none. Great position shall be accorded only to service. Poverty shall be abolished by the power of modern science released within the organised State. The barriers of Class shall be destroyed and the energies of every citizen devoted to the service of the British nation.[13]

It all sounds perfectly harmless and even worthy.

For a man like William Joyce, joining such a movement

was thrilling. An oddball and misfit in so many areas of British life, he had now found a context in which he could be part of something big and, to his mind, meaningful. Being a Blackshirt was fun too, particularly in the early 1930s. Some members were stimulated by the radicalism of the movement. John Beckett, who left the Independent Labour Party to join the BUF, wrote in his 1938 autobiography: 'I found in the British Union of Fascists far more sincere and earnest socialist convictions than I had seen in the Labour Party for the past ten years.' Beckett estimated that among the BUF, 'about 20 per cent of the membership were mainly conservative in outlook but the great majority were either converted socialists or young people who certainly ten years before would have found their way into the socialist movement.'[14]

The Blackshirt movement also offered a 'band of brothers' ambience which was attractive to many young men. Memories of Blackshirt life emphasise the unifying aspect of the BUF. Even Irish republicans and Irish unionists, claimed John Charnley in his autobiography, put aside their differences within the BUF:

> There were ... the two Ashworth brothers from Belfast, the older of the two vehemently anti-Sinn Féin, and yet, surprisingly the closest of Blackshirt companions with Mick Carter [an Irish nationalist from Dublin]. They had fought on opposite sides in Ireland but Mosley bonded them together in common endeavour ... In many a BUF branch, Southern Irish Catholics and Northern Protestants worked together amicably.[15]

Significantly, William Joyce's bitter feelings towards Irish nationalism – he too was an 'Orangeman' when it came to Ireland – softened within the BUF, where he would encounter working-class Irish Catholics who felt unable to join the Communist Party because of its professed atheism. William had fought against any form of independence in

Ireland, yet as a Fascist he was to write that the English should now accept the Irish state, in the greater cause of reconciliation between England and Ireland: 'What is so welded together in race and tradition is not to be burst asunder ... Let the Treaty of 1922 stand.'[16]

The Mosleyite organisation was to provide what would now be called a 'whole lifestyle experience', with Blackshirt clubs, Blackshirt entertainments, holiday camps, outings, Blackshirt merchandising such as cigarettes and brooches, and Blackshirt reading material, from tabloid-newspaper-style publications to intellectual quarterlies. Photographs from the Blackshirt holiday camps in Sussex have something of a Boy Scout–Girl Guide quality, as well as a certain note of social improvement, whereby slum kids were given a seaside treat. (Sir Oswald, more accustomed to swimming by the Côte d'Azur, was astonished by the coldness of the English Channel.)[17] The BUF also attracted an unexpected number of women – about 30 per cent of active Blackshirts were female: many women claimed that, in the BUF, they had an outlet of equality and opportunity not available in conventional political parties.[18] Sexual chemistry was not absent, either, and it was predictable that William would encounter his life's true soulmate among these female fascists.

Margaret Cairns White was a pretty and vivacious brunette who was, like William Joyce, partly of Irish descent. (At least one grandfather was Irish, though her mother was of Italian descent – a fact of which she was proud.) Margaret was described by J. A. Cole, who became her confidant during her detention in the British Zone of Germany in 1945–47, as 'a good-natured, intelligent girl who saw the Depression and wasted lives around her and wondered that the human race did not do better.' Others, notably British Intelligence, were later to describe Margaret as too much of a good-time girl, and a little tarty: the *Daily Mirror* featured a saucy picture of her as a nightclub dancer, which she seems to have been for a short time.[19] People generally liked Margaret: Heather, William's eldest daughter, found her to be a warm-hearted stepmother, and she struck James Clark, who knew her in Berlin, as a jolly Lancashire lass. She was certainly much more of an extrovert than Hazel.

Margaret's father was the manager of a textile warehouse; she herself became a secretary to a Lancashire fabric firm, Morton Sundour Fabrics. The textile industry was vulnerable to vagaries in the global economy. On top of low-cost Asian competition, the invention of the artificial fabric nylon in 1930 dealt another blow to the cotton mills of Lancashire.

Politics interested Margaret from her teenage years, and she was eager to see political change. She would have been acquainted with the squalid conditions of life at the time, which George Orwell described in *The Road to Wigan Pier*: 'In such places as these a woman is only a poor drudge muddling among an infinity of jobs. She may keep up her spirits, but she cannot keep up her standards of cleanliness and tidiness. There is always something to be done, and no conveniences and almost literally no room to turn around.'

Margaret's family was not severely afflicted by poverty, and she herself had a job; but she could see the signs of decay all around, and perhaps glimpsed a gloomy future for herself if things did not change. She had been vaguely interested in the Communist Party at one point, but this interest was dispelled by the charisma, and possibly the sex appeal, of Oswald Mosley.[20]

In her early twenties, Margaret travelled from Manchester to Carlisle to hear Mosley speak and was dazzled by his dynamism and vigour. She found that the Fascist leader 'put into words all I had been trying to think'. She signed up to the British Union of Fascists forthwith and committed herself to Fascism, *con brio*.

Margaret White first encountered William Joyce through official correspondence: he was the BUF's propaganda director, and she was seeking permission to hold a debate at her firm at which she would be BUF speaker: Margaret's opponent was her boss's son. She wrote to William in his official capacity for such permission; he rather gracelessly refused. But this led to more correspondence, and when William was booked to speak at Dumfries on 7 February 1935, Margaret went with a coachload of other Manchester Blackshirts to hear him.

Margaret was late in arriving at the meeting, and William was already on his feet. He stopped speaking and looked at her. 'I tried to get in quietly,' she wrote, 'but he stopped speaking, stared at me and waited till I had sat down. I cursed him and felt awful but soon got so caught up in what he was saying that I thought of nothing else.'[21] She had been impressed by Mosley as a speaker, but she was riveted by Joyce. She had expected an aggressive person because of some of the language he generally used, but what she now saw and heard was 'a man charged with energy, dominating the audience so that everyone else there seemed subordinate to him and only half alive, raking the rows of listeners with his oratory, stirring them with his fierce scorn, suddenly arousing a burst of nervous laughter with his vicious wit.'

Seen for the first time, William's appearance might not have amounted to much, but as A. K. Chesterton said, when he spoke, it was as though a different personality took him over.[22] Afterwards, the two met. William was grave but self-possessed and uttered the fey words that she always remembered as forming part of their semi-ethereal encounter: 'Whence came you?' He told her later that from the moment she had walked into the hall he had said to himself: 'I'm going to marry that girl.'

For her part, Margaret immediately decided to follow William on the next leg of his speaking tour to Kirkcudbright in Scotland. He acknowledged her presence but then artfully carried out the most successful seduction plan of all: he ignored her a little. Margaret was accustomed to men being attracted to her, and paying attention to her: she always had her pick of boyfriends and she had several putative fiancés waiting in the wings, including a Scottish doctor and a couple of chaps in Manchester and Carlisle. But she had set her heart on William Joyce, the 'Mighty Atom', with his energy, vehemence, blarney and passion.

Margaret tracked William to London, where he was in the throes of moving out of home and saying farewell to his daughters. His marriage was over after eight years. He was moving into a flat with John Angus Macnab, whom he had first met in the 1920s, and with whom he had struck up a lifelong friendship. Macnab was the son of a distinguished Harley Street eye-doctor who had impulsively rushed off to join the First World War in 1914 and promptly been killed. John Angus had gone to the famous public school Rugby and was an Oxford graduate. Like William, he was quintessentially a schoolmaster, full of Latin scholarship and jolly japes.[23]

Macnab was an accomplished mountaineer – and could shin up and down drainpipes – and was religious by temperament. He would later become a devout Catholic. Macnab also got along terrifically well with Margaret.[24] One might have expected that Macnab, with his religious inclinations, would have urged William to try and make a go of his first marriage. Not so: he regarded William's first marriage to Hazel Barr as 'invalid', 'since it was contracted in a registry office' and they were both baptised Christians. He also held the belief, common at the time, that marriages broke down because of 'a matrimonial offence' – that is, adultery – and that Hazel's adultery was the legal cause of the divorce. Angus Macnab is unlikely to have known about William's deflowering of Mary Ogilvy, but he was correct in saying that Hazel had found someone else.

Sometime in 1933 or 1934, Hazel had fallen in love with another member of the British Union of Fascists, Eric Hamilton Piercey, a big, handsome man with a Marcel Proust moustache who appears along with Joyce in a 1935 photograph of the BUF hierarchy. Mosley employed Hamilton-Piercey (sometimes known simply as 'Piercey') as one of the 'Praetorian Guard' of Mosleyite stewards, or 'biff boys', as they were also called. Though these Blackshirt 'toughs' had a reputation for violence, Piercey turned out to be quite a good egg: he performed valiantly at Dunkirk in 1940, sailing a small boat back and forth six times across the Channel to rescue members of British forces stranded on the Continent. He was then promptly arrested under Regulation 18B for having been a Fascist.[25] Piercey also proved to be an excellent stepfather to Joyce's daughters: he and Hazel had subsequent children, but the two Joyce girls became part of the new family.[26] Joyce's younger daughter, in particular, retains fond memories of her mother's second husband as a good father to all the children. After the war, Piercey too became an ardent Roman Catholic.

Now, with his first marriage dissolved, William found a woman who was nearer to his temperament – Margaret was warm and bubbly, and, incidentally, a bit of a boozer, whereas Hazel was always a little detached, something her own grandchildren noticed. And Hazel found a man who was nicer to her than William had been. Piercey was cited as correspondent in the divorce papers, and Macnab claimed that the court initially awarded custody of the children to William, because of Hazel's 'matrimonial offence'. (At that time, an 'adulteress' was not usually given custody of a child.)[27]

William apparently voiced the opinion that mothers were more important to young children than fathers, however, and voluntarily allowed Hazel to have custody of the girls. It may have been that it was too much of a nuisance for him to raise the children, since he was so often on the road, speaking for Fascism. Still, Angus Macnab was outraged by the suggestion, made by Rebecca West in *The Meaning of Treason*, that William had abandoned the mother of his children. 'In point of fact,' wrote Macnab many years later, 'the mother of the two children had deserted him.'[28] Miss West's version of events has often been repeated, too: since William is regarded as a villain, it is usually assumed that he was in the wrong on a particular issue. Morally, perhaps he was; but he had not chosen to break with his children.[29]

The sad side to the breakdown of the marriage was that Heather would say goodbye to her father when she was seven; she would never see him again. As she was attached to William, she should have been permitted – indeed encouraged – to maintain contact with her father. Margaret would have liked Heather to come and visit her dad, but Hazel was not amenable, and, from 1936, the first Mrs William Joyce terminated all connection with her former husband. Even in his last days in the condemned cell, she sent no message of farewell to him. William retained more affection for 'Hay', as he called her, than she did for him, and he looked back on their good times with a certain fondness.[30] For the duration of his association with the BUF, Joyce seemed to get along perfectly well with Piercey in their common Blackshirt endeavours.

Although Margaret had made the running, William was quick enough to propose. He and Hazel had parted in 1935: once a man has been married, it is said, he never again remains unmarried for long. In early 1936, William popped the question almost casually to Margaret. They were attending a rather grand party in Mayfair, given by an aristocratic connection of a BUF member. Margaret knew almost no one there, when William suddenly appeared with another young BUF member, who was later to marry a Jewish girl and renounce Fascism.[31] Joyce rather masterfully replaced the whiskey that Margaret was holding in her hand with a glass of champagne, drew her aside and said: 'I wondered whether you would consider marrying me?'

She was astonished, even dazed, but flippantly replied

that: 'We can try. We can always undo it if we don't like it.' William then announced their engagement to the surrounding company, which included John Beckett and Angus Macnab; everyone was delighted. Margaret was warned, later, that it would be difficult to be married to a genius like William.

William and Margaret started living together in 1936 when Margaret moved into the flat that Joyce was sharing with Macnab at 28 Fawcett Street in Chelsea. For a time, they had to be very careful not to be observed as a couple, since William's divorce was not finalised until February 1937. A divorce could, in this era, be pronounced invalid if the 'innocent party' was seen to be cohabiting, since divorce depended on the concept of a matrimonial offence and was not granted simply because the spouses chose it. Strategies had to be devised to avoid an official known as the King's Proctor, who had the power to nullify a divorce if he thought there were irregularities. So the couple had to be very discreet, even secretive: Macnab was a helpful ally in all this. 'The Master' (as Macnab was nicknamed) liked Margaret, perhaps because he loved William, and he brushed aside any religious scruples he might have had about their cohabitation.

In fact, this strange *ménage à trois* was to be one of the happiest times in Margaret's life, or in any of their lives. They were living in Chelsea, in bohemian circumstances: they didn't have much money, but they didn't seem to need much. They all got along well. John Angus Macnab, with his drolleries and Latin puns, had a calming effect on William: he seemed to be able to pull William back from the excesses and ranting bad tempers into which he could so easily slide. In consequence, perhaps, Macnab saw a different side to William – as a thoughtful listener, quiet, even humble. William had various pet names for John: 'the Master', 'the Macnab' and 'Bonga'.[32] John was absent-minded and could be vague: this William called 'being Bonga-ish'.

Although Fascism is not now considered a noble cause, it

was, at this point, a cause in which the three of them sincerely believed. From early 1936, Margaret was working full time for the Fascist cause, and William was particularly busy, in a frantic round of speaking, writing for *The Blackshirt* and the other Fascist publications (including *Action* and the *Fascist Quarterly)* and tutoring aspiring Blackshirts in the art of political address – another task he had taken on. His classes on rhetoric and public speaking were always full. William wasn't always liked, personally, by fellow Fascists. He could be chillingly sarcastic. His ability to speak, however, was always admired, not least because he could deal with hecklers using repartee and humour.

He also loved being on the road and the applause that his appearances brought him. Moreover, the Fascist publications tracked his triumphal procession around the country. (William's friend John Beckett was now the editor of *The Blackshirt:* he turned it into a lively tabloid paper.) Reports of these meetings in the Fascist publications included: 'Mr Joyce at Bethnal Green. Enthusiastic meeting. National Anthem finishes meeting.' 'Mr Joyce at Rotherham.' 'Mr Joyce at Hexham.'

> The Director of Propaganda, William Joyce, held three excellent meetings last week at Ealing, Oxford and Swansea. At Ealing Mr Joyce's astute wit, turned to good advantage on Jewish international finance and Bolshevik Russia, was greeted with applause throughout the meeting. Speaking to the Oxford YMCA on March 4 to an interested audience that included university officials and undergraduates, Mr Joyce was given a good hearing, and the questions put to him showed that questioners had been following his address with extreme interest.

> William Joyce addressed two highly successful meetings at Edinburgh … the audience loudly applauded Joyce for his speech … at South Shields

> in the Congregational Hall, Joyce had a
> sympathetic hearing ... Reds walked out during
> singing of the National Anthem.[33]

'Reds' – Communist Party activists and their sympathisers – were frequently in evidence; the commencement of the Spanish Civil War heightened awareness, even among the normally insular British public, of the sharpness of ideological conflict between Communists and Fascists.

With these speaking engagements around the country, William was gaining an extensive knowledge of the topography of Britain. He had an almost photographic memory: he would later frighten British listeners over the radio, in his 'Lord Haw-Haw' persona, by his precise knowledge of where the town clock was in Bournemouth or what the layout of the railway station was at Hexham.

Three days after William and Hazel's divorce was finalised, on 8 February 1937, William and Margaret were married at Kensington Register Office, in the presence of the ever-faithful Macnab, and Mrs Hastings Bonora, one of the prominent women in the British Union of Fascists. In contrast to William's first wedding, the whole Joyce family came along. If old Michael Joyce objected to his elder son not marrying in a Church, he overcame his objections.

William was electioneering in east London, and excitedly anticipated winning a council seat for the BUF. But unknown to him, these were actually to be his last days in the Blackshirt ranks. Nineteen thirty-six would be the last promising year for Fascism in Britain. The BUF had a certain grass-roots appeal; but it attracted unfavourable publicity when the large and theatrical assemblies which Oswald Mosley particularly favoured were accompanied by violence: stewards would handle hecklers and objectors roughly and throw them out. The Fascists always maintained that they were attacked first by their Red – communist, or merely left-wing – opponents, and there is some evidence that this occurred.[34] More anti-Fascists than Fascists were convicted of public-order offences, perhaps because the authorities at this time were less hostile to right-wing groups than to communists. The Fascists always maintained that most of their Red opponent were Jews. *The Blackshirt* would publish lists of 'Assailants Against BUF Members' with Jewish names. A typical such list read: 'John Feigenbaum, Hyman Goldstein, Joseph Burgess, Harry Distelmann, Barnett Becow, Barnett Rigrotsky, Michael Goldberg' – all of whom reportedly received court sentences ranging from fourteen days to three months for assault.[35] (Joseph Burgess, incidentally, seems to have been a left-wing Irishman.)

This hostility between Fascists and anti-Fascists came to a head with the 'Battle of Cable Street' in 1936, when seven thousand Blackshirts were met by a hundred thousand anti-Fascists and spectators. Although Mosley, by his own account, ordered the BUF to disperse before marching through the East End of London, with its concentration of Jewish inhabitants, a fracas nonetheless broke out. Eighty people were injured, and a Jewish tailor and his young son were thrown through a plate-glass window. But there were no deaths: in contrast to Continental scenes of street conflict, in Britain deaths from political clashes were extremely rare. All the same, it was ugly: the Blackshirts came to be associated in the public mind with violence and 'extremism'. The Spanish Civil War, which attracted continuous and dramatic reportage in the press, also served to remind the British public of their distaste for such extremism.

The Blackshirts also fluffed their big chance in 1936 with the abdication of King Edward VIII, who forsook the throne to marry the divorced Mrs Simpson. The Blackshirts strongly supported King Edward, with whom they felt a sort of kinship. They thought of him as a 'moderniser'. When he visited the disused South Wales steelworks, surrounded by the unemployed, he said: 'Something should be done.'[36]

They believed he felt a compassion for the poor that few other grandees had shown. When he was in the throes of the abdication crisis, the Fascist papers came out with banner headlines such as 'STAND BY THE KING!', sometimes cobbled up in late editions by the media-savvy John Beckett.

The Blackshirt newspapers took the view that the King's sexual relationships were his own business. (Although this might seem like a surprisingly permissive stance for the time, it might not have been unconnected to the fact that Mosley had a reputation as a philanderer and both Joyce and Beckett had less than regular marital situations.)

At one point, Mosley fleetingly believed that the King might call for him to form a government, but it turned out that Edward did not have the fighting spirit to do so. Instead, the King bent to the pressure of the politicians, and fled. The Blackshirts were hugely disappointed. As Lord Beaverbrook, who also supported Edward, said: 'Our cock won't fight.'[37] The episode also showed that the monarchy, not the trappings of Fascism, provided the British people with their sense of ceremonial, a cathartic ritual and even a symbolic corporatist state.

For the first three years of his involvement with the BUF, William tasted success: he was recognised as a fine speaker and often regarded as a successor to Mosley, who was known as 'the Leader'. William had left behind his dreams of being a Conservative MP, and his academic life, but now had dreams of greater things: perhaps a Fascist state in which he would play a starring role.

But being William, he pushed things too far, rubbing people up the wrong way and allowing his hysterical anti-Semitism to distort genuine elements of political concern. He pushed the Blackshirt movement – partly with Mosley's connivance, or complacency – away from the Italian model and towards the German one. As the 1930s wore on, British

Fascism became ever more influenced by the rise of Hitler. William had always been Germanophile and he was tremendously excited by the rise of Adolf Hitler in Germany.

At the beginning, Mosley himself had declared that anti-Semitism was not part of the Blackshirts' ideology. His 'mission statement' book, *The Greater Britain*, did not mention the Jews at all, and *The Blackshirt* even claimed that the Nazis had no intention of harming Jews and that 'Germany does not intend to discriminate against Jews or interfere with their personal liberty.'[38]

Yet as time went by, the British Union of Fascists (which in 1936 changed its name to the British Union of Fascists and National Socialists) became notably more anti-Semitic. There can be little doubt that Joyce – along with John Beckett, who was a passionate opponent of 'international finance', which he regarded as Jewish – was largely responsible for steering the BUF into more anti-Semitic directions. William even boasted that he took credit for alienating Lord Rothermere from the BUF by enhancing the organisation's anti-Semitic theme: 'Very soon, he [Rothermere] began to express grave concern at the growing anti-Jewish tendency of the movement – a tendency for which I was very largely responsible.'[39]

Within Mosleyite circles, private memos began circulating expressing concern that Joyce's influence was leading the BUF towards an excess of anti-Semitism. William, for all his extreme patriotism, never really assimilated the British, and more specifically the English, mentality; they were not averse to a little private prejudice, but did not care for ranting. In a detailed memoir of the 1930s, *We Marched with Mosley*, Richard Reynell Bellamy – who did not personally dislike Joyce – wrote that 'his rabid verbal attacks on the Jews were harmful to British Union'. Bellamy cited the case of a disgusted Yorkshireman who came along to a Joyce meeting in Leeds to hear how Fascists would save the wool trade – 'But all I have had to listen to is a lot of silly claptrap about Jews.'[40] William had boasted that he increased the membership of the BUF by drawing large numbers of people to meetings, but he could alienate potential members too.

There is a chilling passage in a memoir by the writer Cecil Roberts about William addressing a formal dinner of nobs at the Park Lane Hotel in London. Mosley was due to speak but couldn't make it; William deputised. The audience was composed of right-wing swells who were worried about Communism: they were a promising market for Fascist recruitment. 'Thin, pale, intense, he had not been speaking many minutes before we were electrified by this man,' Roberts recalled.

> Never, in any country, had I met a personality so terrifying in its dynamic force, so vituperative, so vitriolic. The words poured forth from him in a corrosive spate. He ridiculed our political system, he scarified our leading politicians, seizing upon their vulnerable points with a destructive analysis that left them bereft of merit or morality. We listened in a kind of frozen hypnotism ... when he invoked the rising wrath of his colleagues against the festering scum that by cowardice and sloth had reduced the British Empire to a moribund thing, in peril of annihilation.[41]

At the end of his peroration, there was a paralysed silence. People felt throttled. Not a single individual present asked a question, and not one person there felt moved to join the British Union of Fascists thereafter.

By 1937, the government had banned the wearing of uniforms by civilian groups; this was a blow to the BUF. Word went around on the Establishment network that the Fascist movement in Britain was not to be widely reported. Mosley and his associates were not allowed to broadcast on the BBC, which had a monopoly of the airwaves. The Conservatives might have been expected to give some tacit support to Fascist movements where their values converged with those of the Fascists – the upholding of the Empire, for example – but the Tories shunned the Fascist movements, even though certain individual right-wingers broke ranks to join 'patriotic' societies.

Although some individual policemen were more inclined to sympathise with the Right than the Left, and William Joyce had personal friends among the police, the Metropolitan Police commissioner, Sir Philip Game, was privately deeply anti-Fascist and determined to keep tabs on the movement. Moreover, Sir John Simon, who was Home Secretary from 1935, was extremely keen for the police to be alerted to anti-Semitism and to arrest provocative anti-Semites under the Public Order Act.[42]

William did not obtain a seat on the London County Council. Indeed, the election results for the Blackshirts were generally disappointing. Mick Clarke, an East End BUF bruiser, and Alexander Raven Thomson – who had written a book about philosophy and was regarded as the intellectual of the movement – received around 3,000 votes each, or 23 per cent of the votes cast. Charles Wegg-Prosser (who later renounced Fascism and married a Jewish girl) and Anne Brock Griggs, one of the feminist Fascists, both standing in Limehouse, received 19 per cent of the vote, or around 2,000 votes each. In Shoreditch, William Joyce and his running mate 'Bill' Bailey received 14 per cent of the vote, or around 2,500 votes. Elsewhere in the country, the BUF received very few votes.

Immediately after the vote, Oswald Mosley claimed that the British Union 'had done better than Hitler had done in Germany a few years before he came to power: in 1928, in a general election Hitler had polled only 2.7 per cent of votes cast and in 1930, 18 per cent.' Moreover, in the municipal elections at this time, only rate-paying householders were eligible to vote – thus excluding the young and the dispossessed, among whom there were many followers of Mosley.

Despite – or even perhaps because of – William Joyce's energetic efforts in speaking all round the country, Blackshirt numbers had dropped from fifty thousand at the movement's peak in 1934 to about twenty thousand in 1937. Two weeks after the results of this poll, Oswald Mosley called a meeting of his senior staff and told them that, because of a dire shortage of funds, there would have to be a dramatic reduction in the wage bill: the number of salaried employees would be reduced from 143 to 30. Among the two most senior staff to be fired – to their great shock – were William Joyce and his friend John Beckett. William, in particular, was stunned. He was being banished from the movement he loved – he, the star speaker, the Fascist celebrity. Moreover, both Joyce and Beckett, as full-time staff, had also lost their livelihood.

William now had a pattern of being expelled from various organisations: he had probably been asked to leave his school; he had been run out of Ireland; he had been discharged from the army; he had been driven out of the Conservative Party; and now, he had been ejected by Mosley's Blackshirts. This last was the one that rankled most of all, and the one that he most repined in the last year of his life. It was also instrumental in leading him to the Third Reich.

6

Germany Calls

'I never heard Englishmen doubt Irish military valour. What they did doubt was Irish political sanity.'

G. K. Chesterton, *Irish Impressions*

So it was a case of William the terrrible – in trouble again! Out on his ear once more! This time, however, there were voices raised in protest, proclaiming that it wasn't fair that he should be made to leave the Blackshirts, along with 75 per cent of the regular staff.

Margaret Collins, who worked on *Action*, the BUF weekly, and helped out at Blackshirt headquarters (at the Black House on the King's Road), was quite taken aback by this 'purge', as the general redundancy decision was called. 'What astonished me was that it was the best ones who were being got rid of,' she recalled.

> Apart from Joyce, there was John Beckett, who was a first-rate journalist. He was a hundred per cent professional. Angus Macnab went in to see Mosley and to protest about it, but he ended by throwing in his resignation. If they had to have fewer staff, then it should have been the best staff.[1]

Most people in the branches were equally surprised, she said.

Some Blackshirts considered this the end of the Fascist movement, because Joyce was regarded as one of the best-known speakers in England.

William Joyce *was* one of the best-known speakers, but his invective could be deadly, and it was becoming a source of embarrassment for the BUF. In a pamphlet about India – which was privately denounced by other members of the BUF[2] – Joyce described Lord Irwin as 'the phenomenal freak whom it would be indecent to describe as Viceroy' and Stanley Baldwin, the decent but dull Prime Minister who was happiest on his pig farm in Worcestershire, as 'the steel merchant metamorphosed into a squire by casual experiment in pig breeding'. Moreover, in an article on the front page of *The Blackshirt*, he referred to the Tories – who were backing the India Bill, which would prepare the way for Indian independence – as 'one loathesome, fetid, purulent, tumid mass of hypocrisy'. In deploring the loss of India, he referred to 'Tory politicians who have yielded to the noisy fakirs and the chattering babus'; when deploring the supporters of disarmament, he referred to 'the political crimps of Judah and moral anarchy ... dribbling old prelates, verminous Bloomsburgians, myopic printers' hacks, and every sort of old woman, male and otherwise, joined in neurotic crusades of Pacifism designed ... to weaken the Empire.'[3] William had an amazing command of invective – but it could be poisonous.

The Jews, of course, always got it in the neck from William's colourful line of abuse: he described them as 'aliens imported from Palestine', 'hairy troglodytes who crept out of the ghettoes of Germany to seek sanctuary in the British Museum' and 'submen with prehensile toes'. Robert Skidelsky, in his biography of Oswald Mosley, points out that the rough-and-tumble of street-corner meetings were hardly conducted in parliamentary language: Fascists would shout 'Yiddish scum!' and their opponents would counter with 'Fascist murderers!'[4] The language that so horrified genteel gatherings of the middle classes was regarded more robustly in proletarian life. But that was another problem with William: he couldn't distinguish between the coster-monger's rough exchanges and the restraints of the bourgeois drawing room – or he chose not to.

Oswald Mosley did have to fire people: the BUF's revenues had fallen dramatically. And one could see Mosley's point of view in getting rid of Joyce. Joyce might have been one of the most notable speakers for the BUF, but he was also one of the most dangerous because least restrained. Oswald Mosley did come to use anti-Semitic language himself, and he allowed anti-Semitism to flourish within his movement; but even so, William went to odious excess.[5] Moreover, Mosley thought William was disloyal: William called Mosley 'the Bleeder' rather than 'The Leader', behind his back. William also referred to Lady Mosley – the former Diana Mitford and Sir Oswald's second wife – as 'the Huntress', alluding to classical mythology, and implying that there was something predatory about her.[6]

William's own followers took a different line. Peter Morris, the young man from Lincolnshire who had followed his sister Sylvia into the Blackshirt movement, believed that Mosley was jealous of William's notoriety. 'Joyce's charismatic character was stealing Mosley's thunder,' he recalled.[7] The Joyce faction would always maintain that William's real offence within the BUF was to outshine the Leader on the platform. Margaret Joyce also believed that Oswald Mosley wanted a 'showy' sort of Blackshirt movement, with big rallies, whereas William believed in grass-roots recruitment work in the provinces and the outlying areas of Britain, where the most discontent with the established parties lay. Some veterans of this period think there was an element of snobbery too: that Sir Oswald and Lady Mosley regarded William as simply too common, too streetwise, too left-wing and too Irish.

Mosley was charismatic, and his most faithful followers always honoured him as their 'Leader'. Even in the 1960s and 1970s, outsiders with no attachment to his politics described him as a compellingly charismatic personality (and the organisation 'The Friends of Oswald Mosley' still exists). But Sir Oswald also lost many former followers, could be monstrously egomaniacal and allowed competing factions to jostle and back-stab within the Blackshirt movement. Peter Morris, for instance, grew bitterly disillusioned with Mosley and described him as 'a liar'.[8] Peter's sister Sylvia, who was Mosley's candidate at Holland and Boston in Lincolnshire, claimed to have found him out in blatant lies; she, and Peter, sided with Joyce and Beckett when, after the 'purge', they formed a breakaway Fascist movement, the National Socialist League.

In April, a news story appeared in the *Morning Post* under the headline: 'BRITISH FASCIST SPLIT: NEW MOVEMENT FORMED.' 'Dissensions in the ranks of the British Union of Fascists have led to the formation of a rival organisation led by two of Sir Oswald Mosley's former chief lieutenants,' the paper reported. 'The leaders of the new organisation, the "National Socialist League", are Mr John Beckett and Mr William Joyce.' William, with an unerring knack of detecting in others faults that could most appropriately be applied to himself, told the *Morning Post* that the BUF had 'completely failed to win support in the country. Many people who would have joined the Union for its policy were repelled by its methods.'[9]

He went on to blame Mosley's foreign ways – he who was on the brink of embracing a foreign allegiance himself: 'Sir Oswald Mosley's insistence on a personal autocracy and Continental "heel clickings", his borrowing of the insignia of the movement from one country, Italy, and its song from another, Germany, repelled and will repel the majority of Englishmen.'

John Beckett's explanation for the split was more down-to-earth:

> We were expelled from the Union on March 11, without any consultation, consideration or notice –

on grounds of economy ... The real reason was that
we told [Mosley] the truth. Sir Oswald Mosley is
surrounded by flatterers, and it is impossible for
any of the rank and file of the movement to see him
or voice its discontent. He is told that all is going
well in the districts – we know better.[10]

Suddenly, the gang of three – Joyce, Beckett and
Macnab – were gone from Blackshirt headquarters. Certain
gossips thought they were 'no loss'. One 'military type' who
was helping with organisation thought that the movement
was better off without Beckett because of 'the way he treated
that poor woman'. This was an allusion to the office gossip
that Beckett was living with Anne Cutmore – 'living in sin',
as the expression had it at the time – because his previous
wife would not grant him a divorce.[11] In truth, he had two
previous wives, and was known in the organisation as a bit of
a ladies' man – an observation that did not always displease
ladies. Margaret Collins remembered Beckett's 'twinkle in his
eye' benignly, whereas William, although he may have been
an adulterer, was never a flirt.

Joyce and Beckett now launched their own political
movement, the National Socialist League, moving closer to
the concept of the German National Socialist Party. Joyce
and Beckett – resonant of two grand Irish literary names –
were to be supported, to some extent, by a third person
whose name has literary connotations, A. K. Chesterton,
who parted company from Mosley in 1938. Chesterton had
written the first, and quite adulatory, biography of Mosley,
which was much advertised in *Action* and *The Blackshirt*.[12]
He did not join the new National Socialist League, although
he did speak at their meetings on a couple of occasions. And
of course the breakaway faction would be continually
supported by William's most enduring and devoted follower,
flatmate and best friend, John Angus Macnab.

John Beckett was a flamboyant, and finally rather tragic,
character. Like Chesterton, he had emerged from the

trenches of the First World War burning with indignation that the working class endured terrible conditions while rich businessmen lived easy lives. Beckett became the youngest Labour MP in the House of Commons, at the age of twenty-five, in 1925: he was a radical and troublemaker who famously seized the Mace in a dramatic parliamentary gesture. He gradually became disillusioned with mainstream politics: he was deeply frustrated that so little was being done, it seemed to him, for the poor.

It was a constant theme of British Fascists that Labour politicians cut the pensions and dole money of the very poor at the behest of international bankers, who were, in turn, allegedly in the pocket of powerful Jewish interests. These 'international bankers' who oppress the poor have reappeared in each generation under different guises: in the 1930s, they were characterised as Jewish monetary power; in the 1960s, the 'gnomes of Zurich'; in the 1990s, the International Monetary Fund. Beckett was originally one of those left-wing anti-Semites who described the Jews as pitiless moneybags and globalised moneylenders; yet Beckett's own mother, Dorothy Salmon, was Jewish.[13] It was by no means unknown to find Fascist anti-Semites who were themselves partly, or even wholly, Jewish in origin.

Beckett, too, had an inclination for hero-worship, and was looking for a male leader throughout his life. For a few short years, William was that leader, just as, for William himself, Mosley had filled that role. Anne, John Beckett's lover – she would eventually become his legal third wife, when the second Mrs Beckett died – 'loyally tried to like John's new hero, William Joyce, but she only saw a small, square, pugnacious man drinking constantly to keep away the pain behind the eyes.'[14] Anne Cutmore was a very attractive young journalist; she stuck by John Beckett throughout his eccentric career and finally the sad conclusion to his brilliant promise, and became the mother of Francis Beckett, the writer and *Guardian* journalist.

Although Beckett and Joyce would part company after a year – Beckett quit the National Socialist League in 1938 – the Becketts would never utter a word against Joyce. If John disapproved of William's metamorphosis into 'Lord Haw-Haw' – as most of the British Fascists did – he never said so. 'My father had quite a cruel tongue,' says Francis Beckett, the author of a filial and yet clear-headed biography of his father. 'But the only person he never said a bad word about was William Joyce. My parents had very fierce, loyal instincts that you don't desert somebody when he's down. And you can't be more down than having been hanged.'

Angus Macnab was a less prominent member of the National Socialist League, but he always followed where Joyce led. He and William also set up in business together – since William now had no visible means of support – as private tutors: they were both quite good at tutoring, and the little business could have developed if it hadn't been for the turbulence of their politics. They had some glamorous pupils – Bourbon princes and the like – but did themselves no good by refusing Jewish or coloured students. Word about this got around, and eventually the supply of students dried up. This was the only decision of William's that Margaret seems to have disagreed with: she thought it completely daft. In all other political respects, she loyally followed her husband.

William's brothers, Frank, now aged twenty-one – an uncomplicated chap, fond of cricket – and Quentin, just twenty, would also support William in the breakaway Fascist group. Frank had spoken for the Mosley Blackshirt movement on a couple of occasions, mostly at local meetings in Dulwich, but his involvement seems to have been more a matter of general family solidarity than strong commitment.[15] Quentin also became caught up in the fringes of Fascist politics because of his unquestioning devotion to his brother William. Indeed, William seems to have roped his whole family into doing his bidding when it came to political action: he even had his teenage sister, Joan, hand out Fascist propaganda leaflets at Sydenham School for Girls.[16] He also dressed little Robert up in a black shirt. 'Poor Mrs Joyce!' the neighbours in Dulwich used to exclaim. 'With all those terrible children in their black shirts!'[17]

᠃ᠬ

The National Socialist League was set up at 109 Vauxhall Bridge Road in London SW1, with some financial backing from a stockbroker called Alex Scrimgeour, who had been a strong supporter of British Fascism, as had his sister, Ethel, an eccentric spinster who was a doting fan of William's. Indeed, the Scrimgeour funds were an essential element in the launch of the breakaway group. Mr Scrimgeour was disabled, enormously rich and obsessively fearful of Bolsheviks; William had rushed off to see him at his home in Pagham, in Sussex, as soon as the split with Mosley occurred.

According to Richard Reynell Bellamy, who chronicled these events in detail, William

> visited a south-coast town where lived a wealthy old gentleman who in the past had contributed handsomely to the [Blackshirts] and who at the same time was a personal admirer of Joyce for the brilliance of his mind, the distinction of his oratory, and his physical courage. What transpired at this meeting is not known; but Joyce returned to town with a substantial cheque.[18]

Many Mosleyites came along to the first NSL meeting out of curiosity; about a hundred BUF members, some of whom had also been victims of the 'purge', initially joined Joyce and Beckett. The new party set about bringing out a newspaper – the *Helmsman* – and adopted the motto 'Steer Straight'. But it quite soon became evident that the glory days for British fascism, if such they were, were over. The NSL struggled to sustain its followers. The *Helmsman* had only four pages and ran to just two or three editions.[19] When

William sought to have a meeting in his home patch of Dulwich in south London, he was turned away from the local church hall, St Barnabas, by the vicar, the Reverend William Brown, who had a poor opinion of Fascist movements in general, and Willliam's antics in particular.[20] The NSL got a couple of meetings going at Dulwich Library, but this effort never amounted to much.

A former colleague who knew Joyce and Beckett described seeing them in their Vauxhall Bridge Road office in somewhat reduced circumstances: 'Up several flights of uncarpeted stairs. The HQ was on the top floor in a single room, also uncarpeted, the only furniture a desk and two or three chairs. In a corner of the room were a couple of piles of leaflets.' Beckett and Joyce looked like men on their way down. A few weeks later, the same witness saw the two of them at a street corner with a portable platform, on which one of them – he couldn't recall which – was standing and speaking, while the other was heckling him: 'a standard way of trying to attract an audience to the open air.' The Blackshirt veteran thought: 'What a terrible comedown from the great meetings I had heard them speaking at.'[21] When Joyce and Beckett had been part of the Blackshirt movement, they had been salaried officials; now they had to earn their living – John as a journalist, William as a teacher – in the margins of political agitprop. Alex Scrimgeour died in 1938 and, disappointingly, left nothing in his will to the National Socialist League. Ethel, his seventy-two-year-old sister, a health- and fresh-air fanatic who fostered poor children who had tuberculosis, remained utterly loyal to William even to the grave: they exchanged affectionate letters when Willliam was in the condemned-man's cell. Afterwards, Ethel kept up a correspondence with Margaret.[22]

Failure can make a man bitter, and the failing fortunes of the National Socialist League, obvious by the middle of 1938, darkened William's outlook. His pugnacity turned to brooding. According to Beckett, William began to drink more heavily from this time onwards: William had always enjoyed drinking wine, but he had generally been able to moderate his drinking when he chose to do so: Peter Morris, who met William on many occasions, remembered sitting all evening with him over one glass of hock and seltzer.

As his political party failed, the intellectual who could pursue every argument to its logical conclusion became ever more unreasonable in his conduct. Chesterton reported that William would now bring a meeting to an end not only with calls for the British national anthem – he had usually done that – but with the Nazi cry of 'Sieg Heil!' William did not seem to see the contradictions in so many of his own statements and positions: he had accused Mosley of importing 'foreign' gimmicks into British politics yet he used such foreign gimmicks himself whenever it suited him. For instance, he once marched through a small neighbourhood in Evesham, Worcestershire, at midnight, leading a column of Blackshirts singing Mussolini's anthem 'Giovanezza!' because some Italian migrant labourers lived there.[23] After that, he would protest that he was more British than the King. He persisted in referring to Jews as 'aliens', when he must have been conscious that he was an 'alien' himself – in fact he was more 'alien' than British Jews with genuine British passports.

At a National Socialist meeting in 1938, Chesterton expressed the concern that a new war was inevitable. William vehemently contradicted this. 'There will be no war! I trust Adolf Hitler to see to that,' he cried.[24] In justice to Joyce, Lord Beaverbrook was making similar predictions, with his famous 1938 banner headline in the Daily Express: 'GREAT BRITAIN WILL NOT BE INVOLVED IN A EUROPEAN WAR THIS YEAR OR NEXT YEAR EITHER.'[25] Many perfectly respectable people, and virtually all Quakers, were opposed to embarking on a war against Germany. It was the era of appeasement, which was an official policy of the British government, ardently supported by The Times and the BBC:

Winston Churchill was banned from the airwaves because he was challenging the policy of appeasing Hitler.

John Beckett disagreed, however. Barely a year after the launch of the National Socialist League, and soon after the Munich crisis in September 1938, Beckett decided to withdraw from their political partnership. Although he got along with William personally – and they shared a sense of affinity as rebels and outsiders – he felt that the politics of the NSL were going nowhere and was convinced that war was drawing closer. (Beckett would go on to found the British People's Party, an organisation dedicated to 'the abolition of a financial system based upon usury', under the patronage of Lord Tavistock, heir to the Duke of Bedford.) If Joyce denied the liklihood of war, he nevertheless confided to Beckett that if war did break out, he would go to Germany. He had made that decision mentally long before he had committed himself to the action. John Beckett was also one of the very select number of Joyce's connections who knew that William had been born in America. Margaret was informed of her own American status only after her marriage to William – a wife at this time invariably taking her husband's nationality.

In fact, William's sense of allegiance had probably begun to shift from about the middle of 1937. His passionate British patriotism, his harping on about the importance of loyalty to the Crown and his claims that the Jews were 'aliens' who could not be trusted to stand by England, were alchemising into something else. National Socialism was now becoming a more compelling cause than mere patriotism. He had thought the 'big idea' of his life was the British Empire, but the Empire had let him down by its weak concessions to liberals and defeatists. Progressively, it seemed that the Big Idea was elsewhere.

But it was also true that by 1939 William was all washed up in England. The National Socialist League had gradually petered out – within eighteen months of its launch, it had been registered as a drinking club. Although, at a personal level, his wife, Margaret, considered herself happy, it was clear that William had problems. The police had been on to him for some time: he had been in trouble with the police twice in the 1930s, once in Worthing in 1934 when he, along with Oswald Mosley and Eric Piercey, was accused of creating a fracas. They were discharged and the case was dismissed[26] – Mosley successfully argued that they had been set upon – but the incident alerted the authorities to put a watch on William. Throughout the later 1930s, there are police reports of the meetings Joyce addressed, and notes of what he said. In November 1938, he was charged with assault when he gave what he called 'a tap on the head' to a man whom he claimed was causing an obstruction at one of the NSL's meetings.

A third such episode followed in May 1939, during one of the last, rather pathetic little meetings of the National Socialist League. A heckler had shouted to Joyce that if he thought Germany was such a wonderful place, why didn't he ruddy well go there! There was also some provocative singing of the 'Internationale', the anthem of the 'Reds'. In any case, William's temper flared and he struck the man on the face. But again, the case was dismissed because there seemed some confusion regarding evidence. It probably looked to an outsider like the usual street scuffles between Fascists and Communists, whom the moderate British arbitrator would have regarded as being as bad as each other.

MI5, the home intelligence service whose business was the surveillance of questionable British subjects, was also on to Joyce. This was a complicated situation, however, as there is also evidence that William himself often supplied information to MI5.[27] The chief MI5 spymaster, Charles Maxwell Knight, had been in the British Fascisti in the 1920s and knew William from the former's brief involvement with Rotha Linton-Orman. Knight had also been friendly with Hazel and her family.

At one point Maxwell Knight was considered a possible suitor for Hazel, although sexually he had no interest in women, and neither of his marriages was consummated. Maxwell Knight was another bizarre personality. He was the model for Ian Fleming's 'M' in the James Bond stories.[28] He had a fascination for peculiar animals and after the war reinvented himself as a successful nature-writer and broadcaster on gardening. Maxwell Knight understood Joyce very well, and filed a secret report on him in 1934 that remains one of the most insightful profiles ever written about him.[29] Joyce, it said, was

> one of the most fascinating character studies … one of the most compelling personalities of the whole [Fascist] movement … a complex character … His greatest failling is that his mental balance is not equal to his intellectual capacity … It has been alleged that he is a pompous, conceited little creature, but a tendency to agree with this should be weighed up against the fact that he has made his way in his own small world entirely by his own efforts and in the face of very considerable difficulties.

Maxwell Knight emphasized William's 'Celtic' volatility.

William's troubles with the police, and the surveillance under which he was placed, probably caused his father, Michael, to destroy the official papers of his own American naturalisation, which, ironically, might have helped to save William's life later. When Quentin Joyce was about seventeen, in 1934, he witnessed his father burning some official papers, one of which seemed to have the American eagle on it.[30] Michael did this, apparently, because he believed that if it was discovered that William was not a British citizen, he would be in even deeper trouble with the authorities. It was a father's act to protect his son.

It was obvious that MI5 would have files on William Joyce. He was a known Fascist, and from 1937 onwards he was involved in a variety of right-wing organisations which had sprung up like mushrooms in the furtherance of keeping the peace, preventing war or befriending Germany. There were a considerable number of these organisations, the leading one being the Right Club, founded in 1938 by Captain Archibald Ramsay, the Scottish Old Etonian MP. Among the club illuminati were the Duke of Wellington, Mrs Dorothy Eckersley – who would come to play a key role in William Joyce's fate in Berlin – and Anna Wolkoff, the ferociously anti-Semitic daughter of an admiral from the Imperial Russian Navy who would later serve a prison sentence because of her admiration for William Joyce as 'Lord Haw-Haw'.

Then there was the Link, founded in 1937 by Admiral Sir Barry Domvile, a former Director of Naval Intelligence who was married to an aristocratic German wife. Its secretary was Miss Margaret Bothamley, a batty old biddy who adored and mimicked Queen Mary, the German-born wife of King George V: her destiny was also to be rather unexpectedly entwined with William and Margaret Joyce in Germany. The Anglo-German Fellowship attracted many pro-Nazis and anti-Semites – and was infiltrated by Kim Philby, the Soviet spy. It glittered with grand names, such as Lords Airlie, Galloway, Glasgow, Lothian, Redesdale and Londonderry (known as 'the Londonderry Herr'). There were also corporate members such as Unilever, Dunlop and Vickers Steel. Unity Mitford was, arguably, the organisation's most colourful and best-known representative – and there were half a dozen more, many attracting influential personalities.[31]

Apart from his own National Socialist League, William was also involved with such organisations as the Right Club, the Nordic League, the Link and English Mistery. He attended some meetings of others, notably the British Council Against European Commitments, which was an anti-war – at all costs – lobby led by Lord Lymington. And of course he also had his own cultural association, the Carlyle Club, which he had founded in honour of his literary hero,

Thomas Carlyle. He usually organised meetings of this club on a weekly basis: James Clark was brought along to several of the meetings by his mother, Dorothy Eckersley. James recalled that the Carlyle Club consisted mostly of about half a dozen, generally elderly 'Joyceophiles' in search of an ideology. James, as a teenager, was baffled by the proceedings, but in a curious way he was impressed by William's earnest readings from the Master's works, and by his dogged pursuit of high Victorian culture.

William was a very visible candidate indeed on the London scene in the late 1930s, and it is scarcely to be wondered at that in the event of a war against Germany, and Fascism, he would be one of the first public figures to be arrested and interned by the British authorities. Moreover, the spymaster, Maxwell Knight, almost certainly tipped him off that he would be first in line for internment. Margaret would probably be jailed as well.[32] So William made his plans.

Besides, sometime in the summer of 1939, William had ceased to believe that war could not occur between Britain and Germany because Hitler would never countenance it. He always believed – as did Hitler – that war *should* not occur between England and Germany, the 'Anglo-Saxon' powers who were in his view racially cousins. He believed, like Hitler, that the British Empire should rule the overseas world, while Germany ruled Europe.

There had been a rehearsal, in the Munich crisis of 1938, for war breaking out between England and Germany. At this moment, William took the opportunity to renew his 'British' passport, with a view to travelling abroad. On Wednesday 24 August 1938, just four days before British Prime Minister Neville Chamberlain's famous Munich meeting with Hitler, William duly renewed his falsely obtained British passport for a year. This passport stated, fictionally, that he had been born in Galway, and was thus a subject of His Majesty. Only at this point did William confide to Margaret that he had in fact been born in America. This made her, technically, an American too: at this time, a married woman had no option but to hold the same nationality as her husband, although Margaret did have her own valid passport as well. Margaret was surprised at the revelation, but she accepted it. She also colluded in it, because when William once again renewed his British passport, which had been obtained under false pretences, twelve months later, on Thursday 24 August 1939 – eight days before Hitler marched into Poland – she supported the decision.

A. K. Chesterton also claimed that William had decided to go to Germany even before the Munich agreement in 1938.[33] William seems to have cherished some rather fantastic plan of getting into the German navy, 'preferably on patrol boat work against the Russians'.[34] William and Angus also cooked up a scheme, just before Munich, for Angus to take Margaret Joyce to Ireland, and to stay in the Free State until William could arrange for them both to remove to Germany. Macnab even purchased tickets for himself and Margaret to travel from Euston for the mailboat to Dun Laoghaire.[35] Then the news came through that Chamberlain, along with Edouard Daladier, the French Premier, had signed an agreement with Hitler and Mussolini, and 'peace in our time' was declared.

Yet from this period on, William's mind seems to have been fixed on Germany. There was still some discussion between William and Margaret as to whether the Irish Free State, which would be neutral in any coming war, would be a better option for them than Germany. William liked both Dublin and Galway: if he had not been hanged, and had instead served a prison sentence after the war, he would almost certainly have gone to live in Ireland, once he had been freed. Margaret also liked Ireland, but she knew, in the period 1938–39, that Germany acted as a magnet for William. And then, in the summer of 1939, Angus Macnab visited Berlin, almost as if to pave the way for William.

At William's request, Macnab visited a connection of theirs – a journalist called Christian Bauer who worked for *Der Angriff*, the newspaper founded by Joseph Goebbels – and sounded him out. 'What kind of a reception could William expect in Berlin, in the event of war?' Macnab asked whether Goebbels would arrange an immediate naturalisation as a German citizen. Bauer played a shadowy but significant role in the fate of William Joyce, and of Quentin Joyce too: his signal to William was a deciding factor in William's decision. Bauer told Macnab that, on Goebbels' word, 'immediate naturalisation will be available to [William Joyce] in Germany, together with his wife'. Angus Macnab travelled back to London in mid-August 1939 and transmitted this intelligence to William.

And so it was decided that William and Margaret Joyce would take the boat-train from Victoria Station in London for Berlin, via Ostend, on Saturday 26 August. Despite the rehearsals for war that were now evident – the mobilisation of troops, the removal of national treasures to storage – it was still just about normal to be seen going off to the Continent for a holiday. All through the summer, German Railways had been advertising the country as a holiday destination:

> Germany – Land of Hospitality – offers you everything you could wish for your holiday this year. Nearly two thousand miles of unique Autobahn motor roads ... Germany's art and creative spirit are to be seen at their best in the numerous exhibitions and festivals, including Heidelberg, Bayreuth, Salzburg, Munich.[36]

One advert underlined Germany's latest spa acquisitions: 'The Sudeten Germany Mineral Springs – Karlsbad, Marienbad, Franzensbad.'

William held a little drinks party with some of his cronies on the evening of Friday 25 August; he told Angus Macnab that he and Margaret were bound for Germany in the morning. Although Macnab must have been expecting this news, it nonetheless somehow came as a great shock to 'the Master', who was charged with winding up the National Socialist League officially. (There were now only forty people on the NSL's list of members.)[37] William also informed Macnab that he was now throwing his lot in with Germany on a permanent basis: 'I have no intention of using Germany as a temporary haven or refuge, but I am making it my permanent home.' That was certainly typical of William: in the same way that he had made the decision to walk out on his academic life without a backward glance, now he was leaving England for the Third Reich with a similar attitude.

He did not, however, speak in such dramatic terms to his family. He told his brother Frank that he was sure the conflict would be patched up before long and that he would only be in Germany for a few months.[38] Perhaps he intended to say that he would be back in triumph, as the 'Gauleiter of London'.

A little group assembled at Victoria Station that Saturday morning to bid farewell to William and Margaret Joyce. His mother, of course, was there, and his youngest brother, Robert. Frank may also have been present: William's brother Quentin was in Bristol, where he had just started a new job with the Air Ministry. Macnab was, of course, the chief steward of the farewell party.

Margaret, with Angus Macnab, was the first of the group to arrive at Victoria. The ticket had been purchased through a travel agency, but William went to the German embassy first, to obtain a visa, and to exchange pounds sterling for Reichsmarks. He arrived at Victoria only just in time to catch the boat-train. The porter carrying their luggage made some joke about the 'Berlin' ticket labels: 'Blimey, that's a peculiar place to be going just now!' 'Oh, I expect everything will blow over all right,' replied William.[39] Perhaps this was also what he wanted his family to think. 'The little group … was solemn, even sad,' wrote Chesterton, whose informant was Macnab. 'Joyce was composed and resolute in appearance, but one of his brothers declares that tears were very close to his eyes. This is not surprising. Joyce was devoted to his own kin and thrust it out of his mind as he might do, a lover of the country he was in the act of spurning. Here was indeed a tremendous parting of the ways.'

Did Queenie have any inkling that she would never see her first-born again on this earth? Gertrude Joyce would die before the end of the war, in September 1944. Although he caused her much pain, and considerable public humiliation over the years, in her last moments she would feel near in spirit to William, and said she would always be with him. Old Michael Joyce, too, would die without seeing his eldest son again; by contrast to his wife, he was later angry that William had metamorphosed into 'Lord Haw-Haw' – and less forgiving about this than Queenie.

William worried whether he would be arrested at the port of Dover. He fancied that a security official gave him 'a dirty look' as he stepped from train to boat. In fact, it seems that there was a plan in place to arrest William on 3 September 1939.[40] But on 26 August, the Special Defence Regulations were not yet in place; even if the official had suspected that William Joyce, the Fascist agitator, was leaving the country, there was as yet no mandate to effect an arrest. Once on the boat, William relaxed a little more and, smoking a cigarette, watched the white cliffs of England gradually disappear.

'It was one of those beautiful later summer days on which the sun, to have full meaning, must pierce the mists hanging over the azure sea,' he recalled later.

> We kept our eyes fixed upon the Dover cliffs until the haze drew over them that impenetrable veil which, for us, was the end of the old life and the beginning of the new. When we could see no more of the land which we had loved and tried to serve,

I said to my wife, curtly enough, 'Let's go to lunch',
and so we did.[41]

In a way, this journey was a repeat of William's flight from Ireland, when he was just fifteen: he was once more standing on a ship sailing away from ties of kinship, territory and history, bound for a new country which would, he hoped, fulfil his expectations. He had had to leave Ireland, and now he had to leave England. But Germany – 'the Heimat' ('homeland') – was calling.

7

Becoming 'Lord Haw-Haw'

'Radio is the most modern and the most important instrument of mass influence that exists anywhere.'

Joseph Goebbels

There was obviously a plan to arrest William Joyce on 3 September 1939, because on 4 September – the day after the Second World War broke out – the London Metropolitan constabulary 'were endeavouring to find' him. New regulations were just coming into operation which would lead to the internment of anyone thought to be a danger to national security – the notorious 18B internment rule, under which dangerous subversives and harmless Italian waiters alike would be put behind bars.[1] William Joyce was one of the first targets.

The police first made enquiries of Miss Ethel Scrimgeour at Stedham Hall in Midhurst, Hampshire; Miss Scrimgeour was the well-to-do spinster who was known to be Joyce's principal patron. Miss Scrimgeour was tight-lipped and would say little beyond indicating that Mr and Mrs Joyce were 'abroad'. She knew this because they had visited her before leaving and deposited with her some of the possessions they would leave behind – not that William was one for many possessions, as a general rule. However, among the objects left at Miss Scrimgeour's estate was a gun, buried somewhere in the grounds.[2]

The police then made to search the premises of 83 Onslow Gardens, one of those pretty wedding-cake Kensington houses on a square, where William had lived, and tutored, working with 'The Master' Macnab. (Macnab paid the rent on his property from his private means.) But they were told, truthfully, that William Joyce had removed from this address some time previously, to 38A Eardsley Crescent in Earl's Court. At Eardsley Cresent, a basement in what was then a mildly louche neighbourhood, the police found not William Joyce, but his mother, Gertrude, 'Queenie', Joyce clearing out the flat and removing what was left of the William's meagre belongings.[3]

In this task, Mrs Joyce was assisted by two fiery female Fascists, Mercedes Barrington of Twickenham, a former suffragette who became a Blackshirt (and a member of other right-wing groups such as the Link), and Sylvia Morris, the daughter of a Lincolnshire doctor, a beautiful Grace Kelly blonde who had been one of Mosley's political hopefuls before quarrelling fiercely with him and then following William Joyce into the National Socialist League. She was the elder sister of Peter Morris, who was also one of William Joyce's followers.

The police noted that while Mrs Joyce – who was being assisted by her youngest son, Robert, then aged seventeen – was polite and helpful, Miss Barrington, the intrepid suffragette, was obstreperous and challenging. By what right were the police entitled to enter the premises of a private citizen? she asked. Why should they answer impertinent questions about personal friends and relations? The officers of the law were undaunted by this barracking and proceeded to examine the ladies' handbags. They came to the conclusion that Mr William Joyce and his wife had indeed absconded to Germany, and duly reported this intelligence back to headquarters. The news should not have caused undue surprise; after all, the tip-off to William had come from inside MI5.

The police also visited Angus Macnab – William's friend, business partner and political cohort – on 4 September for further intelligence. They asked for William Joyce, or information about his whereabouts: 'the Master's' account of the dialogue which took place gives a droll picture of a PC Plod asking leaden questions:

'Is William Joyce here?'
'No.'
'Has he been here?'
'No.'
'When did you last see him?'
'August twenty-seventh.'
'Where?'
'Victoria Station.'
'What was he doing?'
'Leaving for the Continent.'
'Where is he now?'
'I haven't his actual address.'
'Do you know what country?'
'Germany, I believe.'
'How do you know that?'
'He wrote and told me so from Berlin.'
'Did he, by Jove. Of course you destroyed the letter?'
'No, I've got it here somewhere.'
'When did you get it?'
'About 1st September.'
'If you don't mind, we'd very much like to have that letter.'
'It was a picture postcard. Didn't you come across it in your search?'
'No. Have you hidden it?'
'No. It's here somewhere. Ah, here it is.'
'Thanks very much. We could oblige you to give it up if you don't object. It's more pleasant this way.'

'Certainly, by all means have it.'
'Oh dear, what language is it in? I can't understand it.'
'Oh, sorry, of course it's in Latin. We always use that
for postcards.'
'Coo! You professors!'[4]

Having established that William Joyce was now in Berlin,
the constabulary went on their way.

Unable to collar William, the authorities moved swiftly to
detain his second brother Quentin. Frank would also be
arrested under 18B nine months later, but Quentin was first,
and he was to spend more than four years in prison or in an
internment camp on William's account. Frank's detention
lasted less than a year.[5]

Quentin Joyce bore a certain family likeness to his older
brother William: he was described as a taller and better-
looking version of William, a 'fresh-faced Irishman'.[6] He
shared some of William's gifts: he was a fine linguist, and,
like William, could sit down at a piano and play almost any
melody that was called for. He had the family brains, but by
the time he was a teenager, in the 1930s, the family money
had run out, and there were never enough funds for him to
go on to further education. He was expected to earn his
living once he had finished school.

Quentin was a softer, kindlier man than William. He was
obliging by temperament – perhaps too obliging for his own
good – and would go to some pains to help others.[7] He was
also a dutiful son and would be the mainstay of the family
when William was 'in trouble again'; William caused
Quentin much trouble. Yet 'Q', as Quentin was known in
the family, remained devoted to his elder brother. Rebecca
West, that lynx-eyed observer of human emotions, noted this
at William's trial: 'There passed between [Quentin] and the
man in the dock a nod and a smile of pure love,' she
reported, watching the two brothers during the treason trial.

William had, as has been mentioned, dragooned all his siblings into Blackshirt support (a not unusual phenomenon among British Fascists in the 1930s: there were many examples of siblings joining the movement together).[8] Frank and Quentin had both been involved with the British Union under William's influence, and they both supported him in his National Socialist League. Frank did this in an easygoing kind of way: his Blackshirt mates thought that 'he never pushed himself'. In any case, Frank had got married in 1938, and that disengaged him somewhat from political activity. But Quentin, eleven years younger than William, was always ready to help and run errands for William. William himself described Quentin as a 'simple, trusting lad'.[9]

The Secret Services had written to the Home Office on 5 September 1939 to say that they were most 'particularly anxious' to have Edwin Quentin Joyce interned 'at the earliest possible moment' because he had recently started a job at the Air Ministry and 'serious doubts ... have been cast on his reliability'.[10] Quentin's character was not unreliable in the everyday sense of the word – quite the contrary. But he had been involved in Fascist politics and he had been involved – in his simple, trusting way – with Germany.

Thus it was that Quentin was in his lodgings at 25 Julian Road at Stoke Bishop near Bristol when he was apprehended by one Inspector Carter, on 6 September 1939. The inspector informed him of his right to make his objections to the Advisory Committee appointed for 18B internees; he was then taken in a bewildered state to His Majesty's Prison, Bristol. He had the sum of ten pounds, eleven shillings and tuppence ha'penny on his person, as well as a fountain pen, a cigarette case and a distance gauge. He was very dismayed about being removed from his job, and his superiors initially tried to help him: he had been in the job eighteen months and his immediate superior said that he had 'performed his job in an exemplary manner'. But he lost all opportunity of returning to the Air Ministry, which rankled with him for many years afterwards.

Quentin was indignant, depressed and angry about his arrest: he had, after all, done nothing wrong, and he was being held without trial. He had been a member of a Fascist party, yes, but that was not at the time illegal, and in his eyes such a party was merely a 'patriotic' party. He had visited Germany before the outbreak of hostilities, but so had many others: Germany was a popular holiday destination, and many British people had connections with Germans. Quentin had been befriended by a German journalist and had done a couple of favours for him, which amounted to a bit of entirely innocent personal shopping. The authorities considered it sinister, however: the 'German journalist', Christian Harri Bauer, was more than a journalist. He worked for a newspaper, certainly, *Der Angriff*, but it was Goebbels' newspaper, and British Intelligence had Bauer marked down as a Gestapo agent.

In 1939, under William's influence, Quentin had visited Germany and formed a friendship with Bauer. The authorities described this as a 'close association'; Quentin called the connection 'slight'. Quentin had only thirteen pounds in all for his visit to Germany, and Bauer helped him out with a small loan. In return, Quentin agreed to go shopping in London on Bauer's behalf and buy some commodities which Bauer coveted – namely a Dunhill cigarette lighter and a Jermyn Street shirt. Bauer gave him twenty-one pounds to pay for these goods. Bauer also asked Quentin to send him some stamps, which British intelligence claimed – a little implausibly – was a code for 'maps'. As Quentin tirelessly pointed out, many of the British maps on sale in England (at the map shop Geographia, for example, then in Fleet Street) were not merely available in Germany: the maps in use at the British Air Ministry, Quentin said, were all printed in Germany 'by Heinz & Muller, Nuremberg'. The Air Ministry was using a German atlas, supplied by Gotha Parkus.

In the era before globalised shopping was routine, people did sometimes help one another out by obtaining goods in one country and taking them to another. Women travelling between England and Ireland in the 1930s would have their clothes, even sometimes their lingerie, examined by Customs and Excise for their source of provenance. There was a bossy disapproval of ordinary individuals acquiring possessions above their station, and an all-too-zealous bureaucratic control of personal shopping habits: ironically, fascists and nationalists approved of such controls under the guise of supporting home goods. Be that as it may, it seems that initially Quentin Joyce was imprisoned mostly for being William Joyce's brother, and largely on the pretext of having purchased a West End shirt and an expensive cigarette lighter (plus a few single 'Gold Flake' cigarettes, also added to the indictment) for a German with unappetising political connections. (In fact, the shirt didn't come from Jermyn Street itself, where the finest men's shirts were available: Quentin purchased it at a general store in Ludgate Hill. It cost twelve pounds and was of a pattern known as 'Bengal stripe'.) The Nazi journalist was quite delighted with himself with his smart London shirt.

The price of twelve pounds for a shirt was quite high: a good shirt could be had for 7s.6d – just over one-third of a pound sterling. The hapless Quentin paid a higher price, in the long run.

❦

For the first two weeks of his detention, Quentin had no contact with family or friends, and his parents had no idea what had happened to him. The authorities seemed to take spiteful pleasure in not informing his family of his arrest and detention. It was an anxious time for Queenie and old Michael Joyce: William had gone off to the Continent, and Quentin seemed to have disappeared.

In prison – first in Bristol, subsequently in Liverpool,

then at Wandsworth in London – Quentin was held in unpleasant conditions. He was kept in a dark and dirty cell and treated, not with outright cruelty, but with the tip-lipped secrecy that was so characteristic of the British authorities. He railed against his conditions in his copious appeals to the Advisory Committee. This committee was a board that was drawn from the great and the good and ruled with Kafkaesque omnisience. The prisoner did not know what he was accused of – except that he was considered a danger to the defence of the realm – and did not know how long he would be detained.[11]

Quentin pleaded for some clarification. He was desperately worried about his parents, he said, who were now both elderly.[12] Michael and Queenie were eventually told of his whereabouts a fortnight after his arrest, on 18 September. As soon as they learned of Quentin's detention, they wrote to the Home Office: their letters were distressed, but polite and literate.

Michael Joyce wrote that he was 'completely at a loss' to understand why his son had been arrested. Yes, Quentin had been a member of the National Socialist League, which was now dissolved, but that had not been illegal. 'His sole object was to propagate the idea of friendship between England and Germany,' Michael Joyce wrote. 'The boy is a patriot in the finest sense of the word, and to me it is a crime that he should be detained at all.'[13] Queenie's letter of protest, sent in December 1939, was composed in the handwriting of an educated woman:

> We and our son and many others know that … he is innocent of any hostile act against this country or the Crown. He has been in prison now for fourteen weeks for no cause at all. It is indeed a new departure in British justice to punish an innocent person for the alleged activities of others whom he has neither seen nor heard from since war was declared on September 3rd.[14]

There was more correspondence in this vein, and Quentin's letters often express anxiety about his parents.

Michael and Queenie Joyce were now in reduced financial circumstances, and a secondary consideration in relation to Quentin's arrest was the loss of his income, as he remitted a certain amount to his parents. But the Crown was determined to keep Quentin under lock and key, on the grounds that he had been in contact with an enemy alien who was also a Gestapo spy. Quentin's own suspicion – that it was not the contact with Christian Bauer, but the blood-link with his brother William that had prompted the arrest – seems plausible. The authorities knew that William had disappeared to Germany, and they suspected that he was now somehow in the service of the enemy. Perhaps by holding one brother, they might somehow have leverage over the other. This was quite unavailing, however, as Quentin had no contact with William by this point; none of the family had.

The savageries of Nazi Germany, and of other dictatorial regimes of the mid-twentieth century, have rather overshadowed the lesser injustice of the British special regulations enacted under 18B. But it was an ugly piece of legislation which not only ignored traditions of the English Common Law of *habeas corpus* but was also subject to error. Winston Churchill himself called the legislation 'in the highest degree odious'. When it came to arrest, there was also a class element: nobs who had mingled with Nazis at will – Joachim von Ribbentrop, Hitler's ambassador to the Court of St James, who had no shortage fawning guests at his London parties – were excused, where a minor clerk like Quentin Joyce was picked upon.

'Q' didn't give up. He doggedly went on requesting family visits and asking to be transferred back to London from the north of England; he also fretted about his job. But although he must have been furious with William, he never disowned or denounced his brother, although he did point out, quite truthfully, in his letters – writing a sloping, consistent hand – to the Advisory Board that he was not responsible for his brother's decisions and that he had scant influence over his brother's thinking. The reviewing committee came to the conclusion that 'while the fact of his brother's activities should not be pressed unfairly against Quentin Joyce, it could not be disregarded'.

Initially, MI5 was opposed to the twenty-two-year-old Quentin having any visits at all from his family, whom he was missing badly, but eventually they conceded that his mother and one younger sibling might come to see him.

His father, mother and nineteen-year-old sister Joan did visit him at Wandsworth, for twenty minutes on 8 November 1939, more than two months after his arrest. Isolated for more than eight weeks, Quentin did most of the talking. He asked Joan to request help from members of Parliament and from the 'Liberation League', which assisted political prisoners.[15] As to the whereabouts of his eldest brother, Quentin said that he assumed 'William has done one of his usual mental flips'. The family was accustomed to William behaving eccentrically. Quentin didn't blame William for his own incarceration: he blamed the system.

William and Margaret travelled by train across Belgium, the Netherlands, and into Germany in that golden last week of August before hostilities began. Hitler's armies were preparing their cruel but successful 'Blitzkrieg' – the particularly German strategy for a swift strike and a swift victory – into Poland; and the Poles were bracing themselves for what would be a most heroic and gallant defence, bravely and hopelessly charging against Panzer tanks with their cavalry.[16] Poland had been horribly squeezed by the two dictators, Hitler and Stalin, who had formed a pact which sealed their fate.

But William and Margaret Joyce initially shared that mood of light-headed euphoria which sometimes follows a reckless decision to throw everything to the wind and set out on an unknown new course. Their decision to go to Germany was at once momentous and casual. For two pins, they might have gone to Ireland instead. Margaret thought Berlin would be more 'interesting' than Dublin, which certainly turned out to be the case.

It was wonderful weather, that late August and early September of 1939. Since 1934, the Germans had called sunny days 'Hitler weather'. And it must have been perversely exhilarating to arrive in Berlin in September 1939. Food-ration cards were being issued and there was a bustle of expectant activity. Berlin has always had a certain atmosphere, a particular 'air', which is connected with its geographical position on the northern European plane: it can be very cold in winter, as the winds blow in from Siberia, but the summers and early autumns are glorious, when the numerous lakes and woods around the city provide it with such a luscious natural setting. There was even a popular song which celebrated the particular 'air' of Berlin: '*Was is diese schöne, Durft, Durft, Durft/Dass ist die Berliner Luft, Luft, Luft.*'[17]

William and Margaret found a hotel and checked in; they set to telephoning their contact Christian Bauer – the same man who had effectively landed poor Quentin in jail. Bauer, however, responded rather nervously to the call, when they got him on the line. It turned out to be like one of those holiday connections where people say: 'If you're ever visiting my country, do look me up', and when you call, they hide behind the furniture. Bauer was clearly dismayed that William Joyce had taken him at his word and fetched up in Germany. He said, at first, that he couldn't see William and Margaret immediately; then, reluctantly, he said he would meet them in the evening.

Evening came, and Bauer appeared – accompanied by his fiancée, and driving a car, which was a sign of status, since the private use of motor cars would soon be banned, and was already reserved for the elite. William and Margaret were treated to an alfresco meal at a garden restaurant, the Preussenhof, in the lively Savignyplatz in Charlottenburg, near where they would eventually live. No doubt William told Bauer that he had decided to leave England because, as he would later claim, it had been become 'a colony of Palestine'. And doubtless Bauer, being of the same mind, sympathised.

But it was clear that Bauer was giving the Joyces the brush-off, all the same. At the end of the meal, the young German asked William what his plans were exactly, now that he had arrived in Germany. 'I don't know,' William replied, uncertainly – which was far from being his natural register. What was Bauer's advice? he asked. The answer was both vague and menacing. If there was to be war between Germany and England, both William and Margaret would be interned, Bauer warned. This alarmed Margaret, particularly when she was told that they would be interned in separate camps for men and women. 'Darling, I'm frightened,' Margaret said. 'If I have to be imprisoned, at least let me be imprisoned somewhere where I can understand the language.'

William said that if she wanted to go back to England, they would go. Bauer, relieved that this decision would take them off his hands, took them on a night-time tour of Berlin by car. It was a lovely sight: the Brandenburg Gate, the Reichstag, the famous Berlin Zoo and Tiergarten, the lively Alexanderplatz, the floodlit Pergamon Museum.

But when the Joyces got back to their hotel, Margaret wept from fatigue and annoyance. Their light-heartedness had disappeared. They agreed, that Sunday night, to return to England. William knew he would be imprisoned for his National Socialist activities and his pro-German connections; so be it. William would not have been cowardly in facing the music. But he did think it was more romantic to be in Hitler's Germany than to be banged up in an internment cell in Liverpool.

The next few days turned to farce. When William and Margaret went to the tourist agency next morning to purchase return tickets to England, they found they could get tickets only as far as the German frontier. To travel on to England now, they would require sterling, and they had changed their sterling: this was in itself perhaps a sign that they were burning their bridges behind them. They applied to the British embassy for help, but found everyone busy packing up in preparation for an imminent state of war. The embassy suggested they travel to Cologne and see the British consular officer there, but the Joyces feared they might be apprehended and interned on the way. Another telephone call to Christian Bauer proved fruitless: he had had his call-up papers, said his fiancée, and had already left the house.

The pair were stumped; they walked around Berlin looking for soap, which was already being rationed. William smoked a lot. And then William's excellent memory suddenly came to the rescue. He remembered that their friend Dorothy Eckersley must also be in Berlin: she had been due to travel to Budapest, and had come to Berlin to enrol her son James in a school there. This was a stroke of luck indeed. Without Mrs Eckersley, William's introduction to radio work would not have occurred, and he might never have metamorphosed into Lord Haw-Haw, the best-known media celebrity of his time.[18]

Dorothy Eckersley's life would merit a biography on its own. Beautiul, wilful, an upper-class extremist and glamorous bohemian, Frances Dorothy Eckersley was born into the celebrated literary Stephen family in 1893. She was a colonel's daughter and a cousin of Virginia Woolf. Dorothy's mother was a suffragette and Labour Party radical, but Dorothy determined to go on the stage and trained at the esteemed Royal Academy of Dramatic Art. She toured

America and had two children out of wedlock – both eventually adopted – before marrying a gifted musical scholar, Edward Clark. She gave birth to their son James in 1923; James has played a key role in the making of this book.

Dorothy did not remain with Edward Clark for very long after that: she fell in love with Peter Eckersley, the pioneering chief engineer of the BBC. Peter Eckersley was a very clever and unusual man who has been unfairly overlooked by history. He was an innovative technical thinker and virtually set up the BBC's broadcasting network, but he fell foul of the Calvinist morality of his friend Sir John (later Lord) Reith, the director-general, and was fired for marrying Dorothy, a divorcee.[19]

Dorothy Eckersley had thrown herself into a series of passionate political commitments, initially on the Left. She joined the radical Independent Labour Party, and she and Peter Eckersley gave progressive bourgeois-bohemian parties in their *dernier cri* flat in modernist Swan Court, Chelsea. Peter Eckersley, a member of the progressive Huxley clan – he was related to Aldous Huxley, author of *Brave New World* – felt his generation's disgust and impatience towards the 'old gang' of parliamentary politicians. He shared Dorothy's enthusiasm for the new politics of radicalism.

Dorothy's marriage to 'PPE' gradually went downhill over the next ten years, and her search for fulfilment brought her to ever more radical political extremism. In her search for 'a big idea', she had encountered William Joyce in London Fascist circles, and had attended meetings of the National Socialist League and the Carlyle Club. She had even helped William out on a couple of occasions by standing bail for him when he got into legal scraps.

Dorothy had indeed gone to Germany in August 1939 to enrol her son James at the Humboldt School in Berlin-Tegel. Now virtually separated from Peter Eckersley, she was fired with enthusiasm for the Führer and everything that the 'new

Germany' represented. Hitler's Third Reich had become the progressive model for the world of the 'new man'. James, now aged sixteen, had a full-blown teenage passion for Adolf Hitler and the Third Reich: he was totally smitten by the persona of the Führer, who, he believed, could solve any problem, accomplish any deed and remake the world according to the heart's desire. Hitler had enormous powers to enchant: to Jim, just settling in to his class at his Berlin school, he seemed to be 'Mr Magic'. James even altered his name for a while from the Biblical 'James' or 'Jacob' to the more Nordic and heroic-sounding 'Richard'. A mother and son like this, William reckoned, would surely have connections in Berlin. They did.

Angus Macnab said that Joyce had a prodigious memory, and never forgot anything: not only did he recall Dorothy Eckersley being in Berlin, he also remembered her mentioning that she would stay at the Hotel Continental. He consulted the Berlin telephone directory and found the hotel, in Neustädtische-Kirchstrasse, just off Unter den Linden; the hotel itself now no longer exists, although the street is still there, and still bears the same name. He and Margaret made for the Continental at lunchtime. They entered the dining room, and then walked through a second, and then a third, restaurant area; in that third section of the hotel restaurant, to their delight and surprise, they found Dorothy Eckersley.

Unlike Christian Bauer, Dorothy greeted her friends warmly, and invited them to join her. When William said he was now committed to Germany and needed to earn some money, she was also practical in her suggestions. She said she would introduce him immediately to her friend Dr Erika Schirmer, a lecturer at the *Hochschule für Politik* and a specialist in Anglo-German relations. Erika's brother, Dr Hans Schirmer, held an influential position in the German Foreign Office; indeed, she would take the Joyces to a tea party with Fräulein Schirmer that very afternoon. In

Continental Europe, as much, if not even more than in old-boy-network England, personal introductions counted.[20]

✧

Adolf Hitler, who became William Joyce's Carlylian 'Hero', and thus ordained for hero-worship, did not believe in God, but he did believe strongly in 'Providence' – *die Vorsehung*. 'Providence' ordained a man's destiny, especially a man chosen for a particular role. It certainly seemed that some kind of Providence now propelled William towards his destiny, to metamorphose into 'Lord Haw-Haw'. Although he and Margaret made a last-minute panic-stricken attempt – largely at Margaret's instigation – to return to England, she came to accept that their fate now was to remain in Germany. Long-distance telephone calls were hit-and-miss, and they had no news from London.

Margaret said she felt lonely, helpless and homesick in a foreign capital. Political commitments to an ideology do not always compensate for what the Irish call 'the smell of the nest' and the call of home. In the Soviet Union, Guy Burgess eked out his last days thinking of cricket and yearning for London gossip. Despite his frequently affirmed belief in National Socialism and the Führer, in his first days in Berlin William Joyce felt alien and unsure, and drank a lot of vodka.

But Fräulein Doktor Schirmer's interventions bore fruit. William was summoned to the Foreign Office and interviewed for employment in a somewhat bureaucratic way. William himself had no idea of what he wanted to do, or could do, for a living in Germany: his German was good, but not good enough for him to replace a native. The Reich was already awash with special experts on England. A little translation work was put his way, which was no trouble to him. And then the Foreign Office passed him on to Dr Erich Hetzler, who worked directly for Joseph Goebbels and the Propaganda Ministry. Hetzler had studied at the London

School of Economics, and worked with von Ribbentrop in London.

It was through this connection that William Joyce was given a radio audition. His first audition was, in fact, not a success: he had a heavy cold, and his voice was muffled. Yet a radio engineer heard something unusual in William's voice and suggested that he should be tried again. And so William Joyce made his first broadcast on German radio, reading the news in English – anonymously, of course – on 6 September 1939, just three days after the declaration of war between England and Germany. He read another, and then another, and proved a natural at the microphone. By October, he was signing an employment contract with the German Broadcasting corporation, the *Reichs-Rundfunk-Gesellschaft*, or RRG. Unpredicted, unsought and unscheduled, William had come from nowhere, it seemed, and begun his war.

In the twenty-first century, we are apt to regard radio as just one of several means of instant communication. It does not now have anything like the mass impact of television or the Internet. Radio – 'wireless telephony' – had originally been discovered by the half-Irish, half-Italian Guglielmo Marconi, in 1895, although its functional operation is usually dated to 1906, the year of William Joyce's birth. Until the First World War, it was mainly used for the transmission of military information, but by the early 1920s, it began to extend to radio buffs and technological amateurs. The expansion of radio was driven forward by events: reporting the 1926 General Strike in Britain provided the then British Broadcasting Company with its first opportunity to transmit live news. It was duly rewarded, in 1927, for its support for the government with a royal charter, the name British Broadcasting Corporation and a monopoly. By the 1930s, radio was expanding everywhere, notably in Germany. The Germans had a strong tradition of technical expertise in all spheres of engineering, and moreover, Hitler's regime perceived, from the beginning, just how powerful an instrument of propaganda the wireless could be (rather as our modern-day spin doctors regard television).[21] Radio had played a key role in the 1935 Saar Plebiscite and the 1938 Anschluss when Germany absorbed Austria.

It might seem surprising that William Joyce had never previously shown much personal interest in radio until he arrived in Germany with no real plans. He was nonetheless aware, as shown by his pamphlets, of its power as a means of communication. He had used the press, the pamphlet, and the public meeting exhaustively: anywhere there was a soapbox, he would mount it and begin to speak. But he had never attempted broadcasting. One explanation for this is evident: the BBC, having established its monopoly, carefully excluded anyone who challenged its orthodoxies. (When the war broke out, Sir Oswald Mosley, who had been excluded from the airwaves, was involved in a commercial radio project to set up a radio channel using Continental transmitters.)[22]

By the beginning of the Second World War, the vast majority of households had a radio, or access to one, and families and neighbours would sit around a radio set together. Despite working-class interest in the new medium, the BBC fare was rigidly bourgeois in its output, and on Sunday 'gloomily puritanical'.[23] Many listeners in Britain tuned into Continental-based stations such as Radio Luxembourg or Radio Normandie (if they could get the reception), which provided light entertainment and popular music, even on Sundays.

The German RRG, in accordance with German federal traditions of decentralisation, was originally run by nine regional broadcasting companies. However, when the Nazis came to power in 1933, the first new ministry to be established was the propaganda ministry under Joseph Goebbels, the *Reichsministerium für Volksaufklärung und Propaganda* (RMVP). A broadcasting division was thus established within the RMVP ministry, because, for the Nazis, 'radio is the most modern, most powerful and most revolutionary weapon which we possess in the struggle against an old and perishing world, and in the struggle for the new Third Reich.'[24] Joseph Goebbels, Hitler's principal propagandist – a clever, amoral and wicked man – believed that radio was 'the most modern and the most important instrument of mass influence that exists anywhere.'[25] The heads of German radio were thus instructed by Goebbels that they could make or break opinion.

When William was hired by the overseas service of German radio in September 1939, he was entering a sort of state within a state. This was rather like, at least in aspiration, the World Service (formerly Empire Service) of the BBC, in which scores of different personages mingled. Some of those were media professionals, some were eccentrics, some opportunists, some were misfits down on their luck, some were characters who would do anything for a buck, some were individuals with conflicting loyalties – a German parent and a British, or Irish, parent was a not unusual component among broadcasters and others sympathetic to the Third Reich – and some, like William himself, were ideologues and propagandists who believed that the 'new Germany' represented the new world order.

In structure, it was a many-layered bureaucracy in which each person working for it kept an eye on the daily demands, guidelines and exhortations of Goebbels' propaganda ministry. There were propaganda broadcasts from the Reich in fifty-five languages and to many overseas lands; there were open broadcasts from Germany and there were 'secret stations', which purported to come from elsewhere. English-language broadcasts were considered the most important of all – Hitler, after all, admired Britain most of all, and until well into the war believed that it might be possible for Germany and Britain to work together. We might thus imagine that the all-important English-language section of the Rundfunk was organised with military precision and the famous German thoroughness, but this was not the case. The cast of characters brought together for broadcasting to Britain was apparently most un-Germanly haphazard and *ad hoc*.

～

The story of how 'Lord Haw-Haw' came into existence is now a classic. It began with the Beaverbrook press – then consisting of the *Daily Express, Sunday Express* and *Evening Standard* – which, as soon as war broke out on 3 September 1939, was keen to monitor German propaganda broadcasts. Lord Beaverbrook – the Canadian Max Aitken, the legendary press baron – had set up special gadgetry and listening posts in Surrey for this purpose. Beaverbrook appointed an amusing radio critic who called himself by the eighteenth-century pseudonym of 'Jonah Barrington', although his real name was Cyril Carr Dalmaine. Barrington's true calling was as a musician: he had taught music at English public schools and then become a chorus-master at the BBC. From there, he was hired, almost certainly for a large sum of money (since that was Beaverbrook's style – to pay large sums of money in exchange for the journalist's soul) and lots of media glamour. Lord Beaverbrook was quick to spot a talent and adored gimmicks of any kind.

Barrington became the radio critic of the *Daily Express* in 1934 – a very important job at the time, because of radio's status as the latest and most amazing gimmick. The *Daily Express* was the sharpest and most powerful popular newspaper of the period: whatever it did was considered significant. Every reporter wanted to have a job on the *Express*; as for foreign correspondents – why, the *Express* reporter was regarded as Lord Beaverbook's own special envoy and plenipotentiary. He didn't even have to fill in expenses accounts: he was above such pettifogging details.

Propaganda broadcasts from Germany had commenced

in March 1939, and Jonah Barrington began writing his commentaries on these broadcasts in September. He devised comical names for the various speakers from Berlin (who were being transmitted via Hamburg, Bremen and Zeesen). One he called 'Winnie the Whopper' or 'Winnie of Warsaw'; others 'Ursula the Pooh', 'Auntie Gush', 'Uncle Smarmy, or 'Uncle Boo-Hoo' and 'Weepy'. But he somehow hit the jackpot when he brought to life, on 14 September 1939, the character he named 'Lord Haw-Haw'.

Barrington wrote, in an inspired description of a style of speaking: 'A gent I'd like to meet is moaning periodically from Zeesen. He speaks English of the haw-haw, damn-it-get-out-of-my-way variety, and his strong suit is gentlemanly indignation.' This sentence, identifying the 'English of the haw-haw, damn-it-get-out-my-way variety' was to bestow on Barrington a certain celebrity that would last until his death in 1986.[26]

Later, Cyril Dalmaine said that the invention of 'Lord Haw-Haw' was to hang around his neck: he felt that it 'buried alive' his other achievements. He would much rather have been remembered, he said, for something better. He was a successful composer of music for children's ballets. But from that moment on, Barrington enjoyed splash headlines in the *Daily Express*, was subsequently headhunted, probably at an increased salary, by the *Sunday Chronicle* and the *Daily Sketch*; wrote a comical book, *Lord Haw-Haw of Zeesen*, illustrated by the cartoonist Fenwick, which is now a collectors' item; and was gratefully consulted by legal experts when they were compiling scholarly tomes on the trial of William Joyce.

The invention of 'Lord Haw-Haw' was just one of those moments in media history when a fashion, a fad, a talking point and a comical inspiration are synthesised into a minor cult. By mid-October, Poland was conquered and sub-jugated, and Britain was technically at war with Germany, but it was the period known as 'the phoney war' (in France, similarly, as the *drôle de guerre*, meaning something like 'the funny war'). In fact, nothing very much seemed to be happening at all; perhaps the invention of this 'Lord Haw-Haw' character was an entertaining distraction. Very shortly after Jonah Barrington breathed life into a semi-fictional character, the guessing game began as to the identity of this 'Lord Haw-Haw'.

The British press went 'Lord Haw-Haw' mad. Who *was* Lord Haw-Haw? A German schoolmaster? It was confidently asserted at one point that he was one Rolf Hoffman. A British student in Germany? Perhaps a Scot? Was there a hint of an Irish brogue? Whether his upper-class accent was authentic or not was the subject of much speculation. The novelist Miss Rose Macaulay took issue with the claim that Lord Haw-Haw's voice was 'aristocratic, upper-class, "haw-haw" and so forth'. No, she insisted: 'Lord Haw-Haw speaks excellent English but surely not 'Cholmondeley Plantagenet out of Christ Church.'[27] Lady Cynthia Colville averred that she was sure that this person did *not* speak with a true 'Oxford' accent.

It was hardly surprising that there was so much confusion, since there were several different voices being called 'Lord Haw-Haw'. Two English-speaking broadcasters, Norman Baillie-Stewart and Wolf Mittler, were heard constantly on the German airwaves. Baillie-Stewart was another odd character: he was a Scottish officer, formerly of the Seaforth Highlanders, who had been imprisoned in the Tower of London in 1933 on a charge of selling minor military secrets to Germany. After serving a sentence, he drifted back to Vienna and then moved to Berlin, where he had been given a radio audition, and subsequently worked as a broadcaster. Wolf Mittler was a splendidly handsome, and interesting, bilingual announcer, of Polish-German background, whose mother had been born in Ireland. He was not a Nazi, and was thought of by some as a playboy: his broadcasting style was more Terry Wogan than Joseph Goebbels.[28]

Another candidate for the 'Lord Haw-Haw' title was Eduard Dietze, whose mother was Scottish and whose father was half-German and half-Hungarian. He lived in London as a child and retained perfect mastery over English. As a young man he had worked in America; he began to specialise in radio broadcasting and production in 1929. He became William's direct editorial boss for much of his time in Germany.

The first 'Lord Haw-Haw' could have been any of these: James Clark, who came to work at the Rundfunkhaus (and who worked as a newsreader himself) now believes that the first Haw-Haw was Wolf Mittler. Norman Baillie-Stewart, who also claimed the original title, came to the view that Mittler was probably the voice that Jonah Barrington first heard. Yet, as time wore on, William Joyce would become the definitive 'Lord Haw-Haw', and unlike Mittler, Baillie-Stewart or Dietze, all of whom had relatively pleasant post-war years, would pay the full tariff for his media title.

But for the first months of the Haw-Haw craze – and the boredom of the 'phoney war' – the guessing game went on.[29] The Marquess of Donegall, who wrote for the *Daily Mail*, entered into the sport with characteristic British insouciance, treating German radio propaganda as a tremendous joke. 'Best known to English listeners and very dear to my heart is Lord Haw-Haw, as Barrington has christened him,' he wrote on 2 October 1939.

> Anyone can have the joy of meeting him, for he makes lengthy appearances on the medium-wave band from Berlin. Whoever writes Lord Haw-Haw's stuff is a genius in the art of being unconsciously funny. At times he drops his monocle (I'm sure he has one) and becomes endearing.

In a moment of sharp deductive thinking, Donegall contacted Angus Macnab, whom he had known at Oxford in 1927. The Marquess had heard that William Joyce was one of the 'Haw-Haw' suspects; he also knew that Macnab had been involved in British Fascist movements and would recognise William's voice. So he sent a telegram to Angus Macnab and asked him to come and listen to the wireless with a view to identifying Haw-Haw's voice.

'The Master' Macnab was working as a volunteer ambulance driver at the time: he must have guessed what William Joyce was up to, though, typically, he did not possess anything as newfangled as a radio himself. Macnab didn't care for Lord Donegall but consented to come and listen.[30] He promised he would 'tell no lies', which is not quite the same as telling the whole truth. He was brought to Donegall's London residence, and the two men sat listening on a short-wave set. There were problems with the reception, however, and the static was 'utterly impossible'. Donegall asked Macnab to come to his country home the next day, which Macnab duly did.

In fact, Macnab had, despite the static interference, just made out the words 'This is Hamburg and Cologne'. He knew immediately that it was William Joyce's voice, because William always pronounced 'Hamburg' as 'Hambursh'. Donegall had said dismissively, at this point: 'That is not the man I am talking about anyway.' Macnab kept silent. The next day, at his country home, Lord Donegall had an excellent wireless reception from Germany. Macnab heard this 'Lord Haw-Haw' and recognised the voice as that of Norman Baillie-Stewart. So when Donegall asked: 'Is that Joyce?' Macnab could truthfully say: 'Quite certainly not'. He did not add that the voice heard the previous day, through the static, was indeed William's.

It would be April 1941 before William Joyce was officially identified as 'Lord Haw-Haw', although Hazel, his first wife, had recognised William's voice broadcasting from Germany as early as December 1939. She gave a brief interview to the *Sunday Pictorial*, which was regarded as a downmarket paper at the time. Lord Haw-Haw was, the paper announced, William Joyce, one-time director of the British Union of Fascists.

'Any doubts that Joyce is the man was disposed of by a woman who was interviewed by the *Sunday Pictorial* last night,' the paper stated.

> She is Joyce's former wife, now living in the tiny village of Waldron, Sussex. 'I knew it was William Joyce – my former husband – the moment I listened to his voice,' she said. 'My mother and sister, who knew Joyce well, have written to me. They, too, have recognised his voice.
>
> 'Joyce is the father of two of my children. They are eight and eleven years old. One night I turned on the wireless while they were in the room. Joyce was speaking. My eldest daughter turned pale, and when I asked her what was the matter, she said, "That's W.J., isn't it?" – she always called her father W.J.
>
> 'I am positive he is the man. He even tells the same stories that he used to tell me ...' she went on. 'He is a brilliant linguist, speaking four languages. His friends prophesised a great career for him when he was a private tutor, but I'm afraid he has a queer twist in his make-up.'[31]

Strangely, this made little impact, and the rest of the media went on for many more months playing the game of 'Who is Lord Haw-Haw?' Though there were other voices sometimes playing the Haw-Haw role, William indeed became the character.

At St Ignatius College in Galway: a Confirmation picture, taken in 1915 or 1916. 'Willie Joyce', as he was known in Galway, is third from the right in the back row.

Above: with the Blackshirts. This photograph has been dated 1934. William is at the extreme left. Oswald Mosley is third from the left, and in the centre of the group, looking over Mosley's left shoulder, is Eric Hamilton Piercey, who would marry William's first wife, Hazel, and become 'a very good stepfather' to William's daughters. Photograph: The Friends of Oswald Mosley.

On the platform of the British Union of Fascists. William Joyce, the fiery British Empire patriot.
Photograph: Popperfoto.

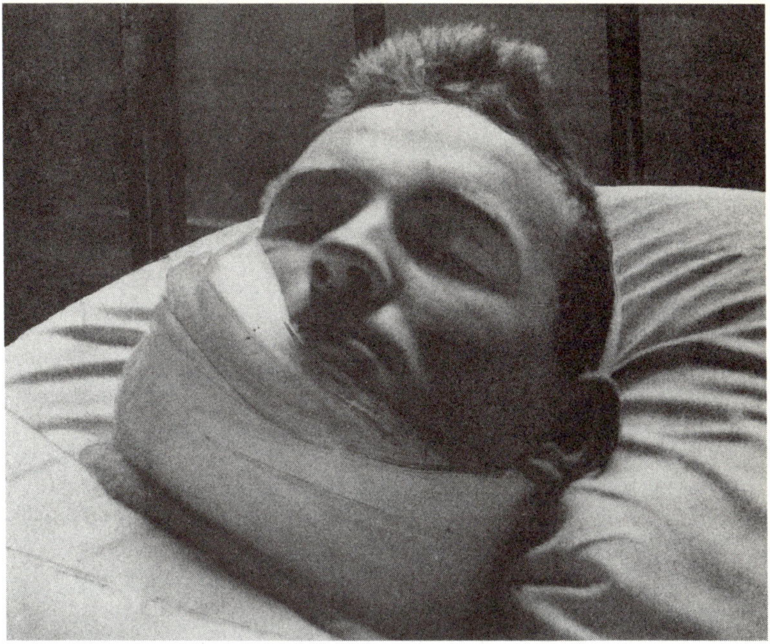

William Joyce in hospital in October 1924, after his neck and face had been carved up by a political opponent when he was stewarding a Conservative Party meeting at Lambeth. He had twenty-six stitches and might have died: the scar marked his face lividly for the rest of his life. He jokingly dubbed it 'The Lambeth Honour'. Photograph: *Daily Mail*. By permission of Atlantic Syndication.

William Joyce, in the Blackshirt uniform of the British Union of Fascists. The scar has been reduced in this photograph by early airbrushing methods. Photograph: The Friends of Oswald Mosley.

'Christiangang', the little Hansel-and-Gretel houses in Kupfermühle, Wassersleben (near Flensburg) where William and Margaret hid out with an Anglo-German couple in 1945. It has been restored by Mr Bodo Daetze, in tribute to the Danish King, Christian IV, who constructed artisans' dwellings at the time of Shakespeare.

The wood at Wassersleben, just by the German-Danish border, where Captain Geoffrey Perry came upon Lord Haw-Haw: William engaged the Allied soldiers in conversation, giving them a tutorial about deciduous and coniferous trees. 'He never stopped talking,' Geoffrey Perry recalls.

The Trial of Lord Haw-Haw: September 1945. William's best friend, John Angus Macnab (first left, in a hat), speaks to a supporter. On the right, carrying a briefcase, is Quentin Joyce, the younger brother who fought so hard to save William Joyce from the gallows. Photograph: Quentin Joyce archive.

Margaret Joyce – 'Lady Haw-Haw' – is arrested, Wassersleben, May 1945, after William has been taken away by the British Army. She blamed herself for William's arrest: if she had gone with him to the woods, he wouldn't have engaged the soldiers in conversation, she reflected in her diary. Her mind was on her lover, Nicky von Besack, at the time. Photograph: *Daily Mirror*.

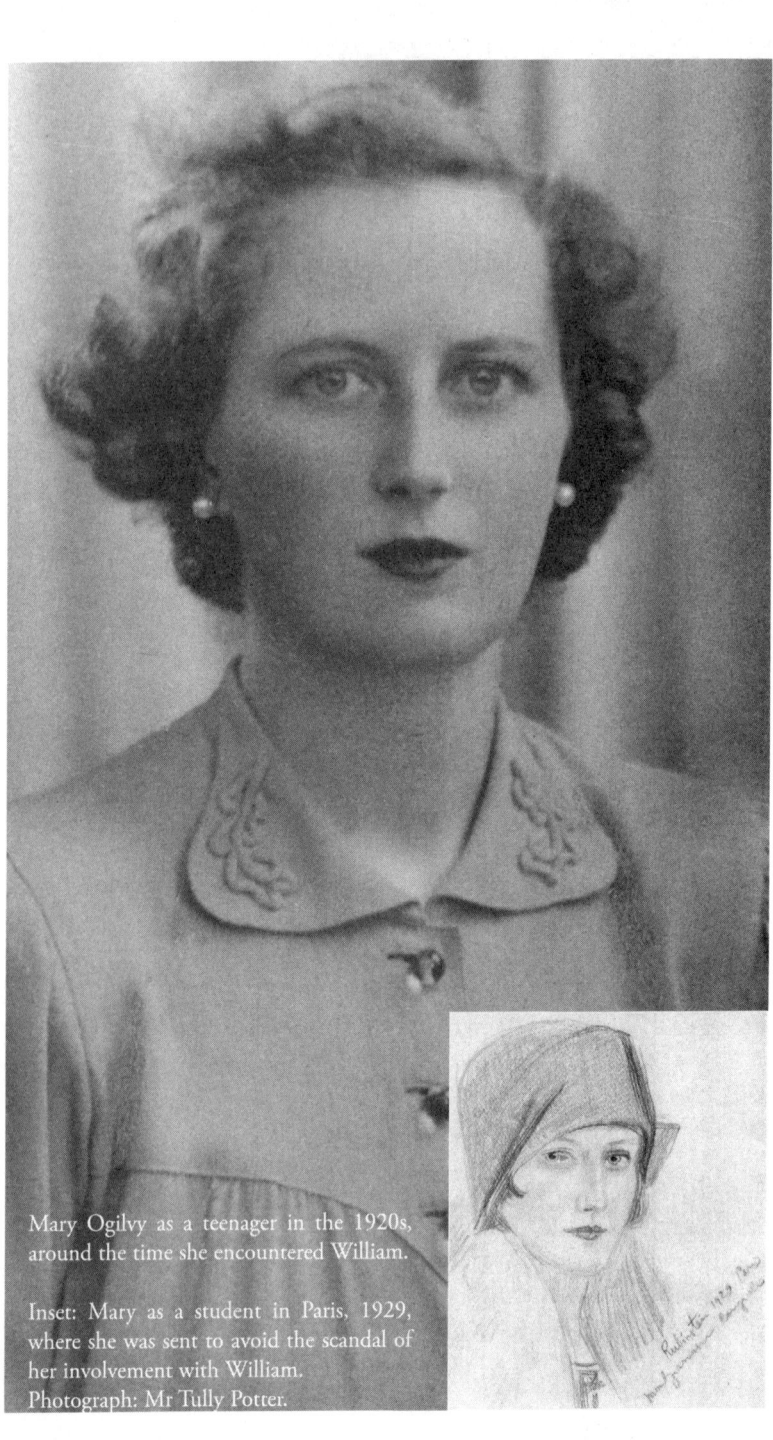

Mary Ogilvy as a teenager in the 1920s, around the time she encountered William.

Inset: Mary as a student in Paris, 1929, where she was sent to avoid the scandal of her involvement with William.
Photograph: Mr Tully Potter.

Frank Joyce's wedding to Edith Ann Ford, known in the family as Ann, in 1947. Left to right: Robert, the youngest Joyce brother, Daisy Young (Ann's sister), Frank, Ann and Quentin. They had put William's execution into the past, and from this period on it was not spoken about. Photograph: Judith Joyce Ware archive.

William's sister, Joan, with her niece Judy, whom she took riding every Sunday on Shooter's Hill. About 1950. Photograph: Judith Joyce Ware archive.

Margaret in her dancing days. She adored dancing, parties and socialising. She had thought of joining the Communist Party in the 1930s, but switched to the British Union of Fascists when she heard Mosley speak.

A picture that William's widow, Margaret, sent from Germany after the war to her brother-in-law Frank. Judy Ware knew Margaret as 'German Aunt Margaret'. Photograph: Judith Joyce Ware archive.

Dorothy Eckersley, cousin of Virginia Woolf, former actress and political radical (first with the Marxists, subsequently with Fascism) during the Second World War. Her connections got William Joyce hired by German radio.

Her son, James Clark, as a very young man in Germany, 1939–40. He had a teenage enthusiasm for the Führer, Adolf Hitler, and also worked at the Rundfunk as a newsreader.

8

A Hit with Hitler: Media Star
of the Third Reich

'Lord Haw-Haw is brilliant.'

Joseph Goebbels, *Diaries*, 11 September 1940

*'The BBC news bulletins were extremely dull
[but] when someone tunes in to Lord Haw-
Haw, the whole room gets up and gathers
round the wireless.'*

Secret military report to BBC, 1940[1]

Even some of William Joyce's Fascist friends thought he was crazy to go to Germany in August 1939. But it turned out to be what could be called a good career move – at least initially. Having failed – or been rebuffed – in so many of his ambitions in England, in Germany he found the work he might have been born to do.

His broadcasting voice, although described as having a rasping quality even by his loyal friend Angus Macnab and often recalled as being 'sneering', 'sardonic', 'sarcastic' and always 'nasal' – he never got over the broken nose from his schoolboy mishaps in Galway – nevertheless also had a striking quality. It could be terrifying: women, notably, who recall having heard it as young children have told me how scary, and yet memorable, it was. Yet it could also be strangely seductive. The 'Lord Haw-Haw' voice had a kind of sex appeal – there was a virility and command about it. Above all, it expressed a 'radio personality'.

Some broadcasters just have a 'radio personality' – the most outstanding and enduring example was Alastair Cooke – and William Joyce was one of them. To listen to the few clips of Joyce that still exist – most of the recordings, either cut on wax, or recorded on tape, were afterwards destroyed – can still be, in a curious way, mesmerising. 'Germany calling, Germany calling,' he would begin, famously. Other English broadcasters – John Amery, for example, who was also to hang as a traitor – had a more polished way of speaking than William. Norman Baillie-Stewart, Wolf Mittler and Eduard Dietze, all early contenders for the 'Haw-Haw' title, were also attractive broadcasters. But William had some extra chemistry. The very high recognition factor of his broadcasting voice was to ensnare him when he was a fugitive.

The Haw-Haw joke continued at high pitch from the autumn of 1939 to the summer of 1940. It is a gallant British attribute to treat serious matters as a great joke, and the Haw-Haw phenomenon duly became an enormous national source of merriment. Lord Haw-Haw made headlines in the British press on an almost daily basis, particularly in the first six months of the war, and entire satirical shows were built around this imagined personality. He was a 'character' on the national stage. He represented both an English toff and an absurd Nazi: the composite caught the public's fancy. By Christmas of 1939, there was a comedy review at the Holborn Empire in London playing to packed houses, called simply 'Haw-Haw', and there were many more stage acts – Arthur Askey had one – and musical reviews on the Haw-Haw theme.[2]

Formal banquets in the City of London were entertained, after port and cigars, with a Haw-Haw impersonator, who was greeted with uproarious laughter.[3] The Haw-Haw craze extended to a prodigious number of cartoons of the imagined Lord Haw-Haw, with his top hat and monocle – ironic, in that William Joyce himself loathed and despised the British upper class: 'the spoilt darlings of Mayfair', as he invariably called them. Within a year there would even be a thriller in which Joyce was the central character: *Lord Haw-Haw is Dead* by Brett Rudledge. William Joyce was flattered by this – and gave a signed copy of the book to an American corres-pondent – although, perhaps prophetically, the Haw-Haw character winds up as a corpse early in the story.

While the press went on treating 'Lord Haw-Haw' as a splendid joke well into the second half of 1940, the BBC and the British authorities in general were more alarmed at the impact of William's increasing popularity. And well they might be alarmed: particularly in the period 1939–40, the German broadcasts showed up the dullness and stuffiness of the BBC services. (Lord Donegall had confessed that he twiddled the knobs of his wireless because it so seldom produced any gaiety in 'these drab days'.) Radio audiences had grown dramatically at the commencement of the war, not just because people were anxious for news, but also because blackouts kept families at home much more, and the wireless became the main source of entertainment.

But at the beginning, the BBC, which had a monopoly on broadcasting in the United Kingdom, did not meet the public demand for such entertainment. The BBC's own historian, Asa Briggs, has said that at the outbreak of war, the corporation

> put on the dreariest programmes imaginable. They really bored people. They consisted of short news bulletins, not telling you anything; very, very long public announcements – as many as an hour's worth – at a time … Virtually no humorous programmes of any kind, no serious music, very, very heavy fare.[4]

The endless public announcements – rather like those scolding reminders at airports nowadays to refrain from smoking – were lugubrious and depressing. A typical announcement went:

> The closing of places of entertainment: all cinemas, theatres and other places of entertainment are to be closed immediately, until further notice. They are being closed because, if they were hit by a bomb, large numbers of people would be killed or injured.[5]

Meanwhile, radio broadcasts from Berlin were boasting that in September and October 1939, there were twenty-five new German films and thirty-three new German plays being shown in the capital of the Reich.[6]

Later in the course of the war, the BBC would prove an invaluable source of objective news to listeners all over Europe, but at the start of hostilities, it was widely criticised for being dull. An organist, Mr Sandy Macpherson, was brought on to produce endless sessions of cinema organ music which people thought achingly tedious. Listeners wrote in to the BBC saying they would rather face Geman guns than any more of the worthy Sandy Macpherson on his organ.[7]

Surveys undertaken in 1939–40 revealed, to the British authorities' alarm, just how popular Lord Haw-Haw was. In January 1940, a survey carried out by the BBC showed that in the previous month, 30 per cent of the adult population of Britain – or about 9 million people – were listening to these broadcasts from the Third Reich. The BBC news was heard by about 50 per cent of the populace, or 16 million people, but a majority of BBC listeners would switch over to Hamburg – the main transmitter – directly after the news. It was calculated that by the end of January 1940, six out of ten Britons were tuning in to hear Lord Haw-Haw. Listeners described him as funny, controversial and a good broadcaster – and anyway, they wanted to hear both sides of the story.[8]

Undoubtedly, Haw-Haw said things that were blatantly offensive to his British listeners: 'Not only invasion, but starvation, stares England in the face';[9] 'Even if England had any prospect of winning the war, she would find herself, when peace was declared, in a disastrous situation';[10] 'We have no time for Churchill's dialectical evasions and rhetorical equivocations. His terminological inexactitudes belong to another world – a world that is crumbling before his eyes.'[11] He also started a running joke asking 'Where is the *Ark Royal*?', this being the only modern aircraft carrier available to the Royal Navy in 1939. The *Ark Royal* was important to Britain's defences, but from September 1939 until June 1940 her whereabouts were not known, and William teased mercilessly over this.[12] (He would be repaid in his own coin: when he was being arraigned for treason in 1945, mocking onlookers would shout: 'Where is the *Ark Royal*?')

Yet these acts of broadcasting provocation revealed something significant about the public: people would rather be shocked than bored. Lord Haw-Haw insulted, outraged, amused and annoyed – but people still listened to him. Moreover, political invective on the wireless was a novelty – nobody on the BBC had ever been heard to lambast those in authority.

The British government considered a prohibition on listening to Haw-Haw, but decided against it, judging that it would cause more trouble than it was worth. In the end, William's provocative taunts may have stiffened resolve in Britain more than they lowered morale. In Germany, the dictatorship took no such liberal view: listening to foreign broadcasts was forbidden, under the most severe penalty. Worse, the ban encouraged the most mean-spirited kind of snooping: the mother of a German airman received word that her son, a Luftwaffe officer, was missing, presumed dead. A few days later, the BBC in London broadcast that he had been captured and was alive. The mother received eight letters from friends and neighbours telling her that her son was alive, because they had heard it on the BBC. The German mother then denounced all eight of her friends to the authorities, for listening to foreign radio, and all eight were arrested.[13]

⤙

There was another aspect of Lord Haw-Haw's broadcasts which has not perhaps been appreciated: he was a trenchant social critic of the condition of Britain. William Joyce has often been described as a nasty character pouring spleen into a microphone. But a close analysis of some of his scripts also reveals a radical critique of British society, elucidating themes which became almost accepted wisdom in the decades after the Second World War. William was a political thinker – daft, chippy and perverse, but nevertheless someone who had read and reflected upon social and political ideas.

For example, he saw health as a political issue at a time when most politicians had nothing whatsoever to say about it. (Conservatives thought it a private matter and many socialists considered it a topic fit only for women.) 'In London, higher medical services, like nightclubs, are open to anyone able to pay extortionate fees,' Joyce announced. 'But there is something radically wrong when everything boils down to money, faith and a bottle of coloured water. The whole layout of the social system is obsolete; only an apathetic public would put up with it.'[14]

He asked in January 1940:

> Where else in Europe will you find a privileged class comparable with the upper nation in England? Look around anywhere in Britain and you will understand what I mean. Go to the slums and there you will find the lowest stratum of the lower nation huddled together in indescribable filth and poverty. Here you will find the permanent underdogs of the capitalist system; recruits for Bostal, Barnardo's hospitals, jails and brothels. Yet it is from the great

majority of decent and honest slum-dwellers and the frugal, industrious working classes that the upper nation expects to draw recruits for the army to fight and to die for King and country. For a country that has confined them to slums.[15]

This propaganda had an impact because it echoed what some people were indeed thinking: it might be better to reform social conditions at home than to embark on a war with Germany. A war against Hitler was far from unanimously supported in early 1940. Many Britons still believed the differences between the two countries could be patched up. It was a shame about Poland, but was that really Britain's business? Some people thought that Hitler was 'only taking what was in his own backyard'.[16]

Joyce hammered home his social message with personal recollections:

It is an unforgettable experience to watch the entrance to a London theatre in the evening: pre-war, of course. Limousine after limousine with extravagantly clad women and their male companions, stepping out of cars like condescending gods and goddesses, whilst the dull and silent crowd composed of the members of the lower nation looks at this brazen display of wealth and leisure. The sight almost reminds one of conditions in the declining Roman Empire, and one is at a loss to say whether the impudence of the upper classes or the meek tractability of the lower is the more astonishing.

The upper nation of the Mayfair type of snob feeds on the lower nation whom it robs. How long is this going to last?

Joyce drew a contrast with Germany, where

There are no unemployed outcasts as in England ... I should like you to contrast the friendly and sympathetic attitude of the party

> members of National Socialist welfare with the
> methods of public assistance offered in England.
> You would be very sorry that you ever condemned
> National Socialism.[17]

William's attacks on the 'Mayfair swells' and the 'rottenness' of the class system that condemned the poor to 'the lower nation' must have had some resonance among working-class listeners. He also uses problems like wartime evacuation to condemn conditions in England:

> The whole nation has been shocked by stories from
> reception areas of verminous people being billeted
> on people, yet the condition of these people cannot
> be blamed on them. The public conscience should
> not allow itself to be lulled into unconsciousness, as
> the wealthy would wish. At Christmas, we should
> help, not give worthless pity to the poor.[18]

He points out that dependants of

> those in the navy and RAF receive a miserable
> allowance, depriving them of a decent living.
> Seamen receive no allowance unless [they are] a
> hundred per cent disabled. The unemployed will
> have a poor Christmas on three and sixpence or
> four shillings.[19]

Themes he had already worked out in Fascist pamphlets were recalled and recycled. The freedom of 'liberal democracy' was mainly the freedom of the rich, he contended:

> The most nauseating feature of all this whining
> about freedom and the traditions of freedom lies in
> the public-school system. This is the cradle of
> sickening snobbery which has so long marred
> English social life. Ability, energy, force of character
> count for nothing unless a man has been to the
> right school. In the Commons today there are more
> than two hundred and fifty representatives of Eton
> and Harrow: Eton has its virtues and Harrow its

vices, but neither can in any sense claim to be representative of the people of England.[20]

Some working-class people said that what they liked about Lord Haw-Haw was his knowledge of poverty and his understanding of the conditions of their lives. Unlike many politicians, he knew the price of a loaf of bread and was well-informed about pensions. A social worker in Liverpool told an academic researcher that 'all soldiers' wives' listened to Haw-Haw, not just for the news but because 'he discussed their hardship, and seemed to be the only person interested in them.'[21]

In 1940, German propaganda broadcasting would appeal to this working-class constituency with the launch of a secret station called Workers' Challenge. William wrote many of the scripts for this station, although he never actually spoke about his work in this area. The dialogue on Workers' Challenge was often peppered with swear words that were shocking in the 1940s ('bleeding' and 'bugger'). The scripts also mocked politicians remorselessly in a way that did not occur in mainstream broadcasting until the 'satire boom' of the 1960s. Many of these scripts bear William Joyce's fingerprints: they use phrases and repeat attitudes that he had used in his writings for *Action*, *The Blackshirt*, and the *Helmsman*. Ernest Bevin, the trade unionist who became minister for labour in Winston Churchill's wartime coalition, was referred to as 'Mr Bleeding Bevin' and 'Hoary Ernie', and vulgar forms of address such as 'old cock' were used: such language was considered dreadfully insulting in this period.[22]

Other expressions come from the rough end of the saloon bar rather than the genteel drawing rooms of the Home Counties: 'Transport House is nothing but a lot of scum, anyhow'; 'To hell with Churchill and his lousy gang of crooks'; 'Put an end to misery, put an end to the bloody war that caused it'; 'Demand peace at once and bash in the interfering bugger that gets in the way.'[23] The message of Workers' Challenge was that workers of the world should unite – under National Socialism. There were other propaganda stations aimed at special interests: a 'Peace' station, aimed at the 'Christian Peace Movement', and of course, separate radio stations aimed at Ireland and Scotland, Irland-Redaktion and Radio Caledonia respectively.

Lord Haw-Haw was listened to with especial enthusiasm in Ireland, even though Irland-Redaktion featured the distinguished writer Francis Stuart, as well as broadcasts in the Irish language. But Irland-Redaktion lacked the common touch, and although Stuart's broadcasts are historically interesting, he never achieved the 'market penetration', as it is now termed, of Lord Haw-Haw.[24]

Whoops of joy and loud cheers often greeted Lord Haw-Haw's commentaries in the land of his ancestors. Announcements from Berlin that a British ship had been attacked were met with approbation, particularly in the west of Ireland:

> According to reports just received, four British merchantmen sailing in convoy were attacked by German long-range reconnaissance planes yesterday a hundred and eighty miles west of Ireland. One merchantman of about seven thousand tons was sunk and another … severely damaged.[25]

Such news was greeted with a huge chorus of 'Hooray!' It may seem unkind to us now that people could cheer at the news that ships were sunk and men's lives lost, but such things often occurred in the context of war, when moral sensibilities are somehow suspended. When the Royal Air Force pulverised Cologne, destroying many beautiful monuments and killing many thousands, the news was greeted with 'jubiliation' in Britain. Only a few older people said they were sorry for civilians such as women and children.[26]

In Ireland, the long memories of Irish peasants being

evicted from their wretched cabins by the British redcoats, or the famines which swept the land at a time that the United Kingdom was the world's richest imperial power, had embittered the Irish mentality, which now savoured a sense of long-delayed retribution.

It has to be added, of course, that Radio Éireann, as Irish state radio was then called, was even duller and more colourless than the BBC in 1939–40; anything provocative seemed a lively contrast. The BBC would not permit dance music on Sunday; Radio Éireann, which took advertising, would not allow lipstick adverts at any time, on the grounds that only fallen women painted themselves. De Valera also shared Hitler's view that jazz was 'degenerate' and, even more offensively, 'nigger music': it was not permitted on Irish radio until well into the 1950s.[27]

᪐

If William and Margaret had been quite timid and uncertain – untypically for William – when they had been wandering about Berlin wondering what to do with themselves, that mood soon disappeared. But once installed in the German broadcasting headquarters – with an office in the old International Programme Exchange on Kaiserdamm (later to move to the Expressionist Haus des Rundfunks in Charlottenburg) – William's ebullience returned. He had started by reading the news, handed to him by the scribes of the 'Englische Redaktion', but soon he was suggesting alterations, making improvements on the sometimes stiff and over-formal English ordained by the broadcasting bosses.[28]

William went into his tutorly mode and even began correcting the work of other English-language presenters. This may have been justified, since the BBC, which monitored the output of German radio from September 1939, had occasion to observe that some of the Reich's broadcasters were not altogether up to standard, or that they stammered and seemed less than fluent. William would have enjoyed putting his colleagues right on matters of grammar and syntax.

Although William Joyce always worked to the orders of his superiors – who, in turn, sought to please Goebbels – he gradually gained more authority over his own scripts. He was perceived to be hard-working by the Germans, and while there were many specialists with formal knowledge of British affairs, William had the tabloid journalist's feel for background information. He knew the gossip about political figures such as Duff Cooper and Samuel Hoare, and made use of it. He also had an unrivalled knowledge of the topography of British life.

It was also said that Joyce made allusions to Ireland, although this has proved impossible to verify. He was supposed to have referred in a broadcast to 'the tinkers in the Ballygaddy Road in Tuam': this was repeated with a great sense of wonder since it showed that Lord Haw-Haw *knew* the Ballygaddy Road in Tuam, and knew that the travelling folk indeed had encampments there at the time.[29] He was also said to mention specific fields in the west of Ireland which belonged to specific, named persons. But it is difficult to know where William's undoubtedly fine knowledge of topography shades into urban myth and legend: indeed, legends arose about Lord Haw-Haw's pronouncements that had more to do with wartime rumour than reported speech.

There arose, in Britain, a legend that Lord Haw-Haw possessed occult powers of omniscience and prophesy: when the bombing began, in September 1940, it was believed that he knew in advance when a certain town was going to be bombed. Mrs Ivy Makin of Manchester, for example, recollected Lord Haw-Haw saying: 'Tonight, our bombers will be coming over Stamford Hill and Stoke Newington, so you have that pleasure to look forward to.' Mrs Makin recalled that:

> We looked at each other in horror and sure enough they came that night and they smashed into Stamford Hill. After that, we started listening

nearly every night to this horrible voice, to see what he was saying and, sure enough, he would mention places like Battersea Power Station, the Oval at Kennington and even one night he said something about Buckingham Palace.[30]

Older readers of the *Daily Express* sent me their recollections of listening to Haw-Haw's 'predictions' during the wartime period. 'We used to listen to the radio every night,' said A. A. Osborne of Sheldon in Birmingham, 'and Lord Haw-Haw had a regular spot every night. He would tell you where you would be bombed, telling you roads and streets which would be bombed, and believe me he was not far out.' Jim Sargant from Hockley in Essex, who grew up in a small village called Stock, between Chelmsford and Billericay, had an extraordinary anecdote from the Haw-Haw legend. He wrote that one morning

> Mum was hanging out the washing and talking over the fence to Mrs Keeble and Mrs Curtis in the next-door gardens, who were doing likewise, when three or four aircraft came out of the sunlight to the east, flying very low over the rooftops. The ladies waved towels or whatever else they had in their hands at that moment. As a laugh, we often used to listen to William Joyce, known as Lord Haw-Haw, who used to broadcast enemy propaganda to Britain from Germany. That evening in his plummy voice, he announced: 'Garman planes flying low over East Angliar today reported housewives waving to them in their gardens.'

The spelling, Mr Sargant adds, is an attempt to indicate the way Haw-Haw spoke.

People came to believe that Lord Haw-Haw not only knew who and what would be bombed – they ascribed to Haw-Haw more power than Reichs-Marschall Goering. At one point in hostilities, it was said that Lord Haw-Haw would 'spare' Glasgow from air raids for five days to give people time to bury their dead. And residents of Glasgow organised their schedules according to the five days' grace that Lord Haw-Haw was supposed to have granted them.[31]

It is true that Haw-Haw was sometimes in possession of information about British prisoners of war, for example, before the British authorities were. Names and addresses of captured British soldiers, sailors and airmen were regularly given out over German radio: these details were seldom inaccurate. For example, Ken Hutchinson of Sale in Cheshire was captured in Libya and 'a German officer took my name and said it would be broadcast so my parents would know I was safe. It was. Lord Haw-Haw persuaded many people to listen to his broadcasts as he read out names of prisoners of war.' Ken's father was a Methodist minister and 'two members of his congregation heard the broadcast and passed on the news to him. This was three or four weeks before the official notification letter arrived reporting me as missing.'[32]

Yet it is clear that Lord Haw-Haw never said some of the things he is supposed to have said. Rumours abound in wartime, especially when news itself is subjected to a degree of censorship. Astrology, recourse to spiritualism, psychics and seances all grow more popular too. Haw-Haw was at the centre of a rumour factory, and in a couple of cases, the British authorities even discovered that people had started 'Haw-Haw rumours' deliberately – perhaps for the same reason that people make hoax '999' calls.[33] According to Martin Doherty, who has published an authoritatative study of Nazi wartime propaganda:

> Normally the [Haw-Haw] rumours took the form of a story that Haw-Haw had referred to some particular town or village and, by mentioning an item of purely local interest, revealed his detailed knowledge of British life and geography – a town-hall clock five minutes slow at Eastbourne, a card school in a munitions factory disrupted by a

German raid, a reference to the Golden Teapot (an
advertising sign) in Londonderry.[34]

It was rumoured that German planes would bomb a
military camp at Honiton, Devon, because Haw-Haw had
announced it. He was also alleged to have mentioned new
buildings at Bradford Grammar School; that he had said that
Fry's factory in Surrey would be a target. In December 1940,
'Haw-Haw rumours were reported to be "extremely prev-
alent",' according to Home Intelligence. Blitzes were
predicted for a range of cities and towns; there were also
rumours that Manchester and Hull would be spared, for
reasons of German strategy. (Manchester was rumoured to be
a candidate as Hitler's 'capital' in the event of an invasion.)
Sheffield, Bognor, Barrow-in-Furness, Oxford and
Tunbridge Wells were also rife with rumours about what
Lord Haw-Haw had allegedly said.

There is a famous urban legend about William Joyce
specialising in mentioning the village or church clock in a
certain locality. But in the official monitors of Joyce's
broadcasts, there is absolutely no mention of particular
clocks being slow or fast. All the experts who have examined
the archives of German radio broadcasts have concluded that
Haw-Haw never made any of these statements about clocks,
or factory sites, or predictions of specific towns as targets.
Terry Charman of the Imperial War Museum, a leading
authority on German propaganda during the Second World
War, says: 'It just never happened. He never said any of these
things.'[35] The BBC personnel and expert stenographers who
recorded the Haw-Haw broadcasts in shorthand and then
transcribed the notes made the same point.[36]

Joyce certainly referred to places that he knew in Britain,
such as Liverpool and Lancashire. He also gave warning
about 'Britain's Danger Zones':

Durham, for instance, contains military objectives
of all sorts. The explosives factories at Birmingham

have already been raided by Germany aeroplanes,
and there are, in addition, other factories such as
Seaham and Bransteth, and armament works in
other parts of the country.[37]

He announced that: 'Absolute safety can be found
nowhere, but there are two or three areas which may be
considered as safer than others.'[38] Here he mentioned central
and north Wales, Perth and Argyle.

Yet, as a Hollywood producer once said, whenever con-
fronted with a clash between truth and legend, the public
generally prefers the legend. The Haw-Haw legend has
persisted quite remarkably. Anywhere you go in Britain, even
today, there is a Haw-Haw story within almost any given
locality: tales are told about William Joyce's alleged super-
natural knowledge about the punctuality of the town clock,
the local promenade or the secret card-games played at a
certain factory. At Whitchurch in Shropshire, there is said to
be a public clock which once had a secret link with 'Lord
Haw-Haw' which has never been satisfactorily explained.[39]

And so, from the obscurity of their washed-up, even
bohemian life, William and Margaret were suddenly
successful radio performers: within a year of arriving in Berlin
without any plans, they had become relatively well paid. By
1940, William was earning 1,200 Reichsmarks a month, with
some bonuses. Lesser stars, including Baillie-Stewart, were
getting between 400 and 600 Reichsmarks; secretaries at the
Rundfunkhaus, who were educated women with bilingual
skills, earned a mere 198 Reichsmarks a month.[40]

And there must have been some gratification, for
William, to have been such a celebrity in England, especially
after being rebuffed so often before. His parents were not
best pleased about William's notoriety as 'Lord Haw-Haw' –
though, as has been noted, his mother was more forgiving

than his father. Michael Joyce thought the entire business deplorable. Queenie suffered on account of William's latest career move, but she still felt loyal to William and loving towards him.[41] Quentin, sequestered at His Majesty's Pleasure, was not permitted to listen to the radio at all. He only learned, through the grapevine, that William was broadcasting for Germany.

Although Joyce never met Goebbels, word got around that the Propaganda Minister was pleased with his performance. Indeed, Hitler was duly informed. 'I tell the Führer about Lord Haw-Haw's success, which is really astonishing,' Reichsminister Goebbels noted in his diary in March 1940. 'He praises our foreign propaganda.'[42] Throughout 1940, indeed, Joseph Goebbels heaps praise on William's work: 'The English are lying to the heavens again, but our Lord Haw-Haw is always ready with an answer for them.'[43] 'That boy's all right! And besides, totally incorruptible.'[44] The Nazi propaganda chief successively described Lord Haw-Haw as 'magnificent' and 'the best horse in my stable'.[45]

By 1940, William's stock was high within the Reichsrundfunk. He had no difficulty in roping Margaret into the act, suggesting that she should broadcast on 'women's issues'. Margaret was growing bored, anyway, staying at home in their modest lodgings, and she did not tolerate boredom easily. She was successfully enlisted, and soon the BBC Monitors began to refer to a genteel *Brief Encounter* type of Englishwoman's voice as 'Lady Haw-Haw'. The role was in fact played by several other Englishwomen broadcasting from Germany on behalf of the Reich.

One of those who was perhaps most often the voice of Lady Haw-Haw was sixty-year-old Margaret Bothamley, who had held a London salon in the 1930s that attracted, in particular, anti-Communists and anti-Semites. She subsequently took herself off to Berlin. Dressed in a Queen Mary toque, beads and drifting finery, she made a bewildering impression on the propagandists of Charlottenburg.[46]

There was also a girl from Jersey, Pearl Joyce Vardon, who had fallen in love with a German officer and impetuously followed him to Berlin. She became a Nazi more from motives of amorous passion than from political ideology, and was hired by the RRG to do some announcing.[47] But Margaret Joyce was certainly one of the Lady Haw-Haw voices, regularly heard on a Tuesday. Much later, Margaret, as William's consort, emerged as the historic 'Lady Haw-Haw': when official papers were released about Margaret Joyce in 1998, the British media called her 'Lady Haw-Haw', as though the title were endorsed by *Debrett's Peerage.*

'Lady Haw-Haw' could be a silly creature, wittering about the pretty clothes available on the Kurfürstendamm, or she could echo Lord Haw-Haw's themes about the living conditions of the poor in England:

> The condition of the poor in England is worse than ever before … Can it be worse when an old woman, scarcely able to stand, must go around picking up bits of garbage in order to make herself a meal? Can it be worse than when children can't go to school on a wet day because they have no shoes? Can it be worse when more than eighteen millions are undernourished?[48]

William and Margaret were a kind of 'power couple' in the hierarchy of Hitler's broadcasters.

William was, Francis Stuart recalled afterwards,

> treated quite regally, which gave me the impression that the Germans thought a great deal of him. As far as I know – I heard this from others – he got rations which the diplomats only got. We got very meagre rations. I think he was highly thought of.[49]

In his autobiographical novel *Black List, Section H*, Stuart describes Joyce sitting in a restaurant known as the *Funk-Eck*, on the corner of the Adolf-Hitler Platz (now the Theodor-Heuss Platz) in Charlottenburg. A character in the book

> pointed out William Joyce to him at a table with others in an inner room, round reddish face with a scar down the cheek, and because of the awe in which he seemed to be held, he supposed must be somebody of great importance in England ...[50]

The restaurant was bombed out during hostilities, but another has arisen in its place as the Biergarten La Torre III. Employees of the Rundfunkhaus – which became dilapidated during the cold-war years, but is now restored to its original glory – still go there for lunch.

People in Berlin generally deferred to William Joyce as the 'Lord Haw-Haw' so much admired by Herr Goebbels, observed John O'Reilly, an Irishman with a picaresque background himself, whose policeman father had arrested Roger Casement in 1916. O'Reilly worked with *Irland-Redaktion* and had an office near Joyce's. He saw William as a bit of an enigma: the professional gasbag could be taciturn in private, and quite stand-offish among his colleagues. William also did himself few favours in terms of his appearance: as well as having unprepossessing looks, his clothes were scruffy. 'Joyce had few friends among the English-speaking colony in Berlin,' wrote O'Reilly.

> He was of a reserved disposition, and I believe I was one of the few people with whom he associated freely, though not talkatively.
> He expressed himself contemptuously about his English associates in the English section. On one occasion he referred to them as 'a bunch of opportunists who had offered their services to Germany in order to avoid the comparative discomforts of a German internment camp.'[51]

He was, O'Reilly continued, 'no less disparaging of those loud-voice, overdressed Yankees who barged and bellowed their way through the restrained atmosphere of the Rundfunkhaus.' There was, indeed, an ensemble of Americans, including Douglas Chandler, known as 'Paul Revere', Leo Delaney, Donald Day, Jane Anderson and Constance Drexler, broadcasting pro-Axis views from Berlin.[52]

Among the occasional contributors to the pro-German airwaves broadcast to America was the poet Ezra Pound, who broadcast from Italy. Pound sent effusive fan letters to William, which the latter treated rather coolly. Pound had been living in Rapallo in Italy since 1908, and was a committed follower of Mussolini, an anti-Semite and a Fascist. His letters to William, bashed out on an old typewriter, the frayed ribbon half-red and half-black, are full of admiration and enthusiasm for the Fascist cause.[53] Pound wrote that he always listened to William and that he would love it if William would sometimes listen to him, and proffer criticism. In his letters to William, Pound refers to the Jews as 'the yidds' and 'the kikes' and signs off 'HEUL [sic] HITLER and nach Vladivostock'. William's replies to these letters are extremely non-committal: he says he is too busy to write Ezra a long letter, but he is duly thankful for the letters he has received. But Pound fired off numerous missives to Joyce – often written in a strange kind of blank verse, and often with his pen dipped in vitriol ('that cunt of all infamy Roosevelt') – but it is clearly an overture to friendship. William, sensing that Pound is even odder than he is, keeps his distance; the Germans were impressed all the same by the status of the correspondent.

John O'Reilly warmed more to Margaret than to William – but then, men liked Margaret. 'She was a complete contrast to Joyce both in physique and temperament,' O'Reilly said. 'She was a tall, good-looking woman with flaming red hair. She was vivacious and ... was ever ready to welcome congenial company.' He described her as 'gay' (in the old-fashioned sense of that word) and 'irrepressible'.

William – who was called 'Bill' by John O'Reilly, and by some other colleagues – himself preferred the company of an American who was not pro-Nazi: William Shirer, the noted American foreign correspondent for the *Chicago Tribune* and later for CBS. Shirer afterwards published vivid diaries about his life in Berlin, as well as his classic *The Rise and Fall of the Third Reich*. At first, William Shirer shunned the other William, condemning him as a traitor and pro-Nazi; yet he came to admire Haw-Haw's 'guts', especially when bombs began to fall on Berlin – William didn't give a damn. Shirer also found Joyce a gregarious drinking companion 'with Irish eyes that twinkle'. Shirer noticed how hard Joyce worked: the latter was forever banging away at his typewriter, giving hell to the 'plutocrats' and 'capitalists' who, he believed, ground the face of the poor.[54]

By the summer of 1940, in addition to his radio work of writing and broadcasting, William was putting together a book with the Wagnerian title *Dämmerung Über England* ('Twilight Over England'). The book was published that September, by the German Foreign Office: a hundred thousand copies were printed. The work is a collection of recycled articles which he had published, during the 1930s, in *Action* and *The Blackshirt*. He always kept some of his old clippings with him in Germany.

Twilight Over England is the authentic voice of William Joyce, Lord Haw-Haw: it is in parts articulate and well informed; in parts irksome, overwrought and pathologically anti-Semitic, to the point of grinding tedium. Shirer described it as 'a hodgepodge of Nazi nonsense about England, studded with obvious truths about its blacker and meaner side.' Yet the book contains a chillingly prophetic passage, written half in irony, and half in sincere avowal:

> When the writer is a daily perpetrator of High Treason, his introductory remarks may command

> from the English public that kind of awful
> veneration with which [highly paid] confessions are
> perused in the Sunday newspapers, quite frequently
> after the narrator has taken his last leap in the dark.

Twilight Over England was republished by the Imperial War Museum in 1992 in facsimile form, forty-six years after the narrator had himself taken his 'last leap in the dark' – for high treason.

Although William was a great success in Germany, and was *the* media star of the Third Reich, throughout much of 1940 he seems to have entertained the fantasy that he might return to England, as a friendly Fascist, when the war was over. And there were indeed plans for him to do so, when the Reich had prevailed. In 1940, he told a British-born colleague, Richard Kupsch: 'A year from now, we will be eating as the guests of a grateful nation.'[55] There were plans to invade the United Kingdom – and Ireland – which the Reichsrundfunk broadcasters took to be imminent in June and July of 1940. In fact, Hitler had an invasion pencilled in for 3 September.

The capture of the Channel Islands in July 1940 was regarded as a fine augury: 'for the first time in history German soldiers have landed on British soil. They met with no resistance,' Lord Haw-Haw said. British refugees were reported to be

> pouring into Dublin and Killarney … There is a
> real danger that people of moderate means may be
> tempted to go to Ireland and stay there. We should
> strongly advise them against any such course. There
> are grave indications that Ireland may be
> transformed into a theatre of war without a
> moment's notice.[56]

Both Britain and Ireland would almost certainly have been invaded had it not been for the extraordinary defence put up by the Royal Air Force in the Battle of Britain, from June to September of 1940. Although much outnumbered, the RAF

Spitfires and Hurricanes went hell for leather against the Luftwaffe's Messerschmidts and Heinkels. Had Reichs-Marschall Goering not decided to switch from aerial battle to aerial *Blitz* over British cities in September 1940, the RAF might indeed have been eventually defeated. The moment for invading Britain passed, and William's fantasy about returning to England in glory necessarily faded from this time on.

9

Life in Berlin

*'Growing up in wartime Berlin, I clearly recall
the atmosphere of unity all around and also the
feeling of well-being it gave me ... it was the
only time in my life I had no doubt that I
belonged.'*

Katrin Fitzherbert, *True to Both My Selves*

In their first days in Berlin, William and Margaret had stayed
in a hotel; they soon moved into a lodging house, near the
Kurfurstendamm. The landlady was friendly, and rushed
into their room soon after midday on 3 September, crying:
'*Jetzt es is Krieg mit England!*' ('Now there is a war with
England!') Then William and Margaret, the landlady and her
husband all shook hands and vowed that 'Whatever happens,
we remain friends'. William reported that not a single
German that he met wanted a war with Britain.[1] Unlike in
1914, there was no joyful welcome for war among the
populace. Indeed, many Germans thought that now that
Poland had been conquered, the war was virtually over. They
only wanted Danzig back, didn't they? Constant 'peace
rumours' broke out in Berlin in 1939–40, when word would
go around that a peace had been negotiated.[2]

Life in Berlin during the early phase of the Second World War was not unpleasant. 'Enemies of the state' or political prisoners were in a different category, but for supporters of the Reich it was a time of infectious optimism. James Clark, who was an impressionable teenager at the time, found the whole tableau of the Reich stunningly glamorous, and Hitler's presence was to many people a comforting reassurance that everything would always be all right.

While the Third Reich turned out to be an atrocious regime, many reporters, not sympathetic to Hitler's Germany, had been impressed by it. 'On first glance, Germany was overwhelmingly attractive, and first impressions disarmed many a hardy anti-Nazi,' wrote an American journalist, Howard K. Smith.

> Germany was clean, it was neat, a truly handsome land … You could search far and wide through Berlin's sea of houses or Hamburg's huge harbour district, but you could never find a slum or anything approaching one … People looked good. Nobody was in rags, not a single citizen. They were well dressed, if not stylishly dressed. And they were well fed. The impression was one of order, cleanliness and prosperity.[3]

William's propaganda boasts, over the radio, that there were no slums in Germany, that you didn't see poor and wretched people begging on the streets, that Germans had much better teeth and free dental care than English people[4] and that German workers could visit spas for the sake of their health were not without foundation.

William and Margaret had chosen a new life, and it did not seem to be a bad one. Although rationing was imposed, from September 1939, and there were night-time blackouts, there were no significant air raids on Berlin for the first year of the war and the normal life of the city continued more or less undisturbed. There was music in the Berlin parks, and shopping in the Kurfürstendamm – Margaret Joyce reported on purchases of washable silk frocks, 'remarkably cheap', and the availability of cyclamen stockings that are 'so bright and gay'.[5] Clothing rations would come later.

It was of course regrettable for the Joyces that once hostilities began, any further contact with Britain was almost impossible. There were no direct postal services between Britain and Germany, only an indirect route via Switzerland. British newspapers arrived via Stockholm, or through Lisbon, but these were of course subject to censorship at source.

In late 1939, William and Margaret moved into a room in the Steifansandstrasse, a tiny street a short walk from the Kaiserdamm, by the Sophie-Charlotte Platz on the U-bahn. The landlady was an eccentric Viennese who rather doted on William but refused his request for a daily bath.[6] The couple ate out a lot and William developed a special liking for a bar–restaurant called Haffners. They also discovered the Press Club at Leipziger Platz, near the Potsdamer Platz underground station: this would be their most frequent meeting place over the following five and a half years. William also liked the *Funk-Eck*, where Francis Stuart had described seeing him: this typically German hostelry welcomed many Funkhaus staff and performers, and Herr Peters, the head cook, had a fine reputation.[7] Indeed, in the first year, William and Margaret were constantly having drinks and meals at Kempinskis, Zum Krone and the Bristol Hotel. Margaret also frequented Gerolds on the Kurfürstendamm, and occasionally the Adlon and the Kaiserhof.

Although her German was not very good, Margaret made more friends in Berlin than William. She was a gregarious type, while he, despite his convivial moments, was still a bit of an oddity: in a behatted age, William always refused to wear a hat. He strode around Berlin in a trench coat, looking like an old IRA man, and carrying a walking stick which bore more than a passing resemblance to a shillelagh.[8] He struck the teenage James Clark as 'fake British, who led an Irish kind of life' in those Berlin years.

In England, William had been so frequently in trouble, and Margaret had been so fervid in supporting his outsider status and Fascist stance, that there had been a togetherness in their marriage: *contra mundum* – 'against the world'. But in Berlin, William was no longer 'agin the government': he was now part of the Establishment.[9] And the basic incompatibilities in their temperaments – and needs – soon emerged.

William liked to work a lot, then to smoke, drink, talk and walk. He was interested in politics, music, chess and reading, but he was indifferent to his domestic surroundings, didn't care for the movies – a great passion in Berlin – and didn't much like parties. He once told Margaret that he found people at parties so predictable – he knew what they were going to say before they opened their mouths. In some respects, his quick brain cut him off from company.

William also had problems at work, despite his grandiose status as Lord Haw-Haw. He was constantly engaged in battles with his bosses about what was and was not allowed to be broadcast. The daily instructions would come from Goebbels' ministry; some of these William considered absurd. Strangely enough, the Third Reich was not run with clockwork efficiency: in the broadcasting field there were constant inefficiencies and incidences of incompetence. Margaret understood that William's nerves were sometimes frazzled by these stresses, but on the other hand she felt annoyed by the situation.

Margaret was outgoing and feminine, and she loved parties and dancing and meeting people. She liked attention from men, and wanted more attention from her husband. She was sometimes lonely and restless, and she, like William, was fond of drink. It was not surprising that the marriage began to fray: Margaret wanted more fun, more attention and – her diaries imply – quite possibly more sex. She often complained that he was sexually 'prudish', for which she blamed his twin inheritance: his Catholic Jesuit education and his Ulster Protestant puritanism. Sexual inhibition is often more a question of temperament than culture: it is possible that William simply had a lower libido than Margaret. He found her mocking and irksome and called her a 'whore'.[10] British Intelligence regarded her as a bit of a good-time girl, which was, at this time, a public-schoolboy euphemism for a nymphomaniac.

Their relationship became quarrelsome and turbulent. William was verbally, and sometimes physically, abusive to her; he certainly admits to shaking her violently on occasions and she said he was sexually jealous and occasionally resorted to beatings. 'Angry because I was late for lunch,' she writes, 'angry because I was not in bed when he came home – he hit me.'[11] William was repeating the pattern of behaviour with his first wife, Hazel, who found his outbursts of temper unbearable. But Margaret could be capricious too. Men fell for Margaret, and on an impulse – or perhaps wanting attention – she would respond to their overtures. She records one episode when, after she had gone off with a young man who was smitten with her, William was incoherent with rage and yet 'extremely gentle'. He just continually asked her, over a period of three or four days: 'How could you?' 'What made you?' 'Is he better than I am?' and other pleadings of the rejected swain.

The stormy marriage of William and Margaret was made worse by living in one-room apartments, although by 1940 they could have afforded better. William would come home late, knock back a couple of schnapps – and then reach for his typewriter. Margaret would fly into a rage and complain that he neglected her. She had been given an office in a different part of town from William's: it was at the Kochstresse in the downtown part of Berlin – whereas William's working area was always in and around Charlottenburg, on the western side of the city. Their vehement quarrels were not unusually followed by 'grand re-unions'. Margaret seemed to like, and even to provoke,

William's displays of jealousy: 'Grand union scene with Will who at last showed faint glimmerings of jealousy.'[12]

In July 1940, William's British passport – temporarily renewed in August 1939 – ran out. An officer of the Gestapo appeared at William's office announcing that the authorities were in the process of conferring German citizenship on the Joyces, and that their papers would shortly be available. They became German citizens on 26 September 1940 and went off to the swish Kaiserhof Hotel to celebrate – and libate, naturally. The couple now acquired the German name 'Fröhlich', being an approximate – but false – translation of 'Joyce'. 'Fröhlich' is a play on the word 'joyful', but the Irish surname 'Joyce' is merely a transliteration of the Irish 'Seoige' (a proper name). Coincidentally – or perhaps predictably, since we often unwittingly follow in our parents' footsteps – William changed nationality just as his father had done. He was six years older than his father had been at his legal switch of allegiance. It is an act of treason for a British citizen to take the nationality of the enemy in wartime; but William Joyce had never actually been a British citizen.

Margaret began staying late at her office, to avoid going home. This soon led to more drinks with colleagues, and then, not unexpectedly, to a flirtation, and then an affair with an attractive German officer, named Nicky von Besack, one of the old Baltic squirearchy. In February 1940, during a 'Phoney War' episode in the North Sea, Berlin's English-speaking editors had been short-staffed, and von Besack was among those called in to help. Margaret had met him just four days previously at a lunch party, and noted his good looks. Even in the bleakest circumstances, Margaret always observed when a man was handsome: it was strange that she had chosen William as a husband, after all. Nicky spoke excellent English and was also a Wehrmacht intelligence officer.[13] From April 1940, Margaret recorded in her diary frequent explosions between herself and 'Will', as she called her husband. It is also clear that the relationship between Nicky and herself was becoming intimate, and throughout 1940 Margaret became more and more obsessed with Nicky, who was no slouch either when it came to liquor: 'Nicky came around looking very well but very drunk.'[14]

Life was very busy for the Joyces. Margaret always seemed to be in a social whirl – she went to the opera, to lunch, tea and supper with friends – and William had his political business to attend to. In January 1941, he was asked to visit a British prisoner-of-war camp at Thorn, in Wartegau, to interview and possibly recruit men who might join the radio service and speak to England. Word had got around that some of the men there were former 'Mosley men' and might be ready to serve National Socialism in exchange for a pleasant billet and an easier way of life. William had not travelled much in Germany, and quite relished the trip: he saw nothing dishonourable or traitorous in luring imprisoned soldiers to speak for the Third Reich against Britain.[15] In fact, he was – though unaware of it himself – following in the footsteps of Roger Casement, who had tried to lure Irishmen to join an Irish rising against the Crown during the 1914–18 war.

William's identity was kept hush-hush, but celebrity is celebrity: he was quite taken aback when one young man rushed out of the interview hut calling out to the whole camp: 'I've just been talking to Lord Haw-Haw!' Among the men he persuaded to serve the Reichsrundfunk were Leslie Banning and Walter Purdy, who had formerly been Blackshirts; William Humphrey Griffiths, who supplied a strong proletarian voice for Workers' Challenge; and Cyril Charles Hoskins, who stipulated that he would not say anything directly anti-British.[16]

Despite the strains in their marriage, William and Margaret moved to a lovely new apartment in February 1941, at 29 Kastanien-Allee, which means 'Chestnut Avenue'.

William had been paid 10,000 Reichsmarks (the equivalent of about £500, a handsome sum of money at the time) by the publisher Santoro for *Twilight Over England* and they could afford to live in a prettier residence. (They did not buy the property – such was seldom the practice in Continental Europe. They rented from a landlady, who provided them with breakfast.) Kastanien-Allee is a charming, tree-lined street, not far from the Rundfunkhaus and halfway between it and the magnificent stadium built for the 1936 Olympics (immortalised by the film-maker Leni Riefenstahl). The 'secret stations' of German broadcasting, which went under the name of 'Concordia', were soon to be transferred to the spacious arcades of the Olympic stadium; Margaret's office would also be moved there.[17] For William, the apartment's main attraction was that it had room for plenty of books.

William's father, Michael Joyce, would have been pleased to see Kastanien-Allee: he always liked a good address. William and Margaret now learned of old Michael Joyce's sudden death, which had occurred on 19 February 1941. They heard the news the following Monday, just as they were moving into their smart new home.[18]

The end of Michael Joyce's life had seen the crumbling of so many of his ambitions. He and Queenie, along with Joan and their youngest son, Robert, had had to move out of 7 Allison Grove, Dulwich, because a German bomb had fallen nearby. The family had been rehoused in a flat nearby, at 86 Underhill Road. After all his aspirations, and all his sleight-of-hand to further them, for both himself and his family, the end of his life was pitiful. Money was short: Michael, who had been flush with funds coming back from America, and had been a well-respected man of property in Galway, was now working as a door-to-door vacuum salesman.[19]

To his credit, he did not complain about this: he and Queenie still felt bitter that events in Ireland had robbed them of their social and financial position; yet, while there was work to do, Michael did it. He wrote cheerful letters to his son Quentin, sequestered in prison under Regulation 18B: 'Do not worry about us, we are too much alive to starve. Joan and I are working and that keeps the wolf off.'[20] He hoped that Robert, who had been dismissed from his trainee job at the BBC because of his connection with William, would 'find something soon'.[21] Joan had been working for the Regional Food Office – part of the Ministry of Food – but was also fired when it was discovered that she was the sister of 'Lord Haw-Haw' and that she had a brother interned under 18B.[22] Joan subsequently found work as a seamstress.

On that Wednesday in February, Joan had been with her father in the Dulwich flat: she heard the siren and the approach of an enemy aircraft. She shouted to Michael, soon after another bomb fell in the Dulwich area: 'Look out, this one is coming our way!' and dived under a table. Michael suddenly had a heart attack, and died. The bomb did not touch the building. The fright did it for him, though heart disease was the organic cause of his death. He was seventy-four.

Quentin, who was at this time in York Internment Camp, was not permitted to attend his father's funeral, although, of course, there was still no charge against him.[23] He had not seen his father since the last family visit to Wandsworth Jail in December 1939. Frank Joyce was also held under Regulation 18B at this time, although he would be released in the spring of 1941, after eleven months.[24] Queenie, who had been an heiress less than twenty-five years previously, and had inherited the equivalent of a quarter of a million pounds, was now in straitened circumstances.

She did not have enough money to cover the funeral expenses of her husband; she also felt tormented by the way the press covered her husband's death. A newspaper published what Quentin described as a 'doctored' photograph of Michael in his coffin.[25]

William learned of his father's death through a foreign press report. He doesn't seem to have been particularly close to his father, but it almost certainly gave him pause for thought and made him worry, as Quentin did, about the plight of his widowed mother. William also knew at this time that Quentin was sequestered under 18B. So was Angus Macnab. A woman called Anna Wolkoff – a White Russian and Fascist sympathiser well known in London – had sent messages to William Joyce through a circuitous and leaky espionage route giving news of family and friends. She was charged, in London, in 1940, with offences against Defence Regulations and sentenced to ten years in prison. The case became notorious because it revealed that a cipher clerk at the American embassy in London, Tyler Kent, was passing on the details of secret exchanges between Churchill and Roosevelt.[26]

William and Margaret were hardly installed in their grand new apartment at Kastanien-Allee when, in the spring of 1941, they began living apart. It seems to have been at William's request. He knew Margaret was seeing more of Nicky. William remained in the apartment and Margaret moved in with a friend in Bülow Strasse, in the Schöneberg area, on the other side of town. For a break, Margaret took herself off for a month or so to the city of Danzig – now Gdansk. She arranged lodgings and made connections, as she always did, and found herself listening to William on the wireless. It was at this point that he announced himself as 'William Joyce, otherwise known as Lord Haw-Haw'. He had his own byline at last, and Margaret was pleased for him all the same. However much she quarrelled with her husband, she was always very proud of his achievments.

When Margaret was in the Danzig area, she saw, for the first and only time, a column of prisoners from a concentration camp in the neighbourhood. She observed that most looked Jewish. It was her only direct contact with anyone from a concentration camp, and she was glad she was in a car and moving fast.[27]

Divorce proceedings commenced. Although William was angry with Margaret for her philanderings, and said he would never trust a woman again,[28] he remained 'quite kind' to her, she notes, and he still wanted to see her for lunch or dinner. He would quite often arrange a rendezvous in town, but annoyed her by refusing to take her to the Press Club, at Leipziger Platz, because she was no longer his wife. Perhaps both of them also enjoyed the element of intrigue. In June, William stormed out of a restaurant after Margaret admitted she'd spent a night of passion with Nicky: 'He told me what he thought of me and then said goodbye.'[29]

The German divorce had to be discreet because the Führer did not approve of the dissolution of a marriage. Joseph Goebbels, also had to feign a disapprobation he can scarcely have felt. Goebbels had a voracious sexual appetite, particularly for film stars, and had fallen in love with the Czech actress Lidia Baarova in 1936. He had planned to divorce his wife, Magda, by whom he had four – later six – golden-haired children. Since Hitler was unmarried ('married to Germany', was his excuse), Magda assumed the role of First Lady of the Reich. Goebbels was forbidden to divorce, and fell into the Führer's bad books for a time. In a bid to re-ingratiate himself with his leader, Goebbels promulgated – with the fiendish Reinhard Heydrich, later deservedly assassinated by the Czechs, although with horrible reprisals – the notorious 'Kristallnacht'[30] in November 1938. Having thus purged his own guilt by tormenting the Jews, Goebbels was duly readmitted to Hitler's favour.[31] Divorce between Joseph and Magda Goebbels was never mentioned again, and others in Nazi circles took their cue. William did not want Goebbels to get wind of his own marital difficulties.

The Joyce divorce was accordingly conducted as quietly as possible. Despite the regime's general disapproval of divorce, in one respect the procedure was liberal: since 1938 the Third Reich had permitted an easy dissolution of marriage where no children were involved. The Joyce case was heard on 12 August 1941; strings were pulled and the lawyers and judge tried to keep proceedings as low-key as possible. The grounds cited were infidelity, on Margaret's part, and cruelty, on William's.[32] Both allegations were justified, but William did not really want to lose Margaret. Nonetheless, he was hurt by Margaret's affair with von Besack: divorce had become a matter of honour.

Once they were outside the courtroom, William and Margaret both burst into tears and fell into each other's arms.[33] To the bewilderment of their lawyers, they then went off arm in arm for lunch at the Kaiserhof Hotel, in Mohrenstrasse. The Kaiserhof – 'of the very highest class', said Baedecker – was Hitler's favourite hotel. (It was destroyed by incendiary bombs in 1943.) After their divorce, William and Margaret became friends again. However, Margaret was now deeply involved with Nick and she made it plain to William. Von Besack himself seems to have been ambivalent: he had recently divorced and signed a paternity order concerning a child he had fathered.[34]

The war had been proceeding with dazzling success for Germany. Over most of the Continent of Europe, with the exception of the Iberian peninsula – which was not unfriendly – neutral Switzerland and Sweden, the Axis powers held sway. Mussolini of Italy had entered the war on Germany's side in June 1940. Britain had escaped invasion by the skin of her teeth and the exceptional valour of the Royal Air Force, but Germany's occupation of Belgium and northern France represented a British nightmare – access to the Channel by an enemy power. The 'New Order' of the swastika was triumphant, and by May 1941, even Winston Churchill was privately extremely depressed: he outlined to his staff a bleak future in which 'Hitler dominated all Europe, Asia and Africa' and in which Britain and America would be subdued into peace on Hitler's terms.

There is a splendid concert hall in the Rundfunkhaus –
'Broadcasting House' – which has been restored to the way it
was in the 1940s. Here, during the Second World War,
musicians would perform wartime concerts broadcast to the
whole Continent. It was also used extensively for rehearsals.

One spring afternoon in 1941, James Clark heard the
sound of music coming from the concert hall, and entered
the upper gallery to satisfy his curiosity. 'I go in,' he recalled.

> The full symphony orchestra is running through a
> tremendous upbeat fanfare, and the conductor is
> pumping it up from take to take, driving the
> performance into the realm of cosmic ecstasy.
> After several times, the waves having risen and
> shattered *con tutti,* I ask a man at the door what
> the piece is. 'The climax at the end of Liszt's *Les
> Preludes,*' he says.

Although James Clark did not know this at the time, this
awesome fanfare had been selected as the musical 'frame' for
the announcement of the invasion of the Soviet Union, and
for every military communiqué that was to follow from the
doomed campaign code-named 'Barbarossa'. James recalls
the amazement he felt at the German thoroughness that
armed a million men for battle and didn't fail to record the
theme music to its triumphal perfection in every radio
loudspeaker in the Reich. Germany had been delayed from
launching the planned spring offensive by unforeseen
involvement in the Balkans and Greece, so it was late June
rather than April when the Wehrmacht marched into Russia,
breaking the Nazi–Soviet pact concocted in August 1939 to
carve up Poland.

When William was captured, in 1945, he gave an
interview to the local Lancashire newspaper from his
mother's home town, the *Oldham Chronicle*, in which he said
that Hitler's great mistake had been to invade Russia.[35]
Hitler had actually invaded on the same day as Napoleon and
made the same error, a hundred and twenty-nine years later.

But in 1941, this had not been the view from Berlin, nor indeed Haw-Haw's own view. In fact, at the time he was delighted, and crowed with pleasure. The 'Barbarossa' campaign was announced with all the glorious fanfare at Franz Liszt's disposal, and was considered a victory almost before it had started. Hitler believed he could flatten the Soviet Union within four months; at one stage, Stalin came near to accepting this assessment.

Lord Haw-Haw was, of course, articulating radio propaganda: the editorial line had been sketched out for him by his direct boss Eduard Dietze, who in turn took the day's 'spin' from Goebbels, or his deputy, at a 'minister conference'. Yet William's authorial voice was full of conviction: it was clear, in these broadcasts, that he believed every word he said, for it perfectly fitted in with his own world-view, which he had outlined so often in the British Fascist newspapers in the 1930s.

'The twenty-ninth of June is recorded indelibly and for all time in the proudest annals of German military achievement,' he announced with joy. 'Its place in history is secure as the day on which the initial victories in a campaign of immeasureable importance was made known.' (Germany moved on 22 June, but the first German communiqués were only given on 29 June.) 'But it must be remembered, even in this hour, that the battle is not for Germany alone. It is for the whole of Europe, and the soul of Europe.'[36] This was certainly Hitler's belief – that his was a pre-emptive strike at Soviet Russia before Russia could 'Bolshevise' Europe.

William echoed his master's voice flawlessly: 'The results of the campaign, so far as they have now emerged, showed beyond any doubt that the Soviet plans for the invasion, subjugation and Bolshevisation of all Europe were nearing completion, when the Führer, with unerring intuition, struck and brought the foulest plot in history to naught.' Two of Stalin's generals, Timoshenko and Zhukov, had, it was true, suggested a pre-emptive strike against Germany in

May 1941, but Stalin had dismissed the notion; he had also ignored the intelligence reports he had received that Germany was about to attack.[37]

Haw-Haw trumpeted Germany's technical superiority, which would allegedly ensure a quick victory. He reeled off statistics about men and machines: 'On the early morning of 22 June, some 160 Red divisions ... the Luftwaffe secured air supremacy ... 1,811 Red machines destroyed at the cost of 35 German planes ... '[38] These were not idle boasts: the Reich's military machine was indeed formidable. The invasion was launched with 3,600 tanks, 600,000 motorised vehicles, 7,000 pieces of artillery, 2,500 aircraft and 625,000 unfortunate horses. Russia was not as ill-defended as was reported, however, and once their war production got under way, it made remarkable headway. Hitler, who was a great admirer of the British Empire, saw Russia as Germany's India: when conquered, it would provide the Reich with all sorts of treasures, and the Germans would run Russia as latter-day *sahibs*.

In Britain, there was a sense of relief, even jubilation, that Russia had now entered the conflict. Communists in Britain, who had until now been advocates of peace and denouncers of the 'imperialist' aims of war, turned overnight into patriotic supporters of war. Subsequently, British people would look ever more benignly on the Communist Party, although they would specify that they preferred home-grown, British Communists rather than foreign Reds.[39]

Lord Haw-Haw now had a new stick with which to beat Winston Churchill. Churchill had himself loathed 'Bolshevism' every bit as much as Joyce until at least 1938, when he began to see that an alliance with Stalin against Hitler might become inevitable. Immediately after the invasion of Russia, Churchill said on the BBC that 'We are resolved to destroy Hitler and every vestige of the Nazi regime ... It follows, therefore, that we shall give whatever help we can to Russia and the Russian people.' William threw himself into an orgy of outrageous anti-Churchill invective – the kind that would have made an entertaining newspaper column in peacetime, taking apart a politician's position: 'Churchill stated "I would pact with the devil to save England." He has pacted with the devil, but the devil is proving as unreliable and unsatisfactory as usual. Churchill has inscribed the hammer and sickle upon the Union Jack.'[40]

Haw-Haw got much propaganda value out of 'the unholy alliance between the premier of Britain and the communist creatures of the Kremlin'. He underlined Soviet atrocities – these certainly existed, as the Katyn massacre in 1940 later revealed – with particular emphasis on attacks against priests and nuns. 'Let Stalin look with his mind's eye on the blood-bespattered faces of the priests and nuns whom his assassins tortured and murdered,' Haw-Haw fulminated. He also denounced the Soviet Union for 'the evil of militant atheism', and 'the criminals of the Kremlin, the enemies of religion, decency and humanity'.[41]

In this line of argument, William Joyce was speaking with his Irish, rather than his English, *geist*: British listeners were not particularly moved either by notions of atheism or by anti-clericalism. But in Ireland, it would, at that time, have aroused people to strong anti-Soviet feelings: the 'godless atheism' of Soviet Communism was strongly denounced by the Irish Church, and by many, if not most, of the Irish people.

William was immensely proud of Germany's successes: he had entered into a zestful feeling of patriotism for the great German Reich, and transferred all the feelings he had once had for the British Empire to Germany. William Shirer noted in September 1940 that when Joyce spoke of the Germans, he used the pronoun 'We' – logically, perhaps, since he now was a naturalised German. But while he crowed with delight about the invasion of Russia – which was to bring unimaginable heartbreak, and to show that the Germans were far from 'thorough' in quite basic elements –

William's real fear was that America would come into the war. By August 1941, he was also privately 'very depressed' – and probably lonely.[42]

Long before it actually occurred, he was alerted to this possibility. When people said to Joyce in 1940 or 1941, 'Herr Joyce, will the war soon be over now?' he replied, 'Yes, I think probably the war will soon be over, as long as America doesn't come in.'[43] The Haw-Haw broadcasts strained every nerve to keep America and Britain apart. Joyce reflected the Reich's strong opposition to President Roosevelt's Lend-Lease Act, passed on 11 March 1941: this gave the United States powers to 'sell, transfer title to, exchange, lease, lend or otherwise dispose of' equipment for the defence of any country associated with the United States' own defence. It seemed a signal of Roosevelt's intention to water down, and finally dissolve, American neutrality.

William's theory was that American capitalism – backed of course by Jewish financiers – was making its bid for world domination: the country was set fair to take over what had been the British Empire. 'Does Uncle Sam really want to save the British Empire for Britain or for Americans?' he asked. 'Does he want the British Empire to be a serious competitor to America or does he want it to be under his control. Your leaders,' he told his British audience, 'are very careful to avoid such questions.'[44]

William was always suspicious of Churchill's closeness to America – Winston was half-American, and had many connections, including financial ones, with the United States – and he believed that Churchill was pursuing every avenue to get FDR on side. He sought, in his broadcasts, wherever possible to drive a wedge between Britain and America.

Joyce perceived that from the spring of 1941 – with the American election well behind Roosevelt – Churchill and Roosevelt were edging closer together. On 9 August 1941, the two men had their first meeting, on board the American cruiser *Augusta,* just off the south coast of Newfoundland. A bond of friendship was established almost immediately. The British–US alliance was sealed by the formation of the 'Atlantic Charter', which was later to become the basis for the United Nations.

Britain needed America's backing: she had already lost more than two thousand ships to German submarines – known as *Unterseeboot,* or U-boats – and aircraft, and many vital foodstuffs and raw materials came to the United Kingdom across the Atlantic. Lord Haw-Haw scoffed at this meeting between the 'plutocracies', the so-called democracies run by money. But privately he knew that good relations between Roosevelt and Churchill were a bad sign for the cause he had so passionately come to espouse: Germany. Even before the Japanese attack on Pearl Harbor, the United States seemed to be moving ever closer to support for Britain at war.

The attack on Pearl Harbor occurred on 7 December 1941; Joyce must have been utterly dismayed by it. Winston Churchill wrote that it was, for him, a moment of 'the greatest joy ... Hitler's fate was sealed'. Joyce must have known, at that moment, that his dreams for the Reich's thousand-year reign were receding out of sight. He certainly confided to Margaret that a war with both Russia and America could scarcely be won. On radio, he treated the Pearl Harbor attack coolly: he played it down, and switched the focus to the Finns, who were, in his view, being delivered into the hands of the Bolsheviks. But he ended on a bitter note:

> Well, England has got her allies now. She has got her losing Bolsheviks and she has got the unprepared Yanks, who can no longer help her as they once did. The Yankees' hands will in future be very full indeed, and so, we think, will England's.[45]

For James Clark, Pearl Harbor shattered his dreams. Until that moment, Clark was a fervent teenage Nazi. He loved everything about the Führer's Germany: he fiercely identified with it, and like a young boy following his favourite football team, marked triumphs on the map where 'his team' had, metaphorically, scored. But Clark remembers so well hearing the news about Pearl Harbor, when the Japanese attacked the American fleet:

> One was always listening to news bulletins in public places, booming away. There was something or other – it wasn't the lead story – on the midday news, blah-blah-blah. It wasn't until we tuned in to the BBC overseas service in the evening, covertly, that we realised that this was Pearl Harbor, in Hawaii, and that Japan had attacked America. And that, for me, totally altered the equation. For although I could argue to myself reasons why I wanted Germany to win the war against the Allies in Europe, I had absolutely no sense of belonging to, or supporting, Japanese aggression.

In his personal life, over this momentous period, William was trying to win Margaret back. She would lunch with him, especially when her lover, von Besack, was away on military service in the Baltic. But when von Besack returned, Margaret was drawn once again to the man she called 'her too-charming Russian': the Baltic squires were historically admixed with Russian blood. She moved to a villa where she and her tall intelligence officer could share what the tabloids call 'a love nest'.[46] She was hoping, according to hints in her diaries, that Nicky would marry her.

William apparently regarded her as a 'fallen woman', though he obviously still loved her. If Margaret's sexual rejections of him hurt him, he was too proud to say so. In any case, to some extent William had cauterised his emotional feelings by his involvement in politics. William would learn to 'console himself', as the French say, however. He took up, during the mid-war period, with a stunning

Finnish 'blonde goddess' – in his words – Greta, whom he dubbed 'unforgettable'.[47] But fundamentally, he was by temperament a one-woman man, and Margaret was the woman. Over the years of their on-off involvement, he always wanted her back.

When Margaret was off with her boyfriend, William spent much of his leisure time time playing chess with, rather unexpectedly, the most prominent of the Indian exiles in Berlin, Subhas Chandra Bose. Bose was another of the strange and colourful characters who formed the repertory of pro-Nazi broadcasters in Berlin. His ideology was a curious mixture of communism, socialism and Indian Fascism: he had fetched up in Berlin, where the Reich helpfully provided him with an Italian passport under the name 'Orlando Mazzotta'. William had refused to teach 'coloured' students back in London in 1938, but now he was grateful for the perverse, intelligent and sometimes grandiose company of the Bengali National Socialist.[48]

Lord Haw-Haw's Christmas broadcast – though underpinned by William's trick of blaming the victim for the aggression – was sombre. 'This is no time for sentiment,' he told his listeners.

> The sternest war in history is being fought and upon its issue depends the destiny of the human race for at least a thousand years to come. What might have been a relatively local conflict has been expanded by the warmongers of Downing Street and the White House, in concert with their Bolshevik allies, into a confligration which envelops the whole world.[49]

Though his reasoning was erroneous, the facts were not in dispute: the conflict was now globalised.

Haw-Haw continued to affirm his belief in his Germany: 'And today, although we in Germany know that the struggle is not over, although we feel that the war has reached its climax, requiring the maximum effort of all, we are able to

celebrate the Christ-tide in the proud and dignified mann
befitting a nation whose fighters by the million are away from
home on the field of battle, conquering the air or ploughing
the deep, with the one, united, indomitable will to victory.'
(William preferred the word 'Christ-tide' to 'Christmas', as
he thought the latter too Popish. 'The Fermanagh blood'
sometimes came out that way with him.)[50]

But he could scarcely resist injecting a little extra kitsch:

> Here in Berlin, I have watched the parents buying
> the traditional Christmas trees for their children,
> and if the range of Christmas purchases cannot be
> all that it was in peacetime, there is something for
> everybody, there is something that we appreciate to
> mark off this time from all others. And, even today
> as I walked through the centre and the suburbs of
> Berlin, and watched the Berliners, I was struck by
> their cheerfulness and good spirits, by their
> contentment and enthusiasm … Supremely
> confident in the Führer, the German people know
> that victory is theirs. That so great a struggle cannot
> be won without sacrifice is plain, but the sacrifice is
> as nothing to the reward.

As William watched Berliners buy Christmas trees for
their children, did he think of his own daughters, now aged
thirteen and ten, growing up in Sussex with their mother in
a new family situation? Did he think of his own mother,
feeling so lonely in her first Christmas as a widow, her three
sons parted from her? Did he think of his brothers, locked up
under Regulation 18B? If he did, he put the thoughts out of
his head, because to dwell on them might have caused him a
moment's hesitation over the path that he had taken.

10

The Turning Tide

'The English speaker, Lord Haw-Haw, is especially good at biting criticism, but in my opinion the time for spicy debate is past. During the third year of the war you must wage it quite differently from during the first year.'

Goebbels, *Diaries*, 23 May 1942

In September 1941, Goebbels, as Gauleiter of Berlin, commanded that all Berlin Jews over the age of six were henceforth obliged to wear the Star of David, represented by a prominent yellow patch sewn on to their overcoats. The regulation applied to the Greater Reich, but Berlin, where so many musicians and people in the arts were Jewish, had always been a little more liberal. And indeed the regulation wasn't rigidly applied in Berlin until 1942 – although Jews could not be served in shops before 'Aryan' customers and did not attend weekly markets.[1]

William and Margaret's divorce had just come through, on 12 September. But as long as her lover, Nicky, was off the scene, the Joyces were friendly. Once Nicky returned, William flew into a jealous rage, and friendly relations were ruptured. On this particular fine September day, they were getting along well, and taking a walk together in the enchanting Charlottenburg area. Out of the blue, a bearded gentleman appeared, walking at an unhurried pace, and with an air of calm. Sewn on the breast of his suit, quite unmistakably, was a prominent Yellow Star. William and Margaret walked towards him, Margaret in a quiet mood. The bearded man passed them by, slowly, almost at a deliberate pace. He had seemed elderly at a distance, but he was not old, just bearded and hatted; he wore the traditional dark garb of the Orthodox Jew.[2]

William said nothing, but something about the man, and the encounter, disturbed him. This was a Jew; he was quite obviously not a 'plutocrat' or a 'Mayfair swell'. He showed no signs of being a subversive Bolshevik, and he was not pulling the strings behind Churchill or Roosevelt. He was not doing any harm to anyone: he was just a man, taking an afternoon walk in the boulevards of Berlin, just like William and Margaret.

Perhaps it was the first time they had seen someone wear the Star of David, and, despite all the anti-Semitic propaganda, the reality of the situation, and the humanity of the person involved, disturbed them. James Clark, who had been subjected, as a teenage boy, to the full blast of National Socialist propaganda about the Jews – 'They were, quite simply, the bad hats; we National Socialists were the goodies' – also saw that elderly Jew taking his afternoon walks in the Charlottenburg area. To this day, sixty years on, Clark remembers the man vividly: his beard and black homburg, his black overcoat and his yellow star, progressing from east to west along the sidewalk in Charlottenburg. To see him like this was a disturbing moral statement, made in silence.

William Joyce had a deep psychological need for dogmatic beliefs, and he clung to his ideologies. On this issue, he was incapable of changing his mind when the evidence before him altered. But the psychological construct was disturbed, just for a moment, when the ideology was effaced by the incarnation of an actual person. That Orthodox Jew was, more than likely, arrested soon afterwards, and hauled off to Auschwitz or Theresienstadt; yet he had borne witness, and his witness was remembered.

The agony of the Jews was only just beginning: in January 1942, at the Wannsee conference, in a bureaucratic language constructed in euphemisms, Reinhard Heydrich drew up the plans for their genocide. It was not coincidental that the war against the Jews would be intensified just as the tide of world war started to turn against Germany. 'Hitler's attitude was – "We may lose but before we do, we will finish off the Jews once and for all."' says Terry Charman, author of *The German Home Front*.[3]

As the tide would gradually turn against Germany in 1942–43, Lord Haw-Haw's star would also wane. Even in May 1942, Goebbels was beginning to believe that a change of approach to propaganda was required. In Britain, Haw-Haw no longer featured as a 'character' in the press: there was too much going on in the theatres of war, too much bombing, and the joke wasn't funny any more. His listener numbers were down, although people still tuned in to hear what he had to say, especially on major occasions. When Cologne was subject to aerial attack by the RAF in May 1942 in the first big bombing onslaught against Germany – Bomber Harris vowed he would wipe the historic city off the map – British listeners wondered what 'clever twist' Haw-Haw would put on this. They were 'gleefully hoping that for once he would be at a loss,' according to Home Intelligence.[4] He wasn't, quite: William had a complicated strategic explanation about Cologne being a reprisal for some of Germany's victories on the Russian front.

Haw-Haw was still a source of wartime rumours, which flourished. It was rumoured, for example, that the *Queen Mary* and *Queen Elizabeth* liners had been secretly sunk at sea; that British criminals had been paid to go to France to carry out secret assassinations with hand grenades; that poison gases had been secretly released in Sussex; that the young princesses, Elizabeth and Margaret Rose, had been evacuated to America; that Éire had been invaded; that Churchill had taken Rudolf Hess with him when he went to see Roosevelt; and there were many more word-of-mouth stories which were the product of fancy and fantasy.[5]

Not all of these rumours were attributed to Lord Haw-Haw, but British Home Intelligence noted that wherever there was a strong wartime rumour or myth, Lord Haw-Haw was frequently linked with it. There had been, of course, many theories about 'Fifth Columnists' allegedly working for Lord Haw-Haw. In 1941, an eccentric film actress called Mary Taverner, sometimes known as Mary Russell Taviner, and at other times called 'Baroness Marovna', claimed that Haw-Haw had three hundred spies working for him in Britain. Joyce rebutted this charge on air.[6] Mary Taverner had once been madly in love with Oswald Mosley, and there had been correspondence, in the 1930s, between herself and Joyce over the relationship.[7]

No evidence has emerged that Joyce had any network of spies feeding him information: he read the papers, he received information from the Propaganda Ministry and he had a remarkable memory. In fact, if William had had better information from close connections in England, he would not have made the major error on air which was greatly to the disadvantage of his brother Quentin. At Macnab's pleading, the liberal independent MP A. P. Herbert had written to Sir John Anderson (responsible for home defence – the 'Anderson shelter' being named after him) asking him to consider Quentin Joyce's case.[8] Herbert suggested that it was unjust that Quentin should be detained because his brother was Haw-Haw.

Not long after this kindly effort to help his brother, William launched one of his demented attacks on Herbert on air. He described Herbert as a man 'whose humour is represented in that well-known organ of British humour,

Punch, controlled by Jews'. Herbert was 'being paid well [for] … serving the interests of his Jewish backers, who exploit British humour to label reason "treason."'[9] A. P. Herbert, who was also a writer, had done nothing more sinister than suggest that people have fun at Easter; William depicted this as an attempt to cover up the fact that the war was going badly for Britain.

✧

William was determined to win back Margaret, and he did so in a romantic way. Nicky had been absent for some time, and she hadn't had any word from him: he took her up and dropped her, it seemed, at his own convenience. Margaret thought von Besack regarded himself as a fool for being in love with her, and tried to shake off the attraction. Or perhaps it suited him to sleep with her when he was back in Berlin on leave and to forget her when he was away. In any case, when she was alone, sometime during the winter of 1941–42, she developed a serious case of gastroenteritis, which was made manifest by a type of dysentery. Her doctor said: 'Take carbon tablets – if you can get them.' Margaret was beginning to discover, along with others, that Germany was perhaps not the well-run state that it had seemed at first sight: there were many shortages, and doctors often had no supplies of medicines, because everything was requisitioned for the army.[10] In fact, there were no carbon tablets to be had.

William learned that Margaret was absent from her office, and called around at the villa to see her: while she was asleep he left a cigar box containing a red rose, and a supply of carbon tablets. She rang and thanked him, and their relations were resumed. William asked her to remarry him, and she agreed. An Anglo-Irish writer, Lavinia Graecen, who has made a study of William Joyce's psychology, claims that William only 'woke up sexually' with his wife, and 'invested all his love and emotional world in her'.[11] Yet a man's conduct can change according to whether his woman is a girlfriend or a wife: when William was in pursuit of Margaret, he could be loving, gentle, romantic and utterly attached; when she became his wife – even for the second time – he was inclined to treat her as 'a halfwit', as she put it.

William and Margaret were duly remarried, in a civil ceremony, on 11 February 1942, two days before the fifth anniversary of their first marriage. 'The deed *was* done!' she confided to her diary. Three days after the wedding, Margaret heard that von Besack was in Berlin: she telephoned him, and he told her that he had been in the eastern territories with a Wehrmacht group that had been completely cut off from contact with Germany by partisans. The first letter that he had received from her was the one saying she was remarrying Will. Despite the remarriage, Margaret remained entangled with Nicky: she continued to write to him when he was at the front, and to stay in touch with him. He continued to blow hot and cold: he seemed to play with her affections. After William's death, she would return to her Baltic lover once more, until he hurt her so badly that she broke with him forever.

William and Margaret continued to have a tempestuous marriage all the time they were in Germany. Wartime, in any case, notoriously increases infidelity and promiscuity, and as the war progressed, sexual morality, even in the apparently prudish Reich, became ever more unstable.

William and Margaret's second marriage occasioned some interesting legal – and even canonical – points. Margaret, though she was every bit as much of a National Socialist as William – and much more precisely a subject of His Majesty – remarried William Joyce when he was a naturalised German. Thus, by her second marriage, she was a full legal German, and thus could not have been charged with treason to the Crown. Canonically, of course, William Joyce, though three times wed, had never been married at all, according to his friend Macnab.[12]

William and Margaret took a second honeymoon in

September 1942. It was William's only full holiday during the war. The choice of destination was between Norway, Turkey and Portugal; William chose Norway. He was ferried there by an army plane, while Margaret travelled overland via Copenhagen and Gothenburg.[13]

Norway was, of course, at this time occupied Reich territory. And while there was some Norwegian resistance to Hitler, there was also a fair amount of collaboration. The most courageous diehards who defended Berlin at the very end, as the Russians were closing in in 1945, were Norwegian Nazis.[14] The race theories which elevated the Nordic type to the very top of the Aryan totem pole were not unflattering to the Scandinavians. Both Norway and Sweden carried out eugenic race practices: Norway through a policy of 'Aryan' baby selection, and Sweden through enforced sterilisations. The notorious Vidkun Quisling was the leader of the Norwegian people: William admired him considerably.

William liked Norway for other reasons. When they were taken to Gotenheim, the alleged location of Valhalla, he thought it looked just like Connemara. The misty fjords reminded him of the many inlets around Galway. He and Margaret also seemed to have been happy there: they didn't quarrel, and they felt romantic. William did his best to get rid of his Norwegian interpreter because he was too much of an intrusion on their togetherness.

In Oslo, they met up with some of the Norwegian National Socialists, at the Viktoria Restaurant, the Quislingites' locale. The Norwegian Fascists were critical of 'the German approach'. William thought them intelligent: he was becoming critical of some aspects of the German approach himself.

Their sojourn in Scandinavia had its amorous moments – William thought back on it fondly from his condemned cell. Yet their usual pattern of boozing, fighting and making up also occurred. 'Got very drunk quarrelling,' is a typical entry in Margaret's diary.[15]

Back in Germany, Berlin was coming increasingly under

aerial bombardment, as were other cities in Germany. The Allied bombing of Germany was now seriously under way; this phase had started when Arthur 'Bert' Harris took over the leadership of Bomber Command in February 1942. An enthusiast of 'area' bombing – the saturation bombing of whole cities, civilians, refugees and all – Harris meant to reduce the Third Reich to smithereens, and much of historic Germany with it. And with American heavy aircraft supporting him – the Flying Fortresses and the Liberators – he was set fair to do so.

When the heavy raids began in March 1943 the Joyces in Berlin faced a daily schedule of air-raid sirens and scuttling to the underground bomb shelters. Life in wartime Berlin was not so dissimilar from life in wartime London, with its famous 'Blitz spirit'. Berliners too displayed a certain stoicism and even black humour during the aerial attacks. The Americans bombed by day, the British by night. William took the air raids as philosophically as he took the threat of being hanged. William Shirer had noticed that Joyce sometimes just ignored the sirens which announced an aerial attack, pounding away at his typewriter amidst the chaos. He was generally the last to seek the shelter, and he impressed Madeleine Stuart – the German girl who was to become Francis Stuart's second wife – with his sang-froid.

'I saw what a courageous man he was,' she recalled.

> When one night there was a heavy bomber attack everybody fled to the *Luftschutzkeller* [air-raid shelter]. But he had remained in the office, gone to the window and looked out at the sky with the bombs falling in the distance. I stayed with him, after he had assured me that the bombers did not, as yet, drop their bombs over residential districts, but concentrated on the industrial surroundings of Berlin.

This was not strictly true, but it was a comforting thing to say. 'I knew little of politics at that time,' Madeleine noted.

'But that night, standing at the dark window, gazing out at the bombs, I was impressed by him and was glad to have shared those few moments with him.'[16]

⤐

From 1942, the Allies were on the offensive and Germany was under increasing pressure – though it could not yet be said to be losing the war. Until El Alamein which began in late October, Rommel was stunningly successful in North Africa. The fall of Singapore in February 1942 had been a huge blow to the British, though, predictably, the news was received with rip-roaring cheers among Irish nationalists; on this particular episode hangs another Haw-Haw legend.

'Each night between 1939 and 1945 it was usual for me and friends to listen to the German radio for the latest news from the fronts,' recalls Joe Roche of west Dublin, speaking for many others of his generation.

> William Joyce was the most popular broadcaster, and the frequent Allied defeats – Dunkirk, Crete, Arnhem – up to 1943 were received with acclamation, and the war map on the wall had the flags adjusted accordingly. At school the following day the wit and sarcasm of William Joyce were discussed.[17]

After the fall of Singapore, William announced that the British Empire was now at an end. Winston Churchill was 'the undertaker of the British Empire,' he proclaimed. Britain, he said, was run by old men in the process of senile decay: 'In England a man cannot be regarded as a serious politican until the first stages of arterial sclerosis have set in, by which time he may be described as a coming man,' he crowed, at the top of his invective form. In rebel Cork, they loved it. Churchill was deeply unpopular in Ireland.[18] The Irish nationalists had not forgotten that Churchill's father, Lord Randolph, had sided with the Ulster Unionists in the Home Rule debates and urged the Ulstermen to 'play the Orange card' whenever necessary, nor that Winston himself had sought the use of the Irish ports in the Battle of the Atlantic: Churchill was to describe Éire as 'neutral, but skulking'.

There was a particular reason for the Irish crowing over the fall of Singapore. The British commander who surrendered a hundred thousand men to the Japanese at Singapore was one Major-General A. E. Perceval. This officer had been, as a young man, with the Essex Regiment, who associated with the Black and Tans in the 1920s in County Cork, when the IRA had fought the Crown forces at Kilmichael.[19] When Lord Haw-Haw 'gleefully announced the fall of Singapore in his newscast of 15 February 1942,' recalls Father Jim Feehan of County Tipperary, 'he jocularly commented: "We are still trying to confirm a rumour that when the Imperial Japanese forces entered Singapore this morning ... their band was playing 'The Boys from Kilmichael'!"'[20] 'The Boys from Kilmichael' was a rebel IRA song.

Again, there is nothing in the official record to the effect that William Joyce made that remark. Since he had been, as a youth, fighting with the Black and Tans himself, it seems perverse, yet it was altogether in character for him to make such a provocative off-the-cuff quip. The episode showed, once again, the legendary, story-telling element of the Lord Haw-Haw phenomenon – and that, despite more recent claims by historians that Ireland's neutrality was discreetly pro-British, there were many nationalist Irishmen who were overjoyed to hear of British defeats between 1939 and 1945.

William had been formally appointed Chief Commentator for England at the Reichsrundfunk in June 1942, at a salary of 1,500 Reichsmarks a month, plus a Christmas bonus of 5,000.[21] Nevertheless, Goebbels was looking around for other ways to vary the propaganda approach, as he had come to think that William was too trenchant and sarcastic in his delivery.

Thus, in 1942, a strange new character appeared on the

broadcasting scene in Berlin. This man would be proposed as William's competitor: in the future, he would also be the angel of death in William's own life. John Amery was the son of a British Cabinet minister, Leo Amery, who was also a friend of Winston Churchill's: John Amery would be sent to the gallows as a traitor immediately before William Joyce, and his case probably made William's irretrievable.

John Amery was a very queer fish indeed: he was even odder than William, and in many ways pathetic and inadequate. He was partly Jewish: his mother was a Hungarian Christianised Jew, which made his anti-Semitism both more contemptible and more pitiful. But he was also peculiar in other ways. From an early age, he was neurotic, uncontrollable and a moral imbecile – his nannies said that, as a child, he simply could not tell right from wrong. From the age of seven, he would draw obscene pictures, often adding a penis to a drawing of a woman. He seduced a young girl when he was fourteen, and frequented prostitutes in his teens, yet he retained his attachment to his teddy bears into manhood. He was gifted at languages and Alpine sports, was described as 'charming and intelligent' by one of his contemporaries and had a great desire to be a film producer, which was in its way enterprising.[22]

But he was always in trouble with money, cars, or women; he committed himself to the Fascist cause in the 1930s, when he came under the influence of the French Fascists Jacques Doriot and Marcel Déat, both of whom had previously been Communists and were subsequently ardent anti-Communists. Amery was obsessively anti-Bolshevik, and shared the common anti-Semitic view that Bolshevism was a Jewish plot.

The German propaganda ministry *imagined* they had rather a coup when John Amery agreed to come to Berlin in August 1942 to collaborate with the Reich. Amery thought he could do the 'Germany Calling' job better than William Joyce. Joyce, he believed, was too pro-German, as Norman

Baillie-Stewart, now demoted to other translating tasks, had been: their blatant bias towards the Reich would never convince the majority of British listeners, he said, and it was crazy to refer to the United Kingdom as 'the enemy'. Accordingly, John Amery was put up at the splendid Kaiserhof Hotel and given his own series of talks on the 'Germany Calling' wavelength, his first broadcast going out in November 1942.

Amery was introduced as 'an Englishman who is speaking to you at his own request and his own free will.' His voice was more evidently upper-class than William's; his message was that Britain should join Germany against the dreaded Soviet Union, and ignore the 'Jew-controlled' media in Britain. His appearance on German radio made some impact on the British media because of his family connections, but almost no impact whatsoever on the British public, who scarcely noticed him: his voice, unlike Haw-Haw's, was well-bred but dull. His anti-Soviet ideas cut no ice either: the British public had now embarked on a love affair with the Russians, whose fortitude they greatly admired.[23]

Obviously, William didn't at all care for John Amery. He was jealous of the kid-glove treatment that Amery – whom he described as 'that quarter-Yid' – received. He warned his boss, Eduard Dietze, that Amery was 'irresponsible' and a silly playboy. This was true enough: in the end, Amery cost the Reich a great deal of money with his various scrapes.

As a broadcaster, Amery was no match for William, who – for all his coruscating invective and pro-German propaganda – was a media professional: the Amery broadcasts lasted only eight weeks. He would depart from Berlin and would eventually seek to set up a renegade British 'Legion of St George' to fight for the Axis powers: he managed about thirty recruits, mainly outcasts and misfits. Like William, Amery had a younger brother who was devoted to him, and fought hard to save him. Julian Amery became a noted Conservative MP: he always voted against the death penalty.

Despite the decline in his ratings, William Joyce was to remain at the helm as the chief broadcaster of the Reich. As time went by, he became exasperated by German officialdom, but he stuck with Germany, all the same, until the whole structure of the state collapsed.

❧

From 1943 onwards, the war was clearly going against the Reich. The Russians, who were almost defeated in 1941, had made a remarkable and swift recovery. Helped by equipment from Britain, by the courage of the Russian people, and by the production of the famous T-34 tank, the Red Army defeated the Wehrmacht at Stalingrad. The Germans, with their Axis allies of Romanians, Hungarians and Italians, had lost two hundred thousand men. Elsewhere, the Wehrmacht was in retreat: there were no more coded preludes from Liszt.

And then the bombing of Germany became relentless: Lubeck, Rostock, Kiel and, most ferociously of all, Hamburg, in July 1943, in an operation ominously code-named 'Gomorrah'. Day after day, and night after night, Bomber Command rained death over this city, which had been, in times gone by, the most pro-British of German enclaves, its rich merchant class Anglophile and Anglophone.[24]

'The combination of high-explosive bombs and large numbers of incendiaries overwhelmed the emergency services in the city,' writes Richard Overy. 'The fierce heat sucked in the surrounding air, working like a giant bellows on the cinders of the city. The fiery storm devoured everything in its path.' Forty thousand people were 'consumed in the inferno'. Albert Speer, the armaments minister, said that Hamburg 'put the fear of God into me'. Goebbels was also rattled. 'This attack definitely shattered illusions ... It is a real catastrophe,' he wrote.[25]

From 1943, the focus of propaganda also began to shift. Goebbels was now more anxious to boost German morale at home rather than to issue boastful threats abroad. Yet even he could not disguise from the people the loss of members of their own families.

A most potent source of bad news were the letters received from German soldiers on the Eastern Front – some were censored, but some managed to get through – sending despairing news. One soldier wrote home: 'They're falling like flies, and no one bothers and buries them. Without arms and legs and without eyes, with stomachs ripped open, they lie around everywhere.' Another reported: 'We're completely alone, without help from outside. Hitler has left us in the lurch ... This, then, is what the end looks like.'[26] Goebbels might vow to his diary that 'The Führer is and always will be the central and focal point of our national life ... As long as he is in our midst and in good health, nobody need worry about Germany's fate.'[27] But the poor infantryman dying in the Arctic cold of Russia's ferocious winter came to think differently.

While William plugged away relentlessly about the greatness of Germany, he could hardly not have noticed that in the streets of Berlin, women were appearing in mourning for their husbands, brothers and sons in ever greater numbers, grabbing desperately for newspapers when they appeared on the newstands. He must also have noticed that by 1943, Germans had stopped using 'Heil Hitler' as a greeting and that the streets of Berlin, which had been so gleamingly clean, were now filthy. He could scarcely have failed to hear stories that people were being summarily executed for 'defeatist talk' or for minor black-market offences – not that that halted the black market. Because of the constant pounding of Berlin by the Allies, William and Margaret were, from 1943, quite frequently shifted back and forth between the German capital and Luxembourg, where there were good broadcasting facilities.

William and Margaret's personal lives were, from 1943, increasingly becoming more rackety. On New Year's Day, Margaret noted that 'William has never seen me so tight'.[28]

Her entanglements with other men enraged William. Aside from Von Besack, other boyfriends now appear in her social calender – a Spaniard, Pablo, a Frenchman, Jean. A British former Mosleyite, Eric Pleasants, claimed in an auto-biography that he had seduced Margaret while William was broadcasting – she had more time on her hands than her husband, anyway.[29] Margaret also socialised with her women friends: lunching with Dorothy Eckersley, playing pontoon with Susan Hilton, an Irish lesbian who shared Margaret's fondness for liquor.[30]

The British people were delighted with the punishment being meted out to Germany. 'Hit 'em harder!' was the popular response to each pulverising raid. Every German should be made to pay in full for the crimes of the Second World War. And yet, although people wanted Germany and the Germans to be tormented, there was not a great deal of corresponding compassion for the Reich's main victims – the Jews. Hitler's war against the Jews did not weaken with the decline of the Reich's fortunes of war. Quite the contrary: after the 'Final Solution' had been outlined at the notorious Wannsee conference in January 1942, the horrible murder machine got into full production.

Everyone in Germany knew, at some level, that the Jews were being persecuted; people abroad knew it too. Arguably, many ordinary Germans behaved no worse, and in some cases better, than other Europeans did. Ursula von Kardorff, a young Berlin journalist who kept a diary from 1942 to 1945, recorded the case of a workman on a Berlin tram standing up to give a Jewish woman – she was wearing the Yellow Star – his seat. 'Come on, have a sit down, my old starry doll!' he said. Immediately, a Nazi Party member reprimanded him: to which he replied, 'I'll do what I like with my own arse, if you don't mind!'[31] But one wonders if, later, he or his family suffered the consequences for this heroic insolence.

'Battling grannies' in working-class areas – possibly

formerly communist neighbourhoods of Berlin – were also seen to taunt Gestapo agents who had come to round up Jews. 'Get off to the Russian front, you daft buggers!' the battleaxes would call out, and the agents of the Reich would retreat. According to von Kardoff, Jews were better protected among the working class, where people in housing estates knew everyone else's business, than among the discreet bourgeoisie, where, under a cloak of privacy, victims could be so much more silently removed.

Yet while it was obvious that Jews were being badly treated, the exact hell that was in store for them was not generally known. Even the degree to which the Jews were being ill-treated in everyday life could surprise those within the Nazi inner circle. Henriette von Schirach, the wife of the former Hitler Youth leader Baldur von Schirach, was distressed to see a group of Jewish women brutally herded into a deportation van at Amsterdam. She was so upset that she mentioned the matter personally to Hitler – she was the daughter of his photographer, Heinrich Hoffmann, and had known Hitler since childhood. She did so at a social gathering at Hitler's mountain retreat, the Berghof. The Führer flew into a temper, declared he didn't want to hear this kind of sentimentality, and stormed out of the room. The other guests said nothing, mortified with embarrassment. The von Schirachs fell from favour after the incident.[32] The persecution of the Jews was at once being planned meticulously, and was yet unmentionable.

In Britain, there was general condemnation of the atrocities carried out against Continental Jews. Although this was another reason to regard the 'Huns' as barbarians, casual anti-Semitism in Britain continued unabated, and was actually quite acute in 1942–43. Even where British people were sorry, in a generalised way, for the persecution of the Continental Jews they grumbled plenty about British Jews. Home Intelligence, which secretly monitored what people were saying in thirteen British regions and reported back to

Whitehall, noted in April 1942 that grumbling about the Jews was commonplace: third on the list, after shortage of crockery and the high price of green vegetables, was 'the preponderance of Jewish names in reports on black-market prosecutions' and 'the skilfulness' of Jews at avoiding military service.[33] Other reasons given for the growth of anti-Semitism are 'the many stories current of Jewish evasion of regulations and duties' and the 'apparent unwillingness of Jewish leaders to take action'.

> The growth of anti-Semitism is reported from widely separated areas ... Infringements of the rationing orders, dealings in black markets and 'deliberate cunning evasions of measures instituted by the government to meet wartime conditions' are said to have aroused strong public feeling.

Allegations are made of 'enormous numbers of young Jews' boasting of evading the call-up: an expression of 'open indignation' is feared unless measures are adopted to 'bring home to this race that they are inviting a similar revulsion to that which they have experienced in other countries.'

In one region, a Home Intelligence officer reported, the comment was heard that 'One thing Hitler has done is to put those damned Jews in their place.' In June 1942, another Home Intelligence region reported such remarks as: 'They [the Jews] rob us while we fight for them.' (There are similar, though less frequent, complaints about gypsies 'Who don't join up ... wander uncontrolled, evade duties and pay no taxes.' As for Jehovah's Witnesses – who were also sent to the death camps of the Reich – they are universally regarded in middle England as a thundering nuisance who have no business knocking on people's doors and disturbing such domestic peace as folks can snatch.)

As reports of atrocities against Jews began to circulate, there was some increase in sympathy for them, albeit in a qualified way: there was apprehension that the Continental

Jews might come to England. There was a slight decline in anti-Semitism in the summer of 1943: in August, it was noted that 'during the last three months, reports of anti-Semitic feeling have declined.' Reports of atrocities against Polish Jews were condemned, yet, paradoxically,

> in the Northern, North Midland, London and South Eastern Regions ... anti-Semitism is still said to be on the increase, particularly among business and working-class people. Criticisms made against Jews are as follows: (a) Jewish names are frequently associated with black-market prosecutions ... (b) They still get the luxuries. (c) You never see Jews in the services. (d) They do nothing towards winning the war; they drive about in cars as if there were no petrol restrictions ... they put the small shopkeeper out of business ... they are rank exhibitionists; they expect more to be done for them than for any other section of the community.

Postal censorship detected sympathy for Jews in Europe: perhaps people who wrote letters were better informed than other people. 'If we don't hurry up and do something, they'll all be killed,' was one prescient remark that was picked up. At the same time, it was noted there was some scepticism about the atrocity stories.

It seemed strange to me that while scores of people in Britain and Ireland wrote to me to recount their memories of listening to Lord Haw-Haw, no one ever mentioned his anti-Semitic jeremiads. I think the sad reason for this is that anti-Semitism was part of everyday life – it was no more remarkable at the time than jokes about mothers-in-law.

&

Quentin Joyce emerged from detention in July 1943, having written a long and eloquent appeal to the Advisory Committee; the letter seems finally to have convinced them that he was not – or was no longer – a security threat to the realm. Quentin was not of a bitter turn of mind, but he regretted losing four years of his life in this way. He had learned Italian, however, making friends especially with the interned Italians: as 'enemy nationals', Italians were arrested and locked up in Britain until 1943, when Italy wisely changed sides. The Italian internees, and their families, remained lifelong friends of Quentin Joyce, and never failed to support and help him afterwards.[34]

Frank Joyce – who had served eleven months under Regulation 18B – had joined the Army, and done well: he was now serving as an army quartermaster. The youngest brother, Robert, had also enlisted and was serving with the Allies in Italy. Their sister Joan was now working as a tram conductress. Quentin, who had been sequestered in London, Liverpool, Yorkshire and the Isle of Man, returned to what was now the family home in Dulwich, a flat at 86 Underhill Road provided by the local council. He would have very much liked to return to the Air Ministry, but this was out of the question.

Quentin had worried a lot about the anxieties that his parents suffered when he was arrested. He had reason to worry. His mother was now a widow, and in indifferent health. She missed Michael a great deal. She did some babysitting for neighbours, and even some house-cleaning.[35] Queenie was liked in the neighbourhood of Dulwich, and was described as a 'nice little person'.

But sometimes, when Mrs Joyce walked along the street in Dulwich, cheeky children would call after her: 'Lady Haw-Haw! Lady Haw-Haw!' It was mortifying for her. The *Evening News*, 29 May 1945, said that 'she went home and cried her eyes out' when this occurred. Quentin resolved to comfort his mother as best he could, and to nurse her back to health.

William did at least bring comfort to one British mother during his broadcasts, if not to his own. Royston Clarke of

Market Rasen in Lincolnshire was shot down over Berlin in February 1944. His mother received a letter from his squadron that he was lost, presumed killed. 'It was made more dramatic for my mother and family as this was my thirtieth and last bombing raid over Germany,' Mr Clarke recalled, 'and she was expecting me on leave the following day.' The lady took it that her son was lost and was, as might be expected, grief-stricken.

Royston's mother worked in a munitions factory, and her colleagues listened to Lord Haw-Haw's broadcasts. While listing prisoners of war, William duly gave names and rank of bomber crews shot down. 'When he broadcast that I had survived and gave my name, rank and number, you can imagine the joy of my mother's department,' Royston said. 'For that British mother, it was as though her son had been brought back to life. He did my mother and me a very great favour.'[36] Sixty years on, Mr Clarke, though no admirer of William Joyce, is still alive to remember the good news that was delivered to his family by 'Jairmany Calling'.

11

The Road to Nowhere

*'The beginning of true knowledge is
certainly self-knowledge, but in most cases,
providentially, it is the end: signed Confucius
W. Joyce aus Brooklyn.'*

Joyce's inebriated reflections on his thirty-eighth birthday, April 1944[1]

From 1943, William and Margaret were on the move.
Because of the bombing of Berlin, they were moved back and
forth to Luxembourg, where there were good broadcasting
facilities. Their marriage was on its usual roller-coaster
course: Margaret was seeing Nicky von Besack again, though
episodically. William took advantage of his sojourns at the
Hotel Alfa in Luxembourg to conduct a liaison – or two.
One of his regular girlfriends at this point was called Lisa.[2]
Margaret actually caught him *in flagrante delicto*, but it
embarrassed him more than it worried either of the women.

As the war moved towards its final phase, casual sex was,
in any in case, increasingly resorted to. 'Berlin is in a strange
mood – a mixture of apathy and pleasure-seeking,' noted
Ursula von Kardoff in her diary for 1944. Strangers
copulated in darkened streets, and even in hospitals, one

256

diarist noted later, 'an erotic fever seemed to have taken possession of everybody. Everywhere, even on the dentist's chair, I saw bodies locked in lascivious embrace. The women had discarded all modesty and were freely exposing their private parts.'[3]

By 1944, the Luxembourg base was becoming vulnerable to the Allies, especially after the Allied landings of 6 June and 'Operation Overlord'. British Intelligence was actively seeking to arrest 'Lord Haw-Haw' as a priority; preparations were already being made to bring him to trial. William must have begun to reflect on the possibility that he would face the ultimate penalty when the Allies won. Indeed, in his usual black-humour way, William constructed an imitation pub in the corner of his office, which he jocosely called 'At the Sign of the Hanging Judge'.[4]

His broadcasts now turned increasingly to the threat of Stalin dominating the post-war world – which was prescient – but no note of apology, regret or repining touched what he said. Quite the contrary: 'National Socialism in Germany is stronger than ever,' he proclaimed in July 1944, after the failed attempt on Hitler's life. With his clever way of finding a smart twist in any story, William argued that it was better that this 'potential source of weakness' – the dissident officers who had courageously tried to rid Germany of Hitler – should be revealed and removed. 'Twenty-five years ago, Adolf Hitler was unknown to the world, although those about him were beginning to realise the power of his personality ... More than ever is it true today – Germany is Hitler and Hitler is Germany.'[5] Hitler had certainly stamped his personality on Germany; as he went down to his own destruction, he sought to drag Germany with him.

After Hitler's fifty-fifth birthday in April 1944, a banner appeared on the streets of Berlin: 'We greet the first worker of Germany – Adolf Hitler.' Graffiti also appeared; one said 'Our walls may break, but never our hearts.'[6] The relentless bombing of Germany had a certain unifying effect on the populace: 'This disaster, which hits Nazis and anti-Nazis alike, is welding people together,' wrote Ursula von Kardorff.

As the Allies advanced across France, the Joyces were evacuated out of Luxembourg and brought back to Berlin, supposedly permanently. In fact, they would soon be on the road again. Radio propaganda was being reorganised all the while; stations were closed down, and fresh stations opened. New personnel were brought in to broadcast, notably British prisoners of war who had – in some cases with John Amery's assistance – turned renegades. A substantial percentage of the British renegades recruited by Amery – although it should be noted that Amery himself only succeeded in recruiting two men – had German mothers, a point not recognised in law, but surely compelling in the emotional loyalties of an individual. The broadcasting scene was changing, but William and Margaret, remained on the job, drunk or sober. From the end of 1944, his broadcasts were also syndicated in the *Guernsey Evening Press*, still evidently pro-German. His warnings about Stalin's encroaching power continued.

Gertrude Joyce died, aged sixty-six, on 15 September 1944, at St Mary's Hospital in Paddington, London. She had not been in good health for some time, but her death still came as a shock to her family. 'The poor dear never had any real peace during the war,' wrote Quentin to his uncle.

> She was worried about William, and the fact that I spent over four years in various prisons and camps without charge or trial upset her very much indeed. Added to this, she had worries about the victimisation of other members of the family.

She had also never really recovered from Michael's death, Quentin wrote.[7] Despite the religious divide, their marriage had been strong.

Some time after Quentin was released in July 1943, he persuaded his mother to take a holiday; although she was reluctant, she did so. She improved, but on returning to London, she collapsed at Paddington Station, and Quentin took her straight to the hospital. Queenie had heart disease, and seemed to be responding to treatment, but then she contracted bronchitis, and died within twenty-four hours. Her last words were; 'Tell William I'll always be with him.' William was not made aware of his mother's death until eight months later.

Quentin, as was his wont, saw to everything in connection with his mother's death. And although he was short of funds, he managed to comply with her final wishes – that she be buried at Chadderton Cemetery in Oldham, Lancashire.[8] He took consolation from the thought that his mother was now 'in a place where no one can do her further harm'. She had had no peace in recent years. 'In the grave at least, she was free from the lying tongues of the scandal-mongers, and all her earthly worries had passed away.'[9]

Quentin said of his mother that 'everyone who knew her, loved her'. It was only those who did not know her who were nasty to her. A friend of the family told the London *Evening News*: 'Mrs Joyce was loved by everybody who knew her. She was always ready to do anybody a good turn. She really died of a broken heart – all because of that one son who was the black sheep of the family.'[10] But the black sheep still remained, one suspects, the favourite child.

⚜

In Berlin, Margaret was noting the retreat of the Reich throughout 1944. She was now illegally listening to the BBC. In February, she was devastated to discover that Nicky, who had just turned 40, had suddenly married someone else – one Fraulein Kutz. He had explained to her the previous year that he could never marry her, Margaret, because she wasn't a proper German.[11] Nevertheless, Margaret still retained a connection with him.

William was realising a boyhood ambition, and enlisting

to be a soldier at last: in September 1944, he made his application to the German Home Guard – the Volkssturm – which, rather pathetically, was composed of young boys and older men who were expected to defend the Reich before the oncoming Russians.[12] In a ceremony on October 22 that was half-desperate and half-farcical, presided over by Reichsminister Goebbels, they were sworn to serve the Fatherland 'until death'.[13] Some of the fifteen-year-old boys among their number bore an expression of doomed, youthful ardour, judging from the archive film of the event.

William was proud to serve Germany in this last desperate throw of the dice, though he couldn't resist a bit of provocative 'codding' when it came to the bureaucracy. The administrative clerk filling out the form for Volkssturmmann Joyce asked him if he had any previous military experience. 'Yes, British army,' he announced.[14] He hoped to get a laugh, but German officialdom was not much given to laughter.

On 14 October, William received his honour from the Third Reich, the War Merit Medal, the *Kriegsverdienstkreuz*, First Class. This was awarded (by Goebbels' deputy, Dr Werner Naumann) for 'extraordinary merit in carrying out general war tasks not directly connected with enemy action': the certificate was dated 1 September 1944 and signed in facsimile by Hitler. Margaret was also to be awarded a medal, the lowest wartime civilian decoration of *Kriegsverdienstmedaille*.[15]

Among the familiar faces which had disappeared from the Berlin scene were James Clark and his mother, Dorothy Eckersley. At the age of twenty, James began to withdraw from the Reichsrundfunk, where he too had done some broadcasting. (He very occasionally stood in for William.) After Pearl Harbor, Clark had had what religious people call a 'crisis of faith'. He was also beginning to feel unhappy about what was happening in Russia and eastern Europe: 'I expected it to be a great crusade to liberate Russia from the Bolsheviks and that there would be a pro-German regime that they would install – a Pétain, as it were, in Russia. But bit by bit it was being treated as a war of conquest.'

Clark kept his doubts to himself, sensing how dangerous a false step could be. The Reichsrundfunk was, he said, a 'hotbed of jealousy – people wanting other people's jobs – and denunciations. And people did disappear suddenly.' His mother arranged matters: Dorothy herself would go on doing some archive work, and young Jim would be confined to their lodgings – a delightful old *pensione* on the Kaiserdamm – allegedly 'unwell'. In this way they managed to survive in Berlin until December 1944 – by means of Dorothy's resourcefulness in gradually selling off her fox furs and couture dresses – and even her underwear.

They were arrested on Christmas Eve by the Gestapo and imprisoned at the Alexanderplatz. They were transported separately, she to a nunnery on Lake Constance, and he to Carinthia in the Alps where they were eventually picked up by Allied Security. James last saw William and Margaret at a coffee house on the Kaiserdamm in July 1944. They exchanged pleasantries, as though nothing at all unusual was happening; William referred affectionately to James as 'the boy'. William could be quite good with young people, in a teacherly kind of way.[16]

But there were days in Berlin like that in 1944, between the bombing and the panic, where life seemed strangely normal. William and Margaret had taken to quarrelling again, and making up again; they did a great deal of lunching at the Foreign Press Club, and a great deal of drinking. William said to Margaret, during one of their spats: 'I have never had such a drunken whore on my hands as you.'[17] They were both faithless.

Although there was a frantic kind of gregariousness in Berlin at this time – the Adlon hotel was packed with revellers – William and Margaret spent a rather bleak Christmas in 1944, dining on trout. They were now seeing a good deal of another Irishman called Edward Bowlby, with whom they spent December 26. Bowlby had also worked as a commentator at the Rundfunk. He had been born in Ireland in 1911 and, like William, had come to England as a boy, in 1922, at the foundation of the Irish State: he sounded, on air, more English than Irish. During the 1930s, he too had been involved with the British Union of Fascists, and at the outbreak of war had been living in Budapest. He had come to Berlin in 1943, and wisely, it would turn out for him, always claimed Irish nationality; although the Irish authorities initially refused him citizenship, he would save his skin by decamping to Ireland after the war.[18]

In January 1945, William was in trouble again. He got into a scrape with the German authorities, which might easily have brought him before a Nazi court. He and Margaret had been having dinner at the Foreign Press Club and, not unusually, had had quite a few drinks. An air-raid siren sounded and, with a French journalist, the couple descended to a bomb shelter for cover. Once in the shelter, William began teaching the Frenchman some English and Irish songs. The air-raid warden bossily told him to stop singing. William teasingly asked the official if he was that scared. Outraged by such insubordination, the warden ordered William to leave the shelter: William retorted with a little light verbal abuse, and then the warden collared him.

The fighting Irishman in Joyce always came out in these circumstances, and there was a tussle.[19] William's lip was slightly cut, and the official received a black eye. The warden departed from the shelter muttering threats, and presently, William received a summons: the charge approximated to 'sub-treason'.

The Joyces thought all this very amusing, but William's boss, Eduard Dietze, was appalled. The bomb-shelter warden was the official driver for the much-feared Roland Freisler, the president of the People's Court. Freisler, a former communist turned Nazi, was an extremely powerful and corrupt lawyer who subverted the law purely to serve Nazi politics.

He had sentenced the July conspirators to be hanged, slowly, with piano-wire; the proceedings were filmed for the delectation of Hitler's court.[20]

William would have been in very serious trouble indeed over the fracas in the bomb shelter had not fate – in the form of the Americans – intervened: in February 1945, the People's Court was bombed, and all the papers relating to William's case were destroyed. Freisler was killed by a falling beam; his driver and other employees were sealed in the cellar and could not be rescued.

❧

In December 1944, Germany had launched its last offensive, driving into the Ardennes, which were lightly held by American and Canadian troops. This offensive was known to the Allies as 'the Battle of the Bulge' and to Hitler, more poetically, as 'Operation Autumn Mist'. Hitler believed it would smash through to Antwerp and the Channel coast and succeed in reversing the Reich's fortunes. Although nothing could now rescue the Reich from defeat, the offensive inflicted eighty thousand casualties on the North American forces and caused tension between the Allies. By mid-January the Battle of the Bulge was over – and the Soviets had taken Warsaw.

The Red Army was now advancing a hundred miles a week. The German population of Silesia, terrified of the oncoming Russians, took to the roads in a mass exodus, moving westward. Many of the refugees were women, since the men had been conscripted. Pregnant women in the eastern parts of Germany hitched themselves into covered horse-drawn wagons, and mothers with small children, or babies at the breast, just started walking. There were pitiful scenes of women trying to stop their babies from freezing to death, starving to death or dying from fatigue. The mass rape of German women was also commencing: more than one and a half million were raped, some of them girls of thirteen or fourteen; some of the women were penetrated with broken bottles.[21]

Then there came the even more ghastly scenes of uncovering the Nazi death camps. On 27 January, the Soviets marched into the largest of these hell-holes, at Auschwitz, near Katowice in Silesia. They found around five thousand tormented, living skeletons: many thousands more had been rounded up by the Nazi guards and forced to walk westwards through the snow, dying from exhaustion, or being summarily shot on the slightest pretext as they struggled to make their way. At Auschwitz, the Red Army also found 'grotesque pyramids of dentures and spectacles, and perhaps most ghastly of all, seven tons of women's hair'.[22]

By 30 January, the anniversary of Hitler's accession to power in 1933, Albert Speer, the architect for whom Hitler seems to have cherished a homoerotic love, was reporting that 'The war is lost'. Even though those around Hitler now knew the end was near, people continued to be executed for 'defeatist talk': a twenty-seven-year-old nurse, Gertrud Seele, who was heard to say at a private party that she 'hated the Nazis', was guillotined as an 'enemy of the State' on 12 January.[23]

⋙

Despite the momentous drama of history going on around them, William and Margaret's last days in Berlin were largely focused on banal details of train timetables, fussing about delays on the U-bahn, worrying about the supply of cigarettes and wondering if there was a decent drink to be had at the club. Life was chaotic: refugees from the East were desperate to get into Berlin, and many Berliners were desperate to get out – although residents were forbidden to leave. The buses had more or less stopped in January; trams and the U-bahn trains were still functioning. The shops were empty. Despite all the war action, there was a great deal of waiting: waiting in queues; waiting for transport; waiting, secretly, for the end. Graffiti appeared on the walls of Berlin: 'Enjoy the war, the peace will be terrible.'[24]

Meanwhile, the Allied forces ravaged German cities, determined to finish the Third Reich off decisively: never again would Germany claim – as she had done after the First World War – that she had not been beaten in battle. The attack on Dresden, on 14 February 1945, in which incendiary bombs killed over thirty-five thousand people by turning oxygen into fire in their lungs, vaporised a cityscape whose name had become synonymous with delicacy, was so destructive of life and architectural beauty, and so cruel to civilians and refugees, that questions were asked in the House of Commons about the morality of the assault. Dresden was pulverised for thirty-six hours non-stop. When Bomber Harris arrived at Chequers, the British Prime Minister's country retreat, and was asked for news of Dresden, he replied: 'There is no such place as Dresden.'[25]

William, having joined Goebbels' Volkssturm, or Home Guard, was, fortunately for him, not really required to do anything more exacting than a little light training. In his broadcasts, he had in the past sneered at Britain's Home Guard – the 'Dad's Army' of legend – for being under-equipped: 'Pikes, forsooth!' he chortled in 1941.[26] Now he was part of the German Reich's equivalent, which was described as 'the last round-up of the old and the lame, the children and the dotards', and was, moreover, woefully underequipped. Some from the Volkssturm would fight to the last man; but many others, wherever they could, slipped away home.

Still, throughout January and February, William continued on his military exercises – though he was handicapped, from early February, by a wobbly ankle caused by an inebriated fall.[27] He now saw that his boyhood dream of soldiering was, as he put it, 'rather a waste of time'. Margaret was now taking opium for her stomach – she suffered much minor ill-health, possibly associated with

265

hangovers. Opium was easily obtained in medical compounds at this time.

The comment going around Berlin now was: 'We know we're going to lose the war – but *when*?' Berliners mocked Hitler with their doggerel: 'No butter with our eats/Our pants have no seats/Not even paper in the loo/Yes, Führer – we follow you!'[28] The received wisdom was that 'The optimists are learning English, the pessimists are learning Russian.' Still, mocking remained underground: Goebbels was continuing to execute bread-rioters.

Plans were made to move the Joyces out of Berlin to northern Germany, from where broadcasts could still be made. Goebbels gave instructions that William and Margaret were to be given safe passage out of the capital. They had been issued with passports under the name of Hansen the previous November. William was to be provided with papers, transport and protection. The orders were: 'The Joyces are at all costs to be kept out of Allied hands.' But then, Goebbels wanted the propaganda broadcasts to go on to the very end. In the last month of his life, he was still planning fresh reorganisations of the radio.

It was in any case necessary, for technical reasons, for the Joyces to leave Berlin. Radio relays from the capital by cable to the remaining transmitters were becoming increasingly difficult. In October 1944, arrangements had been made to move the whole origination of propaganda broadcasts from Berlin's Funkhaus to Apen in north-west Germany; this plan was now becoming operational. William and Margaret, and their Funkhaus colleagues, were told to depart from Berlin on Tuesday 13 March.

⁓

'Seventy-five percent of life is just waiting,' William wrote in the diary he had begun to keep; he regretted that he had not done so previously.[29] His thoughts in his last days in Berlin were volatile. One moment he would be contemplating his own death, courtesy of the RAF ('Are they going to cut off my drink?'); the next, he would be complaining that Margaret was sulking. William began to cast his mind back to his past life: on 4 March, he remembered his first wife, Hazel, and their life in Jubilee Place, Chelsea. He was right to leave Hazel, he concluded, but was he right to leave Chelsea, that favourite London *quartier* of which he once cherished the hope of representing in Parliament? He remembered Hazel's birthday on 6 March, and that of Miss Scrimgeour, his faithful if eccentric patroness. He remembered attending rallies for the United Empire Party – a short-lived political group supporting the British Empire – with Hazel in 1930. He also recalled joining the British Union of Fascists in 1933 and his first days with Margaret in Berlin, in August 1939, and how long ago that seemed now.

William and Margaret quarrelled again, made up, went to bed with other partners, dined quite normally at the Foreign Press Club, slept badly, craved sugar, sat in bomb shelters sharing *sekt* – German champagne – with soldiers, walked in the Tiergarten, walked in the twilight from 'Nollendorf Platz to Potsdamer Platz', observed the swan on the river and the owl in the tree, celebrated eight years of marriage, quarrelled again, and through it all, went on working. William never let up writing, translating and broadcasting, though he grumbled a lot about his bosses now, who 'don't, or won't, realize that after five and a half years, a steady writer needs certain amenities'.

Like virtually everyone else in the beleaguered Reich, the couple thought more and more about food, and indeed yearned obsessively for cigarettes, which were becoming more valuable than money: certain shops in Unter den Linden traded not in cash, but in tobacco. How many long hours had Hitler railed and ranted against cigarettes, which he regarded as such a great evil! Now they were the most useful currency in the 'thousand year-Reich'.

Alcohol also became a necessity, providing momentary comfort among the ruins. A decent wine could make a day bearable. On 8 March, William noted: 'Lunch at Club. Châteauneuf du Pape. Marvellous, RM 6 per glass, but worth far more at present rates.' Sometimes he got so plastered that he didn't care where the bombs fell: 'I believe a bomb fell quite near,' he recorded on the day before his departure, 'but I was indifferent to it, was really drunk ...' William regretted that his exit from Berlin should have been 'so undignified', but in fact it was all rather fitting. The saga of Lord Haw-Haw had been the theatre of the absurd: the protagonist might as well leave the stage pissed as a newt.

Yet the Lord Haw-Haw radio show was not finished quite yet. The broadcasts were to continue from the little town of Apen – with its strategically significant cable links – about thirty kilometres from Oldenburg and about fifty from the Dutch border. Here the technical equipment had been set up, and recording studios installed, complete with a music archive, in a requisitioned hotel. 'Poor Margaret is crying,' William wrote.

> She could not believe that it would ever come to this ... I loathe to think that these may be my last hours in Berlin, a city which I love, despite its swine, and despite the heartaches it has brought me. Berlin is a composite part of my life, and I do not yield it up gladly.

On 7 March, the Americans had crossed the Rhine at Remagen, close to Bonn; William immediately recognised this as a key advance.

Moreover, despite the fanatics of the Third Reich screeching about fighting to the last man, the people of Remagen immediately hung out white flags of surrender. Yet footling everyday anxieties took precedence for the Joyces: William worried as much about the prospective lack of liquor at little Apen as he did about General Eisenhower. Life isn't worth living, he declared, without Bacchus and Lady Nicotine.

The Joyces packed up their bags at the lovely old flat in Kastanien-Allee for the last time. Margaret was miserable about leaving Berlin. William got drunk again and had another fight with Margaret, and she made to leave him once more. He unceremoniously got rid of his Volkssturm uniform and, on Wednesday 14 March, had his last lunch in Berlin. On his final journey on the Berlin S-bahn, he caught a glimpse of Christian Bauer, the very man he had met on his first day in Berlin. 'On the first day and the last!' he remarked, pondering on fate and coincidence. He and Bauer did not speak.

Although, as late as February 1945, William had still imagined there was a chance for a 'diplomatic peace' for the Germans, he now knew what would be in store for them: 'Oh Lord! I pity them in the awakening that is coming. Trouble is that so many decent and innocent people have to suffer.' In their homes, Berliners were confecting white flags from old sheets, and symbols of the Nazi era were quietly erased.[30] With dark irony, the most useful artefact to possess would soon be a Yellow Star of David: the five thousand Jews who had survived by living in secret – protected by Berliners – were often driven to yield up these dubious momentoes in exchange for food. William would notice, soon after his arrival in Apen, that locals were busy cleaning swastikas off the walls and dumping copies of *Mein Kampf.*

And so in mid-March 1945, Margaret and William, together with various other members of the Rundfunk, including William's boss, Eduard Dietze, boarded a train in Berlin. Margaret was left behind while changing trains at Oldenburg, but she managed to find another among the vast mêlée of people, soldiers and refugees on the move. They passed through Bremen, which Margaret noted was 'very badly smashed'[31] and were relieved to reach Apen, their penultimate berth in Germany.

Apen is a pleasing little town, with many canals, flat countryside, tall trees by long avenues and the domestic architecture so beloved of the Dutch style. In this backwater, people just tried to keep their heads down. 'You could see and hear the Allied bombers going over and over, often at low altitudes,' recalled Lisl Kuhlmann, who worked as a secretary for the Rundfunk with William. 'Times were hard. People ate the agricultural produce, root crops and so on. There were many shortages [but] … there was often too much to be done to think about events.'[32]

The broadcasting personnel were billeted with various landladies around the town. William – never too bothered about his immediate domestic surroundings – was content enough with his landlady, Frau Kruse, and relished the 'damned good' fried potatoes and fried eggs which she put before him. The food situation in Apen was better than in half-starved Berlin. Despite his bad ankle and buckled knee, he took the opportunity to do some walking between Apen and Augustfehn, a neighbouring hamlet about a kilometre away. His favourite pastime was walking in the rain: that was how he cleared his head.

Margaret noticed that the countryside was gradually awakened to spring, and this gave her some joy. The weather was marvellous. William marked St Patrick's Day (17 March) without a drink – to his disgust.

William's moods were volatile and his tone often strangely fatalistic. He began to wax religious: the Lord would take care of everything. 'Most of the people are wondering what will happen to them. Perhaps I have the greatest cause; but I feel quite serene. Not a bit worried.' He took an Irish view of matters: things were desperate but not serious. 'The situation is so grave that I should hate to take it seriously.' He had moods of demented *folie de grandeur:* if only he could have advised Hitler ... 'I could have warned the Old Man against most of his mistakes before he made them.'

On his walks to Augustfehn, along the canals, with their willow trees, and across enchanting little wooden bridges, William came to resent the fact that he had never even met Goebbels – or even shaken his hand. If Germany lost the war, it was because there were too many yes-men, William thought: 'The formula "Ja, mein Führer!!!" is largely responsible.' Joyce could still joke, though: when the 'Yankees' crossed the Rhine at Wesel, he quipped: 'Pop goes the weasel!'

All the while, the sound of battle grew closer. He wagered with himself that the war would be over by his birthday – 24 April – and he wasn't far wrong. Stalin was planning to take over Berlin on 22 April, Lenin's birthday. Churchill believed the war could end on 30 April. Speer reckoned, in March, that the German economy would collapse within eight weeks. In his religious mood, William marked the Feast of the Annunciation, 25 March, which is traditionally much revered in Ireland, since it opens the Christian story with Mary's pregnancy: 'The Angel of the Lord declared unto Mary ... ' By chance, Margaret was now trying to get pregnant, and when her period – described as 'Mrs Thing' in William's despatches – arrived, it was a disappointment.[33] Was she 'impregnable', he asked himself. Or was he impotent?

He meant infertile. He had fathered children, but now his fertility seemed to be failing. 'It seems that I have become a human contraceptive,' he said. Well, he reflected then, maybe so much the better. After all, 'It will soon be over now'. It was Margaret, rather than William, who wanted a child. She was coming up to thirty-four: a time when a woman's biological clock starts ticking more loudly. She was thinking of the future; William was thinking of the past. 'Today I have sad and haunting memories,' he wrote in his diary.

> I yield nothing of my political opinions, nor do I believe that I have acted wrongly, but I hate the idea of dying as England's enemy – or of being

> despised by those among whom I was once
> regarded as an ardent patriot. A damned nuisance.

Margaret was despatched back to Berlin, briefly, to carry out a business errand for her boss; suddenly, as the train took her off, William was stricken with tenderness for her. After all their fighting and bickering, their drunken exchanges, their faithlessness, now, it seemed to him, the idyll of their marriage commenced. He thought about other women: he remembered, particularly, Mary in London, the Young Conservative he had seduced back in 1930. He thought romantically of his Finnish Valkyrie, Greta-Lisa. But when Margaret was gone, he lamented how empty Apen seemed without her and how much he was still in love with her. He began calling her, fondly, 'Peggy'. Would he see her again? The end was near, he felt: 'Oh, God, restore her to me,' he prayed. The faster Germany lost the war, the more religious, in a fatalistic way, William became. With the bombing raids getting ever nearer, and louder, sleep was elusive.

William watched the funeral of a suicide – 'horses draped in black looked queer and sinister' – and thought: 'Damn it! I wish I could go out like a man – with plenty of drink and a good cigar.' Many Germans were now killing themselves, horrified by what the future might hold. The various means of self-slaughter were favourite topics of conversation in Berlin, and many of the leading Nazis – along with some army personnel (who were not necessarily Nazi Party members) – took their own lives. But not William: like Winston Churchill, he thought suicide unnatural. Anyway, he was now animated by his love for Margaret:

> How my mind and body burn for Margaret when
> she is away and not safe … Ah! Well! – how I thank
> God that I clung to her – that I always took her
> back. I hope she will realize, before the end, what
> she has meant to me.

Still he went on broadcasting, working, talking and

writing. 'Europe's fate will be sealed in the east.' 'Churchill has surrendered not only Europe, but his own country, to the menace of Bolshevism.' He went on doing his 'Germany Calling' broadcasts. He could not do otherwise: his work had been the life of him, and his compulsion to speak would be the death of him.

In Berlin, Margaret saw her boss, Eduard Dietze, went to the Press Club for the last time, slept alone at the apartment in Kastanien-Allee. On 30 March, she noted glumly that 'My DANZIG is in Russian hands'. She hated 'the English', too, for bombing the places she loved.

⌘

Easter fell on 1 April in 1945, and it became obvious that, as the military situation worsened, the team would have to leave Apen. 'Pity,' he remarks pithily, 'I like the place very much'. The drink situation had much improved in the latter days at Apen, and he had tasted the pleasure of liquor for breakfast. Being on the move again, leaving most of their belongings behind, was 'a damned nuisance', yet he seemed to accept whatever was now in store.

On Easter Sunday, he wondered if it would be his last: maybe so, maybe not. The chess player who could only play a defensive game, and would never attack was now showing his character: 'The immediate future is shrouded in mystery. The ultimate future – well – have three guesses!' There was around him, he noted, 'a feeling of relief that the climax is coming. The people want peace.' There was a scramble among the local population to destroy pictures of Adolf Hitler. This would not save the town from being thoroughly trashed by the Polish divisions, who were the first to arrive among the liberators. More than fifty years later, the less-than-polite manner in which the Polish troops treated Apen was recalled with pursed lips by those who remember it; but it could hardly have been otherwise.[34]

Besides, much worse things were happening elsewhere in the last weeks of the war. On 13 April, a group of Jews who had escaped from the death-march from Auschwitz were rounded up near the town of Gardelegen, and chased into a barn. Some escaped, but the rest were burned to death. Two days later, British tanks entered Belsen and were shown around by the camp commandant, Josef Kramer, as though it was a tour of inspection of a holiday site.[35] On 16 April, half a million shells, rockets and mortar bombs were fired on Berlin by the Red Army, while sixty German suicide planes crashed into the bridges over the River Oder in a bit to halt the Soviets.

The Canadians took Arnhem, the Americans captured Nuremberg and the French entered Stuttgart. On Hitler's birthday, 20 April, twenty Jewish children who had been taken to Auschwitz for medical experimentation were hanged, when the British forces were only a couple of miles away. This group included two five-year-olds and three seven-year-olds.[36]

The Apen group decamped to Hamburg. William and Margaret left behind four copies of his old National Socialist newspaper *The Helmsman*, a history book, *The 19th Century and After*, and three library tickets for Kensington Library, which William had kept since 1939. They were now bound for Hamburg, where William and Margaret were briefly lodged at the Atlantic Hotel, overlooking the sparkling bay the Alster sea-lake. They subsequently moved to the equally comfortable Vier Jahreszeiten, near a local radio station. William noted that the food at the Four Seasons could still be very good: there was plenty of fish from the Alster, and the wine kept flowing. When bombs fell over Hamburg, William was more concerned that he would lose the bottle of wine he had just opened than that he would lose his life. They learned of President Roosevelt's death: this would momentarily fill the demented Hitler's head with the notion that the war could be turned around. Goebbels had given Hitler one of William's favourite books: Carlyle's *Life of Frederick the Great*. In this biography, the Prussian King's fortunes are reversed by the sudden death of the Tsarina of Russia; Goebbels was also providing Hitler with favourable astrology charts.

William was more realistic: FDR's death wouldn't change a thing. 'Militarily, the war is now lost,' he averred. The weather was intoxicatingly good: the Alster was beautiful; and 'anyhow, we can laugh'. He was spending his money freely by mid-April because 'Now it is only a matter of weeks, possibly of days.' As the RAF Mosquitoes and De Havillands pounded Hamburg, William experienced a perverse excitement: 'Crash! Crash! Crash! … The culminating moment has a wild thrill in it, like the peak of the crescendo in a great piece of music.'

Soon it would be his thirty-ninth – and last – birthday, on 24 April. He had begun to think about Ireland again, vaguely wondering if there was a chance he could make it to the still-neutral country. (Éire had not joined Argentina in declaring war against Germany in March 1945; Argentina was the fifty-third nation to do so.) Goebbels, too, had speculated on whether it might be possible to get his Lord Haw-Haw to Ireland by U-boat; but this was absurd. William thought of England too. After all his passionate German patriotism, he now came to feel that he could never be really at home in Germany. Had it all been worthwhile? 'I think not,' he wrote. 'National Socialism is a fine cause, but most of the Germans, not all, are bloody fools … England means so much to me, and I am old.'

William's syndicated broadcasts were still running in the *Guernsey Evening Press*, and on the eve of his birthday the headline over his piece proclaimed: 'WHAT MANKIND OWES TO HITLER'S GERMANY.' 'The German armies in the field remain unbroken,' the report read, 'and … they will continue to fight so long as they possess weapons and munitions.' There was a particle of truth in this: on the Eastern Front, German divisions were still putting up a fight. Surrender to the Allies in the west was now a welcome prospect for the civilian population; surrender to the Red Army in the east was regarded with terror.

Margaret regretted that she wasn't able to get William a birthday present – she still cared about him, through all the quarrels. Still, he managed to enjoy his birthday. He happily traded his bread allowance for cigarettes and drank a bottle of German champagne before retiring and sleeping well. The next day, he and Margaret were quarrelling again, and his idyll of 'Peg o' My Heart' was momentarily forgotten. She had become 'sexually useless' to him – she seems to have frequently suffered menstruation problems. She had lost her hold on him, he ranted: 'Our days in Apen have been unhappy mainly because she has developed all her worst traits.'

Bremen fell to the Allies, and rumours abounded that Goebbels had been killed. 'A few of us now are running the whole propaganda service in north Germany,' William speculated. Among his everyday companions now was the ineffable Miss Bothamley, one of his cronies from the Fascist-salon days in London before the war. She was an eccentric old doll; she annoyed William by telling him that he was the main man, while she was the main woman – on the radio waves. 'Good Lord, how conceited some people are,' he wrote.

The Joyces were still in Hamburg in the last days of April when Reuters released a report – accurate, too – that Himmler was trying to negotiate with the Western Allies and that Mussolini was dead, killed by the Italian partisans, and hung upside down in a public square in Milan. Margaret wrote: 'BBC confirmed Mussolini rumour and gave gloating description of how he was hung and then his body was thrown in a Milan square and riddled with bullets. The BBC calls these people patriots.' It was Mussolini, after all, who got them all interested in Fascism in the first place.

William made his famous drunken, almost comical, last broadcast on 30 April, the day his Führer and Eva Braun, now Mrs Adolf Hitler, committed suicide in the Berlin bunker by putting his 7.65 mm Walther pistol to his temple, his bride Eva Braun, slumped to his left, smelling of almonds, having died from a phial of prussic acid. Much of what people recalled about the Lord Haw-Haw broadcasts was a myth. But his last, plastered words are often remembered quite accurately more than half a century after his death, his Irish accent showing through the slurred phrasing and the odd emphases of his cadence.

> I have always hoped and believed that in the last resort there would be an alliance, a compact, an understanding between England and Germany. Well, at the moment, that seems impossible. Good. If it cannot be, then I can only say the whole of my work has been in vain.
>
> I can only say that I have day in and day out called the attention of the British people to the menace from the east which confronted them. And if they *will* not hear, if they are determined *not* to hear, I can only say the fate that overcomes them in the end will be – the fate they have merited. More I cannot say.
>
> Now in this most serious time of our modern age, I beg you to realise the fight is on. You have heard something about the Battle of Berlin. You know that, there, a tremendous, world-shattering contest is being waged. Good. I will only say that the men who have died for the Battle of Berlin have given their *lives* to show that whatever else happens, Germany *will* live. *No* coercion, *no* oppression, *no* measures of tyranny that any foreign foe can introduce will shatter Germany. Germany *will* live because the people of Germany *have* in them the secret of life: *en*durance. *Will* and *purpose*. And

therefore I say to you in these last words – you may
not hear from me again for a few months – I say, *Es
Lebe Deutschland*. Heil Hitler – and farewell!'[37]

William and the remnants of the Reichsrundfunk had
plundered the cellars at the Hamburg Funkhaus: they ate
and drank everything in sight. This was not *Twilight Over
England*, as William had predicted, but the *Götterdämmerung*
of 'Germany Calling', half-tragedy, half-farce. At four o'clock
the following morning, he was driven away from Hamburg,
which was about to surrender to the British troops.

William Joyce had indeed fulfilled his Faustian compact with
what was a truly demonic regime: he broadcast until the
radio lines went down. He complained, in the final days of
April, how hard his masters were working him. And yet he
had become addicted to his broadcasts, to airing his opinion.

Though Goebbels was now dead – having put an end to
himself, his wife Magda and their six children – his
instructions were still being followed. William and Margaret
were to be taken from Hamburg, by car, towards Schleswig-
Holstein, which the remnants of the Third Reich still held.
There was a plan to take them from the Flensburg border
area to Denmark, and thence, possibly, to neutral Sweden,
where they might have found shelter, at least for a time. They
might even have gone on to Ireland from Sweden, if they
could have found a passage.

Flensburg in Schleswig-Holstein is a Hanseatic city on
the Baltic, only a few kilometres from the Danish border. As
the Third Reich collapsed, Admiral Doenitz, named as
Hitler's heir, conducted the last rites of the fallen regime
from there. Beyond Flensburg, virtually straddling the
border with Denmark, is a seaside resort called Wassersleben,
and within this village is a hamlet called Kupfermühle –
'Coppermill'. It is most picturesque, looking out on the

calm, tideless Baltic Sea, and surrounded by wooded copses of tall birch, silver beech and green pines.

By mid-May the British occupying forces were in control of this whole area of Danish Germany, and formerly German-controlled Denmark: the documents of surrender were signed on 7 May. William and Margaret had made it to Denmark, very briefly on 5 May, but they felt uneasy: the Danish (mainly communist) resistance was active and on the lookout. The couple were not going to make it across the strip of sea to Sweden.

When they stopped over in Flensburg, they had seen a sign 'to Wassersleben', and the place had meant something to them: Ted Bowlby, the Anglo-Irishman, had a fiancée who hailed from there. And so the Joyces came to rest in this tranquil little place by the Baltic: in Maytime, the blossom all around was quite stunning. There were some British Tommies in the area; despite the formal 'no fraternising' regulations, they were not too unfriendly towards the locals.[38] Berlin was now in the hands of the Red Army – as were Prague, Vienna and Budapest. But in Wassersleben, people there just wanted to get back to their ordinary lives. At Whitsun, they even managed to hang out the traditional bunting of the season.

At Kupfermühle, there is a little cluster of artisans' dwellings called Christiangang, Hansel and Gretel cottage-houses originally erected by the enlightened King Christian IV of Denmark in the sixteenth century. This was where a couple calling themselves Wilhelm and Margaret Hansen came to lodge with their English-born landlady, Frau Asmussen, and her more elusive husband, Fred. The 'Hansens' stayed there quietly for much of the month of May. Frau Asmussen got on especially well with Margaret. They gossiped, drank gin and even sometimes chatted with British Tommies together. Indeed, the British soldiers were delighted to find an attractive Englishwoman like Margaret in this little backwater and frequently visited for drinks.[39]

Wilhelm 'Hansen' seemed to like walking. He liked to walk in the woods, pick up pieces of timber to burn in the landlady's stove – this being the main source of heating and cooking during the end-of-war shortages – and chop the wood slowly and deliberately.

A neighbour of the Asmussens, Frau Paula Bebensee, got to know the Joyces fairly well during that month. She paid scant attention to the fact that they seemed English: there were so many different nationalities coming and going, this didn't seem particularly peculiar. Paula Bebensee thought Margaret was a very nice – *sehr nette* – person though she did notice that she was fond of gin.[40]

Then, one day, there was a report of a shooting incident in the woods, and Herr Hansen was removed, in handcuffs, by the British military. Paula Bebensee kept her children inside while the military jeep carried off neighbour Hansen. It only took about ten minutes. The British military then returned and told Frau Bebensee that it was safe to let her children out of the house to play again. Then they arrested 'Frau Hansen', although they did not put the lady in handcuffs, Paula noticed.

What strange synchronicity of fate was now to bring Lieutenant Geoffrey Perry into William Joyce's life, as the fatal encounter with destiny? Lieutenant Perry had been sent to Germany towards the end of the war to assist with the interrogation of German prisoners, since he was German – speaking: indeed – oh, poetic justice – Geoffrey Perry was born into a German Jewish family as 'Horst Pinschewer'. He and his brother had come to England as teenage refugees because of Hitler's persecutions. He had now come to regard himself as British, although technically he was not yet a British subject. He enlisted in the British Army and was commissioned to help launch a free German press at the end of hostilities. One of Geoffrey's first adventures in Germany in 1945 was to walk into the Hamburg studios where Joyce had made his last, inebriated broadcast.

Geoffrey was then directed to proceed to Flensburg, along with Captain Adrian Lickorish of the Reconnaissance Regiment. And on 28 May, it happened that the two men in British army uniform went out into the Wassersleben woods to collect firewood together.

What Providence prompted another man, a certain 'Herr Hansen', also on the same errand of firewood-gathering, to choose to address Perry and Lickorish, perversely, in French, informing them that there were more twigs and branches near to him? The man collecting pieces of wood didn't just address the British officiers, he engaged them in conversation. He started to chat to them and give them a tutorial on the difference between coniferous and deciduous forests. As he was speaking, the soldiers exchanged a word or two with one another, and then Lieutenant Perry said to the man: 'You wouldn't by any chance be William Joyce, would you?'[41]

William reached to pull out his false passport, which described him as 'William Hansen', but, not unreasonably, Perry thought he was reaching for a gun, and shot William through the hip, flooring but not seriously wounding him. William protested that he was not armed, and afterwards wrote that Perry had 'blazed away' at him unreasonably. As the wound was superficial, this could not have been the case; indeed, Geoffrey Perry was criticised for not killing William Joyce outright and saving everyone the trouble of a trial.[42]

As Lord Haw-Haw was driven off in the army jeep, Geoffrey Perry recalls: 'He couldn't stop talking.' He gave them chapter and verse on the political situation, and the coming domination of all of Europe by Stalin. After nearly a month's silence, William was bursting to speak: his need to do so surpassed even the need to survive.

12

The Dramatic Last Days

'Never was there a more perfect voice for a demagogue, for its reverberations were certain to awake echoes in every heart tumid with the same desire ... That was the reason why he was in the dock: that, and Irish history.'

Rebecca West reporting the trial of
William Joyce, 'Lord Haw-Haw'

As the Second World War came to an end, the hunt commenced for war criminals, and the press was on the watch for the whereabouts of 'Haw-Haw'. In the west of Ireland, there were tales of 'sightings': he had been 'seen drinking potcheen at Rosmuc; poaching salmon at Ma'am Cross; cycling into Galway for the pictures.'[1] There was tremendous excitement when the news broke that 'Lord Haw-Haw' had been captured on 29 May: it was greeted with splash headlines in the popular newspapers. (Norman Baillie-Stewart, captured on 21 May, had also received quite a good show, but it was still much inferior to William's.)

'WE'VE GOT HAW-HAW!' splashed the *Star* – one of the

main London newspapers of the time – on 29 May 1945. 'CAUGHT IN MANHUNT: WIFE, TOO.' The almost casual apprehension of William in the woods of Wassersleben was heightened to 'a widespread manhunt by British Second Army security and intelligence men. So intense was the search that every person moving through the Second Army was very closely interrogated by the security experts.'

William had been branded a traitor long before he set foot in an English court – he had even branded himself as such. The word was now bandied about promiscuously under pictures of William on a stretcher at Luneberg: 'Traitor in striped pyjamas.' Death by hanging for William was now being predicted by the *Daily Express*. It was being suggested by some correspondents to newspapers that anyone who was convicted of collaborating with Germany should be hanged publicly, upside down, and strung across in a row across the River Thames. This was the hot flush of post-war fever: it was perhaps understandable too, as the horrors of Belsen and Buchenwald were simultaneously being revealed. In France, more than nine thousand alleged collaborators with the Germans were shot, in most cases without benefit of judge or jury.[2]

The hullaballoo in the media about the 'traitor' Joyce probably played a key role in the decision to put him on trial for high treason. On the plus side, one could say that he had the satisfaction of being treated like celebrity from the moment of his arrest. In Ireland, especially, anyone associated with William was touched by his celebrity. As he went under the surgeon's knife to remove the bullet with which Captain Perry had plugged his buttock, *The Irish Times* was proud to report: 'DUBLIN MAN OPERATED ON "HAW-HAW"'. An Irish doctor, Lieutenant Colonel Martin Fallon, wrote to his sister, Mrs Eileen Brown of 58 Ranelagh Road, Dublin, that 'I operated on him, and he is my patient now': this compensated the soldier-surgeon for the loss of Himmler, 'who was being sewn together in his blanket when

I called at his house.'³ (Himmler had committed suicide with a cyanide pill that had been concealed in his tooth.)

Later it transpired that William had been nursed back to health by two Irish nurses, Miss Maureen Murphy of Galway and Miss Peggy Slattery of Kildimo, County Limerick, and that he had been reading a book by Christine Longford, *The Earl of Straw*, while lying in his bed at Military Hospital Number 74.⁴ Yet the newspapers liked to play on the theme of the famous man who is bereft: the *News Chronicle* described William as 'the loneliest man in Europe': Margaret had been refused permission to visit him in his hospital cot, and was being held separately.⁵

Soon after his surgery, Joyce was flown to Brussels and kept there under military surveillance while he continued to recuperate. During this period the British Parliament rather hastily revived a statute of 1351 to ensure that William would get his 'just deserts'. The extant law of 1695, which required at least two witnesses to an act of treason, or two separate acts of treason for which there were two separate witnesses, was regarded as being not sufficiently copper-bottomed for Joyce. The Treason Act of 1945 thus received the Royal Assent, conveniently, the day before Joyce was brought back to England.⁶

As William was sitting in the aeroplane with Commander Len Burt of Scotland Yard, sharing a cordial cigarette or two, a guard got up and asked Lord Haw-Haw for his autograph, which he graciously bestowed. Burt warmed to Joyce, and wrote affectionately about him in his memoirs. Of all the traitors or villains he had ever known, he said, he liked William Joyce best: 'thin, shabby, scar-faced and lame.' He liked him 'for his courage and blazing sincerity', and for his sentimental patriotism: as they passed over Dover, William exclaimed: 'The white cliffs of Dover! God bless old England on the lea' – whatever that may mean. Burt also liked Joyce for what he regarded as his gallantry towards his wife, because William had insisted: 'She had nothing to do with anything I did. I know you won't try to pin anything on her.'[7]

&

If there is a hero in the saga of William Joyce, it is his brother Quentin. From the moment William touched down on British soil, it was Quentin who carried the main burden of responsibility for managing William's affairs. Quentin was aged twenty-seven in May 1945, and by force of circumstance – and of character too – he had assumed the role of the head of the family. Frank was still overseas, serving as a Quartermaster in the British Army of the Rhine; Robert, 'Bobbins', was a soldier in Italy; and Joan, William's only sister, was planning her own wedding at this time.

In any case, it was generally to Quentin that all the siblings turned for a sense of family responsibility and leadership. 'On the subject of your status,' Joan wrote to him, 'you are brother number one on whom we shall always rely, and for whom we would, if the necessity arose, make a Joycean sacrifice.'[8] She meant that the others would die for 'Q', as he was called in the family. It was Quentin who had sorted out their mother's meagre financial affairs after her death: although she had in her time been something of an heiress, she had scarcely £100 in her bank account at the end of her life.[9] It was Quentin who signed the death certificates and made all the arrangements for his mother's burial in Lancashire, as was her wish. It was Q who sorted out his father's papers, too, and who was, most competently, able to give evidence at William's trial that Michael F. Joyce had undoubtedly been a naturalised American. Finally, it was Quentin who made all the arrangements for the defence witnesses at William's trial, even down to their hotel accommodation.

Quentin would have been justified in resenting, even hating, his brother William: it was because of him that

Quentin had spent more than four years in the prime of life in prisons and internment camps. Yet Q never blamed William: he blamed the system, and to some extent prison radicalised him, making him more resentful against injustices.[10]

From May 1945, Quentin devoted every waking hour to strategies for rescuing the brother he had hero-worshipped from boyhood. William himself was, strangely, more philosophical about his own prospects: he had moments of hope but was fairly sure that he was 'for the rope', as he told Commander Burt on the journey back to England. Quentin wouldn't even contemplate this possibility. In this endeavour, Q teamed up with Angus Macnab, 'the Master' (known also to William as 'Bonga' or 'Good Old Bonga').

Angus Macnab, described by Rebecca West as another oddity – 'a black Highlander ... plainly foredoomed to follow odd bypaths' – also loved William with that deep, abiding love that can exist between men and which is not sexual. He too had been interned under Regulation 18B, though he had served for some time beforehand as a wartime ambulance driver. (He was apparently an atrocious driver, his mind being on Latin texts or religious conundrums rather than the road.)

It would be Quentin and Macnab together who unfailingly attended Criminal Court Number One at the Old Bailey, the Appeal Court in the Strand and finally the House of Lords at the Palace of Westminster for the final appeal; it was they who most regularly and faithfully visited William in prison – first Brixton, then Wormwood Scrubs and finally Wandsworth – every day until the end.

Margaret was not brought to England until November 1945: until then she was kept in a women's military camp in Brussels. For some time, William was not sure where she was, or what had become of her. Even when she was allowed to visit, towards the end, it was a visitation across a table, and through a wire-mesh grille: no touching was permitted. This was not so much a matter of security as principle: prison regulations designed to be austere. Miss Scrimgeour told Margaret she thought that the lack of privacy and closeness was 'awful'.[11]

When William Joyce landed in England, at the weekend, he was brought to Bow Street Police Station. He was immediately charged with high treason by the station officer: 'You are charged that you did commit high treason between September 1939 and May 1945 ... By adherence to the King's enemies.' Joyce apparently heard the charge calmly, said 'I have taken cognisance', made his bed on a rubber mattress in the cells and went to sleep.

He appeared before the magistrate at Bow Street on Monday 18 June: there was an immense crowd of press and public curious to catch a glimpse of the celebrated Lord Haw-Haw. At this time, Bow Street, in the Covent Garden area, was surrounded by tenement buildings, and press photographers inveigled, or possibly paid for, balcony positions in an effort to get pictures of William exercising in the yard below. He could not be seen, however, in the 'fifteen-yard strip of concrete'.

This court appearance was also a brief formality: the court was told that the charge was high treason and the magistrate, Sir Bernard Watson – whom William thought was kind – asked the prisoner if he was legally represented, and if he had funds to engage his own lawyer. William replied 'No' to both questions and agreed that legal aid be arranged for him. The case was remanded for later procedure at the Old Bailey, and William was conveyed to Brixton Prison hospital – he was still being treated for his wound and also for a scalp infection. It was there, on 26 June, that Quentin, along with Macnab, saw him for the first time since 1939. Although he looked shaky – reporters had described him as 'thin and yellowish' – Q and John were astonished by his cheerfulness. He would indeed remain cheerful throughout this last six months of his life.

On 27 June, Quentin wrote to a friend that

> William is making steady progress in his state of
> health, and when I saw him yesterday he seemed
> much better. He still suffers a certain amount of
> pain but in view of the seriousness of his wound
> and his badly sprained ankle, he is doing well.[12]

Apparently the sprained ankle, the result of an inebriated fall
in Berlin, caused more difficulty than Captain Perry's
gunshot. Over the course of the next few months Quentin
would write to friends and relations: 'William is very
cheerful and in good spirits', 'William is in magnificent
spirits', 'William is in very good form.' The prison regime
suited William: it was regular; it was quasi-military; all his
everyday worries were taken care of; he could read, write and
drink a moderate amount of beer; and he was plied with gifts
of cigarettes.

In jail, first on remand, and finally under sentence of
death, William became a very nice person. Regrettably, he
remained unrepentant in his National Socialist views, but he
was kindly, thoughtful, considerate of others, humorous and
calm about his fate. The warders seemed to like_him very
much. He also received shoals of letters from well-wishers –
many from Ireland, he was pleased to note. Although
Quentin asked for letters to William to be preserved for the
sake of the family, they were all destroyed at the end of
William's life, in accordance with regulations.[13]

The trial was due to commence in July 1945, when
Europe was recovering from the destruction of nearly six
years of war, and Britain was engaged in a general election
which, by British standards, was mildly revolutionary, for it
seemed to be about to sweep away the old Tory England of
pre-war times and usher in fresh young Labour radicals like
Michael Foot, Roy Jenkins and the fiery Barbara Castle. The
trial did not in fact start until September, so as to allow the
copious amount of documentation to be prepared.[14]

Quentin took it upon himself to help prepare the lawyers' papers as much as he could. Quentin was not as highly educated as William had been: Q had been sent to a good school, Mercer's at Holborn, but had no university degree. Nonetheless, Quentin educated himself in the intricacies of the law in researching his brother's case.

The authorities had known for some time that William had been born in America: he had announced it in *Twilight Over England*, published in 1940. This fact worried them, and intelligence papers were being prepared on Joyce from 1944 onwards.[15] The simple truth was that William was never British at all, however ardently he wrapped himself in the Union Jack and advocated the cause of the British Empire. He was an American: he had been born in America of naturalised American parents. His father had been solemnly sworn to American nationality in 1894 and, as was pointed out during the course of the trial, 'naturally', at that time, a wife took the nationality of her husband: this made his mother, also, technically an American. (She was described as an alien when visiting her home town of Oldham in 1917.) However, his father had claimed to be British.[16]

As the Crown prosecution was wrestling with the awkward fact that they would have a US citizen in the dock, so Quentin was building all his hopes on it. He knew that William was an American, but he also knew that he would have to prove this fact in court. He wrote to everyone he could think of, trawling for witnesses.

Quentin wrote his letters from the 'not very comfortable' little flat that he shared with his sister Joan, at 86 Underhill Road in Dulwich. Unbeknown to Quentin, British Intelligence shared in much of his correspondence: they opened virtually every letter that arrived at his address, read it, copied it, passed on the information to the prosecution, and resealed it. They also opened most of the correspondence with the lawyers who had been assigned to the case, Messrs Ludlow & Co. of Broad Street, Covent Garden.[17] The State had developed the habit in wartime – as governments generally do in time of war – of prying into the lives of its citizens, and indeed controlling many aspects of civil life; they saw very little amiss with continuing to do so in peacetime.

Quentin started with the older members of his family: his uncles, Gilbert Brooke, resident in Chapel-en-la-Frith in Derbyshire, and Pat Joyce of Killour in The Neale, County Mayo, who had inherited the family farm.[18] He wrote to his 'dear Uncle Gilbert' on 11 July that he was 'once again hoisting the distress signal' over William's forthcoming trial. Nonetheless, he noted that

> We are pretty confident of success. We have been fortunate enough to have the services of a very fine solicitor who has gone to endless trouble with the case and given unstintingly of his time to ensure that everything humanly possible has been done to prepare a cast-iron defence.

Quentin's unstinting work for the lawyers – and the touching sense of appreciation he and John Macnab showed to the law firm afterwards – made the case, for the lawyers in question, one of the most rewarding they had ever taken on.

C. V. Head, who had been selected on the taxi-rank principle as the legal-aid solicitor, was most diligent in his labours; the advocates that he briefed, Gerald Slade, King's Counsel, Derek Curtis-Bennet and James Burge were all highly esteemed lawyers. Mr Slade had a fine reputation in criminal and civil cases and was the Recorder of Guildford; Mr Curtis-Bennet was a distinguished and experienced silk; and James Burge had been a deputy judge advocate in the RAF during the war. For the prosecution, the leading counsel would be the handsome and clever Sir Hartley Shawcross, the rising star of the post-war Labour Party, who would also perform with very great distinction as a prosecutor in the Nuremburg Trials.

Yet, Quentin told his uncle Gilbert that if the defence could convince the jury that William truly was an American, they would be sure of 'a hundred percent' success. He was concerned that the prosecution would say that there was no proof that the William Joyce in the dock was the son of the Michael Joyce who had become an American citizen at Hudson County, New Jersey, on 25 October 1894, since there might be many Irishmen called Michael Joyce who became Americans. Thus he was entreating Uncle Gilbert to come to London, to enter the witness box and swear that William was indeed his nephew, and the son of Michael and Gertrude Joyce. 'I cannot tell you how sorry I am, my dear uncle, that you should be dragged into this case,' Q added, with the courtesy that was his wont. 'I am very sorry that you are to be worried in this way, but I am sure that you appreciate how very critical the position is ... '[19]

Gilbert certainly did not want to be brought into the limelight as the uncle of Lord Haw-Haw – a fact he was desperate to keep secret. He informed the local constabulary that he was 'worried to death about this case because, living as he did in a small village, the fact that he was a relative of William Joyce would become a source of local gossip' and this would reflect adversely on him.[20] Moreover, he had never greatly approved of his sister's marriage to an Irishman and a Roman Catholic, and he considered the marriage unhappy – which, incidentally, it had not been. Gilbert wrote a not unfriendly letter to Quentin, but signalled that he would not be much use in the matter.

Quentin grumbled to a friend that Gilbert was probably more use to the prosecution than to the defence. He had been hopelessly vague about everything: he had got mixed up as to whether he had been in America in 1903 or 1906, and he had said he didn't know whether Michael Joyce was an

American citizen or not. 'The whole thing was so damnably obscure and obviously an unwilling effort that I don't think it would be of the slightest use,' Quentin said.[21]

Quentin was also in correspondence with his Irish uncles – his father's brothers – John in America and Pat in the Ballinrobe area of Mayo. John did not prove very useful: he said he was too old to travel to England and was not confident about making a statement in court. His letter wished Quentin well but it was not particularly warm-hearted: maybe Uncle John still bore some animus against William for his connection with the Black and Tans in Galway during the 1920s.

Uncle Pat in Mayo proved to be the best of the collateral relations: he wrote seven or eight times to Q and did what he could to search out documents and affidavits. He tracked down the whereabouts of William's baptismal certificate and tried to locate his late brother's bank manager, and generally showed affection and support for 'poor Willie' and his situation. Uncle Pat expressed the hope, above all, that 'Willie will get a fair trial', though he seemed doubtful that this would prove possible.[22]

He also assured Quentin that 'the Irish government was taking a great interest in the case'. People in Ireland were fascinated by the trial of Lord Haw-Haw but the State distanced itself from any involvement in it. Many Irish civil servants and political personnel had been privately horrified by Éamon de Valera's much-publicised visit to the German legation in Dublin to offer condolences for Hitler's death in May 1945: the official view was growing that Ireland should not be seen as sympathetic towards Nazi sympathisers.[23] Edward Bowlby, Joyce's colleague in the Rundfunk, who had been born in Ireland and had lived in the country until he was eleven, was turned down several times in his application for an Irish passport after the war. He finally obtained one in 1947, but the State was not keen to accept him initially.[24]

The Irish high commissioner in London, John Dulanty – a career diplomat who was privately pro-British – stated coldly that 'Joyce is not a citizen of Éire under any of the several categories that constitute citizenship.'[25] The American authorities made no attempt to claim William either, and limited themselves to providing the background documentary information about Michael F. Joyce's naturalisation.

Quentin followed every trail imaginable in an effort to establish his parents' American status. From address to address, he sought out old connections of his parents, sometimes without luck. He also had a large amount of incoming mail to deal with – much of it monitored by British Intelligence – from both well-wishers and ill-wishers, on the subject of Lord Haw-Haw.

Old friends and family connections wrote to Quentin, offering their help and support. Among these was Emily Holland, who, with her husband Frank, had been close friends of Quentin's parents in the United States. She offered to do anything she, or her husband, could to help. 'My heart has been heavy ever since William's case came up,' she wrote.

> I have known him from a baby a few months old,
> so your sorrow is my sorrow. Your mother was a
> brave woman – I hope we may all be as brave and
> pray that God will help us all. My love to Joan and
> Frank and Robert, wherever they may be. Yours
> lovingly, Emily Holland.[26]

Mrs Holland, and her husband Frank, who now lived in retirement at Hoath, near Canterbury, could certainly assist William's case: they could testify in court that the William Joyce in the dock, whom they had known since he was a baby, was indeed the American-born son of Michael and Gertrude Joyce. Quentin, always courteous and 'sorry that it should have become necessary to trouble you in this matter', asked them to do so, and they willingly agreed. Quentin had found his key witness. Frank Holland, though he seemed elderly, and quavered when he spoke, immediately convinced the court that the accused was the same person as the American child he had known in Brooklyn in 1908.[27]

Quentin's second witness was also an old friend of the family: the retired policeman Bernard O'Reilly, who now lived in Liverpool. O'Reilly had known Michael Joyce in Galway, where Michael had always had good relations with the RIC (which, on the foundation of the Irish State in 1922, was replaced by the Garda Síochána). O'Reilly had also helped Queenie Joyce in the footling offence of not having registered as an alien when she visited her own home town of Oldham in 1917, to prove her mother's will, which was to leave over £7,251 to her and two of her brothers – a sum in excess of £220,000 by current values.[28]

Bernard O'Reilly, though an elderly gentleman as well, was only too willing to support the Joyces. The first thing he did was to start a Holy Communion novena (a nine-day cycle of prayer, performed, in this instance, with the sacrament of the Eucharist).[29] He would travel to London, accompanied by his daughter. Quentin, as usual, consulted train timetables and arranged accommodation, at the Tuscan Hotel on Shaftesbury Avenue. He apologised to O'Reilly for not putting him up in the Dulwich flat: 'You know how cramped our quarters are.'

Among the letters that Quentin received, and responded to, were warm and compassionate letters from two young women: one was from Sylvia Morris, the beautiful young Fascist from Donnington in Yorkshire, the doctor's daughter and former Mosleyite who had helped Queenie to clear out William's London flat in September 1939.[30] The other was from Margaret Wood, an attractive young woman who still lived near the Joyces in Dulwich. Margaret Wood's letters to Q were warm, friendly, sensible and kindly, but also concerned with everyday life, and restrained. The letters were thoroughly English: quietly supportive of Q, but downplaying the drama of what Q constantly referred to as 'this matter of life and death'. Margaret Wood obviously hoped that Quentin would be successful, but she did not dwell on the Haw-Haw theme, and tried to interest him in a range of other topics: her parents' visits to a West End show and the tedium of office work.

Q liked Margaret Wood a great deal, and kept up the friendship with her, but his consuming focus for the time being was William. He would not suffer a word to be said against his brother, and he engaged in a blazing row with a policeman, outside Mornington Crescent tube station, one evening in July when the copper made some casual remarks about William Joyce being a traitor and that public opinion demanded that he should hang, or that he should have been shot out of hand.

Quentin wrote a heartfelt letter of complaint:

> You must be aware ... that Mr William Joyce is on remand and that his case has not yet been tried and that comment on the case which is sub judice is contempt of court and an extremely serious offence.

The policeman, Constable Hilditch, wrote back promptly with an anxious statement of withdrawal:

> I tender you without any reservation whatsoever my humble and sincere apologies ... I do hope for my sake you will let this drop as you know I have nearly finished my service so would not like my pension in any way jeopardised.[31]

Quentin agreed: honour had been satisfied. But the episode had upset him because he knew that this was what many ordinary folk were saying. Since William had been charged at Bow Street, the newspapers had become more circumspect and had stopped throwing the word 'traitor' around, but there was undoubtedly a substantial number of people who were firmly of the view that Lord Haw-Haw was a traitor who deserved to be 'strung up'. Quentin was receiving letters and cards to that effect: these were generally anonymous and were sometimes embellished with a drawing of a gallows.

⁓

The trial of William Joyce commenced at the Old Bailey on Monday 17 September 1945: that September was a golden month before the onset of a harsh winter. There were queues around the block for the public gallery: some people had slept on the pavement overnight. The restaurants around the Old Bailey were full at lunchtime: an Irish law student from Dublin who attended the trial had to go as far as Piccadilly for lunch.[32] More than fifty reporters were present from Britain and overseas. This was described, at the time, as an extraordinary number of journalists gathered in one place: space in the public gallery had to be made to accommodate the press.[33]

It had been regarded as a complex trial, and from 1946 until the present the case of *Rex v. Joyce* has accumulated many weighty volumes of print in the legal profession. It remains to this day a contentious case which is, in the words of a London lawyer, 'not only a useful but an indispensable precedent on the question of allegiance to the Crown'. It was to set a significant precedent: if a British journalist were to broadcast for an enemy in time of war, the case of *Rex v. Joyce* would be invoked. In the winter of 2001, the *Law Gazette* of London considered the possibility of British Muslims adhering to foreign powers being tried under the rules of the Joyce case.[34]

At this time, Britain was in the throes of changing governments. As a result, three Attorneys-General were involved in the trial: Sir Donald Somervell of the coalition government in May; Sir David Maxwell-Fyfe, of the Churchill 'caretaker' government; and finally Sir Hartley Shawcross, for the Labour government. Even though the trial itself was all over in less than three days, the transcript of the trial filled more than a hundred and sixty closely printed pages.

The case threw up a great deal of intricate detail beloved by legal experts. There was a substantial amount of scholarly disquisition on precedent: 'The case I have in mind, m'lud, is In re Perton, 1885', 'Personally, I do not think that ... *Protectio trahit subjectionem et subjectio protectionem* points to such a conclusion' and suchlike. There were no end of references to important sources and precedents: to *Halsbury's Laws of England*, common-law jurisdiction, Admiralty jurisdiction, Section 11 of the 1870 Foreign Enlistment Act, the statutes of King Edward III, the notorious case of Peacham in 1615, *Phillimore's International Law*, *East's Pleas of the Crown*, *Coke's Report*, the legal tomes of Blackstone, the Aliens Act of 1920 and much more besides – all prefaced by exquisite exchanges with 'my learned friend'.

As doctors revel in a truly unusual illness, so lawyers relish the recondite complexities of the law: *Rex v. Joyce* offered a feast for legal appetites. But it boiled down to this: Sir Hartley Shawcross, who looked like a matinée idol and spoke with the polish of a West End actor, contended that Joyce had wrapped himself in the Union Jack many times over and, in claiming a British passport, owed allegiance to the Crown. He said that exact precedent was less significant than common sense, for which there had always been flexibility in English law.

Sir Hartley's opening statement for the Crown summed up the case for the prosecution: treason, he said, was the most serious of crimes, and Joyce was a man who had 'claimed and asserted the rights to British citizenship and had clothed himself in the full status of a British subject'. This was undeniably true: Joyce had affirmed his Britishness more emphatically than any true-born Englishman. He had the blood of Ulster flowing in his veins, and the passions of Ulster transmitted to him by his mother: his Britishness was the Britishness of an Orangeman, not the Britishness of an Englishman – extreme, inflated, vehement and violent. What was, perhaps, most piquant of all was that the point at issue was whether William was an 'alien' – he who had worked that word to death when writing about Jews in his writings in *Action* and *The Blackshirt*. The man who had charged British Jews with being, in essence, aliens, was now hanging his hopes of survival on the possibility of being pronounced an alien himself.

Gerald Slade, who would later become a judge, was acknowledged to have put up a most estimable, and extraordinarily detailed, defence in arguing that William was in fact an alien. Slade knew the law and displayed his knowledge of it to great effect. He brought forward the witnesses – there were seven in all, including Frank Holland, Bernard O'Reilly and Quentin himself – and sought to prove beyond all doubt that Joyce had been born in America of naturalised American parents. Slade's argument was that, regardless of whether Joyce affirmed a thousand times that he was British, he was still in law an American, just as if any of us shouted a thousand times that we were Chinese, this would not make us Chinese.

But Sir Hartley's moral and metaphorical truth carried more weight with judge and jury than Slade's legalistic defence. Moreover, Sir Hartley's handsome appearance, which seemed particularly stunning in that immediate postwar time when people in general looked grey and pinched, impressed the court more than Mr Slade's drier personality.[35]

In the dock, William looked small and unprepossessing, but he never lost his sang-froid. He took a detached, sometimes faintly amused interest in the proceedings and was intrigued by the technical aspect of the debate. The schoolmaster in him was engaged by the pedantry and strategems of court procedure. He was amused, at one point, when the award that he had received from Hitler on 1 September 1944 was described as the 'Iron Cross': it was in fact the *Kriegsverdienstkreuz,* the 'War-merit Cross'. William said only three words during the proceedings: 'Not guilty, sir.' He had his own private musings: he called Sir Hartley 'Hotcross' and sometimes 'Hotcross Buns'.[36] Characteristically, William suspected 'Hotcross' of having Jewish blood: Shawcross did have some foreign blood, as it happens – it was Danish.

Quentin truly believed that when William's American citizenship was established – as it was – William would at least escape the death sentence. The looks that he exchanged with William were full of hopeful affection. It was an enormous shock to him when, at the end of the third day of the trial, Mr Justice Tucker more or less directed the jury to find Joyce guilty on the third count of treason: that he had adhered to the King's enemies between 18 September 1939 and 2 July 1940.

William Joyce had been charged with three counts of treason, but the first two were dropped, essentially, because they could not be made to stand up. The first count was that he had acted as a traitor during the war. This charge was vulnerable to the challenge that, from 1940, Joyce had become a German citizen and his British passport had expired. The second count was that he was guilty of a treasonable act by taking German citizenship, since it was judged treasonable to do so during wartime; this charge too was apparently difficult to sustain. The third charge was the most precise and narrow: that Joyce had broadcast for the enemy, while still holding a British passport, between 19 September 1939 and 2 July 1940. The judge, Mr Justice Tucker, who had branded Joyce a 'traitor' in the previous case of Anna Wolkoff, in 1940, directed the jury to concentrate on this count. Mr Tucker directed the jury as a matter of law that Joyce continued to owe allegiance to the Crown throughout the currency of his passport. Although falsely acquired, this passport was intended to signify allegiance. It was evident to most observers that the jury was intended to convict.

The jury duly retired to consider their verdict at 3.37 PM on 20 September and returned to Number One Court at the Old Bailey at 4 PM. The foreman of the jury duly informed the clerk of the court that Joyce had been found guilty on the third count of high treason, by a unanimous verdict.

Mr Justice Tucker donned the black cap – William wittily called it the 'vampire chapeau' – which judges then wore to pronounce sentence of death, and proceeded to do so. William was utterly composed, but Quentin's eyes were wet with tears. The press was delighted to be able to run splash headlines about Haw-Haw's forthcoming hanging. In Mayo, Uncle Pat reflected bitterly that this was no more than you could expect from England when an Irishman was in the dock.[37]

Quentin was once again overwhelmed with letters of condolence, distress and gloating vengeance. One man offered to take William's place at the gallows – as though this could be permitted. Frank wrote from the British Army of the Rhine, where he was now stationed:

> My dear Quentin … I was completely astounded when I heard the news, but surely the appeal must be successful, pray God it will be. I think you have been splendid, Q, and I admire you so very much, also dear old John … Things must come right. *Nil Desperandum.* Always yours.[38]

Bernard O'Reilly wrote to say that he was 'overwhelmed' – but that, in view of the appeal, there should be no cause for despondency. Perhaps the most touching communication that Q received was an anonymous note: 'God help you and bless you, from a mother who lost her son in this terrible war.'

Quentin turned his attention to the question of an appeal. He believed that everything now depended on this, and devoted himself as much to it as he had to the original trial.

William also showed a certain degree of optimism, though there also runs, through all that he said or wrote, a sense of acceptance of his fate. 'I am in good health and excellent spirits,' he wrote on 19 October, to Aubrey Lees, one of the old BUF members, 'and am fortified against whatever the future may bring, with the complete and, I might say, epic unity with which my wife has honoured me and by the knowledge that I am to you, my friends, what I was.'[39]

William was not permitted to read the newspapers in prison – although clippings were given to him. This might have seemed like a deprivation to a man who loved current affairs, yet perhaps it was for the best. He now read more fiction. He felt himself to be 'scandalously lucky' for the richness of his reading fare: John Buchan, C. S. Forester, Arnold Bennett, Dennis Wheatley and his old favourite, A. J. Cronin. He even absorbed himself in *Gone With the Wind*. Margaret loved this book, though he could not match her enthusiasm for it: 'My objections are not so much as to the sickly idealising of the South, as to the odious personality of the heroine, who is as a real woman as a chocolate liqueur is to a tumbler of vodka, or a Steinhägen,' he told her. 'But there, darling, let's not quarrel!' Sometimes it amused him to spell 'quarrel' as 'kwarrel'. He also conceded that his dislike of Scarlett O'Hara was being 'Brookish', by which he meant both austere and pompous. 'Probably an Orange chromosome at work!' he opined.

Among certain Catholics, the battle for William's soul now commenced. A Roman Catholic priest, Father Edmund Marshall-Keene – a convert from Anglicanism, and formerly a Captain Dunkerton – began to correspond with William.[40] He asked if he might visit William, with a view to bringing him back back to the Church of Rome, his baptismal faith. For Catholics at that time, a cradle Catholic must die reconciled to Mother Church if he was to save his soul. William dissented from this judgement, as he had done since the age of fourteen, but he said he had nothing against seeing

Father Marshall-Keene, and instructed Quentin to arrange a visit. William would talk to the priest, correspond quite copiously with him, and accept the priest's blessing in a friendly spirit.

The Joyces' priest cousin in America, Father Martin Stanton, would become most exercised about this issue, and wrote from Jersey City about the necessity of the sacrament of reconciliation. Earthly life ends soon anyway: what about eternity? 'My father, who was a saintly man, was [William's] godfather,' Father Martin wrote.

> He would have considered it a great disgrace if his godchild, for whom he stood sponsor, were to cut himself off from the Church and the sacraments …
> I also express the heartfelt wish that William be reconciled to the Church … that he may make certain his eternal salvation.[41]

Angus Macnab also worried fretfully about William's soul. But he knew William well enough to acknowledge that he was not one for a deathbed conversion. 'He professed himself to be a Protestant,' Macnab recalled in the 1970s. William was not intolerant of the Church of Rome: he said that, for millions of people, it was an excellent religion. It just wasn't for him, and he had a certain joshing contempt for 'canonical jiggery-pokery'. He was also taken up with another quasi-spiritual philosophy, known as gestalt. This is a form of psychotherapy – invented by a Jewish German, Fritz Perls – that takes a holisitic approach to mind–body balance. It emphasises 'personal growth' and – in William's own version of it at least – had a Buddhist element: after our death, he believed, we are absorbed into an undefined spiritual life whereby our being lives on. William certainly believed he would live on in spirit; he also believed that his mother's presence was near him.

Father Edmund battled on patiently, and was permitted many visits: the conversations between the two were obviously interesting, and William nominated him as a visiting chaplain. But Edmund never got his man: William was determined to die an Anglican. Still, the priest was able to reassure Angus Macnab, afterwards, that he was certain that William's soul was redeemed.[42]

⁓

The appeal against the sentence of death on William Joyce was opened on 30 October at the Court of Criminal Appeal in the Strand, before the Lord Chief Justice, Mr Justice Humphreys, and Mr Justice Lynsky. Quentin looked dreadful at this stage: his eyes were red and puffy, suggesting sleeplessness and weeping. In fact, he wasn't well. He was suffering from some form of glandular fever, which – perhaps presciently – was affecting him around his neck, as though a noose were tightening around it.[43] John Mayes, an Englishman who had been a merchant seaman during the war, was present at the appeal. Joyce, he said, 'held his head high, with a resolute smile of indifference' during the proceedings. Mayes recalled William's 'commanding gaze', which somehow compensated for his facial disfigurement. Joyce's counsel, Slade, 'quiet, patient and cool in manner, made point after point seemingly unanswerable in terms of existing case law', according to Mayes. Sir Hartley Shawcross struck Mr Mayes as 'loud and brash in argument, but [he] never seemed to be doing so from true substance.'[44] The benches were packed with young barristers and law students.

After a little more than a week, as the light of the year was fading into a dingy November, William's appeal was dismissed. It was said that no new evidence had emerged, although Judge Humphreys asked such probing questions that Quentin dared hope, again, that he was sowing new doubts in the minds of the judges. But once again, Sir Hartley had won the day when he said that 'the incalculable advantage of the whole system of British law is that its principles are capable of adaptation to the new circumstances perpetually arising.' The Lord Chief Justice agreed.

The defence team, with Quentin now in a state of great concern, asked leave to appeal to the House of Lords: this took place in the second week of December. The House of Commons, which had been bombed during the war, was still occupying their lordships' chamber, so the appeal was heard in the royal Robing Room at Westminster. Once again, the case of William Joyce drew crowds of Lords and Commoners. William had the impression that by now, Slade was suffering from nervous strain but that Curtis-Bennett was 'good'.[45] Five law lords sat for three days; on 18 December their verdict was announced. William's final appeal was dismissed, with one law lord, Lord Porter, dissenting. Their lordships said they would give their reasons at a later date, although William himself would never learn of the reasons, except in the great gestalt of his spirit after death.

A crucial element in Lord Jowitt's reasoning was that

> the special value to the enemy of the appellant's services as a broadcaster was that he could be represented as speaking as a British subject, and his German workbook showed that it was in this character that he was employed, for which his passport was doubtless accepted as a voucher.[46]

In common sense, this was accurate: William was valuable to Germany because he seemed so very British, and the Reich had initially accepted him as a Galway-born British subject.[47] Yet a question mark hovers over the *Rex v. Joyce* trial. Was it fair, or was it a show trial? Was it wartime revenge – Britain's *épuration?* Legal opinion has remained uneasy about the verdict to this day. In 1975, Sir John Foster told Ludovic Kennedy that the verdict had not been properly arrived at.[48] Geoffrey Robertson describes the Joyce trial as a case of a capital offence turning on 'the merest technicality', which is clearly unacceptable.[49] Some critics have even gone so far as to describe the killing of Joyce as 'judicial murder'.

William – who was not present when their Lordships pronounced – was not too surprised at the final verdict, and his letters remained full of jokes and 'codding'. As the House adjourned, he contemplated the view over the Thames and Lambeth Bridge. What a wonderful winter afternoon it was: 'crimson sun on the water, mist, leafless trees, a picture that stirred my heart with memories of the Heimat.' He still called Germany 'the Homeland'.

As Christmas approached, William knew that there would now be no reprieve from the gallows – and so did a despairing Quentin. Indeed, William knew this by 28 November, when John Amery, his radio competitor in Berlin, was tried for treason at the Old Bailey – and sentenced to death within the space of eight minutes. The charge against Amery went beyond mere broadcasting: he had been only an occasional broadcaster, but he had travelled around the Continent trying to recruit men to fight against Britain.

Efforts were made by Amery's family to save him, by providing psychiatric reports showing that he was a moral imbecile – which indeed he was. He was almost certainly unfit to enter, as he did, the plea of 'guilty' to the charge of treason. But Amery insisted on pleading guilty, and the death sentence automatically followed.[50]

There was one chance for Amery of escaping the gallows: a royal pardon, which was in the gift of the home secretary. Amery might have been spared the gallows if the home secretary, James Chuter Ede, one of the new Labour intake who had come up through the safe ranks of municipal authorities, had agreed to recommend the King's pardon. Chuter Ede was new to the job and thus more reliant on his civil servants than an experienced statesman might have been; his principal civil servant, the permanent secretary at the Home Office, Sir Frank Newsam, strongly argued against granting Amery a pardon. It would, he said, look weak. It would also appear as though John Amery had been spared because he was the son of a distinguished Tory political family.[51] So Amery was doomed; and once Amery had been hanged – the sentence was carried out on 19 December – Joyce was bound to follow.

Thus William Joyce followed his Berlin adversary to the execution chamber. William's cousin Father Martin Stanton had written that he prayed that William 'will die holily and bravely in the spirit of St Thomas More, the Chancellor of England, who went innocent to the block with God in his heart and a jest on his lips.'

Though he was far from saintly, William maintained his sense of humour to the end. Although he admitted to Margaret that their predicament was 'hardly a laughing matter', he added, 'I should not be myself if I did not see the humorous side of the present situation.'[52] On one occasion, Quentin's glandular swellings were so acute that he had to wear a bandage, and he arrived to visit William with his neck in a medical halter. 'Tut!' cried William. 'Fancy coming to see me in that condition! Don't you know necks are a very sensitive subject in this quarter?'[53]

His last letters to his wife Margaret are by turn loving, joking, rueful, personally (but not politically) repentant, ironic, sarcastic, and full of puns, wordplay, intellectual showing-off, occasional sanctimoniousness and tutorial advice: he loved to teach. He encourages Margaret to learn French, and says her German is now very good (which it wasn't). 'I do wish I had taken the trouble more often to EXPRESS my admiration of your many talents and virtues. I have been an ungracious wretch, but blame the chromosomes, dear!'[54] He sometimes signed himself 'Wandsworth Will'.

It seemed that once sex – and perhaps alcohol – had been, by force of circumstances, removed from their relationship, so was the combative element. William was tender and contrite towards her:

> All you say of my bad habits is justified. When I curse myself for your predicament, I was not thinking of any fundamental decisions, but simply of my gross irresponsibility in getting so incontinently caught. No incarceration without representation! That will be your plaint.

He could never resist jesting. When he was attending the Old Bailey he quipped that he was now 'something in the City!' In his letters, he calls a priest by the cod-Irishism 'prasht', and uses big words, just as he did as a schoolboy. He describes his old boss, Eduard Dietze as a 'squamous cuttlefish' and refers to skin trouble as 'cutaneous sesquipedalianism'. He also indulges in his sideline hobby of medical diagnoses: when Margaret is unwell, he writes that it 'looks to me as if a stray staphylococcus might have been at work ... the bloodstream needs purifying.' He discourses playfully upon the difference between a cyst and an abcess: 'The cyst occupies a higher place than the mere abscess in the eruptive hierarchy. The cyst ... originates with a rebellious local gestalt demanding, not, like a tumour, complete autonomy, but a quite irregularly constituted Borough Council.' He calls Margaret's cyst 'Cyril the Sod'.

When Margaret had a period – she habitually suffered from menstrual troubles – he wrote: 'the corpus luteum and the hormones have reached a gentleman's agreement.' In Margaret's case, especially latterly, a period was a reminder of disappointment: she had wanted a child. William had not: thus the menstruation agreed with this gentleman. When she had a period after a delay of some weeks after they had been physically parted, he quipped: 'Fate did not play the joker!'

Lyrically, he remembers their best times together,

especially the Christmases: 'Anyhow my darling, on Sylvester [New Year's Eve] I may as well admit I shall be thinking with affection of our old club Leipziger Platz ... ' He wishes that they had spent all their Christmases in Germany alone, instead of having had others present: 'Our Weinachtan were wonderful but I could have made them better if I had not been a pig. But I know that you have forgiven me. There's nothing I want or miss, but you dear.' Again, he apologises for having brought misfortune on her; 'I know that you have forgiven me, altho' I have not forgiven myself.' He thinks back to Berlin, romantically, seeing it now as a lovely city in ruins, its people suffering: 'I love Berlin more than I can say.' He remembers a special afternoon he and Margaret spent together on an Oslo fjord, and their happy days in London before the war, at Onslow Gardens, a flat rented by Macnab.

He counsels Margaret to go and live in Ireland after he has gone: 'Ireland is the only place to live.' But not Mayo, he says: 'it's depressing'. The outskirts of Dublin are mentioned as a possibility: 'Dublin ... has been touched by the Renaissance.' But the best option of all for him is Galway: 'I prefer Galway by far.' He would be glad to see any part of Eyre Square again in Margaret's presence: 'God grant we may! ... Galway is surely *ein schönes Städchen*' ('a pretty little town'). He often thought of Galway now, and the great Atlantic Ocean, which symbolised the mystery of the infinite to his boyhood eyes. If Margaret would go to Galway, walk down by the Spanish Arch and out towards Salthill, he would walk with her in spirit, in the great gestalt that awaited him.

He encouraged her to become a writer, but cautioned her not to grow too fond of 'the cratur' – an old Irishism for the bottle of whiskey. 'Enjoy yourself but never let the cratur be master,' he wrote, 'else it may dim that fine perception which our preternatural means of communication will require.' As the days progressed towards 3 January 1946, the appointed day of his death, he began to call Margaret 'Freya', a name associated with Nordic mysticism:

> My own dear Freya, in the courts of the morning, I
> shall be waiting for you, ready to embrace you ...
> Freya, I just want to keep on saying, I love you, I
> love you, I love you, I shall always be with you ...
> My dearest Freya, darling comrade of eternity ...

His pet-names for Margaret also include 'Mae' and 'Mother Sheep'.

William told Margaret that he could not find words to express his admiration for Quentin, and he now charged his ever-reliable brother with the worldly care of Margaret, and asked his other siblings to 'make her one with them'. On the eve of his execution, William wrote to Q:

> My very dear Quentin, to you, my beloved brother
> and sure comrade, I write this little letter: but it is
> also addressed to Frank, Joan and Robert. There is
> no need for me to write to each of you individually.
> We are all one, in this life and beyond. And my
> sweet Margaret is also of your company. I charge
> you with her, as flesh of our flesh and blood of our
> blood: but I know that this is something which I
> need not stress ... It has not been my way to speak
> my deep admiration for you as a family. But you
> have been aware of it. Words cannot express my
> feelings for you: but you are worthy of our parents.
> That God spared them the ordeal which they
> would have endured had they lived, we must be
> thankful. They would have been with me in every
> way: but they would, in the decline of their lives,
> have suffered much.[55]

Do not, he asks, be unhappy about him, 'dear children'. Be proud that he died for a cause he believed in. 'In the name of our parents and our cause, I salute you and pray that God's blessing may be upon you.'

The last farewell between the siblings was of course

tearful, but William helped them with his joviality. Quentin wrote: 'I saw my brother for the last time yesterday. Another brother [Robert] accompanied me. William was in magnificent spirits, as he has been throughout.'[56] Robert, regarded as a mere child by William, was in fact 'beside himself' with grief. Robert was not yet twenty-four.

To Macnab, William wrote a letter of great tenderness on the morning that he died: 'Beloved John,' he wrote,

> I am now so far moved away from all earthly things that the remaining minutes of my life seem like tenants who have not paid their rent … Thank you for your devotion to me and above all for your prayers. More I will not write, save to say that when we meet again, we shall regret nothing that has happened now.[57]

Macnab wrote afterwards that 'In his last days, although in perfectly good health, his actual body seemed spiritualised … his flesh seemed to have a quasi-transparent quality. Being with him gave a sense of inward peace, like being in a quiet church.'[58]

William Joyce had not led a good life; he had been on many occasions horrid, nasty, selfish, arrogant and unforgivably prejudiced. Yet there was something redemptive about his walk to the gallows, which was shaky but brave. It was a Sidney Carton death: *It was a far, far better thing that he did now than he had ever done.* And he went to a far better rest after his restless life.

Immediately after he was executed, the Lord Haw-Haw story was mentioned no more. But from Ireland, where there has always been sympathy for a hanged felon, came many messages of condolence. 'I have heard your brother spoken of as a hero everywhere I have gone,' an Englishwoman wrote to Quentin Joyce, from Mullingar, County Westmeath, three days after the hanging. 'In the cathedral here he was referred to from the pulpit and men and women almost wept.'[59]

EPILOGUE

Post-Mortem, Post-War

'The man who was born American, lived a German, and died a British traitor will at the end become what he really was all along – an Irishman from Connemara.'

Ludovic Kennedy, 1975

William Joyce said dreadful things sometimes, and his last public utterance was ill-judged and appalling. 'I defy the Jews who caused this last war,' he stated, with breathtaking inappropriateness, before going on to warn the West against the 'aggressive imperialism of the Soviet Union'.[1] But the question remains: should a man be executed, essentially, for what he *says*? Unlike other traitors and spies of the mid-twentieth century – Philby, Burgess, Maclean and Blunt – William Joyce was not responsible for a single British death, unless you count the suicide case of a woman who was allegedly so depressed by the sound of Lord Haw-Haw's voice that she put her head in the gas oven.[2] As a member of the public wrote in a letter to Quentin Joyce in September 1945: 'After all, people did not have to listen to him if they did not so desire.' A correspondent to the *Manchester Guardian* – which had opposed the hanging of Joyce – wrote:

'No matter how much we may detest what a man believes we have no right to put him to death for expressing that belief.'[3] Touchingly, too, John Amery's mother, Florence, wrote to the newspaper to ask that Joyce's death be spared, now that 'her beloved son' had paid the penalty for his foolishness.[4]

It might also be said that Joyce was hanged for his celebrity. Other British broadcasters for the Nazis, such as Margaret Bothamley, his colleague in Berlin and companion in Hamburg and Flensburg, got off virtually scot-free: the lady walked with a year's suspended sentence. Even though she was one hundred percent a British subject of the King, she was not charged with high treason, presumably because she was not a celebrity. She was also older, and a woman, though these facts carry no weight in law.

The law can be an awkward tool and the criminal-justice system is not always imaginative in fitting the penalty to the offence. The most fitting penalty for William would have been to bring him on a guided tour of the death camps of Belsen, Auschwitz and Treblinka, and to show him the consequences of the anti-Semitism upon which the Third Reich had been constructed. To make him tour the Nazi death camps of the Third Reich, and ask him, repeatedly – '*Now* do you think that "the Yids" benefited from the Second World War? *Now* what have you to say about the Jews as so-called oppressors?'

As it was, Joyce was dismissive of the death camps, as was Margaret. His laughing hard-heartedness about Belsen and Buchenwald – he quipped that the Jews thrived in adversity, and made jokes about Belsen to Margaret – was lamentable.[5] If he had been made to witness the truth, this would have been, in some measure, fitting to the offence. His anti-Semitism seems worse to me than the charge of treason: in a sense, he was always 'true to himself'.

His trial was most unfair, it seems to me, in that the prosecution, thanks to the surveillance of British Intelligence, was in possession of most of the private correspondence of the defence, while the defence had no access to the private papers of the prosecution. That pall of cheapness – of lingering questions about tactics and procedure – will always hang over the trial of William Joyce. Even Hartley Shawcross, whose scintillating performance in court carried the day, said afterwards that the Joyce trial was not one of which he was especially proud. And there will always be some Britons who take the view of the historian A. J. P. Taylor, who said that Joyce was hanged for making a false statement on a passport – the usual penalty for which was a fine of two pounds.[6]

Shortly after William's execution, Quentin fell ill again – a recurrence of the 'influenza complicated by painful swelling of the glands of the neck'. When his brother's neck was broken, Quentin's neck went into pain. William's brother spent most of the rest of January 1946 convalescing in a cottage in Suffolk, with Aubrey Lees and his wife, Ella, former members of British Union of Fascists. Lees, like Quentin, had done time under Regulation 18B.[7] Before taking this rest cure, Quentin, along with Macnab, gave a series of small gifts and momentoes to the legal team, whom they felt had served William valiantly: Messrs Head, Slade, Curtis-Bennett, Burge, and the solicitors' clerk, Joan Mildner, were most affected by this gesture, and wrote to Quentin to the effect that they had loved working with William.

The solicitor, Mr Head, was particularly pleased with the gift given to him: a cigarette box which had originally belonged to Tsar Nicholas II of Russia, and had originally been presented to Major Francis Trelawny, a British officer who had served at the Imperial Court in 1916. Major Trelawny had been the friend of – and suitor to – John Macnab's widowed mother; the cigarette box had been left to Macnab as a personal souvenir of Russia's slain emperor. Head wrote that it would always be a precious souvenir of a trial which held such pleasant memories for him. 'William Joyce ... was always the perfect client,' wrote the solicitor. 'My sister and her fiancé, who attended the Central Criminal Court trial, paid a tribute to his courage.' Miss Mildner, the solicitors' clerk, a woman in her early twenties, wrote to Quentin to say that she was 'very touched to think that your brother had even noticed me, when he had so much to occupy his mind.' William had described her as intelligent-looking: 'I only hope that I will fulfil his expectations,' she continued, adding, 'I ... only pray that your brother's treatment in the next world will be more merciful than it was in this.'[8]

Quentin's gracefulness – much aided by John Macnab – brought to William's exit a sort of gentlemanly courtesy. At the end, there was also a sense of closure, as we say now: those who had been involved with William began remaking their lives, differently. 'The Master' Macnab had married, at the beginning of 1945: his bride was Catherine Collins, sister of Margaret Collins. The two Catholic sisters had worked together at the British Union of Fascist headquarters back in the 1930s. Quentin was best man at the wedding, and Margaret Collins (who was married to Alexander Bowie, the cartoonist for *The Blackshirt)* was the matron of honour. The Macnab marriage turned out very happily, according to Margaret Collins, who still speaks tenderly of 'John and Cath'. They never had a moment's disharmony over the next thirty years, she said.[9]

The Macnabs went to Franco's Spain, where they settled in Toledo. They carried out translation work, they taught English and they had four children, one of whom died in infancy. Macnab also wrote a book about bullfighting, *The Bulls of Iberia*; the English critic Kenneth Tynan regarded it as the definitive text on the subject.[10] John Macnab never again returned to England – he always felt that he was vaguely under surveillance by the British authorities because of the fact that he had been sequestered under Regulation

18B. But he corresponded with A. K. Chesterton, who planned to write a memoir about William Joyce but never did. Macnab died in March 1977, and Catherine some years later; their daughters, son and grandchildren became integrated into Spanish society.

William's sister Joan – he nicknamed her 'Little Wolf', as she could be sharp-tongued – married in February 1946, a month after his execution. She and George 'Ted' Barker, a London policeman, had been courting for some time, and had indeed already deferred their wedding because of William's trial. William never met Ted Barker: the Joyce family went to some trouble not to let it be known that Lord Haw-Haw's sister was marrying a policeman, since this would certainly not have been helpful for Ted. Ted had known Quentin very slightly before the war.

And so Joan and Ted went ahead with a quiet wedding ceremony at Camberwell Registry Office on 9 February, with Quentin once again doing duty as best man. Although in those days, weddings did not usually follow for at least six months after a family death, William had forbidden them to defer the ceremony once again on his account

Joan and Ted had a happy marriage. Joan went on to run a haulage company, and to indulge in her great passion for horses – she had learned to ride as a girl in Galway. She and her husband had no family, but Joan became a fond aunt to Frank's step-daughter Judy, who remembers Joan with great affection as a clever and cheerful woman, who took her riding nearly every weekend. Joan and Ted Barker had a mildly Bohemian lifestyle – they kept a pet monkey at one stage – and perhaps because of this, would later drift away from Quentin and his wife.

William's daughters, Heather and Diana, grew up as part of the new family that their mother had made with Eric Hamilton Piercey, the handsome Blackshirt who had been a comrade of William's in the British Union of Fascists. Hamilton Piercey turned out to be a kindly father to the

Joyce girls, and there were three new half-siblings, to whom Heather and Diana felt close. Both Hazel and Hamilton Piercey became converts to the Catholic Church, and later they emigrated to Canada, where Hazel died in 2001.

For Quentin, life continued to be a struggle for some time after William's death. He took his responsibilities to William seriously, and wrote copiously to William's widow, Margaret, who was still held on the Continent – first in Brussels, and subsequently in Sennelager, a civilian POW camp for suspect Nazis and their re-education in the Westphalia. He approached the Irish high commission in London to plead that Margaret be permitted to settle in the Irish Free State – as it was called until 1949 – just as William had wanted her to do. Margaret was initially keen to go and live in Ireland, and Quentin, as ever, wrote an eloquent letter to Mr Dulanty, the high commissioner, explaining his sister-in-law's attraction to the Emerald Isle, her ancestral link with it (one grandfather had been Irish, which would qualify her automatically for Irish citizenship) and her resolve not to be controversial or to be a charge on the Irish State. Dulanty was cordial in response, but he had to refer the matter back to Dublin, and the application was lost in the bureaucratic process.[11]

Margaret was released from post-war internment in Germany in January 1948; she settled in Hamburg for a time, and amended her name to Margaret Brooke-Joyce, to emphasise the Brooke connection, which had meant so much to William. In post-war Germany, she renewed, for a time, her relationship with her old boyfriend Nicky von Besack – although he was now married. When his wife became pregnant, it hurt her terribly – she, who had been unable to conceive herself – and she finally ended the relationship for good.[12]

She worked for a food company, the Deutsche Maizena Werke. She also did some translating work and produced a paper on German refugees who had fled from the East; the paper was published by the Göttingen Research Committee in 1952. Margaret stayed in Germany until the 1950s, but when she was permitted to return to England, in 1955, she gladly did so, and reapplied for British nationality, which was granted to her.

Despite her acts of treason, Margaret was never prosecuted: the authorities quietly let the whole matter drop. They had political fears that the widow Joyce might prove a rallying point for veteran Fascists. The letter of the law was not invoked in Margaret's case perhaps because it seemed too complicated to do so: Margaret was married to William twice, for the second time when he was indisputably a naturalised German, although she had broadcast while he was still living under his false British passport; the whole thing was a legal minefield. Quentin continued to do try to do his duty by Margaret as he had promised William, but she visited Quentin's family home only once. He had signed his letters to her 'Your loving brother' at the time of William's death.

In 1962, Margaret married her second husband, Donald John May, who was eleven years her junior; she was fifty-two years old.[13] Characteristically, they had met in a pub. Their wedding took place in Gibraltar: Donald May had a domicile, and an accountancy job, in Morocco. He was described in the newspapers as 'a bit of a rolling stone': in fact, he also had a minor criminal conviction in England in connection with impersonating an officer. But he may have been fun, as such characters often are, and Margaret liked fun. Margaret Brooke-Joyce May died in 1972, in west London, from hepatic cirrhosis due to chronic alcoholism. She had not carried out William's counsel to rebuff 'the crathur'. Donald May died in the 1990s.

Margaret wanted to write – she had an idea for a novel in Berlin – but somehow never got down to it, though her diaries are lively. She did help J. A. Cole, who had been the chief interrogator at Sennelager internment camp, where she had been held, to write the first biography of William Joyce in 1964. Cole's biography has remained a fine primary source because the material came directly from Margaret. She did not know everything about William's life, however, and what she knew was only William's version; and she did not then know much of what has emerged subsequently.

❧

In the years directly following William's execution, Quentin was still dealing with the aftermath of the event. Quentin helped research William's case after the execution, often without any recompense or acknowledgement.[14] Quentin also corrected some of Rebecca West's errors of fact about William's life: she incorporated the corrections into the book versions of her reportage (which had originally been written for the *New Yorker),* without ever acknowledging that he was the source. Quentin could never even get a letter published in the London *Evening Standard* on points of information about his brother's case.[15]

Undoubtedly, doors were closed against Quentin Joyce because of the Haw-Haw connection. He struggled on with very little money, and became desperate to find a regular job. He had been doing some freelance work in magazine publishing and had learned to lay out pages and to do sub-editing work. Although he managed to get some work here and there, it was all very precarious. His friendship with Margaret Wood turned into a courtship – William had suspected that Q was in love with the Dulwich girl who had been so steady in her support of him.

Margaret, a pretty girl who had worked briefly as a mannequin, had been married previously in a hasty wartime marriage, and she had a young son, John, who was born in 1944. She also had some difficulty getting a divorce from her first husband, who initially took their son to live with him in Scotland. But in the late 1940s, Margaret Wood went to live with Quentin when he moved from 86 Underhill Road to a maisonette in nearby Sydenham. (All the Joyces lived either in south London or in north Kent.)

Margaret subsequently obtained her divorce, and she married Quentin in August 1950. Little John came to live with them both: he later took the name 'John Quentin Joyce'. John grew to love Q as a true father, and wept more at Q's funeral than at any bereavement he has attended before or since.

In May 1952, a son, Michael Kevin Quentin Joyce, was born to Margaret and Quentin: the Irish middle name of 'Kevin' was a sentimental link with 'the old country'. By now Q had a steady job, writing for the *Investors' Guardian* in the City of London; he had put his days of railing against the wickedness of the capitalist system behind him. He also, largely at his wife's insistence, put behind him the whole drama of Lord Haw-Haw.

From the early 1950s, Quentin Joyce constructed another life for himself. Those who had known him in the days when he had followed his brother into the British Union of Fascists, and then into the National Socialist League, never saw him again. He lost contact with Macnab in Spain – although in any case Macnab was paranoid about the British authorities opening his mail.

The only tenuous connection with the William Joyce days that Q maintained was a very occasional afternoon tea at A. K. Chesterton's home, when Chesterton would discourse upon world politics to the assembled company: he was, in the later 1950s and 1960s, involved in running his League of Empire Loyalists, a group campaigning for the return of the Empire and for opposition to the European 'Common Market'. John and Michael, as young schoolboys, would be brought along to these events – and were bored rigid by the grown-up talk. But this was Quentin's last link with any form of political activity. He did remain loyally friendly with the Italians who had been interned with him – either as supporters of Mussolini, or simply because of their nationality – under 18B. But these friendships were of a personal rather than a political nature.

A man's destiny is quite often shaped by his wife: a wife may push a married man towards fulfilling ambitions, or she may provide a nest for him against the world. With Quentin, Margaret provided a fortress against the world. They built a happy home life together: their children and grandchildren remember Q as fun, easy-going and entertaining. The grandchildren in particular remember him as someone who could always make them laugh. Quentin's family not only loved him, they admired him: his easy ability to open up a piano and play it, his gift of languages and of writing, and his loyalty and forbearing nature. In short, Quentin was a gentleman. When he died in 1989, the letters of condolence fulsomely singled out that quality in him: his gentle-manliness and gentleness.

Quentin achieved a sense of contentment, but the price of this serenity was that the past was sealed. Once Quentin and Margaret had married, and he had got a steady job and a home of his own, William Joyce and the legend of Lord Haw-Haw was never again mentioned in Quentin's family. He kept his own archive, his correspondence about William's trial and all his documents about his own term of internment, in a series of boxes tucked away in a loft: this archive was preserved when the family moved house and other items were thrown out, but it was not opened again until after the death of Quentin's Margaret in January 1997.

When John and Michael were growing up, the Haw-Haw connection was never alluded to or spoken about. Michael discovered, at the age of about thirteen, that Lord Haw-Haw was his uncle. Later, it became an accepted fact that the parents knew that the children were aware of this fact, but nonetheless, Margaret did not want the subject discussed. Whenever the topic of Lord Haw-Haw came close to open discussion, Margaret would find a way of distracting Quentin. 'Come here, Q,' she would say, 'I want you in the kitchen a moment.'[16]

When William's daughter Heather was reburying her father in Ireland in 1976, she telephoned Quentin, although she knew him only slightly. She asked him to come to Galway for the reburial service, but he was called away from the phone by Margaret. 'Drop it, Heather,' he told her. That ceremony was quite widely reported – it appeared in all the London papers, and there were television reports on it too. Quentin's memory must have travelled back to all he had been through with William, but he complied with Margaret's wishes and did not go public about his connections with the notorious Lord Haw-Haw.

In one sense, Margaret was right, and she was acting in Quentin's best interests. Quentin had to go forward and reinvent his sense of self. The pull of William's personality had been so strong, in Quentin's young life, and so all-enveloping during the course of trial, that the only way to be free of it was to shake it off completely. His wife was determined to help him do so, partly by ensuring that the links with the Haw-Haw past were cauterised. If Q had married a woman who wanted to wallow in the Haw-Haw story, he would never have moved on.

Quentin did not deny what had occurred in that he made no attempt to change his name, for example, or even to modify it: his first name was 'Edwin' and he might easily have chosen to use this name in his byline for the *Investors' Guardian*. Yet his family believes that the memory of William's trial, and the connection with a man hanged as a traitor, kept Quentin from pursuing the heights of ambition. Quentin earned a decent living and he raised and supported his family successfully. But for many years the family income was modest, and he might have achieved more, with his gift for language and communication, and his personal charm and popularity with friends and colleagues. To the end, the shadow of William Joyce held him back a crucial bit: Q never quite wanted to be so successful that he would draw attention to himself as 'Lord Haw-Haw's brother'.

Joan and Ted's more Bohemian way of life was very different from the respectable and regular home life of Margaret and Quentin. Margaret found it unforgivable that Joan and Ted would fail to show up for Sunday lunch: they often phoned from the local hostelry at the last minute to cancel – the carousing of their cronies could be heard in the background. Joan died of cervical cancer at the age of fifty-eight, in December 1978. She had ignored the early symptoms of the illness, but faced her death bravely, her step-niece recalled. Ted Barker lived on for many more years.

Robert, the youngest brother whom William had affectionately dubbed 'Bobbin', did reasonably well in army life, but after being demobbed in the 1950s became something of an oddity. He was described as a quiet type of man by those who met him, and always neatly turned out. But he was secretive and mysterious, and drifted away from contact with his family. He never acquired a home of his own, but lived with various landladies. He also had a weakness for drink. In 1975, unbeknownst to his siblings, he married an older woman, Marjorie Guard (née Butler) in Croydon, South London. Marjorie predeceased Robert, and he became unsettled with grief. She left him her estate, but the proceedings disappeared mysteriously. He ended his life alone, in a mobile home in Hastings, in 1986. It was some days before the body was discovered and the exact date of death could never be established.[17] Frank Joyce thought there was something suspect about Robert's death – the mobile home had almost no possessions in it, and there was no cash. Was he a victim of foul play? No one ever knew, or enquired. Robert would never speak about William and refused at all times to discuss either politics or religion.

Frank and Quentin stayed in contact, and remained brotherly to the end of their lives. Frank had been first married in 1938, to Eva Weeks; this marriage came apart during the war, with no great repining on his part. He subsequently married Edith Mary Ann Ford, in 1947, and settled down in Sidcup in Kent, where, like his father, he flourished in the building trade. Frank had no children, although Ann, his second wife, had a daughter, Judy, from her first, wartime marriage. Judy regarded herself as Frank Joyce's daughter – she was crestfallen to find out that she was not his biological child but she still thinks of him as her real father. 'He was a lovely, lovely man,' Judy recalls. She loved the Joyces: they were all so 'clever and beautifully mannered', and 'had such personality'. Frank and Quentin together were 'a riot'. Yet, they none of them ever talked about the dark shadow of the hanging. Judy only came to know gradually that there had been 'another brother'.

Frank's marriage to Ann was very happy, and Ann was friendly, too, with Joan. Frank became a pillar of the golf club and an upstanding Freemason, and remained, until his death, from lymphatic leukaemia, in 1991, as he always had been – bluff and cheery. William had nicknamed him 'Old Seal' and had thought him very sound. Since Frank had figured only very briefly in the trial, and his first name was not particularly unusual, his association with Lord Haw-Haw faded out of memory. If anyone knew he was Lord Haw-Haw's brother, they did not mention it. With Frank's funeral, the last of the Joyce siblings passed from this earth.

The post-war lives of other characters in the William Joyce story varied as much as any human pattern of life varies. Eight days after Joyce's execution, Norman Baillie-Stewart, who claimed to be the original 'Lord Haw-Haw', was sentenced to five years' imprisonment on the charge of aiding the enemy. This was something of a contrast to William's capital sentence, although the judge called Baillie-Stewart 'one of the worst citizens that any country has ever produced'. He served three years in London, Yorkshire and Parkhurst on the Isle of Wight. After his release, in October 1949, he was aided by the Quakers, who provided him with false papers to go to Ireland, where he settled under the name of James Scott, married a young Dublin girl, had two children and lived contentedly until his death on 7 June 1966.[18]

Wolf Mittler, the handsome and charming bilingual German – whose mother had been born in Ireland – and who more convincingly fitted the original voice that Jonah Barrington dubbed 'Lord Haw-Haw', had a picaresque life from 1943 onwards. Mittler was never a Nazi, or even a supporter of the Reich. Because of his lack of political 'reliability', in 1941 he was moved to a special short-wave radio station, whose broadcasts were aimed at Allied forces in the Mediterranean and North Africa; the calling signal for this station was 'We'll Meet Again'. His regular programme, *Anzac Tattoo*, was popular with British and Commonwealth forces in North Africa, but he overstepped the mark by introducing jazz and offended by interviewing Canadian prisoners of war sympathetically.

From 1943 Mittler was more or less on the run in Italy, where he was helped by the Italian partisans, and he had many adventures, until escaping into Switzerland. After the war, he worked for Allied media in Rome, and eventually rejoined Bavarian Radio in the 1950s. He had a long and happy family life; when he died in November 2002, his wife Birgitta sent friends a memorial card bearing the words: 'In memory of a wonderful man.'[19]

Francis Stuart, the Irish broadcaster whom William had known briefly in the Irland-Redaktion, returned to Ireland in 1948 and became a full-time writer, publishing the cult novel *Black List H* in 1971. He married Madeleine, his long-time companion, in 1954: she died subsequently and he married yet again. In 1996, he was elected to the Irish academy of letters, Aosdána, and was nominated as a *saoi,* or wise elder. He was fiercely criticised by the poet Maire MacEntee (Mrs Conor Cruise O'Brien) for his attachments to the Third Reich and alleged anti-Semitism; he denied the claims. But Stuart, who had earlier been married to Maud

Gonne's daughter Iseult, and had had the patronage of W. B. Yeats, was always accorded in Ireland the honour due to a venerable bard. He died in Ireland, aged ninety-seven, in February 2000.[20]

John O'Reilly, the Irishman who had been friendly with William in Berlin, had extraordinary adventures during the Second World War: in his early life he had been a customs' official, seminarian, hotel receptionist, potato picker, interpreter, steel worker, broadcaster and spy. He had led a group of Irish potato workers from Jersey to Berlin. After the war, he managed to escape retribution, travelled widely, ran hotels and pubs in Ireland and England and in 1952 sold his memoirs to the *Sunday Dispatch* for a large sum of money. His wife in Ireland died in an abortion scandal, in April 1956, known as the Nurse Cadden case.[21] O'Reilly himself died in 1971 and was buried at Dean's Grange Cemetery on the same day as the former Taoiseach, Seán Lemass.[22]

Sylvia Morris, one of the most ardent of William's followers in the National Socialist League, and who wrote regularly to Quentin at the end of William's life, had an unusual life afterwards. In the late 1940s, she fell in love with a highly strung Jewish actor, whose wife had committed suicide, and who was the father of three children. Sylvia went to live with the actor, who, a few years later, had a very serious nervous breakdown and was committed to an insane asylum. Sylvia cared for his children and brought them up herself: when she was old, they repaid her care with warmth, whether or not they knew she had once been a Blackshirt, and subsequently a National Socialist intimate of William Joyce. She died in the late 1980s after a fall; her memory is still cherished by her brother Peter.[23]

Ethel Scrimgeour, the rich spinster who, with her brother Alec, had financed William Joyce and the National Socialist League just before the war, and to whom he wrote many grateful letters from prison, concentrated her attentions on another of her interests – the fight against TB.

(Health and efficiency often went hand in hand with a tendency towards Fascism during the 1920s and 1930s.) A former nurse at Bart's Hospital, she took poor and orphaned children from London into her Sussex home, fostered them, and administered her own TB 'cure', which consisted of fresh air and a faddish diet. The children seem to have flourished: one of them was Trevor Aston, who became a distinguished academic. Miss Scrimgeour herself died in 1953, aged eighty-eight, from the effects of scurvy: despite her focus on diet, she neglected to give herself enough Vitamin C.[24]

The half-Scot Eduard Dietze, William Joyce's bilingual boss – he once called him his Mephistopheles – and the head of broadcasts to the British Isles, stayed by his post at the Rundfunk until the end. He made a last broadcast on the German home service on 5 May 1945, asking Germans to 'maintain a certain dignity towards the Allies, and not to lose all honour' as the war terminated. Dietze was arrested, and Allied military authorities regarded him at first as a British subject by birth who had assisted the enemy. But he was released on condition that he would never again enter Britain. He returned to German broadcasting in 1950 and built a successful career as a television executive. Not least of his achievements was to report Royal Ascot for German television, unhindered by the security services. He died, aged fifty-one, in 1960, of a heart attack: his wife Edith, who had often been his collaborator in his radio career, survived until 1993.[25]

Edward Bowlby, the Anglo-Irishman who had worked alongside the Joyces in Berlin and Hamburg, made a new life in Ireland after the war. He chose to use one of his other Christian names, Charles, and became a teacher at Aravon School in Bray, Co. Wicklow – a very smart prep school for pupils going on to English public schools or to upper-class Protestant schools in Ireland. He was one of the founders – with the British diplomat Sir John Maffey – of the

Leprechauns Cricket Club. He died after returning to England in 1959.

Geoffrey Perry, the young solider who had shot and wounded William Joyce in the woods at Wassersleben, never appeared at the trial: his superior, Captain Lickorish, was briefly interviewed instead. It might have looked a little incongruous if the British soldier who shot William was not yet, technically, British himself. Geoffrey was already an accomplished photographer before joining the army and after the war went into the magazine industry, and started his own business, Perry Press Productions. In 1952, he launched *Family Circle,* a supermarket magazine, and later, *Living,* its stablemate. He also started up the highly successful *Business Traveller.*

He became a magistrate and a prisoner visitor. He married and had two children, and when his wife died in 2001, he set about compiling his memorabilia into a charming autobiography that invaluably reproduces every document that he has saved, from his childhood days in Germany onwards.[26] He is now retired and lives partly in Florida. His attitude to Joyce is generous: he does not think the trial was fair or the outcome just. His attitude to Germany is also characteristically generous. 'I don't judge Germans by the Nazis,' he says. 'You will find fanatics anywhere.'[27]

Charles Maxwell Knight, the MI5 spymaster who had many contacts with William Joyce, surfaced after the war as a nature writer. His obituary in *The Times* in 1968 omitted all mention of intelligence activities, but praised his works such as *Pets Usual and Unusual, Bird Gardening* and *Cuckoo in the House.*[28] One of his bird books, *Talking Birds,* was illustrated by David Cornwell, who became the spy writer John Le Carré.

Heather Iandolo, William's eldest daughter, became a schoolteacher, married and had four children. His second daughter, Diana, also married and had a family. In 2003, Heather completed a religious book she had been working on for some time, on the subject of the prophecies of the Old Testament being fulfilled in the New.

Dorothy Eckersley, who had really made it possible for William and Margaret to survive in Berlin at all, and then to gain a foothold in broadcasting, was arrested at Christmas 1944 by the Gestapo, as was her son James Clark. They had not been pulling their weight over the past two years – indeed, James had gradually and surreptitiously withdrawn from microphone work from early 1942, with some assistance from a fictitious doctor's certificate that had some-how been wangled by his enterprising mother. They were held at the Alexanderplatz prison for some weeks, while the Flying Fortresses blasted central Berlin, and then transferred to internment camps in the south and in Austria. After being held in British camps – she in the Ruhr, he in Italy – they were brought back to England in November 1945 and charged with aiding the enemy. At the Old Bailey, both pleaded guilty to the charge. Dorothy was sentenced to twelve months in prison; James Clark was 'bound over to keep the peace'.

Her imprisonment in Holloway Women's Prison – to her, who had been a glamorous stage star during the First World War and a former social figure – came as a rude shock. But she made the best of it: she became friendly with her prison visitor, and when she came out of prison, took instruction for conversion to the Roman Catholic Church. 'She needed something big in her life,' her son said. Dorothy Eckersley died in 1971, chagrined that the Catholic Church, after Vatican II, seemed about to begin compromising with the modern world.

At their trial, the jury heard that James had read the scripts given to him – he had, on some occasions, been the voice of Lord Haw-Haw – and that in the early period he had been 'hysterically' pro-German. The judge said that James, who was only sixteen at the outbreak of the war, and not yet seventeen when he began broadcasting, had never been a traitor: 'I think you were caught up with many others in that abominable and most insidious propaganda which was imbued with the so-called tenets of the Nazi youth organisation.' James went to live with an aunt, who had been, coincidentally, an actress at the Gate Theatre in Dublin in the company of Micheál Mac Liammóir and Hilton Edwards. He went into publishing and had a long and successful career with Hutchinson, Thames and Hudson and Paul Hamlyn. In 2003, he celebrated his eightieth birthday surrounded by his family and grandchildren, and this author is indebted to him for the 'local colour' and very special insight he has given her into the Lord Haw-Haw story in Germany.

❦

William Joyce had hoped that he would go down in history as a thinker and prophet who had warned the world against Bolshevism; he believed the wheel of history would turn and National Socialism would once again come back into its own. His prophecies were wrong; and although in the immediate aftermath of his execution the Haw-Haw name dropped out of the public realm, his celebrity returned and endured, in peculiar and quirky ways, as legend. His voice is played regularly in broadcast clips about propaganda, or treason trials, and he is remembered, at the grass roots, in the genre of the urban myth. During the course of my researches for this book, people would come up to me and tell me odd tales about how William Joyce was connected to their locality: he was supposed to have had a secret hideaway in Herne Bay, Kent, from where he sent signals to Germany; he is supposed to have haunted a house in Suffolk; he is remembered as a pre-war character in a small village in Scotland, which he graced with a visit. He also retains a certain profile as a hate-figure: in 2002, the *Sun* placed Lord Haw-Haw at the top of their list of '100 Britons we Love to Hate'.[29]

And in north County Mayo, at the Heritage Centre on

the beautiful promontary of Clew Bay, from where the ships once departed to take poor Irish emigrants to the New World, a prize exhibit is 'Lord Haw-Haw's Cradle'. This cradle – which came from the pub at Ayle where Michael and Queenie Joyce had been hosts – hangs very splendidly from the rafters, nicely positioned over the gloves worn by James Connolly, Irish republican, trade unionist and communist, at *his* execution. The ensemble is a neat visual metaphor of the strange inclusiveness of the stream of life and of Irish history.

Envoi
The Last Possessions of William Joyce

Delivered to the Metropolitan Police on arrival in prison:

One brown fibre suitcase containing:
One book by Horace
One dark-brown waistcoat
One check jacket, one pair check trousers, one white vest, one grey pullover, one blue shirt.
Three handkerchiefs, one pair of foot supports, one box of contraceptives, two boxes containing three files of text.
One box of digestive tablets. One book *Portrait of a Village*; one book *Armies of the Revolution*; one book *British Classical Authors*; one book *Dr Faustus*; one *Rasher's Parliamentary Almanac*; one hotel receipt; one nail file; one keyring for keys and one white metal ring thereof; one ten-pfennig piece.
One black fibre suitcase containing:
One sign, fish-shape; one wooden box shaving soap and forty-four safety razor blades; two odd slippers; two hairbrushes; two toothbrushes; one enamel mug.
One tin of toothpaste, one face flannel, one shaving brush, one tube of skin paste, three combs, one pair

of pyjama trousers, one blue-striped shirt, one striped shirt, two pyjama jackets, one pair of pants, one sock, one tube of shaving cream, four soft collars, three ties, one wooden coat-hanger, one tablet of soap, one nail brush, one book *Der Kleiner Bilder Duden,* fifty-eight safety razor blades, one tablet of shaving soap, one pair of bootlaces, one metal ashtray, three German tobacco couples, three hairslides, one ear pendant, one collar stud, seven German coins.

Effects collected after his death from Wandsworth Prison by William Joyce's brother Robert:

One overcoat, one pair of shoes black, one necktie, one handkerchief, one scarf cotton, two pairs socks, one pair pants, short, one vest, two shirts.[30]

Whatever else had motivated William Joyce's life choices, it was clearly not worldly gain.

NOTES

[1] William Joyce, *National Socialism Now*, London, 1937.

[2] A. K. Chesterton's notes, Sheffield University archive.

[3] The list of writers with casual anti-Semitic reflexes is well known and, in this instance, by no means complete. Noël Coward's offence was minor, but its removal was telling: in 'The Stately Homes of England', recorded in 1938, there was a sly dig (a reference to selling off hereditary possessions 'with some assistance from the Jews') which was tactfully removed in post-war versions. Many books appeared during the 1920s and 1930s which accused the Jews of Bolshevism and of monopolising the media and the professions (see bibliography). The eugenicists, including Karl Pearson and Sydney Webb, criticised the Irish and the Jews for being 'dysgenic' – having too many children in conditions of poverty, in effect (see Daniel Kevles, *In the Name of Eugenics*, London, 1985).

[4] British Home Intelligence reports are available at the British National Archives-Public Record Office, Kew, hereinafter known as TNA-PRO.

[5] Home Intelligence, TNA-PRO INF 1/292.

[6] It was common to portray the Irish as chimpanzee-like creatures in cartoons in the nineteenth century. In his autobiography, Bob Geldof recalls the persistence of anti-Irish notices in landladies' windows up until the 1960s.

[7] William Joyce, *Fascist Educational Policy*, National Socialist League, undated pamphlet. Held in the Quentin Joyce archive.

[8] This theme appears repeatedly in William Joyce's writings. See *Twilight Over England*, Berlin, 1940, and *National Socialism Now*. His early broadcasts from Germany underline the superior social welfare system of Germany, and his broadcast about the very poor state of teeth in England was made on 8 September 1940 (BBC Monitors, Imperial War Museum).

[9] Author's correspondence with McNeil Sloane, February and March 2003.

[10] William Shirer, *Berlin Diary*, New York, 1940, entry for 28 August 1940. Harry Flannery, another American correspondent in Berlin, and a committed anti-Fascist, nonetheless wrote of William: 'I did not find him unlikable.' See Harry W. Flannery, *Assignment to Berlin*, Michael Joseph, 1942.

[11] Angus Macnab's notes, Sheffield University archive.

[12] Sarah Ebner, interview with Heather Iandolo, *Daily Express*, 11 February 1995.

PROLOGUE: A HANGING AND TWO BURIALS

[1] William Joyce's prison letters, Forman archive. This passage also appears in J. A. Cole (ed.), *Lord Haw-Haw and William Joyce: The Full Story*, London, 1964 and has been quoted in several Irish outlets.

[2] See C. E. Bechhofer Roberts (ed.), *The Trial of William Joyce*, London, 1946; J. W. Hall (ed.), *The Trial of William Joyce*, London, 1946; Rebecca West, *The Meaning of Treason*, London, 1949.

[3] 'Buckingham Palace and Whitehall were flooded with appeals for clemency when the wartime traitor William Joyce was about to hang in Wandsworth jail in 1946.' *The Times* of London, 8 February 1995. Leslie Harries had been a member of Mosley's British Union of Fascists and corresponded with Quentin Joyce. But many non-Fascists also wrote letters of protest, and the *Manchester Guardian* opposed the death penalty to which Joyce was sentenced.

[4] Correspondence to the author from Lord Jenkins, March 2002.

[5] See Adrian Weale, *Patriot Traitors: Roger Casement, John Amery and the Real Meaning of Treason*, London, 2001.

[6] TNA-PRO 2/250.

[7] James Chuter Ede in the *Dictionary of National Biography*.

[8] Hartley Shawcross, *Life Sentence: Memoirs*, London, 1995.

[9] A. J. P. Taylor protested against Joyce's sentence on several occasions. He wrote in *English History 1914–1945* (Oxford, 1965): 'Technically, Joyce was hanged for making a false statement when applying for a passport, the usual penalty for which is a small fine. His real offence was to have attracted to himself the mythical repute of Lord Haw-Haw.' In his collection *British Prime Ministers* (London, 1998) Taylor wrote: 'He was hanged before the House of Lords had even stated their grounds for rejecting his appeal. He should have been fined two pounds for making a false statement when applying for a passport.' Taylor wrote several

letters to the newspapers protesting about the Joyce case; in the 1980s, he told Patrick Marnham of *The Spectator* that the whole thing was a 'judicial murder'. See also A. J. P. Taylor's letter to the *Guardian*, 21 February 1979.

[10] See Albert Pierrepoint, *Executioner: Pierrepoint*, London, 1974.

[11] To use an Irishism, William Joyce died in the best of health. Less than three weeks before he died Angus Macnab wrote: 'William is amazingly cheerful and I don't think his health has ever been better.' TNA-PRO KV 2/236/4.

[12] TNA-PRO HO45/22405.

[13] This claim was made in David Seabrook, *All the Devils are Here*, London, 2002.

[14] *Galway Advertiser*, 22 January 1976.

[15] Father Padraic Ó Laoi, *Father Michael Griffin*, Galway, 1994. The late Father Ó Laoi remains a respected figure in Galway.

[16] 'FORGIVE AND FORGET PLEA AS LORD HAW-HAW IS BURIED', *Daily Telegraph*, 21 August 1976; 'IRELAND CALLING! IRELAND CALLING!' *Guardian*, 24 January 1976; 'LORD HAW-HAW GOES HOME', *Daily Mail*, 23 January 1976.

[17] Although Joyce opposed Sinn Féin bitterly as a teenage boy, in his thirties he took a mellower view and accepted Home Rule for Ireland, though not the total separation of a Republic: 'Rather than that Ireland should separate from England, it were better that Englishmen should accept an Irish government … Let the Treaty of 1922 stand, but let it stand for both parties. England has undertaken not to interfere in the domestic affairs of the Free State. So be it. There must, however, be no rupture of the Treaty and Britain cannot afford to recognise an Irish Republic' (*National Socialism Now*). In Germany, he went along with German broadcasting's pro-Irish nationalist and anti-British remarks: 'I have lived in a town wrecked by military operations,' he said on 31 January 1940 (Hamburg wavelength), 'that, by the way, was an Irish town in 1920 after the Black and Tans had been let loose on it.'

1. BLOOD AND SOIL: THE FAMILY HERITAGE OF WILLIAM JOYCE

[1] Quoted in Hall, Rebecca West, et al.

[2] William Wilde, *Lough Corrib, its Shores and Island (with notices of Lough Mask)*, Dublin, 1867.

[3] Joyce, *Twilight Over England*.

[4] Quentin Joyce, William's brother, told his family about this

Heidelberg link. It is believed that Dr William Brooke's brother may have been at Heidelberg.

[5] Terence De Vere White, *The Parents of Oscar Wilde*, London, 1967.

[6] General Gordon's letter to *The Times* appears in Robert Kee, *The Green Flag*, London, 1972. On the dire conditions of the population of Mayo see J. F. Quinn, *History of Mayo*, Ballina, 1986, and *Cathair na Mart*, the journal of the Westport Archaeological Society.

[7] See Joseph Lee, *The Modernisation of Irish Society*, Dublin, 1973.

[8] Joyce, *National Socialism Now*.

[9] See Norman Stone, *Europe Transformed: 1879–1919*, London, 1983.

[10] See Monsignor James Horan, *Memoirs 1911–1986*, Belfast, 1992.

[11] Tithe applotments of Killour Townland, Griffiths Evaluation, 1855. Kindly provided by Adrian Martyn, genealogist in Galway.

[12] Vere Foster, *The Nation*, 10 June 1882, quoted in Gerard Moran and Raymond Gillespie, *Galway: History and Society*, Dublin, 1996.

[13] Father Patrick Grealy, quoted in Moran and Gillespie.

[14] Interview with Daniel McGing, August 2001.

[15] Described in Ralph Richardson, *Ireland in 1880*, London, 1881.

[16] The notorious Maamtrasna murders are described in Jarlath Waldron, *Maamtrasna: The Murders and the Mystery*, Dublin, 1992. Local feeling was still so strong in Connemara in 1992 that a whispering campaign was orchestrated against the late Father Waldron.

[17] Irish judicial statistics for 1880 quoted in Richardson.

[18] Bernard O'Reilly was the Galway RIC man who defended Michael Joyce. Cole, Rebecca West and TNA-PRO KV 2/246.

[19] Jacob Riis, *How the Other Half Lives*, New York, 1971 (first published 1890).

[20] See Ronald H. Bayor and Timothy J. Meagher, *The New York Irish*, New York, 1999.

[21] See Riis.

[22] Statements in the Derek Curtis-Bennett archive. William said his father was first a freight-checker with the Pennyslvania Railroad. He then got work in the building industry where he worked with a relative by marriage, Naughton. Material relating to this also in TNA-PRO KV2/245.

[23] Interview with Heather.

[24] Copy at the New York Municipal Archives, Chamber St, New York 10007.

[25] See Loretto Dennis Szucs, *They Became Americans: Finding Naturalization Records and Ethnic Origin*, New York, 1989. See also Bayor and Meagher on the power base of Irish-Americans.

[26] Frank Holland, who appeared at the William Joyce trial, said he was advised by Michael Joyce to become an American citizen for reasons of

business advantage. Statement from Frank Holland in the Derek Curtis-Bennett archive.

[27] Ulster Historical Foundation. Also Census of England and Wales, 1881, 1901.

[28] According to Derek Denton of Oldham, a research paper on Dr Brooke is being prepared by a local historian.

[29] With thanks to Colonel Henry Brooke, genealogist, and Viscount Brookeborough.

[30] According to family letters in the Quentin Joyce archive. Also interview with Gilbert Brooke at National Archives. TNA-PRO KV 2/248.

[31] Family source. Also Quentin Joyce's letters about his parents' mutual devotion in the Quentin Joyce archive.

[32] TNA-PRO KV2/247.

[33] A cousin of William Joyce's was told by her mother that everyone in the family was worried that William weighed 'no more than a bag of sugar' at birth. This remains anecdotal as the weight of an infant at birth was not recorded in New York at this time, but it is congruent with his size as an adult.

[34] *Hamburger Fremdenblatt*, 6 October 1944. TNA-PRO KV 2/247.

[35] Letter from Martin Stanton in the Quentin Joyce archive.

[36] TNA-PRO KV2/245.

[37] There are several studies available at the Brooklyn Special Collection at the Brooklyn Public Library on the rise of Jewish Brooklyn in the years before the Second World War. See Brian Merlus, *Brooklyn: The Way it Was*, Brooklyn, New York, 1995 and Wendell Pritchett, *Brownsville, Brooklyn, Blacks, Jews and the Changing Face of the Ghetto*, Chicago, 2002.

[38] Ibid.

[39] Michael Joyce's was renting property to the RIC in Mayo from July 1910. Copies of rental agreements in the Derek Curtis-Bennett archive.

2. A JESUIT BOYHOOD; A TIME OF TROUBLES

[1] Letters in the Quentin Joyce archive.

[2] See Cole, for which Margaret Joyce was the main source.

[3] Interview with Heather.

[4] Macnab's notes, Sheffield University archive. Macnab testified in notes to A. K. Chesterton that Mrs Joyce was conscientious in fulfilling her promise to raise her children as Roman Catholics.

[5] Tourmakeady, Co. Mayo, November 2001: one local man claimed that certain Protestant landowners still refused to sell property to Catholics up to 1930.

[6] Interview with Heather.

[7] Interview with Daniel McGing, August 2001.

[8] Emily Brooke's will was issued on 1 May 1917. She left £7,311.0s.5d gross (net £7,2511.0s.5d) – almost a quarter of a million by today's values. Probate Office, High Holborn, London.

[9] Kathleen Murphy of Loughrea, born 1908, recalls Patrick Pearse and Thomas Ashe cycling around Tourmakeady before the First World War. Interview, December 2002.

[10] The school roll at Scoil an Linbh Íosa, held at Francis Street, Galway.

[11] Seventy-eighth report of the Commissioners of National Education Ireland, 1911–12, kindly supplied by Dr Deirdre Raftery, Education Department, University College Dublin. Dr Raftery also referred me to other education material.

[12] Interviews in Galway.

[13] With thanks to Eamonn Waldron for supplying the deeds of his house at 1 Rutledge Terrace, from the Registry of Deeds, Dublin. The deeds were finally signed 13 November 1913. The house had been purchased from the Rev. John A. Carr and Mary Carr, who would have been Protestant gentry.

[14] Letters to the *Oldham Chronicle*: Mrs Butterworth, 27 February 1976 and Mrs Buckley, 5 March 1976.

[15] Kevin Sullivan, *Joyce Among the Jesuits*, Columbia University Press, 1958.

[16] Joyce, *Twilight Over England*.

[17] Interview with Frank Canavan, Principal, and archive papers supplied by Father Fergus O'Donoughue SJ, editor of *Studies*, Dublin.

[18] The priests' obituaries appear in the *Irish Province News*, 1925–1990, Jesuit Archive, Leeson Street, Dublin. Father Henry Foley's liberal-minded sermons sometimes appeared in the *Connaught Tribune* from about 1912–1921.

[19] William Naughton's memorandum about William Joyce was provided by Mrs Patricia Naughton, Galway. An interview with Mr Naughton also appeared in the *Sunday Press*, Dublin, January 1976.

[20] Recollections of William Joyce: from an unbroadcast interview by Ronan Kelly, producer of RTÉ Radio 1's *Morning Glory*, with his uncle Tom McDonough, and other classmates of William's, shortly before Mr McDonough's death in 1996; and Arthur Miles-Webb TNA-PRO KV2/249.

[21] Ronan Kelly's unbroadcast interview, 1996.

[22] Cole.

[23] Macnab's notes, Sheffield University Archive.

[24] Ibid.

[25] Michael d'Arcy, *Iognaid (Ignatius)*, 1982.

[26] E. L. Kineen, *The Irish Times*, 8 March 1941.

[27] Robert Brennan, *Allegiance*, Dublin, 1950.

[28] Peadar O'Dowd, Galway Historical Society.

[29] Ronan Kelly's unbroadcast interview, 1996.

[30] There are many horrified reports in *The Irish Times*, particularly during the first six months of 1921, about the horrific acts, not of the Black and Tans, but of the Irish 'rebels'. 'BOMBS THROWN IN DUBLIN. CROWN FORCES ATTACKED'; 'THE CO. GALWAY AMBUSH – CIVILIAN SHOT DEAD'; 'MALICIOUS DAMAGE IN TIPPERARY'; 'FORCES OF THE CROWN WERE ATTACKED IN DUBLIN LAST NIGHT AND IN AT LEAST TWO INSTANCES BOMBS WERE THROWN AT LORRIES CARRYING MEN'; 'AUXILIARY POLICE ATTACKED'; 'SOLDIERS IN PERIL. ATTEMPT TO BLOW UP TROOP TRAIN': headlines from just one day, 20 January 1921. But Lady Gregory's *Journals*, edited by Lennox Robinson, give poignant accounts of country families who were victims of the Crown forces.

[31] Interview with Galwegian whose father was in the Old IRA, July 2002.

[32] Douglas V. Duff, *On Swallowing the Anchor*, London, 1954.

[33] Ó Laoi.

[34] Jane Beatty, lecture given to the Loughrea Literary and Historical Society, 3 March 1998.

[35] Speaking to Proinsias MacAonghusa on the RTÉ programme 'Féach', 29 March 1976.

[36] TNA-PRO KV2/245.

[37] Quentin Joyce archive and Joan Joyce's birth certificate.

[38] Interview with son of IRA lieutenant, July 2002. The IRA lieutenant was born in 1893 and died in the 1980s. Family requests anonymity.

3. FROM ERIN TO EMPIRE; FROM ANTI-FENIAN TO ANTI-SEMITE

[1] Personal note in Margaret Joyce file, PRO KV 2/346.

[2] Peter Hart, *The IRA and its Enemies: Violence and Community in Cork 1916–1923*, Oxford, 1998.

[3] Recalled by a contemporary in the Proinsias MacAonghusa RTÉ programme 'Féach', 29 March 1976.

[4] Ministry of Defence records on Private William Joyce, Number 5265132, as supplied on 10 September 2002, with permission from next of kin.

[5] Michael and Queenie were formally cautioned by the police for not registering as aliens when they visited Oldham in 1917 to prove her mother's will. This emerged as evidence of William Joyce's nationality

during the trial. Queenie was very irked that she was expected to call herself an 'alien' in her own home town and mentioned it to her family on several occasions (William's notes to Derek Curtis-Bennett). Bernard O'Reilly of the Galway RIC fixed matters for the Joyces with the Lancashire constabulary (Quentin Joyce archive).

[6] Cole, and Francis Selwyn, *Hitler's Englishman*, London, 1987.

[7] Taylor, *English History*.

[8] Macnab's notes, Sheffield University archive.

[9] Family source.

[10] See Mrs Stanley Gardiner, *We Two and Shaumus*, Duckworth, 1913.

[11] Interview with Daniel McGing, August 2001.

[12] Irish National Archives, Bishop Street, Dublin. File Number D4761.

[13] *Illustrated London News*, 21 January 1922.

[14] John Charnley, *Blackshirts and Roses: An Autobiography*, London, 1990.

[15] *John Bull*, 7 January 1922. There were a lot of press snippets like this, implying that those who had fought in the war were impoverished, while those who had made money were rewarded.

[16] Macnab's notes, Sheffield University archive.

[17] Ibid.

[18] Battersea address given on his Ministry of Defence records. For histories of Battersea, see Patrick Loobey, *Battersea Past*, at Battersea Public Library.

[19] Mentioned in his prison letters, Forman Archive.

[20] See Loobey.

[21] George O'Riordan's views from William's application to the Foreign Office, TNA-PRO CSC 11/150.

[22] Dr Arthur Chandler, archivist of the University of Surrey (which took over from Battersea Poly), provided me with background and access to the Battersea Poly students' magazine.

[23] School roll at St Ignatius. Frank also went to the Mercy Convent after William.

[24] Michael Joyce's claims for compensation involved him in a long wrangle with the authorities of the new Irish state. The papers relating to this are under file 395/45, 'Claim for Destruction of a House', and Criminal Injury Books, Co. Mayo: 1920–21 IC 74/46 and Criminal Injury Papers 1920 IC 76/38 at the Irish National Archives. The paucity of compensation rankled with the Joyces for the rest of their lives and added to William's general chippiness. In a comment on a student's essay on Ireland, in the early 1930s, William wrote: 'Long before the "Black and Tans" appeared, my parents had been reduced to abject poverty by Sinn Féin burnings (compensation awards were reduced to about 25%).' Sheffield Archive.

[25] Eamonn Waldron archive.

[26] *Oldham Chronicle*, 27 February 1976.

[27] Irish census of 1911, 1918.

[28] Michael Joyce's letters in the Quentin Joyce archive.

[29] *The Times*, 29 March 1919.

[30] See Neil Baldwin, *Henry Ford and the Jews*, London, 2001.

[31] See *Morning Post*, 18 January 1922, 'JEWRY IN POLITICS'; 25 January 1922, 'ALIENS IN ENGLAND – GENERAL PRESCOTT-DECIE ON JEWISH INFLUENCES'.

[32] *Morning Post*, 19 January 1922, 'COMMUNISM AND IRELAND'; 6 January 1922, 'IRISH AFFILIATION WITH MOSCOW'. There were many reports and articles in this vein.

[33] *Morning Post*, 19 January 1922, 'BOLSHEVISM IN IRELAND: A STATE OF ANARCHY'.

[34] Letters in the Quentin Joyce archive make it clear that William was never a full member of these early Fascist groups.

[35] William expresses this in a letter to Captain Lewis, 20 May 1932, Sheffield University archive.

[36] Recalled in *The Blackshirt*, 8 June 1933.

[37] Macnab's notes, Sheffield University archive.

[38] *Evening Standard*, 23 October 1924.

[39] Macnab's notes, Sheffield University archive.

[40] *The Irish Times*, 21 June 1945. In the Irish Military Archive on William Joyce.

[41] *Daily Mail*, 24 October 1924.

4. A MARRIED MAN

[1] Noted in a profile of Joyce written, almost certainly by Charles Maxwell Knight, for MI5. TNA-PRO KV 2/245.

[2] Pearson's death is mentioned in Macnab's notes, Sheffield University archive.

[3] Interview with Douglas Trew, 1905–2003, October 2002.

[4] TNA-PRO KV 2/245.

[5] Macnab's notes, Sheffield University archive.

[6] Letter from British Fascisti in the Quentin Joyce archive.

[7] William's prison letters, Forman Archive.

[8] According to Margaret in Cole.

[9] William's exam questions kept by his mother, in the Quentin Joyce archive.

[10] Interview with Heather.

[11] Ibid.

[12] Records at Birkbeck University.

[13] *Fascist Quarterly*, Vol. II, No. 3, July 1936.

[14] Unfortunately, the archive copy of this magazine is missing from the British Library, and at the time of writing Birkbeck's archive is inaccessible during building reconstruction.

[15] *Review of English Studies*, Vol. IV, 1928.

[16] Quentin Joyce archive.

[17] TNA-PRO CSC 11/150.

[18] Ibid.

[19] Interview with Heather.

[20] William's letter to his pupil Captain Lewis, 1932, Sheffield University archive.

[21] Macnab's notes, Sheffield University archive.

[22] Heather Marsden-Smedley, *The Times of Kensington and Chelsea*, January 1973, now missing from all relevant libraries. It was subsequently reprinted as *A Place Called Chelsea*, City Journals Ltd, London, 1974. With thanks to Philip Marsden for supplying me with a copy.

[23] Joyce, *Twilight Over England*.

[24] Marsden-Smedley.

[25] William's letter to his pupil Captain Lewis, 1932, Sheffield University archive.

[26] Interview with Heather.

[27] TNA-PRO KV2/245.

[28] King's College archive.

[29] Winston Churchill, *Great Contemporaries*, London, 1937.

[30] T. O. Lloyd, *Empire to Welfare State: English History 1906–1967*, Oxford, 1970.

[31] See Piers Brendon, *The Dark Valley: A Panorama of the 1930s*, London, 2001.

5. WITH THE BLACKSHIRTS: THE 'MIGHTY ATOM'

[1] Recollection by school contemporary in Galway.

[2] Family source.

[3] Macnab's notes, Sheffield University archive.

[4] Date noted in TNA-PRO KV 2 346/No. 3.

[5] See Colin Cross, *Fascism in Britain*, London, 1961.

[6] Noted in Nicholas Mosley, *Beyond the Pale*, London, 1983.

[7] See James Drennan, *B.U.F, Oswald Mosley and British Fascism*,

London, 1934. 'James Drennan' was the pseudonym of W. E. D. Allen.
[8] See Richard Lamb, *Mussolini and the British*, London, 1997.
[9] See Julie Gottlieb's fascinating study *Feminine Fascists* (Manchester, 2000) detailing the number of former Suffragettes drawn to Fascist movements in the 1930s. For Leese and other Fascist groups, see the authoritative works of Richard Griffiths (*Fellow-Travellers of the Right: British Enthusiasts for Nazi Germany*, London, 1980) and Richard Thurlow (*Fascism in Modern Britain*, Sutton, 2000).
[10] Interview with Francis Beckett, author of the John Beckett biography *The Rebel who Lost his Cause: The Tragedy of John Beckett, MP* (London, 1999). See also John Beckett's revealing papers at the Sheffield University archive.
[11] Interview with Peter Morris, Liverpool, June 2002.
[12] 'THE FASCIST "PROFESSOR" – MR W. JOYCE EXPLAINS A MISTAKE', *New Chronicle*, 26 January 1934.
[13] *The Blackshirt*, 8 February 1933.
[14] Beckett's papers, Sheffield University archive.
[15] Charnley.
[16] Joyce, *National Socialism Now*.
[17] See J. A. Booker, *Blackshirts on Sea*, London, 1999.
[18] Gottlieb.
[19] *Daily Mirror*, 9 May 1940.
[20] Cole and Selwyn.
[21] Cole.
[22] A. K. Chesterton's notes, Sheffield University archive.
[23] Interviews with Margaret Collins Bowie, Macnab's sister-in-law, in August 2002. Macnab once reprimanded members at a very rowdy BUF meeting near the Elephant and Castle, who had shouted anti-Royalist abuse, as 'utter cads', which somewhat flattered the rough proletariat and brought a round of applause. He wrote a 'funny' column in *The Blackshirt*, called 'Jolly Judah', making jokes about the Jews. It was anti-Semitic, but seldom vicious. Example: 'Judah Rules the Waves … the Queen Mary is to be the first transatlantic liner equipped with a synagogue and one of the principal holdings in the Cunard Company is that of Mr J. B. Kosher. Evidently the Jews are preparing to become a maritime nation' (28 February 1936).
[24] Macnab's letters to Margaret in prison are very affectionate: TNA-PRO KV 2/346.
[25] See Cross, Gottlieb, and A. W. Brian Simpson, *In the Highest Degree Odious: Detention Without Trial in Wartime Britain*, Oxford, 1992. Piercy's performance at Dunkirk was reported in the Mosleyite bulletin *Comrade*, 1940, and reprinted in the July 1989 issue. 'On May 28 1940 … Piercey and fellow BU member CPP Dick, owner of an open

bridged forty-foot motor launch *Advance*, learned from the Admiralty that there was an acute shortage of crews for the Dunkirk evacuation and all boats taken over by them had left. An official report states that Dick and Piercy ... volunteered to take themselves to Sheerness and then by persistence took *Advance* to Dunkirk. In a non-stop ferry service throughout the Dunkirk evacuation they brought back hundreds of British soldiers to our shores. What the official report did not reveal was that on their final return they were arrested under 18B Defence Regulations and taken to Walton Gaol.' The Dunkirk episode is also described in Charnley. Details about Hamilton-Piercey's arrest under 18B: TNA-PRO HO 144/21564.

26 Family source.

27 Macnab's notes, Sheffield University archive.

28 Ibid.

29 Family Division of the High Court of Justice, High Holborn, London, Folio No. 46 of 1937. Hazel was indeed the 'matrimonial offender', at least technically.

30 William's diary, PRO KV 2/25/2, copyright Forman Archive.

31 Cole. The BUF member who was later to marry a Jewish girl may have been Charles Wegg-Prosser, a Catholic who stood for Mosley in East London, apparently to appeal to the Irish vote. Later, he renounced his Fascist past and married into the Jewish faith. Undated article in William Joyce file, Box G2.5329, Irish Military Archives, Cathal Brugha Barracks, Dublin.

32 William's nicknames for Macnab appear in his letters. Macnab was called 'Angus' by his wife Catherine, but was also sometimes known as John. He signed his letters to Margaret 'Master'.

33 Articles from *The Blackshirt*, tracked week by week, particularly 1936.

34 Oswald Mosley wrote in his autobiography (*My Life*, London, 1968), 'They attacked and we defended.'

35 *The Blackshirt,* 22 June 1933.

36 King Edward VIII's words were reported as 'Something should be done' (not 'Something must be done') in the *Illustrated London News*, 28 November 1936.

37 Quoted in David Irving, *Churchill's War: The Struggle for Power*, Australia, 1987. Beaverbrook, like Mosley (and Churchill), supported the King.

38 *The Blackshirt* claims it is 'lying propaganda' that the Nazi Government are persecuting the Jews (1 April 1933): 'Dr Goebbels, minister of Propaganda, has offered a challenge to anyone who can name one single Jew who has met his death in the course of the national revolution ...'

[39] Joyce, *Twilight Over England*.
[40] R. R. Bellamy, unpublished manuscript in the Sheffield University archive.
[41] Cecil Roberts, *And so to America*, London, 1946.
[42] See Mike Cronin (ed.), *The Failure of British Fascism*, London, 1996.

6. GERMANY CALLS

[1] Interview with Margaret Collins Bowie, August 2002.
[2] There was, according to Nicholas Mosley, much disapproval inside the BUF about William's pamphlet on India, which was thought over-arching.
[3] Quoted in Nicholas Mosley.
[4] Robert Skidelsky, *Mosley*, London, 1981. For an almost comical recollection of the rough-and-tumble of Jewish radicals versus Fascist streetfighters in the 1930s, see Derek Jameson's autobiography *Touched by Angels*. Jameson writes that it was almost *de rigeur* for young Jews to be communists in working-class London life of the 1930s.
[5] Nicholas Mosley (in *Beyond the Pale*) and John Warburton of The Friends of Oswald Mosley (in an interview with the author, November 2002) both make the claim that William sought to make the British Union much more anti-Semitic than Oswald Mosley liked.
[6] Quoted in Jan Dalley, *Diana Mosley: A Life*, London, 1999.
[7] Interview with Peter Morris, June 2002.
[8] Ibid.
[9] *Morning Post*, 13 April 1937.
[10] Ibid.
[11] Francis Beckett, *The Rebel who Lost his Cause*.
[12] A. K. Chesterton, *Oswald Mosley: Portrait of a Leader*, London, 1937.
[13] Francis Beckett, *The Rebel who Lost his Cause*.
[14] Interview with Francis Beckett.
[15] *The Blackshirt*, 20 September 1936, 'Dulwich. Two fine meetings at Dulwich Library and Triangle. Frank Joyce spoke'; October 24, 'Dulwich. Good meeting outside Library. Frank Joyce spoke.'
[16] Interview with Mrs Doris West of Broadstairs, formerly Dulwich, who was a schoolgirl with Joan Joyce.
[17] Interviews with neighbours at Allison Grove, Dulwich, summer 2002.
[18] R. R. Bellamy, unpublished manuscript in the Sheffield University archive.
[19] Two copies of *The Helmsman* are available at the Wiener Library, London W1.

[20] Brian Green, *Dulwich: The Home Front 1939–45*, Dulwich Society, 1995.

[21] Francis Beckett, *The Rebel who Lost his Cause*.

[22] William's letters to Miss Scrimgeour from his prison cell are in the Forman Archive. They have a respectful tone. Her letters to Margaret show how Ethel Scrimgeour adored William, almost as a replica son.

[23] The Evesham episode is described in A. K. Chesterton's papers, Sheffield University archive and also referred to in Cross.

[24] Quoted in Nicholas Mosley.

[25] See W. J. West, *Truth Betrayed*, London, 1987.

[26] *Worthing Gazette,* 19 December 1934, 'FASCISTS ACQUITTED AT ASSIZES'.

[27] There are several files at the British National Archives at Kew on this. See also Peter Martland, *Lord Haw-Haw: The English Voice of Nazi Germany*, Secret History Files, National Archive, London, 2003. Joyce is known to have passed information on to the security services as well as having been the object of their surveillance.

[28] See Anthony Masters, *The Man Who Was M: The Life of Maxwell Knight*, Basil Blackwell, 1984. See also Joan Miller, *One Girl's War*, Co. Kerry, 1986.

[29] Maxwell Knight's profile of William is in TNA-PRO KV2/245.

[30] Quentin's recollection of this emerged in the trial of William Joyce and is referred to in the standard texts (Hall, Bechhofer Roberts, Rebecca West). 'When Quentin was about 16 years old, his father destroyed some documents saying "This will save a hell of a lot of trouble". "He was taking papers out of an old tin box at the time, and shortly afterwards I saw him burn a number of papers. One of the documents which I remember seeing looked like an American eagle embossed on it"' (Derek Curtis-Bennett archive).

[31] For an extraordinary and detailed description of these right-wing organisations see Griffiths, *Fellow Travellers of the Right*. These included doctors organisations constituted to stop immigrant (usually Jewish) incomers. They also showed an alarming tendency among English animal-lovers to dislike Jews, arising from hysterical objections to kosher butchering methods.

[32] William Joyce's tip-off almost certainly came from Charles Maxwell Knight, according to John Beckett (Francis Beckett, *The Rebel who Lost his Cause*). Both W. J. West (in *Truth Betrayed*) and A. W. Brian Simpson (in *In the Highest Degree Odious*) also write that Maxwell Knight was the most likely candidate. Simpson points out that Joyce had supplied Maxwell Knight with information about communists and this tip-off was the *quid pro quo*. See also Adrian Weale, *Renegades: Hitler's Englishmen*, London, 1994.

[33] A. K. Chesterton's notes, Sheffield University archive.

[34] Ibid.

[35] Cole, with supplementary information from A. K. Chesterton's and Macnab's papers at Sheffield University archive.

[36] *Vogue*, 1939.

[37] According to a note from Angus Macnab in the Quentin Joyce archive.

[38] Frank Joyce told John Charnley that William had said he would be back in a short while (see Charnley, *Blackshirts and Roses*).

[39] See Cole and also Selwyn.

[40] Derek Curtis-Bennett archive.

[41] Joyce, *Twilight Over England*.

7. BECOMING 'LORD HAW-HAW'

[1] See Simpson. During his trial, William's defence lawyer Derek Curtis-Bennett was passed the following unsigned note: 'You can sub-poena the Special Branch of the Yard on when Joyce left England. He was checked out at ports by Home Office emigration. A detention order under 18B was to have been served on him on September 3, 1939. Weeks later the special branch found that he had been checked out of the country and that his wife had been too' (Derek Curtis-Bennett archive).

[2] See Cole.

[3] TNA-PRO KV 2/247.

[4] Macnab's notes, Sheffield University archive.

[5] *Daily Mirror*, 4 June 1940; TNA-PRO HO144/22158; see also Simpson.

[6] Rebecca West's description in *The Meaning of Treason*.

[7] Family sources.

[8] See Charnley.

[9] William's prison letters, Forman archive.

[10] TNA-PRO HO 45/25690. Most material relating to Quentin's arrest and imprison-ment is in this file, supplemented here with material from the Quentin Joyce archive

[11] See Simpson.

[12] TNA-PRO HO 45/25690.

[13] Ibid.

[14] Ibid.

[15] Ibid. The MPs he named included Captain Ramsey – not a wise choice in view of Ramsey's involvement with extreme right-wing groups

(see Thurlow, *Fascism in Britain*). The conversation was monitored by a warder: perhaps this shows Q's naïvety.

[16] See 'Poland 1939' in Robert Cowley, *No End Save Victory*, London, 2002.

[17] Recalled by James Clark.

[18] William and Margaret in Berlin: Cole; A. K. Chesterton's papers; Horst J. P. Bergmeier and Rainer E. Lotz, *Hitler's Airwaves: The Inside Story of Nazi Radio Broadcasting and Propaganda Swing*, London, 1997; and James Clark.

[19] See Myles Eckersley, *Prospero's Wireless: A Biography of P. P. Eckersley*, Hants, 1998.

[20] Recalled by James Clark.

[21] See W. J. West. As West points out, Neville Chamberlain declared war by radio in September 1939.

[22] See Eckersley.

[23] Asa Briggs, *A History of Broadcasting*, London, 1995; Tom Hickman, *What Did You Do in the War, Auntie? The BBC at War*, London, 1995.

[24] See Bergmeier and Lotz for details on the structure of German radio.

[25] M. R. Doherty, *Nazi Wireless Propaganda, Lord Haw-Haw and British Public Opinion in the Second World War*, Edinburgh University, 2000.

[26] See Jonah Barrington's obituary, *Daily Telegraph*, 26 September 1986.

[27] *The Times*, 8 January 1940.

[28] See Bergmeier and Lotz; also private information from James Clark.

[29] On 9 October 1939, the *News Chronicle* claimed Lord Haw-Haw was believed to be Dr Helmut Hoffmann 'a German teacher who caused an outcry in Scotland by his lectures on Nazi-ism to students at Coatbridge Secondary school'. The newspaper said that Lord Haw-Haw was 'voted radio comedian No 1 by British listeners'. The *Sunday Express* on 29 January 1940 claimed that he was 'said to be a former London insurance chief, Henry Williams Wicks'. The *Daily Express* on 14 February 1940 claimed it might be 'Hans Fritsche ex-German consular official'.

[30] Macnab's notes, Sheffield University archive.

[31] *Sunday Pictorial*, 17 December 1939.

8. A HIT WITH HITLER: MEDIA STAR OF THE THIRD REICH

[1] Quoted in Doherty. This academic study contains a voluminous amount of material on press and public response to the Haw-Haw phenomenon.

[2] See Doherty and Bergmeier and Lotz. The Western Brothers performed a hilarious double-act on the theme of Lord Haw-Haw of Zeesen, which is reproduced on the CD accompanying the Bergmeier and Lotz study.

[3] The clip of a formal banquet being entertained by 'Lord Haw-Haw' (with his friend Adolf) is reproduced on the Ludovic Kennedy TV documentary 'Lord Haw-Haw', broadcast on 29 December 1975, and available from the BBC archives.

[4] Speaking on 'Germany Calling', BBC Radio 4 documentary, 4 May 1991.

[5] Ibid.

[6] German radio broadcast on 7 November 1939 on the Zeesen wavelength.

[7] Quoted in Hickman.

[8] Doherty.

[9] Bremen wavelength, 1 July 1940.

[10] Breslau wavelength, 21 December 1940.

[11] Bremen wavelength, 2 June 1940. This broadcast jeered at Dunkirk and Churchill's boast that defeating Hitler would be an easy business. It was true Winston Churchill was over-confident at the start of hostilities.

[12] Mention of the Ark Royal first appears on German airwaves, Hamburg wavelength, on 28 September 1939.

[13] This story is quoted in Shirer, entry for 4 February 1940.

[14] Hamburg wavelength, 5 November 1939. This passage begins as a commentary on *The Citadel* by A. J. Cronin, an author William Joyce greatly liked.

[15] Hamburg wavelength, 22 January 1940. The BBC Monitor was nick-naming Joyce 'Sinister Sam' at this point.

[16] Most ordinary British people, according to George Orwell, had little interest in what they regarded as Continental political quarrels. See his 1945 essay on P. G. Wodehouse in *The Essays of George Orwell*, London, 1984.

[17] Hamburg wavelength, 22 January 1940. He added to his point about the unemployed a castigation of the Duchess of Hamilton who was 'fussing over animals'.

[18] Hamburg wavelength, 18 December 1939.

[19] Ibid.

[20] Hamburg wavelength, 10 December 1939. In this broadcast he adds that he was astonished when he first came to England to hear men asking one another what school they had gone to. The theme of social inequality is consistently strong in the broadcasts 1939–42.

[21] This study was carried out by Liverpool University's Social Science

department and is quoted in Doherty. It was endorsed by Mass Observation findings.

[22] Mr Bleeding Bevan appears on the Workers' Challenge wavelength, 10 August 1940; 'Hoary Ernie', 9 February 1941; 'old cock', 27 August 1940.

[23] The first of many mentions of 'bugger': Hamburg wavelength, 5 July 1940.

[24] See David O'Donoghue, *Hitler's Irish Voices: The Story of German Radio's Wartime Irish Service*, Belfast, 1998.

[25] Breslau wavelength, 20 March 1941.

[26] Home Intelligence, TNA-PRO INF 1/292.

[27] Maurice Gorham describes Radio Éireann's restrictive output well (and the Irish public's dislike of Churchill) in his memoir *Forty Years of Irish Broadcasting* (Dublin, 1967).

[28] William very quickly got into his stride and began using his own tone of voice: a broadcast about the Tories on the Hamburg wavelength on 28 September 1939 could only have been written by Joyce, though it carries no 'by-line'. 'It is a waste of time to try to analyse very deeply the thought processes of Paleolithic crustaceans who move feebly now and then in nice easy chairs in the Carlton Club.' His childhood liking for 'big words', his excoriation of the Tories and his knowledge of the Carlton Club all come into the picture.

[29] The story goes that when De Valera warned over the radio that Ireland would resist invasion, Lord Haw-Haw replied the next day: 'De Valera couldn't even drive the tinkers out of the Ballygaddy Road in Tuam, let alone resist the power of the Third Reich.' This story was told to me as a local legend by Ger Delaney of the South Mayo Genealogical Society, and it has been repeated in several other versions in correspondence from other Irish sources. But, as with many Haw-Haw legends, there is no mention of it in the official records. Lord Haw-Haw was said to have apologised when a German bomb accidentally fell on a field in the West of Ireland in 1940. No one was killed but it was said that William named the field's owner. Again, there is no such record in the BBC monitors of the broadcasts, but it remains a legend in the Galway region. (There is a broadcast denial that German bombs would ever fall on Ireland, even by mistake.)

[30] Interviewed on 'Germany Calling', BBC Radio 4, 4 May 1991. William Joyce certainly gave out news before such news had been released in Britain, or when certain aspects of news were censored altogether. For example, on 15 September 1940 on the Bremen wavelength, in the middle of the Battle of Britain, he announced that: 'Today Dover was once more the scene of vigorous air attacks which were directed primarily against barrage balloons there. The British defence was

vigorous but attempts to cut off this district by firing salvoes were unsuccessful. Speedy Stukas were able to break through this iron curtain without losses and attack their objectives.' Most of the planes shot down were Spitfires, he added. This was indeed news to many people in Kent.
[31] Doherty.
[32] Letters to the author from A. A. Osborne, Jim Sargant and Ken Hutchinson will be deposited with the University of Sheffield.
[33] Doherty.
[34] Ibid.
[35] Interview with Terry Charman.
[36] The BBC personnel who monitored the German broadcasts were interviewed for 'Germany Calling', BBC Radio 4, 4 May 1991. Lorna Swire asked all her colleagues also working on monitoring and they agreed with her that the clocks, and so on, were never mentioned by Haw-Haw. The 'clocks' legend remains a mystery.
[37] *News Review*, Hamburg wavelength, 1 July 1940.
[38] Ibid.
[39] I was confidently informed by a member of the Conservative Party at Dover that there was a known William Joyce connection with Whitchurch in Shropshire. Lorna Sage in her autobiography *Bad Blood*, published in 2000, writes that 'Joyce's Clock Factory' in Whitchurch was owned by a cousin of Lord Haw-Haw. I have not been able to trace any family link between the Mayo Joyces and the Whitchurch Clock Factory.
[40] Bergmeier and Lotz.
[41] Family source.
[42] Joseph Goebbels, *Goebbels Diaries*, London, 1948. Quoted in Doherty.
[43] Ibid., 6 January 1940.
[44] Ibid., 22 August 1940. Goebbels added to this reflection that William 'genuinely wanted to serve England', which, in a perverse way, had some truth.
[45] Ibid.
[46] Bergmeier and Lotz; also personal information from James Clark.
[47] The lovestruck case of Pearl Vardon, woman broadcaster, is mentioned in Doherty.
[48] Calais (Hamburg group) wavelength, 5 February 1941.
[49] John Bowman interview with Francis Stuart, RTÉ Radio 1, 29 January 1976.
[50] Francis Stuart, *Black List, Section H*, London, 1975.
[51] *Sunday Despatch*, 13 July 1952.
[52] See Bergmeier and Lotz, and John Carver Edwards, *Berlin Calling: American Broadcasters in Service to the Third Reich*, Praeger, 1991.
[53] Ezra Pound's letters appear in Bergmeier and Lotz, and in John Tytell, *Ezra Pound: The Solitary Volcano*, New York, 1987. William thought

that Ezra Pound had 'a screw loose', as he mentions in his letters to Margaret from prison (Forman Archive). Pound's letters are at the Beinacke Rare Book and Manuscript Library, Yale University. With thanks to James Clark who has shown me a copy of this collection. After the war, Pound was judged to be mentally unfit to stand trial and spent twelve years in an asylum near Washington. When Ernest Hemingway received the Nobel prize for Literature in 1954, he announced that Ezra Pound should have been the recipient. Pound was released from hospital in 1958 and died in Venice in 1972.

[54] Shirer.

[55] Richard Kupsch, 'Germany Calling', BBC Radio 4, 4 May 1991.

[56] Bremen wavelength, 2 July 1940.

9. LIFE IN BERLIN

[1] Joyce, *Twilight Over England*.

[2] Observed by Shirer.

[3] Howard Smith, *Last Train from Berlin*, London, 1942.

[4] Bremen wavelength, 8 September 1940.

[5] 'What Berlin is Wearing', 2 April 1940. Margaret was also heard to broadcast as 'Frau Frohlich'. Some contemporaries described her as a 'compulsive babbler' without much of a microphone voice (Bergmeier and Lotz). She may have felt she was tolerated on sufferance because of William.

[6] Cole.

[7] Recalled by James Clark. The Joyces were obviously treated royally at the *Funk-Eck*: 'They killed the fatted calf for us,' Margaret noted on 18 October 1940.

[8] John O'Reilly's memoirs, *Sunday Dispatch*, 13 July 1952.

[9] According to Margaret's diary, Goebbels favoured William with a fine box of cigars on 22 August 1940.

[10] This is mentioned several times in her letters, and in Joyce's diary. William also had affairs with other women, but this seems usually to have been on the rebound from Margaret's rebuffs.

[11] Margaret's diary, 2 January 1940, TNA-PRO KV/246/8.

[12] Ibid., 11 January 1940.

[13] Bergmeier and Lotz.

[14] Margaret's diary, 10 August 1940.

[15] Cole, Selwyn, Bergmeier and Lotz.

[16] See Bergmeier and Lotz. See also John Borrie, *Despite Captivity: A Doctor's Life as a Prisoner of War*, London, 1975.

[17] James Clark's recollections.

[18] Margaret's Diary, 24 February 1941.

[19] Described in William's letters, Forman Archive.

[20] Quentin Joyce archive. Although Michael Joyce talks about 'keeping the wolf off', he did not die penniless. He left £650 at his death (*Daily Sketch*, 29 September 1943), which was a respectable sum of money at the time.

[21] Quentin Joyce archive.

[22] Ibid., and Simpson.

[23] Notes in Quentin Joyce archive.

[24] Simpson.

[25] Quentin Joyce archive.

[26] The story of Anna Wolkoff and Tyler Kent is one that fascinates conspiracy-theorists because of the complicated backgrounds of both protagonists, and because it revealed much about Churchill's relationship with Roosevelt before they officially became allies. See Ray Bearse and Anthony Read, *Conspirator: The Untold Story of Churchill, Roosevelt and Tyler Kent, Spy*, London, 1993.

[27] Margaret's diary, 15 April 1941.

[28] William's diary, 7 May 1941, Forman Archive.

[29] Margaret's diary, 9 June 1941.

[30] Twenty thousand Jews were imprisoned, ninety-one were killed and mobs attacked Jewish shops, shattering the glass (*kristall*) fronts.

[31] See Anja Klabunde, *Magda Goebbels*, London, 1991, and Ralf Georg Reuth, *Goebbels*, London, 1993.

[32] Cole.

[33] Ibid.

[34] Margaret's diary, 10 July 1941.

[35] *Oldham Chronicle*, 5 June 1945.

[36] Luxemburg wavelength, 29 June 1941.

[37] Bullock, *Hitler and Stalin: Parallel Lives*, Fontana, 1998.

[38] Luxemburg wavelength, 29 June 1941.

[39] Home Intelligence, TNA-PRO 1/292.

[40] Luxemburg wavelength, 20 July 1942.

[41] Luxemburg wavelength, 29 June 1941.

[42] Margaret's diary, 19 August 1941.

[43] James Clark.

[44] Calais (Hamburg group) wavelength, 2 March 1941.

[45] Breslau wavelength, 8 December 1941.

[46] Cole.

[47] William's diary.

[48] See Cole.

[49] Luxemburg wavelength, 25 December 1941

[50] Macnab's notes, Sheffield University archive.

10. THE TURNING TIDE

[1] See Kershaw, *Hitler: Nemesis 1936–45*, London, 2000.

[2] This episode is described in Cole.

[3] Interview with Terry Charman, Imperial War Museum.

[4] Home Intelligence, TNA-PRO INF 1/292.

[5] Ibid.

[6] Mary Taverner's claim was made in the London *Evening Standard*, 27 March 1941. William rebutted her on air on the Breslau wavelength, 2 April 1941.

[7] See Dalley, which contains some priceless invective from William in the form of letters about Mary Taverner.

[8] A copy of Macnab's letter to A. P. Herbert is in the Quentin Joyce archive.

[9] Breslau wavelength, 2 May 1941.

[10] Cole.

[11] Lavinia Greacen did some preliminary work for a biography of William Joyce. I believe that her theory is correct, and it correlates with my own 'feminine intuition' on this matter.

[12] Angus Macnab wrote at length in his notes at the Sheffield University archive of the 'canonical' entanglements of William's marital status. Macnab claimed that William died a bachelor, canonically, as he was never sacramentally married, a valid point in Anglican as well as Catholic canon law at this time.

[13] The date of their trip to Norway was stamped in Margaret's passport, TNA-PRO KV 2/346/1. She was provided with two passports, one as Margaret Joyce, 'commentator', and one as Margaret Hansen, 'housewife'.

[14] See Anthony Beevor, *Berlin: The Downfall 1945*, London, 2002.

[15] Margaret's diary, 22 September 1942.

[16] Madeleine Stuart, *Manna in the Morning: A Memoir 1940–1958*, Dublin and London, 1984.

[17] Letter to the author from Joe Roche, to be deposited with Sheffield University.

[18] Breslau wavelength, 17 February 1942.

[19] See Hart.

[20] Letter to the author from Father Jim Feehan.

[21] Bergmeier and Lotz.

[22] See Weale, *Patriot Traitors*. Margaret mentions the arrival of John Amery in Berlin in her diary – the Joyces clearly thought it a significant development. See also Rebecca West for a well-observed portrait of Amery, a pathetic and vacant man.

[23] Home Intelligence, TNA-PRO INF 1/292.

[24] Richard Overy, *Why the Allies Won*, London, 1995.

[25] Goebbels, *Diaries*, 29 July 1943.

[26] For the soldiers' reports see Kershaw, *Hitler: Nemesis*.

[27] Goebbels, *Diaries*, 8 April 1942.

[28] Margaret's diary, 18 January 1943.

[29] Eric Pleasants, *Hitler's Bastards*, unpublished autobiography (supplied by the Friends of Oswald Mosley).

[30] Susan Hilton's sad story is told in O'Donoghue. She was also an alcoholic.

[31] Ursula von Kardorff, *Diary of a Nightmare: Berlin 1942–1945*, London, 1965.

[32] Kershaw, *Hitler: Nemesis*.

[33] Home Intelligence, TNA-PRO INF 1/292. These files cover all the quotes mentioned in this section.

[34] Letters in the Quentin Joyce archive.

[35] Interview with Judith Fitton of Dulwich, January 2003, who was babysat by Mrs Joyce during the war. She recalls that Queenie also did some cleaning for her mother.

[36] Letter to the author from Royston Clarke.

11. THE ROAD TO NOWHERE

[1] Quoted in Cole and by permission of the Forman Archive.

[2] Cole.

[3] Beevor.

[4] James Clark.

[5] German European Services in English, 21 July 1944.

[6] Terry Charman, *The German Home Front*, London, 1989.

[7] Quentin Joyce archive.

[8] Thanks to Derek Denton of Oldham for information about Queenie's burial place.

[9] Quentin Joyce archive.

[10] *London Evening News*, 29 May 1945.

[11] Margaret's diary, 2 March 1944.

[12] See Anthony Read and David Fisher, *The Fall of Berlin*, London, 1992.

[13] Although William's card was issued on 21 December 1944, Margaret noted that he joined on 22 October. Before his trial he told his lawyer that he was forced into the Volkssturm (statement in the Derek Curtis-Bennett archive).

[14] Cole.

[15] His Reich honour, the Cross of War merit, was exhibited at the Trial of William Joyce, and pictured in Hall. Margaret was also awarded an honour by the Reich, which is displayed in the British National Archives, TNA-PRO KV 2/346/9.

[16] James Clark.

[17] Margaret's diary, 2 November 1944.

[18] TNA-PRO KV 2/250/2.

[19] Cole, with supplementary recollection from James Clark.

[20] Roland Freisler was notorious: see Louis L. Snyder, *Encyclopaedia of the Third Reich*, Ware, 1998.

[21] See Beevor, and Read and Fisher.

[22] Martin Gilbert, *The Second World War*, London, 1989.

[23] Derrick Mercer (ed.), *Chronicle of the Second World War*, Harlow, 1990.

[24] Read and Fisher.

[25] John Colville, *The Churchillians*, London, 1981.

[26] Luxemburg wavelength, 16 February 1942.

[27] Noted in Margaret's diary, 10 February 1945.

[28] Charman, *The German Home Front*.

[29] All following quotes from William Joyce are from his diary, original held at TNA-PRO KV 2/250/2; much of it has been reproduced in Peter Martland's excellently helpful *Lord Haw-Haw*, which documents all the material held at the British National Archives. Copyright of the diary belongs to the Forman Archive, and extracts are quoted here with permission.

[30] Gilbert, *The Second World War*.

[31] Cole.

[32] Interview with Lisl Kuhlmann, Apen, October 2002.

[33] Margaret marked her menstrual period in her diaries. Her problems with menstruation may have been related to disappointment at childlessness.

[34] Local interviews, October 2002.

[35] Gilbert, *The Second World War*.

[36] Ibid.

[37] Taken from the CD recording included with Bergmeier and Lotz.

[38] Geoffrey Perry, *When Life Becomes History*, London, 2002.

[39] Even at the end, Margaret's sex-appeal is evident. The soldiers fairly buzzed around her, and she notes in her diary how delighted they are to come and drink with an Englishwoman.

[40] Interview with Frau Bebensee, Flensburg, January 2003.

[41] Interview with Geoffrey Perry, May 2003. Also see Perry, *When Life Becomes History*.

[42] James H. Hodge (ed.), *Famous Trials*, London, 1954.

12. THE DRAMATIC LAST DAYS

[1] *Irish Press*, 8 June 1945. In file G2/5329 in the Irish Military archives.

[2] P. Novick, *The Resistance Versus Vichy: The Purge of Collaborators in Liberated France*, London, 1968.

[3] *The Irish Times*, 9 June 1945.

[4] Ibid., 17 July 1945. In the Irish Military archives.

[5] *News Chronicle*, 29 May 1945.

[6] See Selwyn.

[7] Leonard Burt, *Commander Burt of Scotland Yard*, London, 1969.

[8] Letter from Joan to Quentin, undated, Quentin Joyce archive. Possibly early 1946.

[9] Queenie Joyce's bank statement, Quentin Joyce archive.

[10] Michael Joyce (born 1952), Quentin's son, believes that Quentin was driven more by a sense of injustice, arising from his own internment, than by pure devotion to William. It seems to me to have been both. Quentin did have a sharpened sense of injustice after his own internment, but he did show enormous devotion to William too. He even argued with the prison authorities about supplying William with extra food (they refused). Letters referring to this are in the Quentin Joyce archive.

[11] Ethel Scrimgeour wrote to Margaret, 'It must have been trying not to be allowed to see him in private – touch him, even clasp his hand – Even *I* felt that. You are both so wonderful and brave' (PRO KV2/346, No. 4). Stewart McLaughlin, historian of Wandsworth, says at that time there was a deliberate policy of austerity to reduce 'emotionalism'.

[12] Quentin Joyce archive.

[13] Quentin's letter of request for the preservation of William's correspondence is in the Quentin Joyce archive.

[14] The accounts of William Joyce's trial come from a variety of contemporary newspaper reports, the two standard textbooks cited, Hall and Bechhofer Roberts – containing verbatim transcripts of the case – as well as the more colourful and descriptive report by Rebecca West. Other legal books are mentioned in the bibliography. I have also drawn on Selwyn's *Hitler's Englishman*, a particularly clear account of the complex case. The archive of Derek Curtis-Bennett QC, who worked on the case with Gerald Slade, has also been most illuminating.

[15] See under TNA-PRO KV 2/245–2/250.

[16] See Hall.

[17] The authorities obtained copies of most of Quentin's incoming mail, but since they were not to know where Quentin posted his letters, they did not have all the outgoing mail.

[18] Quentin's letters to his family are in the Quentin Joyce archive.

[19] Quentin Joyce archive.

[20] TNA-PRO KV 2/247.

[21] Quentin Joyce archive.

[22] Ibid.

[23] Robert Fisk, *In Time of War: Ireland, Ulster and the Price of Neutrality*, London, 1983.

[24] TNA-PRO HO 45/25789.

[25] *Sunday Despatch*, 31 May 1945. In the Irish Military archives.

[26] Quentin Joyce Archive.

[27] For a brilliant description of Frank Holland in the witness-box, see Rebecca West.

[28] TNA-PRO KV2/246.

[29] Letter stating this in the Quentin Joyce archive.

[30] Letters from Sylvia Morris, Quentin Joyce archive. For Sylvia Morris's political career, see Gottlieb.

[31] Quentin Joyce archive.

[32] Interview with Judge Conor Maguire, an Irish law student at this time, March 2002.

[33] *Manchester Guardian* and other newspapers for September 1945 reported conditions of crowding for the press. Rebecca West reported that everybody in London wanted to be at the Trial of Lord Haw-Haw.

[34] 'British Muslims who join the Taliban may face jail. But there are many problems with the Mediaeval law of Treason', Victoria MacCallum, *Law Gazette*, London, 22 November 2001.

[35] Rebecca West claimed that Slade was a temperance campaigner in his spare time.

[36] This joke appears several times in William's prison letters, Forman Archive.

[37] Quentin Joyce archive.

[38] Ibid.

[39] All extracts from William's letters are reproduced from the Forman Archive.

[40] Information on Father Edmund Marshall-Keene from an interview with Heather. First an Army captain, then a parish priest, he later became a Cistercian monk.

[41] Quentin Joyce archive.

[42] Macnab's notes, Sheffield University archive.

[43] Rebecca West.

[44] Correspondence with Mr Mayes, March and April 2003.

[45] William's prison letters, Forman Archive.

[46] O. Hood Philips, *Leading Cases in Constitutional Law*, London, 1957.

[47] Ibid.

[48] Ludovic Kennedy TV documentary, 'Lord Haw-Haw', BBC, 29 December 1975.

[49] Geoffrey Robertson, *Freedom, the Individual and the Law*, London, 1993.

[50] Weale, *Patriot Traitors*.

[51] Ibid.

[52] From William's prison letters, Forman Archive.

[53] From an article written by Quentin Joyce and rejected by the *Evening Standard*, Quentin Joyce archive.

[54] All the following quotations from William's prison letters to his wife are from the Forman Archive.

[55] Original in Quentin Joyce archive, copyright Forman Archive.

[56] Quentin Joyce archive.

[57] Sheffield University archive, copyright Forman Archive.

[58] Macnab's notes, Sheffield University archive.

[59] Quentin Joyce archive.

EPILOGUE: POST-MORTEM, POST-WAR

[1] Quoted in Bergmeier and Lotz, Cole, Selwyn, and others.

[2] 'HEARD LORD HAW-HAW, KILLED HERSELF', *Daily Mail*, 18 January 1940.

[3] John Wardle, *Manchester Guardian*, 31 December 1945.

[4] *Manchester Guardian*, 31 December 1945.

[5] In justice, it should be pointed out that it took a long time for the implication of the genocidal crime against the Jews to sink in. In 1945, people walked out of cinemas in protest in Britain when newsreel about Belsen was being shown (Kee, *1945: The World we Fought for*, London, 1985). Irish nationalist newspapers dismissed the pictures from the concentration camps as British propaganda (Fisk).

[6] Taylor, *British Prime Ministers*.

[7] TNA-PRO HO 45/255728.

[8] Letters from the legal team, Quentin Joyce archive.

[9] Interview with Margaret Collins Bowie, sister of Catherine Collins, August 2002.

[10] Tynan's endorsement is on the jacket of Macnab's book

[11] Dulanty's correspondence, Quentin Joyce archive.

[12] Mentioned in Bergmeier and Lotz.

[13] 'HAW-HAW WIDOW TO WED ENGLISHMAN', *Daily Express*, 6 June 1962.

[14] Quentin provided Hall with copious amounts of background for his book on the Trial. Hall thanks other sources in his introduction but

forbears to thank Quentin. Quentin saved Hall from several howlers, including an outrageously silly claim, based on mistaken identity, that William had once had a shop in Bristol where he sold rubber truncheons. (Quentin Joyce archive.)

[15] Quentin also corrected some of Rebecca West's errors of fact by writing a letter to the *Evening Standard* after she had published extracts from her report of the trial. Shabbily, the *Evening Standard* refused to publish Quentin's letter – being the brother of a man hanged for treason – but passed the letter on to West so that she could benefit from his corrections. (Quentin Joyce archive.)

[16] Interview with Angela Joyce, Quentin's daughter-in-law.

[17] It is noted on Robert's death certificate that exact date of death could not be ascertained.

[18] Bergmeier and Lotz, and *Daily Telegraph* obituary.

[19] James Clark, and communication from Frau Mittler. Mittler wrote a memoir in German, *Anzac Tattoo* (Munich, 1996).

[20] Obituary of Francis Stuart, *The Times*, 2 February 2000.

[21] See Terry Prone, *Irish Murders*, Dublin, 1992.

[22] John O'Reilly's picaresque life is narrated in David O'Donoghue's remarkable study *Hitler's Irish Voices.*

[23] Interview with Sylvia Morris's brother Peter, June 2002.

[24] With thanks to Bob Ratcliffe of Midhurst, Sussex, who wrote a play which featured the eccentric Miss Scrimgeour. See also Paul Thompson, 'The Life and Death of Trevor Aston', *History Workshop Journal*, Issue 39, 1995.

[25] Bergmeier and Lotz, and James Clark's recollections.

[26] Perry, *When Life Becomes History*.

[27] Interview with Geoffrey Perry, May 2003.

[28] Obituary of Maxwell Knight, *The Times*, 27 January 1968.

[29] 'YU.K. 100 BRITONS WE LOVE TO HATE', *Sun*, 23 August 2002. No. 1: 'Lord Haw-Haw. Nickname given to William Joyce who broadcast sneering messages from Germany during the Second World War.' Runners-up: James Hewitt, Jeffrey Archer, Robert Maxwell, Arthur Scargill, Prince Edward. Mosley comes No. 17 between George Galloway and Jonathan Aitken. The Cambridge Spies are No. 27.

[30] Listed in the Quentin Joyce archive.

Select Bibliography

Anderson, Gerald D., *Fascists, Communists and the National Government 1931–1937*, University of Missouri Press, 1983

Baillie-Stewart, Norman (with Murdoch, John), *The Officer in the Tower: The Dramatic Life-story of the Last Englishman to be Imprisoned in the Tower of London*, London, 1967

Baker, David, *Ideology of Obsession (A. K. Chesterton)*, IB Tauris, 1996

Baldwin, Neil, *Henry Ford and the Jews*, London, 2001

Barker, Ernest, *Ireland in the Last Fifty Years: 1866–1918*, Oxford, 1918

Barnes, J. S., *The Universal Aspect of Fascism*, London, 1929

Barrington, Brendan (ed.), *The Wartime Broadcasts of Francis Stuart, 1942–44*, Dublin, 2000

Barry, Tom, *Guerrilla Days in Ireland*, Dublin, 1962 (first published 1949)

Bayor, Ronald H. and Meagher, Timothy J., *The New York Irish*, New York, 1999

Bearse, Ray and Read, Anthony, *Conspirator: The Untold Story of Churchill, Roosevelt and Tyler Kent, Spy*, London, 1993

Bechhofer Roberts, C. E. (ed.), *The Trial of William Joyce*, London, 1946

Beckett, Francis, *The Rebel who Lost his Cause: The Tragedy of John Beckett MP*, London, 1999

Beevor, Antony, *Berlin: The Downfall 1945*, London, 2002

Belloc, Hilaire, *The Jews*, London, 1922

Bennett, Richard, *The Black and Tans*, Severn House, 1976 (first published 1959)

Bergmeier, Horst J. P. and Lotz, Rainer E., *Hitler's Airwaves: The Inside Story of Nazi Radio Broadcasting and Propaganda Swing*, New Haven and London, 1997

Billig, Michael, *Fascists: A Social Psychological View of the National Front*, London, 1978

Birrell, Augustine, *Things Past Redress*, London, 1937

Bolitho, Gordon, *The Other Germany*, London, 1934

Booker, J. A., *Blackshirts On Sea*, London, 1999

Borrie, John, *Despite Captivity: A Doctor's Life as a Prisoner of War*, London, 1975

Bosworth, R. J. B., *Mussolini*, London, 2002

Boyce, George D., *Ireland 1828–1992*, Blackwell, 1992

Boycott, Charles Arthur, *Boycott: The Life Behind the Word*, London, 1997

Boyle, Andrew, *The Climate of Treason*, London, 1979

Brendon, Piers, *The Dark Valley: A Panorama of the 1930s*, London, 2001

Brennan, Robert, *Allegiance*, Dublin, 1950

Briggs, Asa, *A History of Broadcasting*, Oxford, 1995

Briggs, Asa, *The Golden Age of Wireless*, Oxford, 1965

Brown, William, *War and Peace: Essays in Psychological Analysis*, Adam and Chas Black, 1939

Bullock, Alan, *Hitler and Stalin: Parallel Lives*, Fontana, 1998

Burleigh, Michael, *The Third Reich: A New History*, London, 2000

Burt, Leonard, *Commander Burt of Scotland Yard*, London, 1969

Carlyle, Thomas, *Heroes, Hero-Worship and the Heroic in History*, London, 1872

Charman, Terry, *The German Home Front*, London, 1989

Charnley, John, *Blackshirts and Roses: An Autobiography*, London, 1990

Chesterton, A. K., *Oswald Mosley: Portrait of a Leader*, London, 1937

Chesterton, A. K. (with Leftwich, Joseph), *The Tragedy of Anti-Semitism*, London, 1946

Chesterton, G. K., *Irish Impressions*, London, 1919

Churchill, Winston, *Great Contemporaries*, London, 1937

Churchill, Winston, *The Second World War*, London, 1948

Cole, J. A., *Lord Haw-Haw and William Joyce: The Full Story*, London, 1964

Colville, John, *The Churchillians*, London, 1981

Cowley, Robert, *No End Save Victory*, London, 2002

Cronin, Mike (ed.), *The Failure of British Fascism*, London, 1996

Cross, Colin, *Fascism in Britain*, London, 1961

Dalley, Jan, *Diana Mosley: A Life*, London, 1999

De Vere White, Terence, *The Parents of Oscar Wilde*, London, 1967

Dennis Szucs, Loretto, *They Became Americans: Finding Naturalization Record and Ethnic Origin*, New York, 1989

Doherty, M. R., *Nazi Wireless Propaganda, Lord Haw-Haw and British Public Opinion in the Second World War*, Edinburgh University, 2000

Drennan, James, *B.U.F., Oswald Mosley and British Fascism*, London, 1934

Duff, Douglas V., *On Swallowing the Anchor*, London, 1954

Duggan, John P., *Neutral Ireland and the Third Reich*, Dublin, 1989

Eatwell, R., *Fascism*, London, 1995

Eckersley, Myles, *Prospero's Wireless: A Biograpy of P. P. Eckersley*, Romsey, Hants, 1998

Edwards, John Carver, *Berlin Calling: American Broadcasters in Service to the Third Reich*, Praeger, 1991

Fisk, Robert, *In Time of War: Ireland, Ulster and the Price of Neutrality*, London, 1983

Fitzherbert, Katrin, *True to Both My Selves*, London, 1997

Flannery, Harry W., *Assignment to Berlin*, Michael Joseph, 1942

Fleming, Lionel, *Head or Harp*, London, 1965

Forester, C. S. (with Balchin, Nigel et al.), *Fatal Fascination: A Choice of Crime*, London, 1968

Fry, Leslie, *Waters Flowing Eastward*, Paris, 1933 (also 1965 version with introduction by D. Fahey)

Fry, Michael, *Hitler's Wonderland*, London, 1934

Gardiner, Mrs Stanley, *We Two and Shaumus*, Duckworth, 1913

Gilbert, Martin, *History of the 20th Century*, London, 1998

Gilbert, Martin, *The Roots of Appeasement*, London, 1966

Gilbert, Martin, *The Second World War*, London, 1989

Gill, Anton, *A Dance Between Flames: Berlin between the Wars*, London, 1993

Goebbels, Joseph, *Goebbels Diaries*, Lochner, Louis (ed.), London, 1948

Gottlieb, Julie, *Feminine Fascists*, Manchester, 2000

Griffiths, Richard, *Fellow Travellers of the Right: British Enthusiasts for Nazi Germany*, London, 1980

Griffiths, Richard, *Patriotism Perverted: Captain Ramsey and the Right Club and English Anti-Semitism 1939–40*, London, 1998

Gross, John, *A Double Thread*, London, 2001

Grundy, Trevor, *Memoir of a Fascist Childhood*, London, 1998

Gwynn, Denis, *The Life of John Redmond*, London, 1932

Hall, J. W. (ed.), *The Trial of William Joyce*, London, 1946

Hart, Peter, *The IRA and Its Enemies: Violence and Community in Cork 1916–1923*, Oxford, 1998

Hastings, Max, *Bomber Command*, London, 1979

Heffer, Simon, *Moral Desperado: A Life of Carlyle*, London, 1995

Hickman, Tom, *What Did You Do in the War, Auntie? The BBC at War*, London, 1995

Holmes, Colin, *Anti-Semitism in British Society*, London, 1979

Hone, Joseph, *The Moores of Moore Hall*, London, 1939

Irving, David, *Churchill's War: The Struggle for Power*, Australia, 1987

Jameson, Derek, *Touched by Angels*, London, 1988

Jowitt, Earl, *Some Were Spies*, London, 1954

Joyce, William, *National Socialism Now*, London, 1937

Joyce, William, *Twilight Over England*, Berlin, 1940. Reprinted in facsimile by the Imperial War Museum, London, 1992 with an introduction by Terry Charman

Kardorff, Ursula von, *Diary of a Nightmare: Berlin 1942–55*, London, 1965

Kee, Robert, *1945: The World we Fought For*, London, 1985

Kenny, Mary, *Goodbye to Catholic Ireland*, London, 1997 (with full annotation), and Dublin, 2000

Keogh, Dermot, *Jews in Twentieth-Century Ireland*, Cork, 1998

Kershaw, Ian, *Hitler: Hubris 1889–1936*, London, 1998

Kershaw, Ian, *Hitler: Nemesis 1936–45*, London, 2000

Kilroy, Thomas, *Double Cross: A Play about William Joyce and Brendan Bracken*, London, 1986

Kitson, Arthur, *The Bankers' Conspiracy which Started the World Crisis*, Oxford, 1933

Klabunde, Anja, *Magda Goebbels*, London, 2001

Knight, G. E. O., *In Defence of Germany*, London, 1933

Knightley, Phillip, *The Master Spy: The Story of Kim Philby*, New York, 1998

Kushner, Tony, *The Persistence of Prejudice: Anti-Semitism in British Society during the Second World War*, Manchester, 1989

Lamb, Richard, *Mussolini and the British*, London, 1997

Lane, A. H., *The Alien Menace*, London, 1929

Lee, Joseph, *The Modernisation of Irish Society*, Dublin, 1973

Le Quesne, A. L., *Carlyle*, Oxford, 1982

Lewis, Wyndham, *Count your Dead – They are Alive: Or a New War in the Making*, London, 1937

Lewis, Wyndham, *Left Wings Over Europe*, London, 1936

Lloyd, T. O., *Empire to Welfare State: English History 1906–1967*, Oxford, 1970

Loveday, Arthur, *World War in Spain*, London, 1939

Lucas, James, *Last Days of the Reich: The Collapse of Nazi Germany, May 1945*, London, 1986

Lunn, Kenneth and Thurlow, Richard, *British Fascism*, London, 1980

Lustgarten, Edgar, *Prisoner at the Bar*, London, 1952

Lustgarten, Edgar, *Time of My Life*, London, 1970

McLaughlin, Stewart, *Wandsworth Prison: A History*, HMP Wandsworth, 2001

Macnab, John, *The Bulls of Iberia*, London, 1957

Mark, Jeffry, *Analysis of Usury: With Proposals for the Abolition of Debt*, London, 1935

Marlow, Joyce, *Captain Boycott and the Irish*, London, 1973

Martland, Peter, *Lord Haw-Haw: The English Voice of Nazi Germany*, Secret History Files, National Archive, London, 2003

Marwick, Arthur, *Britain in the 20th Century*, London, 1984

Masters, Anthony, *The Man who was M: The Life of Maxwell Knight*, Basil Blackwell, 1984

Merlus, Brian, *Brooklyn: The Way it Was*, Brooklyn, New York, 1995

Miller, Joan, *One Girl's War*, Co. Kerry, 1986

Moore, George, *Hail and Farewell*, Colin Smyth, 1985

Moore, Des, *Offbeat Ireland*, Dublin, 1981

Moran, Gerard and Gillespie, Raymond, *Galway: History and Society*, Dublin, 1996

Mortimer, John (ed.), *Famous Trials*, Book Club, London, 1986

Mosley, Diana, *A Life of Contrasts*, London, 1977

Mosley, Nicholas, *Beyond the Pale*, London, 1983

Mosley, O., *My Life*, London, 1968

Mosley, O., *The Greater Britain*, London, 1932

Nathan, P., *The Psychology of Fascism*, London, 1943

Nicolson, Harold, *Diaries and Letters, 1939–45*, London, 1937

Ní Scannlan, Eibhlín, *Land and People: Land Uses and Popular Change in Connemara in the 19th Century*, Connemara West & Dúchas Heritage Centre, 1999

Noakes, Jeremy (ed.), *Nazism 1919–1945, Volume 4: The German Home Front in World War II*, University of Exeter, 1998

Novick, P., *The Resistance Versus Vichy: The Purge of Collaborators in Liberated France*, London, 1968

O'Donoghue, David, *Hitler's Irish Voices: The Story of German Radio's Wartime Irish Service*, Belfast, 1998

Ó Laoi, Padraic, *Father Michael Griffin*, Galway, 1994

O'Malley, Charles, *Glancing Back*, London, 1933

Overy, Richard, *Interrogations: The Nazi Élite in Allied Hands, 1945*, London, 2001

Overy, Richard, *Why the Allies Won*, London, 1995

Perls, Frederick et al., *Gestalt Therapy*, London, 1972

Perry, Geoffrey, *When Life Becomes History*, London, 2002

Phillips, O. Hood, *Leading Cases in Constitutional Law*, London, 1957

Pierrepoint, Albert, *Executioner: Pierrepoint*, London, 1974

Pritchett, Wendell, *Brownsville, Brooklyn, Blacks, Jews and the Changing Face of the Ghetto*, Chicago, 2002

Quinn, J. F., *History of Mayo*, Ballina, 1996

Read, Anthony and Fisher, David, *The Fall of Berlin*, London, 1992

Reuth, Ralf George, *Goebbels*, London, 1993

Richardson, Ralph, *Ireland in 1880*, London, 1881

Riis, Jacob A., *How the Other Half Lives*, New York, 1971 (first published 1890)

Roberts, Cecil, *And so to America*, London, 1946

Robertson, Geoffrey, *Freedom, the Individual and the Law*, London, 1993

Robertson, Nora, *Crowned Harp: Memories of the Last Years of the Crown in Ireland*, Dublin, 1960

Roth, Andreas, *Mr Bewley in Berlin: Aspects of the Career of an Irish Diplomat 1933–1939*, Dublin, 2000

Rudlin, W. A., *The Growth of Fascism in Great Britain*, London, 1935

Rutledge, Brett, *The Death of Lord Haw-Haw*, New York, 1940

Sapper, *Bulldog Drummond at Bay*, London, 1935

Selwyn, Francis, *Hitler's Englishman*, London, 1987

Senger, Valentin, *The Invisible Jew*, London, 1980

Sewell, Dennis, *Catholics*, London, 2001

Sharf, Andrew, *The British Press and Jews under Nazi Rule*, London, 1964

Shawcross, Hartley, *Life Sentence: Memoirs*, London, 1995

Shirer, William L., *Berlin Diary*, New York, 1940

Simpson, A. W. Brian, *In the Highest Degree Odious: Detention Without Trial in Wartime Britain*, Oxford, 1992

Skidelsky, Robert, *Mosley*, London, 1981

Smith, Howard, *Last Train from Berlin*, London, 1942

Snyder, Louis L., *Encyclopaedia of the Third Reich*, Ware, 1998

Somerville, E. O. E. and Ross, Martin, *Irish Memories*, London, 1925

Speer, Albert, *Inside the Third Reich*, New York, 1982

Spurr, Michael Adrian, *Becoming Blackshirts: Ideology, Culture and the British Union of Fascists*, Unpublished thesis available at Sheffield University Library

Stokesbury, James L., *A Short History of World War II*, London, 1980

Stuart, Francis, *Black List, Section H*, London, 1975

Stuart, Francis, *States of Mind: Selected Short Prose 1936–83*, Dublin and London, 1984

Stuart, Madeleine, *Manna in the Morning: A Memoir 1940–1958*, Dublin and London, 1984

Sullivan, Kevin, *Joyce Among the Jesuits*, Columbia University Press, 1958

Taylor, A. J. P., *British Prime Ministers*, London, 1998

Taylor, A. J. P., *English History 1914–45*, Oxford, 1965

Thurlow, Richard, *Fascism in Britain: A History 1918–1985*, London, 1987

Thurlow, Richard, *Fascism in Modern Britain*, Sutton, 2000

Trevor-Roper, Hugh (ed. and introduction), *The Goebbels Diaries*,

London, 1978

Tytell, John, *Ezra Pound: The Solitary Volcano*, New York, 1987

Vassiltchikov, Marie, *The Berlin Diaries 1940–45*, London, 1985

Waldron, Jarlath, *Maamtrasna: The Murders and the Mystery*, Dublin, 1992

Ward Price, George, *I Know These Dictators*, London, 1937

Ward Price, George, *Year of Reckoning*, London, 1939

Weale, Adrian, *Patriot Traitors: Roger Casement, John Amery and the Real Meaning of Treason*, London, 2001

Weale, Adrian, *Renegades: Hitler's Englishmen*, London, 1994

Webster, Nesta, *World Revolution: The Plot Against Civilisation*, London, 1922

West, Rebecca, *The Meaning of Treason*, London, 1949

West, W. J., *Truth Betrayed*, London, 1987

Wheatcroft, Geoffrey, *The Controversy of Zion*, London, 1996

Wilde, William, *Lough Corrib, its Shores and Island (with notices of Lough Mask)*, Dublin, 1867

Wilson, A. N., *Hilaire Belloc*, London, 1984

Wolf, J., *Nazi Germany*, London, 1934

Yeats-Brown, F., *European Jungle*, London, 1939

INDEX

367